Graphic

D0874332

STAR TREK®

THE KEY COLLECTION: VOLUME 3

CHECKER BOOK PUBLISHING GROUP

6/2016   2-6-06

HW

Graphic

"Our galaxy, the one which includes Earth, is approximately 10,000 light years in diameter and 12,000 light years in depth at the center. Our galaxy has not yet been fully explored by the Federation's starships–there are still vast unknown areas even in the sector assigned to the U.S.S. Enterprise. By conservative scientific estimate, its uncounted millions of suns and planets include at least several billion planets quite like Earth–more than enough adventures for even an unusually long television run."

Excerpt from "The Star Trek Guide," the in-house series production bible for STAR TREK, the Original Series.

STAR TREK®

THE KEY COLLECTION: VOLUME 2

CONTRIBUTORS:
STAR TREK created by Gene Roddenberry
Artwork . . . Nevio Zaccara and Alberto Giolitti

EDITORIAL CREDITS:
Publisher . . . . .Mark Thompson
Managing Editor . . . . .Constance Taylor
Graphic Design . . . . .Cheryl Amburn
Graphic Design . . . . .Angie Dayton
Graphic Design . . . . .Trevor Goodman
Graphic Design . . . . .Mike Gregg

TM, ® & © 2005 Paramount Pictures. All rights reserved. STAR TREK and related elements are trademarks of Paramount Pictures. Checker Book Publishing Group authorized user.

Originally published by Gold Key Comics 1972, 1973, 1974

Checker Book Publishing Group
228 Byers Road, Suite 201
Miamisburg, OH 45342

Visit STAR TREK at www.startrek.com
Visit Checker at www.checkerbpg.com
Printed in China

I've been a Star Trek fan for a long time. Even though the Original Series TV show had been relegated to the land of re-runs by the time I was born, I enjoyed all of the many incarnations that followed. I used to watch The Next Generation with my dad when I was a kid, and ended up having a big crush on Worf... when I was about 11 years old I painted a water-color picture of him, which I proudly presented to my dad. He thought it was an acorn wearing a yellow shirt.

My point is that, even though my foray into the world of Star Trek art was short lived, there's something about the Star Trek legacy that sparks inspiration in an infinite variety of areas, in an infinite variety of people. Whether you wear your collectors-edition Ferengi ears to your cousin's wedding, write a graduate-level thesis on the physical impossibility (or possibility) of Warp 10, or compose a song based upon Romulan musical theory, Star Trek finds itself surrounded by fans because of it's ability to integrate so many aspects of human experience and interest within the confines of a TV show. Or a comic book.

There was a short period of my life that I had cable television, which is the only time I've ever been able to watch any of the Original Series episodes -- and now that I don't have cable, there's no more Spock or Uhura or Bones or Sulu for me. That's one of the things I like best about this project....I get to sit around and read Star Trek comics and get my Original Series fix in book form. Sure, it's a comic that's pretty easy to make fun of, especially when the only "alien" thing about a species is a goofy haircut, and when you notice things like inconsistencies in character design (there's a panel where Spock has...gasp! Regular Ears!). And it's not quite the same as hearing Kirk's impassioned, staccato speeches or watching Scotty's face contort as he yells for more power. But, really, when you think about it, Star Trek and comic books go together like Kirk and space girls. Gene Roddenberry's vision of a better world is alive and well within these pages, and these comics retain that inimitable Original Series fusion of camp, drama, and ethics that we all expect and love.

Constance Taylor, Managing Editor
Checker Book Publishing Group

TABLE OF CONTENTS

STAR TREK
15c
STAR TREK
BEHOLD THE IDOL WHO DEMANDS THE DEATH OF THE THREE STRANGERS!

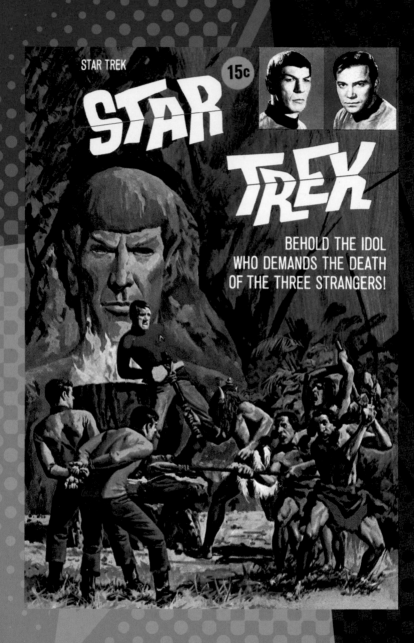

Chapter 1
The Cosmic Cavemen

[Originally Published in 1972]

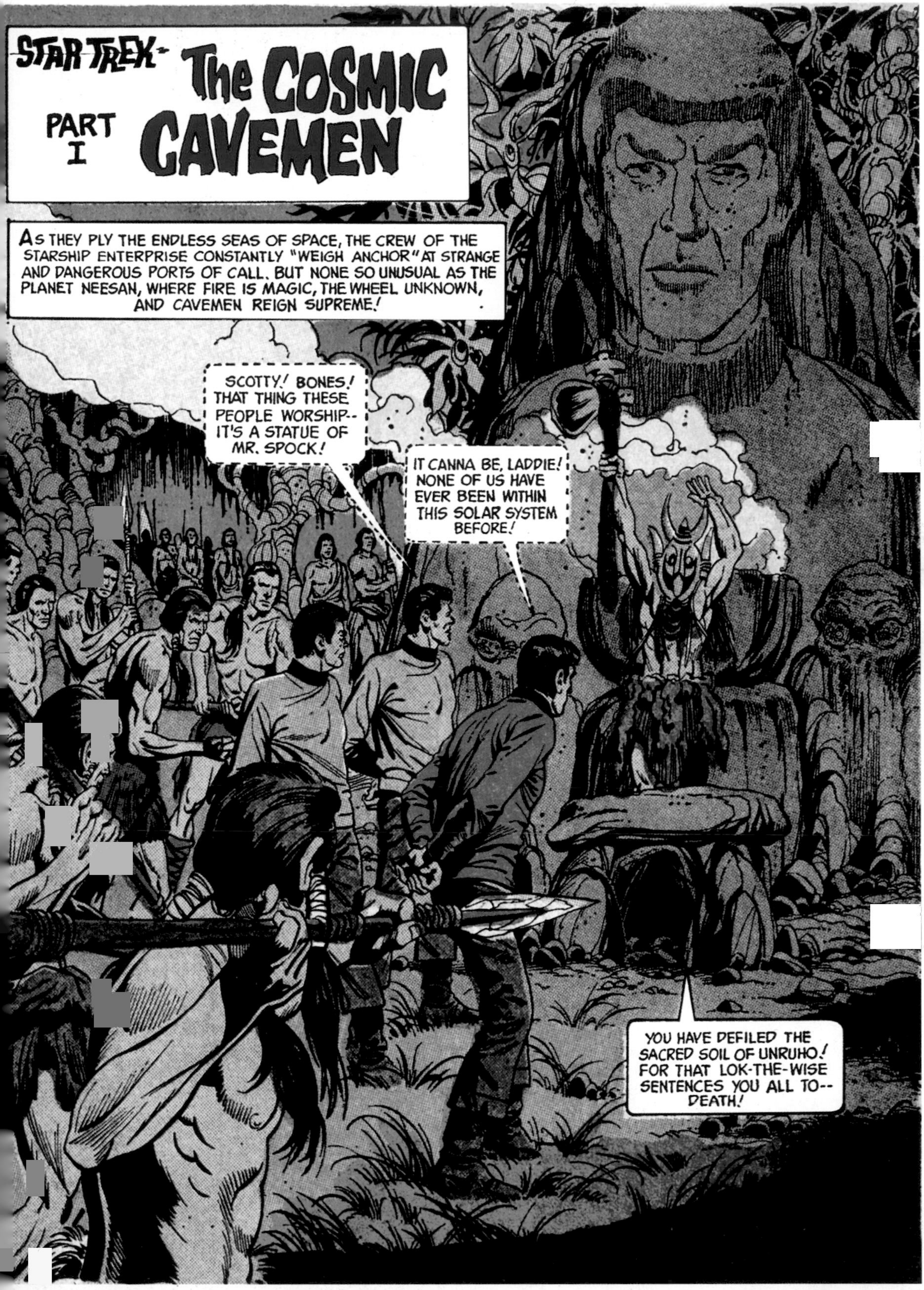
STAR TREK - The COSMIC CAVEMEN
PART I
AS THEY PLY THE ENDLESS SEAS OF SPACE, THE CREW OF THE STARSHIP ENTERPRISE CONSTANTLY "WEIGH ANCHOR" AT STRANGE AND DANGEROUS PORTS OF CALL. BUT NONE SO UNUSUAL AS THE PLANET NEESAN, WHERE FIRE IS MAGIC, THE WHEEL UNKNOWN, AND CAVEMEN REIGN SUPREME!
SCOTTY! BONES! THAT THING THESE PEOPLE WORSHIP-- IT'S A STATUE OF MR. SPOCK!
IT CANNA BE, LADDIE! NONE OF US HAVE EVER BEEN WITHIN THIS SOLAR SYSTEM BEFORE!
YOU HAVE DEFILED THE SACRED SOIL OF UNRUHO! FOR THAT LOK-THE-WISE SENTENCES YOU ALL TO-- DEATH!

aptain's Log, Stardate 19:24.3 . . DATA REF . . 17.00-17.25

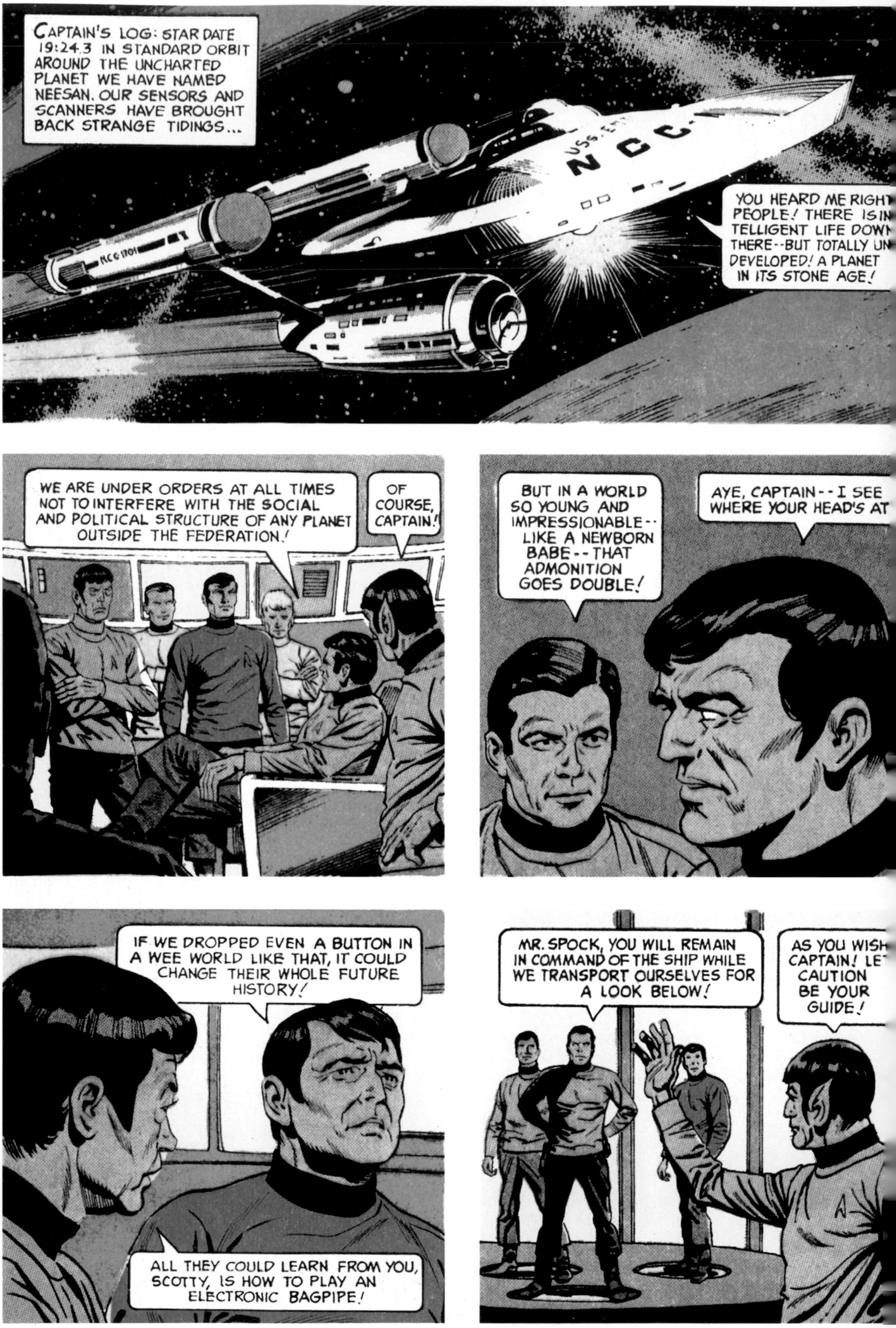
CAPTAIN'S LOG: STAR DATE 19:24.3 IN STANDARD ORBIT AROUND THE UNCHARTED PLANET WE HAVE NAMED NEESAN. OUR SENSORS AND SCANNERS HAVE BROUGHT BACK STRANGE TIDINGS...
U.S.S. ENT
NCC
NCC 1701
YOU HEARD ME RIGHT PEOPLE! THERE IS IN TELLIGENT LIFE DOWN THERE--BUT TOTALLY UN DEVELOPED! A PLANET IN ITS STONE AGE!
WE ARE UNDER ORDERS AT ALL TIMES NOT TO INTERFERE WITH THE SOCIAL AND POLITICAL STRUCTURE OF ANY PLANET OUTSIDE THE FEDERATION!
OF COURSE, CAPTAIN!
BUT IN A WORLD SO YOUNG AND IMPRESSIONABLE--LIKE A NEWBORN BABE--THAT ADMONITION GOES DOUBLE!
AYE, CAPTAIN--I SEE WHERE YOUR HEAD'S AT
IF WE DROPPED EVEN A BUTTON IN A WEE WORLD LIKE THAT, IT COULD CHANGE THEIR WHOLE FUTURE HISTORY!
ALL THEY COULD LEARN FROM YOU, SCOTTY, IS HOW TO PLAY AN ELECTRONIC BAGPIPE!
MR. SPOCK, YOU WILL REMAIN IN COMMAND OF THE SHIP WHILE WE TRANSPORT OURSELVES FOR A LOOK BELOW!
AS YOU WISH CAPTAIN! LET CAUTION BE YOUR GUIDE!

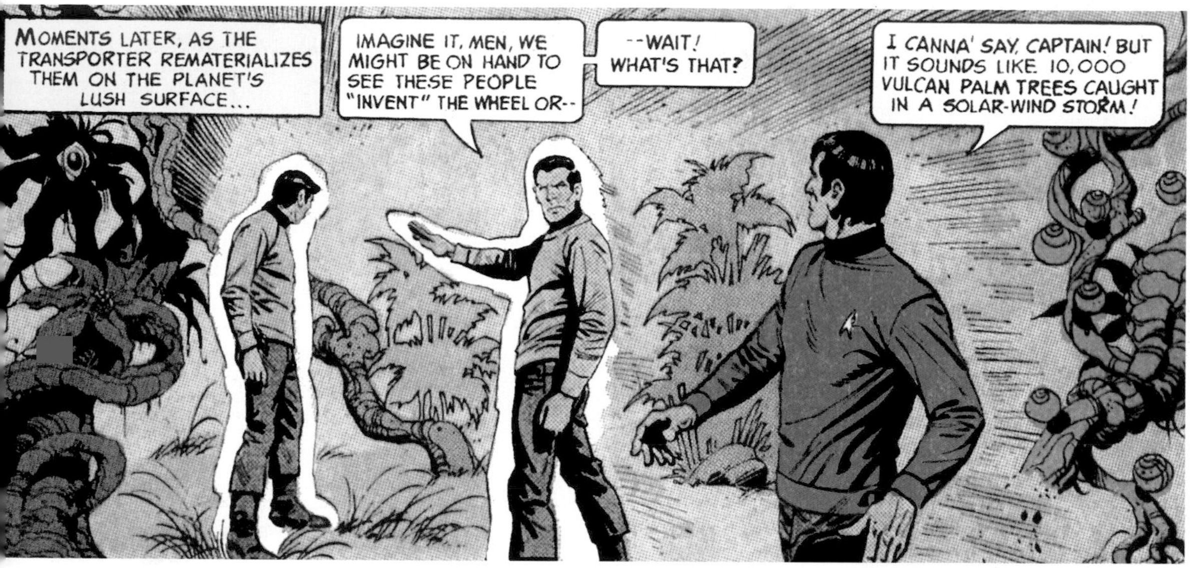
MOMENTS LATER, AS THE TRANSPORTER REMATERIALIZES THEM ON THE PLANET'S LUSH SURFACE...
IMAGINE IT, MEN, WE MIGHT BE ON HAND TO SEE THESE PEOPLE "INVENT" THE WHEEL OR--
--WAIT! WHAT'S THAT?
I CANNA' SAY, CAPTAIN! BUT IT SOUNDS LIKE 10,000 VULCAN PALM TREES CAUGHT IN A SOLAR-WIND STORM!

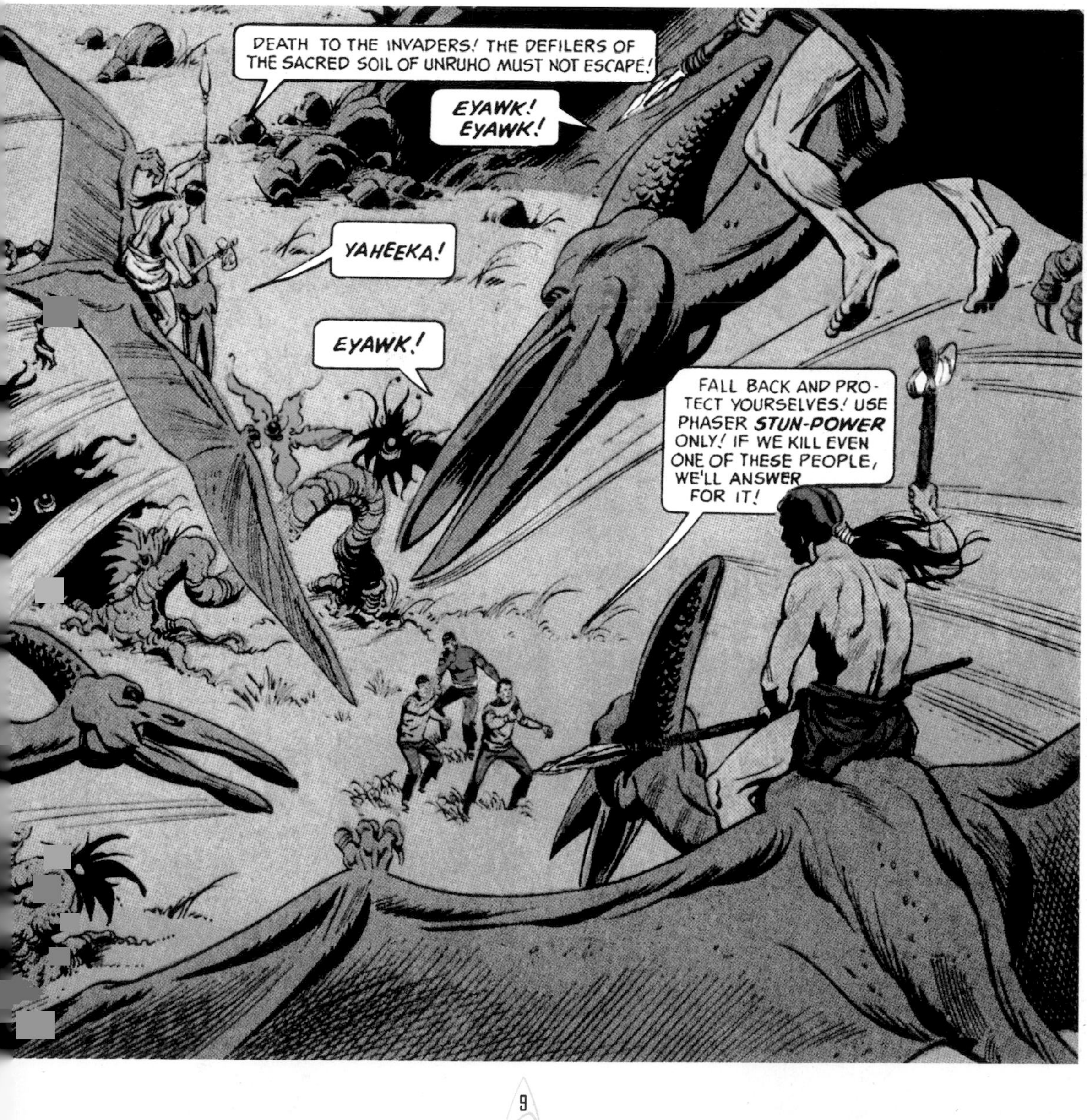
DEATH TO THE INVADERS! THE DEFILERS OF THE SACRED SOIL OF UNRUHO MUST NOT ESCAPE!
EYAWK! EYAWK!
YAHEEKA!
EYAWK!
FALL BACK AND PROTECT YOURSELVES! USE PHASER STUN-POWER ONLY! IF WE KILL EVEN ONE OF THESE PEOPLE, WE'LL ANSWER FOR IT!

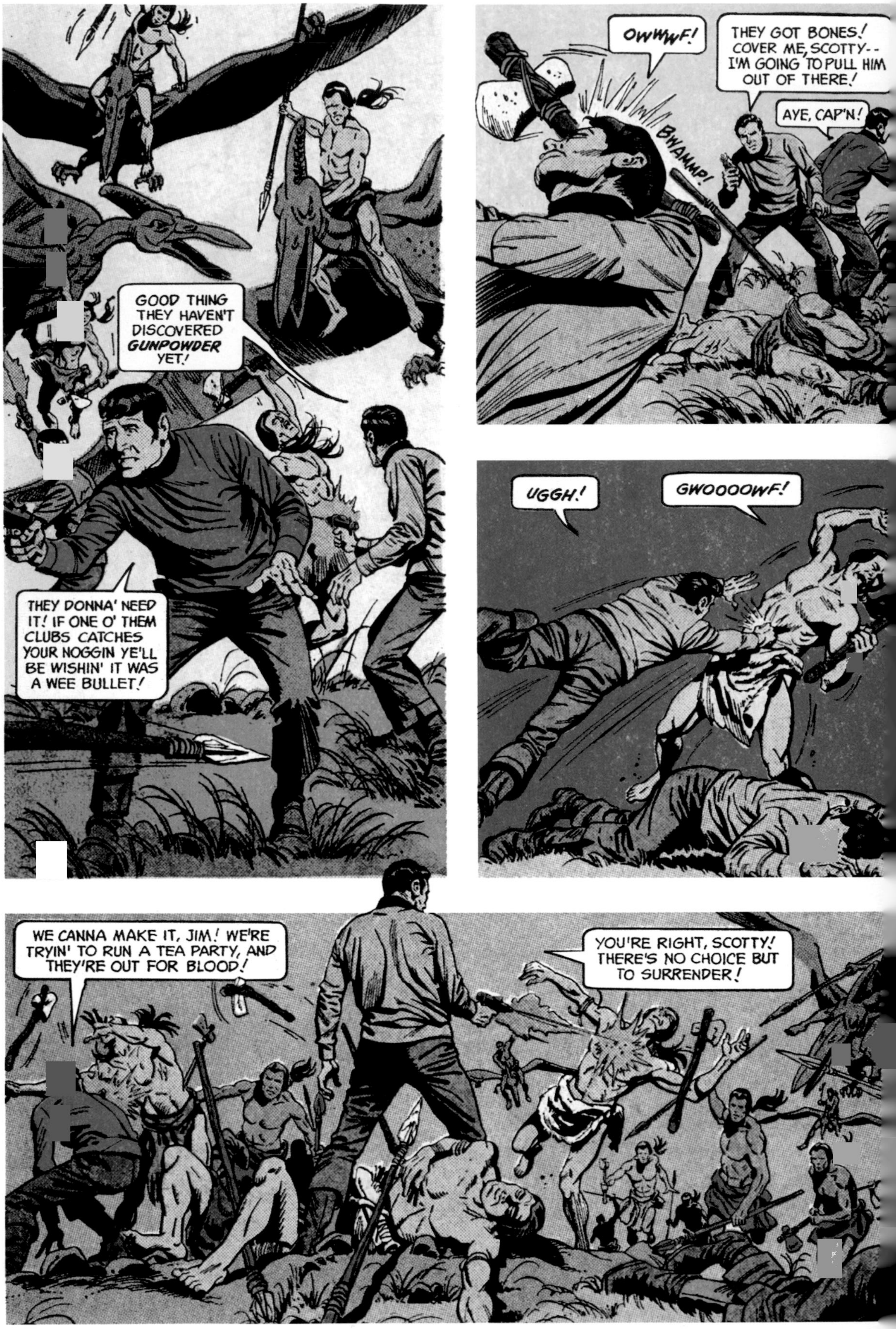
GOOD THING THEY HAVEN'T DISCOVERED GUNPOWDER YET!
THEY DONNA' NEED IT! IF ONE O' THEM CLUBS CATCHES YOUR NOGGIN YE'LL BE WISHIN' IT WAS A WEE BULLET!
OWWWF!
BWAMMP!
THEY GOT BONES! COVER ME, SCOTTY-- I'M GOING TO PULL HIM OUT OF THERE!
AYE, CAP'N!
UGGH!
GWOOOOWF!
WE CANNA MAKE IT, JIM! WE'RE TRYIN' TO RUN A TEA PARTY, AND THEY'RE OUT FOR BLOOD!
YOU'RE RIGHT, SCOTTY! THERE'S NO CHOICE BUT TO SURRENDER!

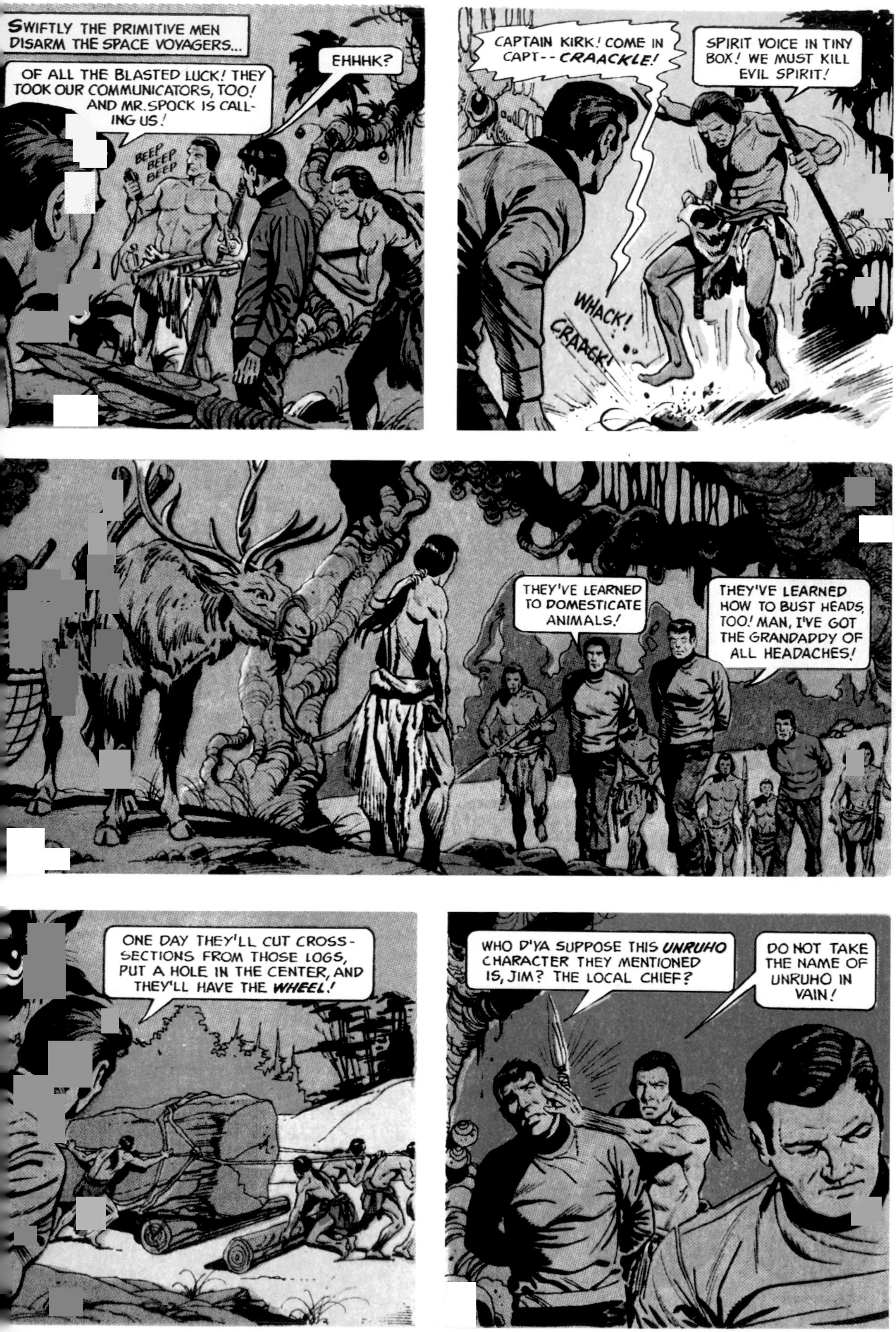

SWIFTLY THE PRIMITIVE MEN DISARM THE SPACE VOYAGERS...
OF ALL THE BLASTED LUCK! THEY TOOK OUR COMMUNICATORS, TOO! AND MR. SPOCK IS CALLING US!
EHHHK?
BEEP BEEP BEEP
CAPTAIN KIRK! COME IN CAPT-- CRAACKLE!
SPIRIT VOICE IN TINY BOX! WE MUST KILL EVIL SPIRIT!
WHACK!
CRAACK!
THEY'VE LEARNED TO DOMESTICATE ANIMALS!
THEY'VE LEARNED HOW TO BUST HEADS, TOO! MAN, I'VE GOT THE GRANDADDY OF ALL HEADACHES!
ONE DAY THEY'LL CUT CROSS-SECTIONS FROM THOSE LOGS, PUT A HOLE IN THE CENTER, AND THEY'LL HAVE THE WHEEL!
WHO D'YA SUPPOSE THIS UNRUHO CHARACTER THEY MENTIONED IS, JIM? THE LOCAL CHIEF?
DO NOT TAKE THE NAME OF UNRUHO IN VAIN!

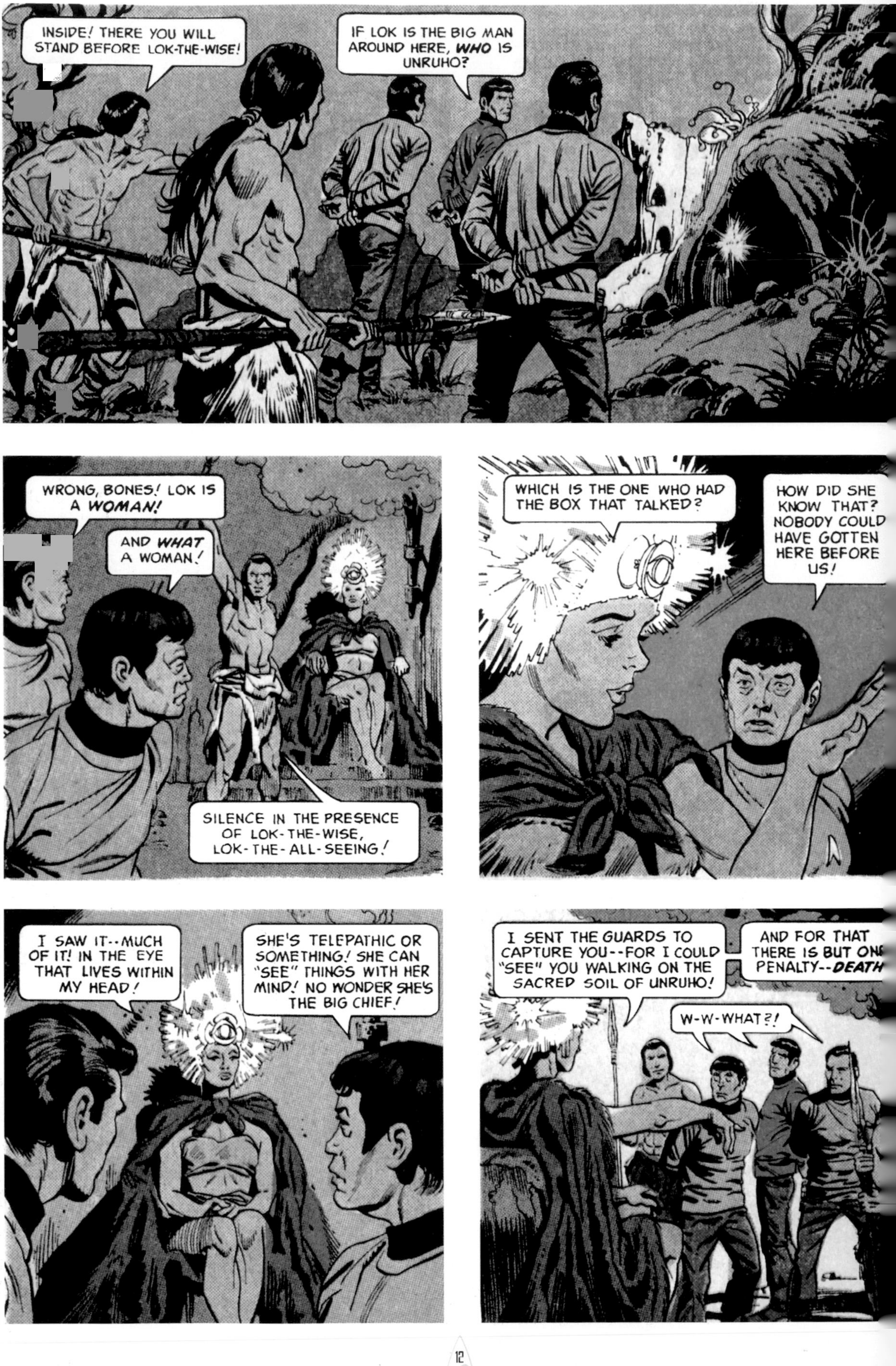

INSIDE! THERE YOU WILL STAND BEFORE LOK-THE-WISE!
IF LOK IS THE BIG MAN AROUND HERE, WHO IS UNRUHO?
WRONG, BONES! LOK IS A WOMAN!
AND WHAT A WOMAN!
SILENCE IN THE PRESENCE OF LOK-THE-WISE, LOK-THE-ALL-SEEING!
WHICH IS THE ONE WHO HAD THE BOX THAT TALKED?
HOW DID SHE KNOW THAT? NOBODY COULD HAVE GOTTEN HERE BEFORE US!
I SAW IT--MUCH OF IT! IN THE EYE THAT LIVES WITHIN MY HEAD!
SHE'S TELEPATHIC OR SOMETHING! SHE CAN "SEE" THINGS WITH HER MIND! NO WONDER SHE'S THE BIG CHIEF!
I SENT THE GUARDS TO CAPTURE YOU--FOR I COULD "SEE" YOU WALKING ON THE SACRED SOIL OF UNRUHO!
AND FOR THAT THERE IS BUT ONE PENALTY--DEATH
W-W-WHAT?!

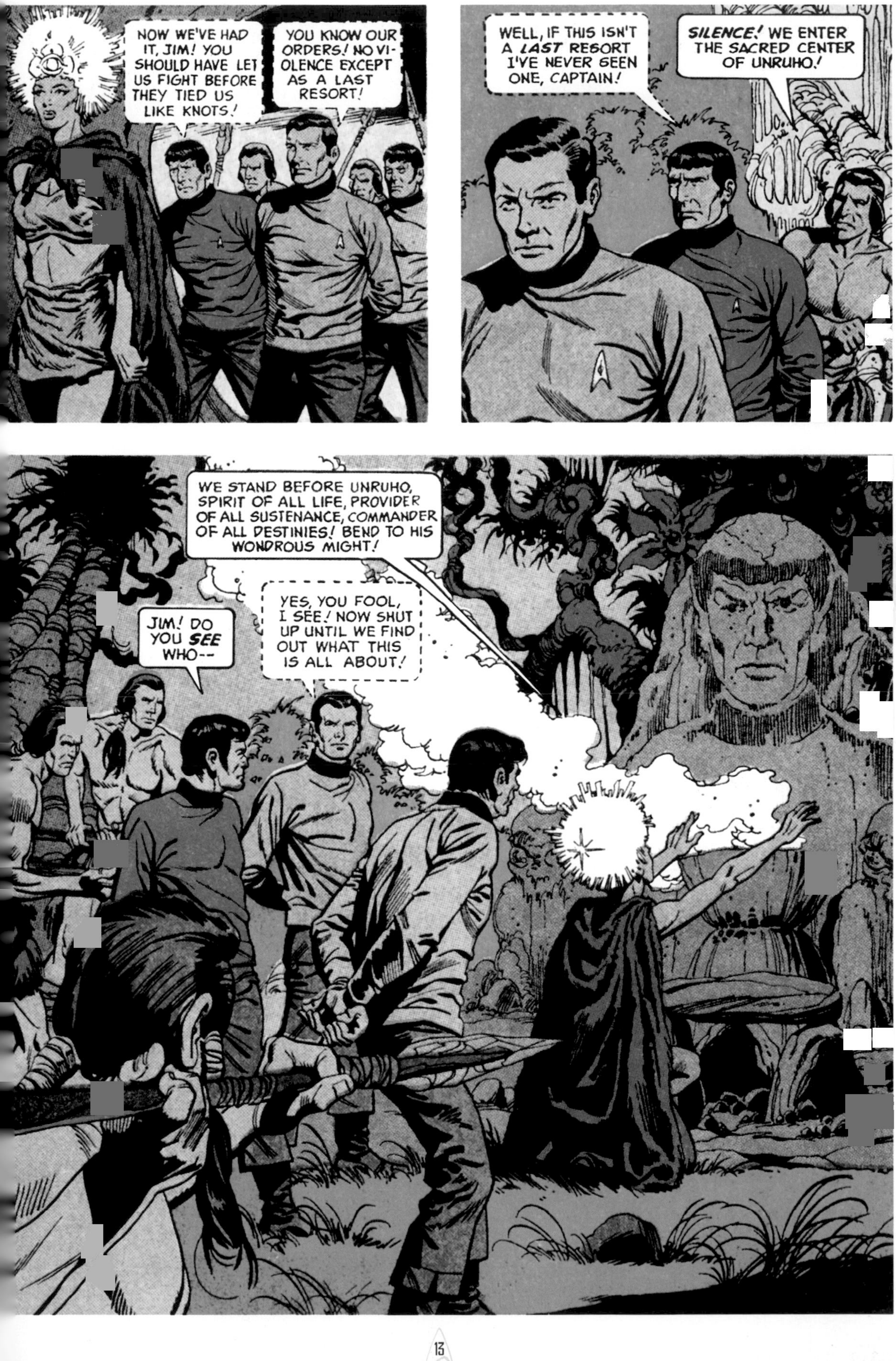
NOW WE'VE HAD IT, JIM! YOU SHOULD HAVE LET US FIGHT BEFORE THEY TIED US LIKE KNOTS!
YOU KNOW OUR ORDERS! NO VI-OLENCE EXCEPT AS A LAST RESORT!
WELL, IF THIS ISN'T A LAST RESORT I'VE NEVER SEEN ONE, CAPTAIN!
SILENCE! WE ENTER THE SACRED CENTER OF UNRUHO!
WE STAND BEFORE UNRUHO, SPIRIT OF ALL LIFE, PROVIDER OF ALL SUSTENANCE, COMMANDER OF ALL DESTINIES! BEND TO HIS WONDROUS MIGHT!
JIM! DO YOU SEE WHO--
YES, YOU FOOL, I SEE! NOW SHUT UP UNTIL WE FIND OUT WHAT THIS IS ALL ABOUT!

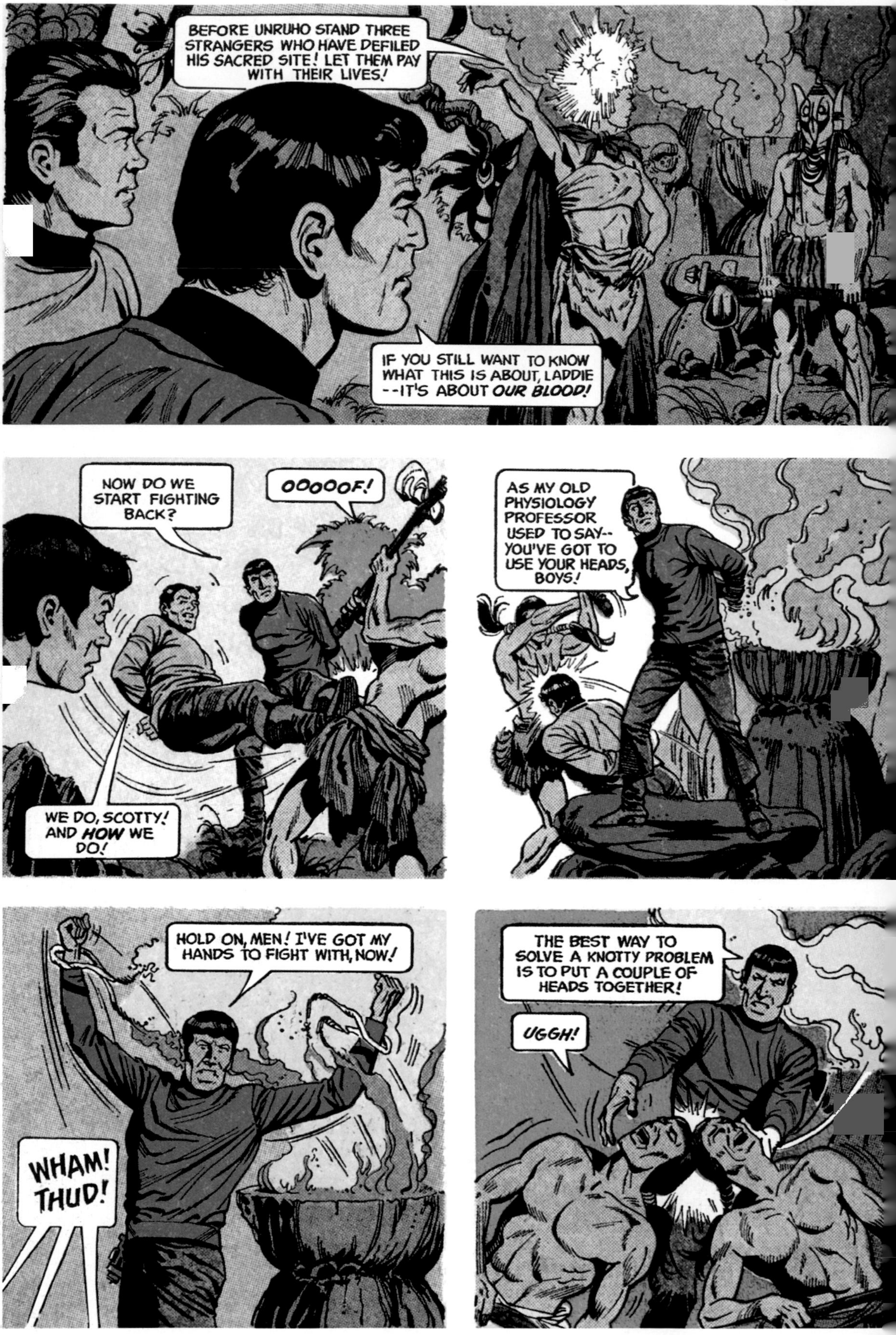
BEFORE UNRUHO STAND THREE STRANGERS WHO HAVE DEFILED HIS SACRED SITE! LET THEM PAY WITH THEIR LIVES!
IF YOU STILL WANT TO KNOW WHAT THIS IS ABOUT, LADDIE --IT'S ABOUT OUR BLOOD!
NOW DO WE START FIGHTING BACK?
OOOOOF!
WE DO, SCOTTY! AND HOW WE DO!
AS MY OLD PHYSIOLOGY PROFESSOR USED TO SAY-- YOU'VE GOT TO USE YOUR HEADS, BOYS!
HOLD ON, MEN! I'VE GOT MY HANDS TO FIGHT WITH, NOW!
WHAM! THUD!
THE BEST WAY TO SOLVE A KNOTTY PROBLEM IS TO PUT A COUPLE OF HEADS TOGETHER!
UGGH!

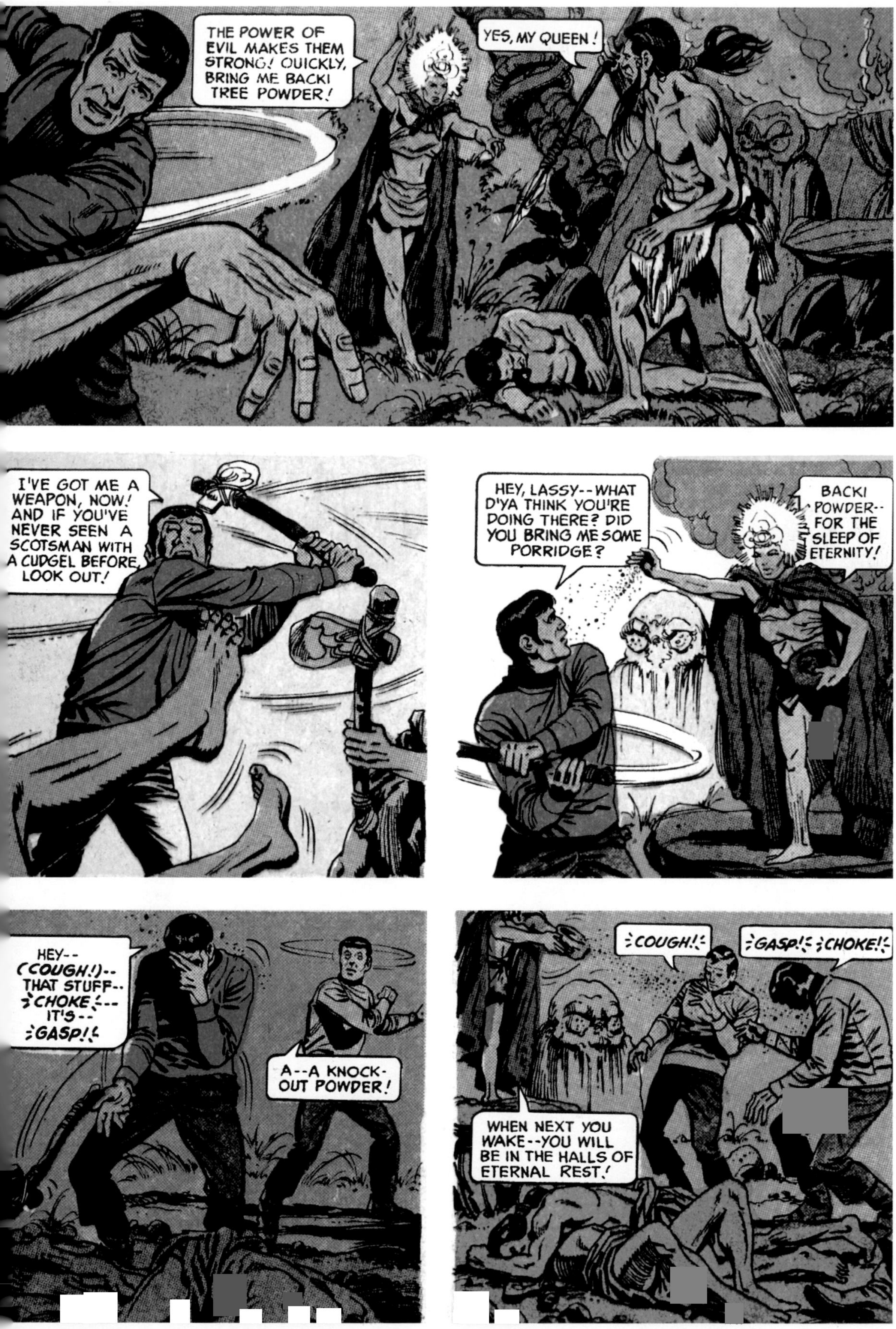
THE POWER OF EVIL MAKES THEM STRONG! QUICKLY, BRING ME BACKI TREE POWDER!
YES, MY QUEEN!
I'VE GOT ME A WEAPON, NOW! AND IF YOU'VE NEVER SEEN A SCOTSMAN WITH A CUDGEL BEFORE, LOOK OUT!
HEY, LASSY--WHAT D'YA THINK YOU'RE DOING THERE? DID YOU BRING ME SOME PORRIDGE?
BACKI POWDER--FOR THE SLEEP OF ETERNITY!
HEY--(COUGH!)--THAT STUFF--CHOKE--IT'S--GASP!
A--A KNOCK-OUT POWDER!
COUGH!
GASP! CHOKE!
WHEN NEXT YOU WAKE--YOU WILL BE IN THE HALLS OF ETERNAL REST!

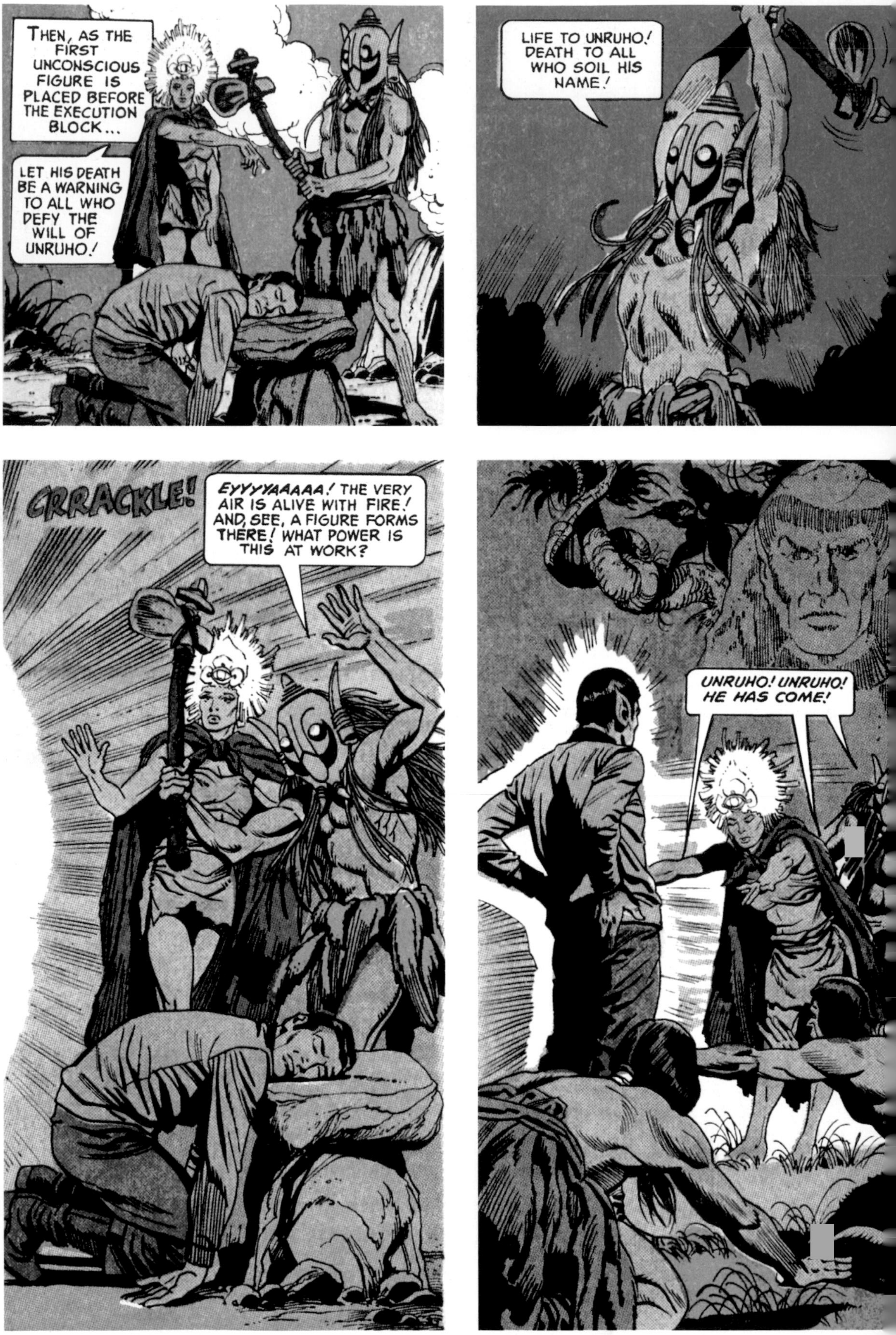
THEN, AS THE FIRST UNCONSCIOUS FIGURE IS PLACED BEFORE THE EXECUTION BLOCK...
LET HIS DEATH BE A WARNING TO ALL WHO DEFY THE WILL OF UNRUHO!
LIFE TO UNRUHO! DEATH TO ALL WHO SOIL HIS NAME!
CRRACKLE!
EYYYYAAAAA! THE VERY AIR IS ALIVE WITH FIRE! AND, SEE, A FIGURE FORMS THERE! WHAT POWER IS THIS AT WORK?
UNRUHO! UNRUHO! HE HAS COME!

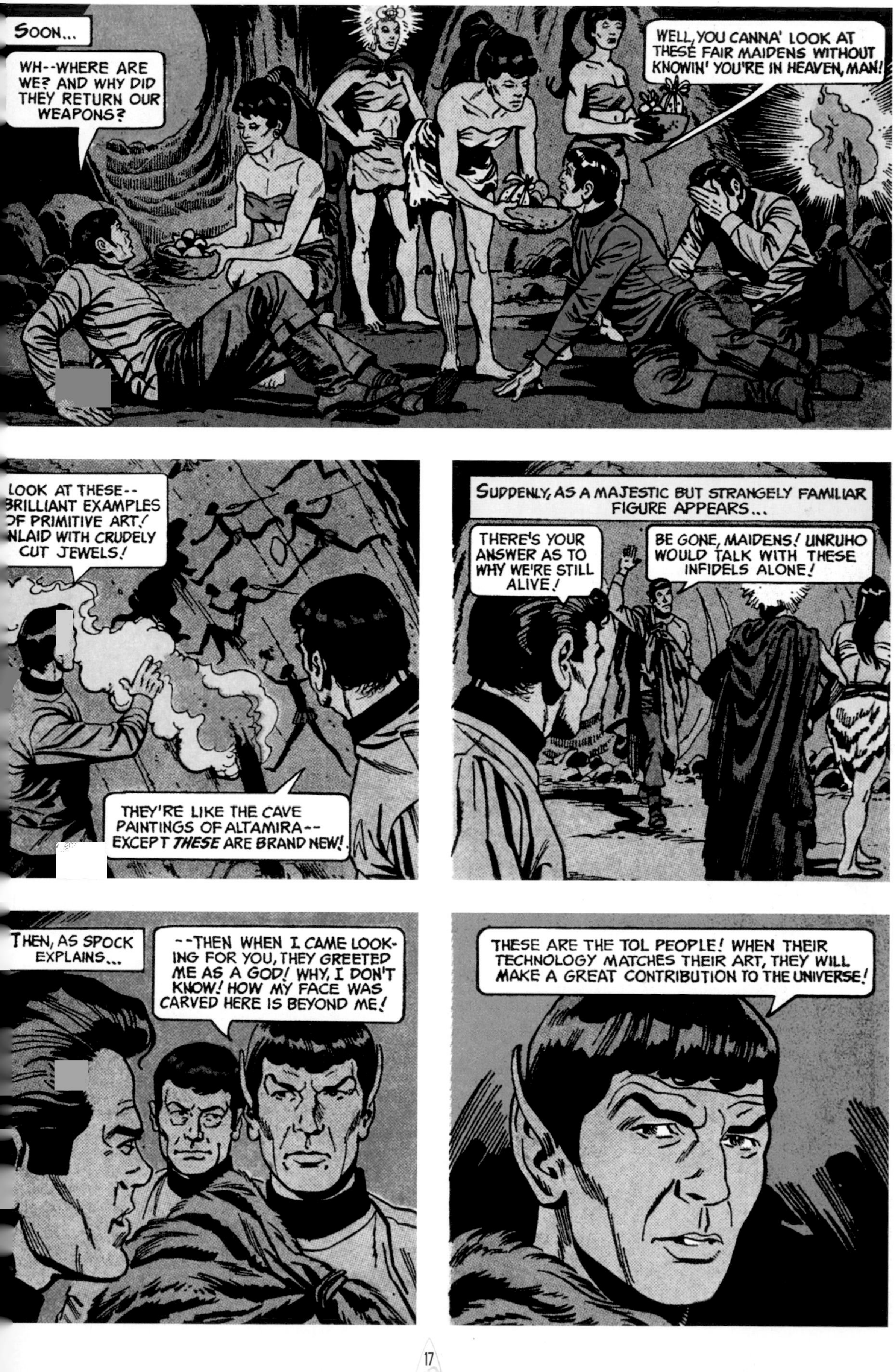
SOON...
WH--WHERE ARE WE? AND WHY DID THEY RETURN OUR WEAPONS?
WELL, YOU CANNA' LOOK AT THESE FAIR MAIDENS WITHOUT KNOWIN' YOU'RE IN HEAVEN, MAN!
LOOK AT THESE-- BRILLIANT EXAMPLES OF PRIMITIVE ART! NLAID WITH CRUDELY CUT JEWELS!
THEY'RE LIKE THE CAVE PAINTINGS OF ALTAMIRA-- EXCEPT *THESE* ARE BRAND NEW!
SUDDENLY, AS A MAJESTIC BUT STRANGELY FAMILIAR FIGURE APPEARS...
THERE'S YOUR ANSWER AS TO WHY WE'RE STILL ALIVE!
BE GONE, MAIDENS! UNRUHO WOULD TALK WITH THESE INFIDELS ALONE!
THEN, AS SPOCK EXPLAINS...
--THEN WHEN I CAME LOOKING FOR YOU, THEY GREETED ME AS A GOD! WHY, I DON'T KNOW! HOW MY FACE WAS CARVED HERE IS BEYOND ME!
THESE ARE THE TOL PEOPLE! WHEN THEIR TECHNOLOGY MATCHES THEIR ART, THEY WILL MAKE A GREAT CONTRIBUTION TO THE UNIVERSE!

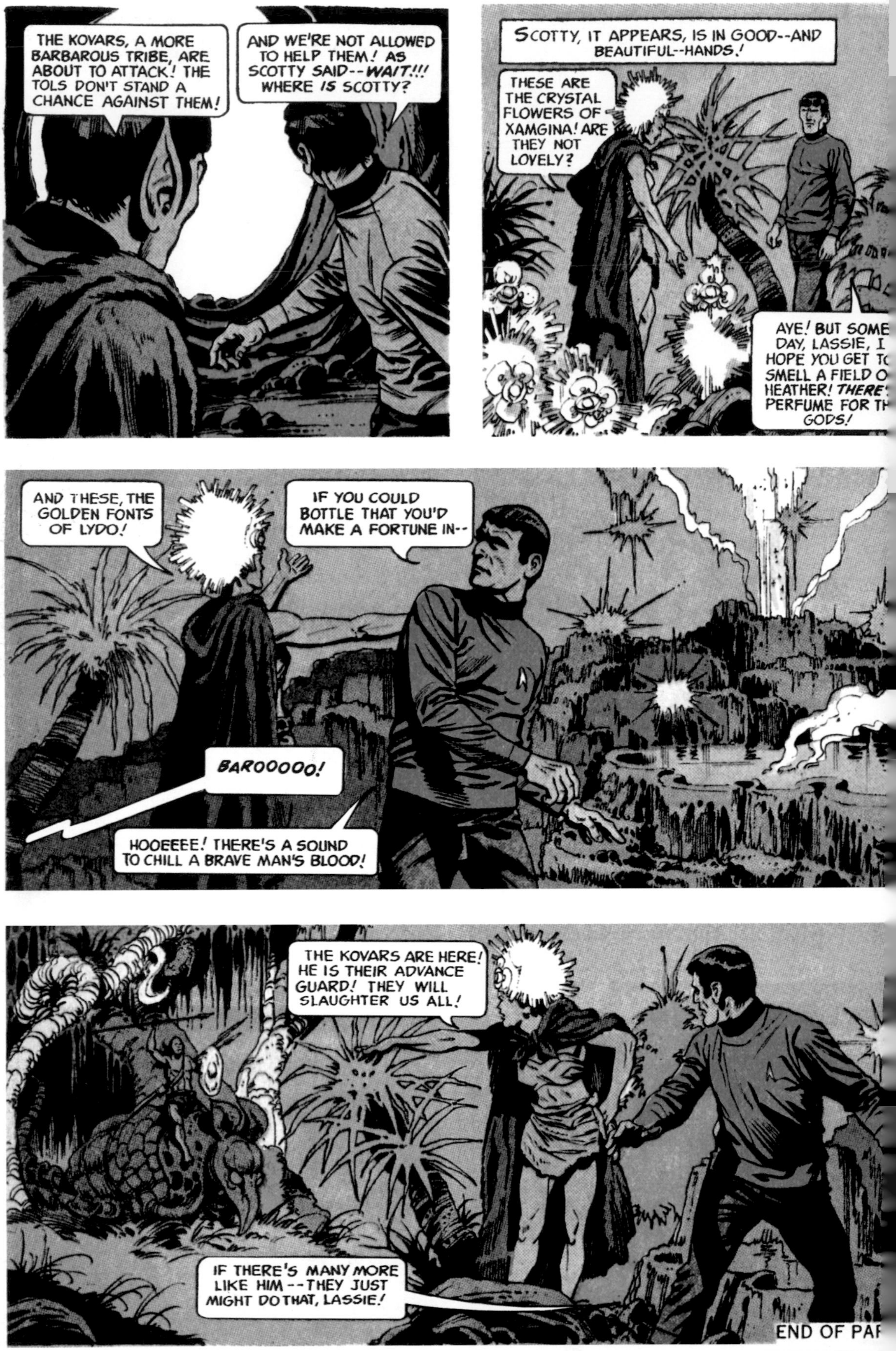

THE KOVARS, A MORE BARBAROUS TRIBE, ARE ABOUT TO ATTACK! THE TOLS DON'T STAND A CHANCE AGAINST THEM!
AND WE'RE NOT ALLOWED TO HELP THEM! AS SCOTTY SAID--WAIT!!! WHERE IS SCOTTY?
SCOTTY, IT APPEARS, IS IN GOOD--AND BEAUTIFUL--HANDS!
THESE ARE THE CRYSTAL FLOWERS OF XAMGINA! ARE THEY NOT LOVELY?
AYE! BUT SOME DAY, LASSIE, I HOPE YOU GET T SMELL A FIELD O HEATHER! THERE' PERFUME FOR T GODS!
AND THESE, THE GOLDEN FONTS OF LYDO!
IF YOU COULD BOTTLE THAT YOU'D MAKE A FORTUNE IN--
BAROOOOO!
HOOEEEE! THERE'S A SOUND TO CHILL A BRAVE MAN'S BLOOD!
THE KOVARS ARE HERE! HE IS THEIR ADVANCE GUARD! THEY WILL SLAUGHTER US ALL!
IF THERE'S MANY MORE LIKE HIM--THEY JUST MIGHT DO THAT, LASSIE!
END OF PA

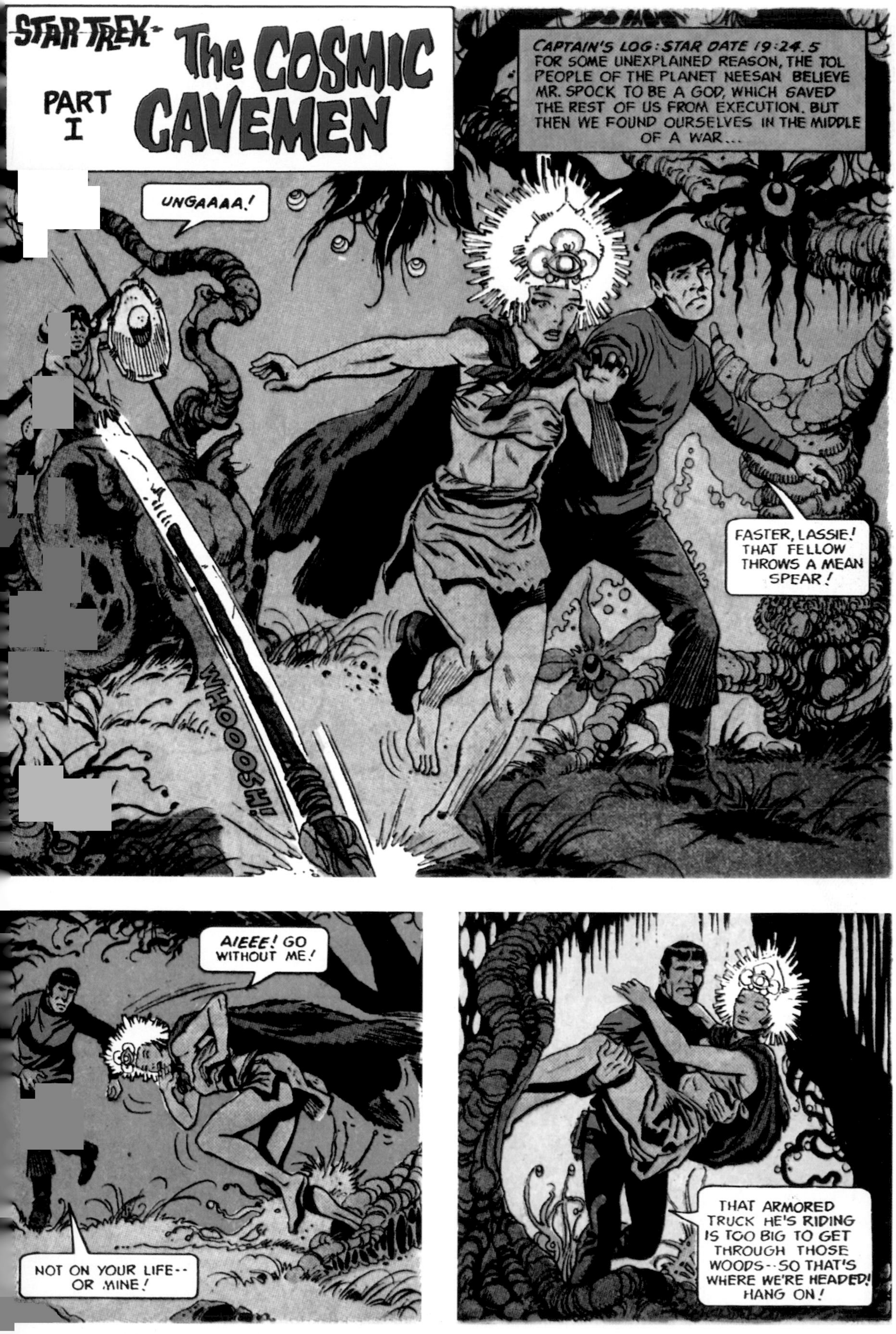
STAR TREK -
The COSMIC CAVEMEN
PART I
CAPTAIN'S LOG: STAR DATE 19:24.5 FOR SOME UNEXPLAINED REASON, THE TOL PEOPLE OF THE PLANET NEESAN BELIEVE MR. SPOCK TO BE A GOD, WHICH SAVED THE REST OF US FROM EXECUTION. BUT THEN WE FOUND OURSELVES IN THE MIDDLE OF A WAR...
UNGAAAA!
WHOOOOSH!
FASTER, LASSIE! THAT FELLOW THROWS A MEAN SPEAR!
AIEEE! GO WITHOUT ME!
NOT ON YOUR LIFE-- OR MINE!
THAT ARMORED TRUCK HE'S RIDING IS TOO BIG TO GET THROUGH THOSE WOODS--SO THAT'S WHERE WE'RE HEADED! HANG ON!

LATER...

THAT'S ALL THERE IS TO IT, MEN-- WE HAVE TO *LEAVE* BEFORE THE MAIN BATTLE BREAKS!

AGREED! OTHERWISE WE WOULD BE INVOLVED-- AGAINST ORDERS!

BUT I CAN'T DENY MY DIVINITY NOW OR THE TOLS WOULD KILL US!

KNOW THIS, TOL PEOPLE! I MUST DEPART WITH THE OTHERS! BUT REMEMBER THAT I SHALL ALWAYS BE WITH YOU IN YOUR STRUGGLE TO SURVIVE!

I'M NOT ONE TO RUN OUT ON A LASSIE IN HER TIME OF NEED! BUT I CANNA' DO OTHERWISE NOW!

GO IN PEACE-- AND LOVE!

GET A MOVE ON-- SCOTTY!

MOMENTS LATER, ABOARD THE STARSHIP...

I DON'T MIND ADMITTIN' THAT I LEFT THAT GIRL WITH A HEAVY HEART!

YES--AND A LIGHT *WEAPON BELT!* SHE TOOK YOUR *PHASER*, YOU FOOL!

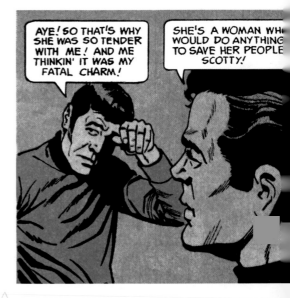

AYE! SO THAT'S WHY SHE WAS SO TENDER WITH ME! AND ME THINKIN' IT WAS MY FATAL CHARM!

SHE'S A WOMAN WHO WOULD DO ANYTHING TO SAVE HER PEOPLE, SCOTTY!

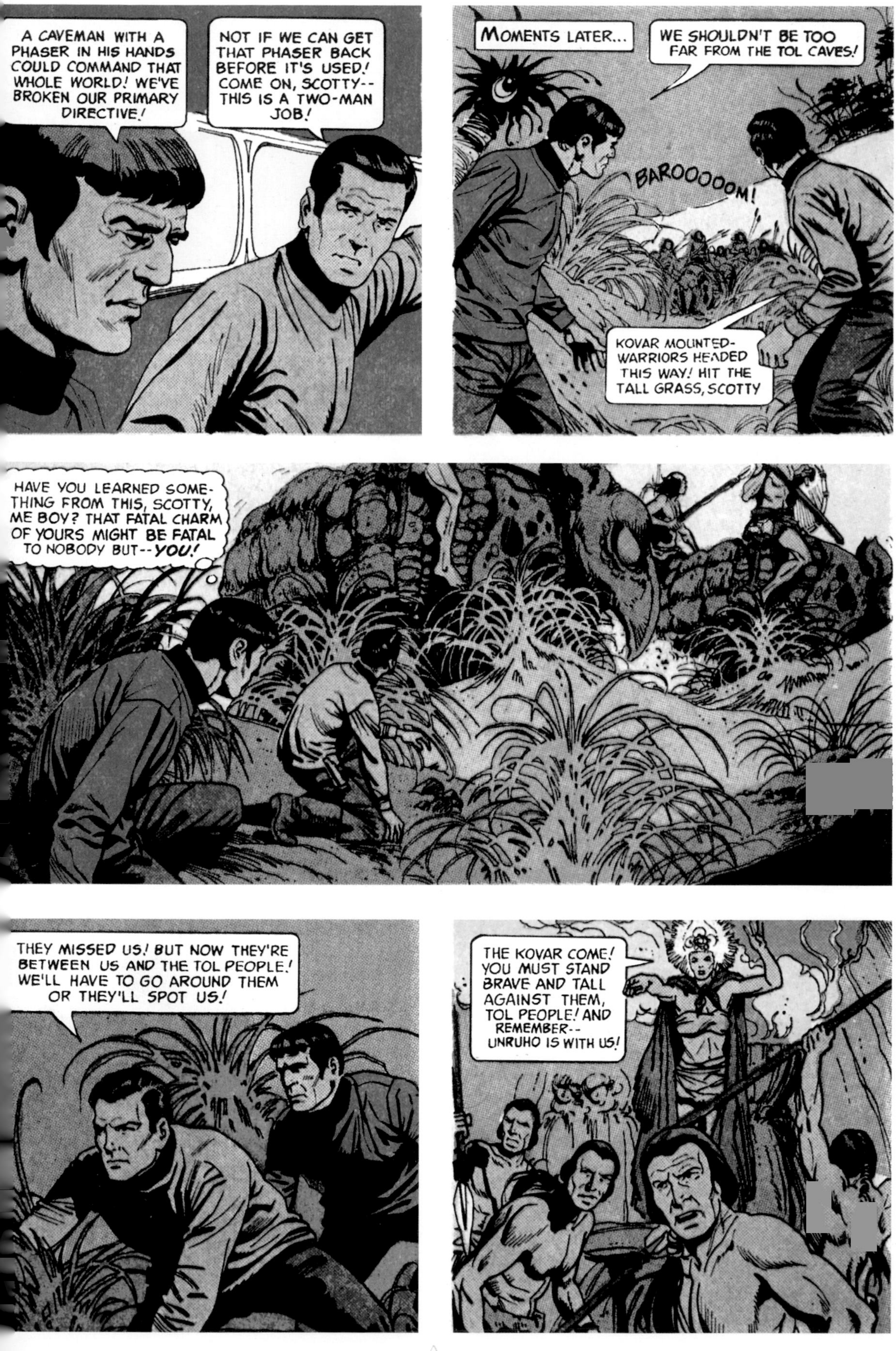
A CAVEMAN WITH A PHASER IN HIS HANDS COULD COMMAND THAT WHOLE WORLD! WE'VE BROKEN OUR PRIMARY DIRECTIVE!
NOT IF WE CAN GET THAT PHASER BACK BEFORE IT'S USED! COME ON, SCOTTY-- THIS IS A TWO-MAN JOB!
MOMENTS LATER...
WE SHOULDN'T BE TOO FAR FROM THE TOL CAVES!
BAROOOOOM!
KOVAR MOUNTED-WARRIORS HEADED THIS WAY! HIT THE TALL GRASS, SCOTTY
HAVE YOU LEARNED SOMETHING FROM THIS, SCOTTY, ME BOY? THAT FATAL CHARM OF YOURS MIGHT BE FATAL TO NOBODY BUT--YOU!
THEY MISSED US! BUT NOW THEY'RE BETWEEN US AND THE TOL PEOPLE! WE'LL HAVE TO GO AROUND THEM OR THEY'LL SPOT US!
THE KOVAR COME! YOU MUST STAND BRAVE AND TALL AGAINST THEM, TOL PEOPLE! AND REMEMBER-- UNRUHO IS WITH US!

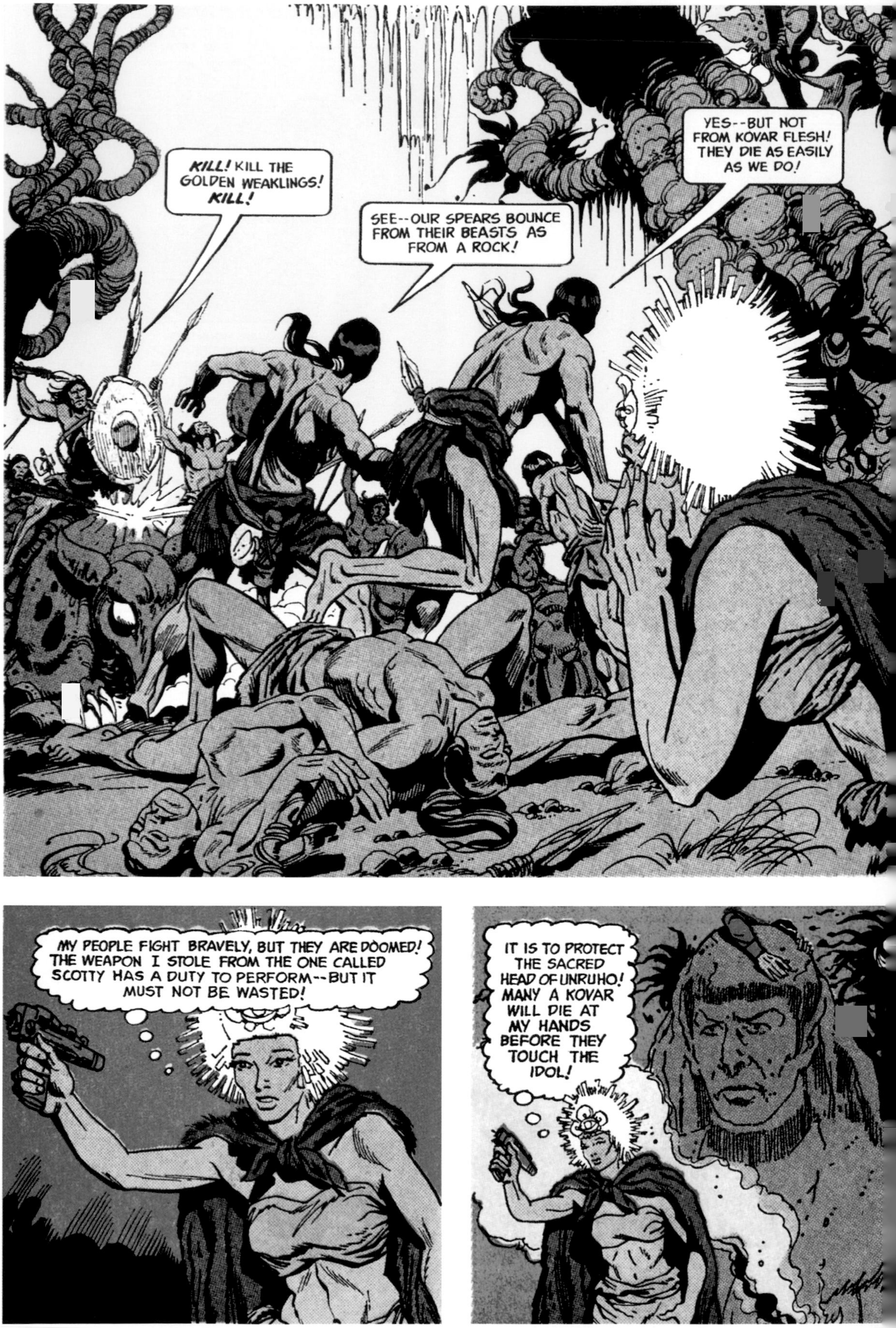

KILL! KILL THE GOLDEN WEAKLINGS! KILL!
SEE--OUR SPEARS BOUNCE FROM THEIR BEASTS AS FROM A ROCK!
YES--BUT NOT FROM KOVAR FLESH! THEY DIE AS EASILY AS WE DO!
MY PEOPLE FIGHT BRAVELY, BUT THEY ARE DOOMED! THE WEAPON I STOLE FROM THE ONE CALLED SCOTTY HAS A DUTY TO PERFORM--BUT IT MUST NOT BE WASTED!
IT IS TO PROTECT THE SACRED HEAD OF UNRUHO! MANY A KOVAR WILL DIE AT MY HANDS BEFORE THEY TOUCH THE IDOL!

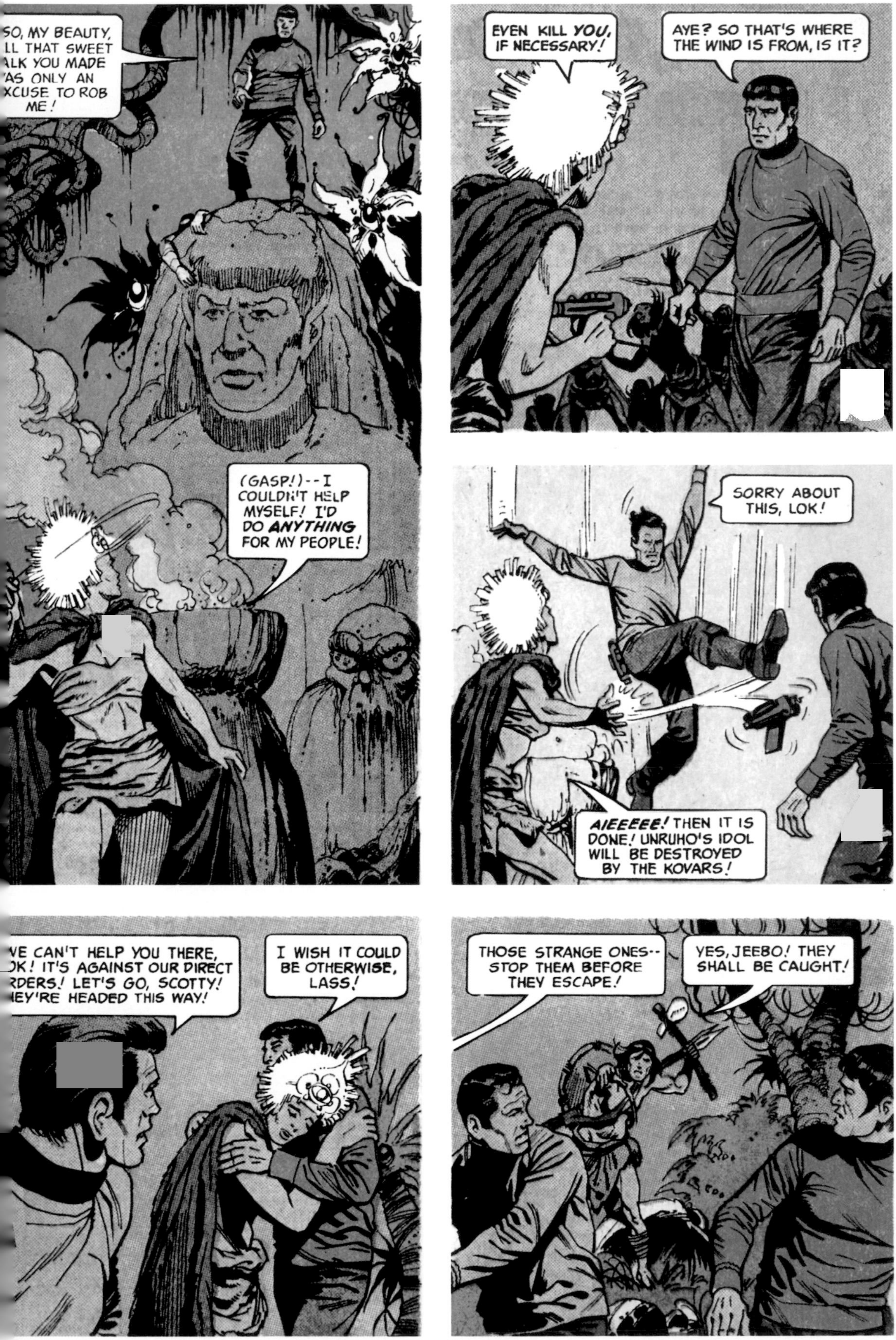

SO, MY BEAUTY, LL THAT SWEET ALK YOU MADE AS ONLY AN XCUSE TO ROB ME!
(GASP!)--I COULDN'T HELP MYSELF! I'D DO ANYTHING FOR MY PEOPLE!
EVEN KILL YOU, IF NECESSARY!
AYE? SO THAT'S WHERE THE WIND IS FROM, IS IT?
SORRY ABOUT THIS, LOK!
AIEEEEE! THEN IT IS DONE! UNRUHO'S IDOL WILL BE DESTROYED BY THE KOVARS!
VE CAN'T HELP YOU THERE, OK! IT'S AGAINST OUR DIRECT RDERS! LET'S GO, SCOTTY! HEY'RE HEADED THIS WAY!
I WISH IT COULD BE OTHERWISE, LASS!
THOSE STRANGE ONES--STOP THEM BEFORE THEY ESCAPE!
YES, JEEBO! THEY SHALL BE CAUGHT!

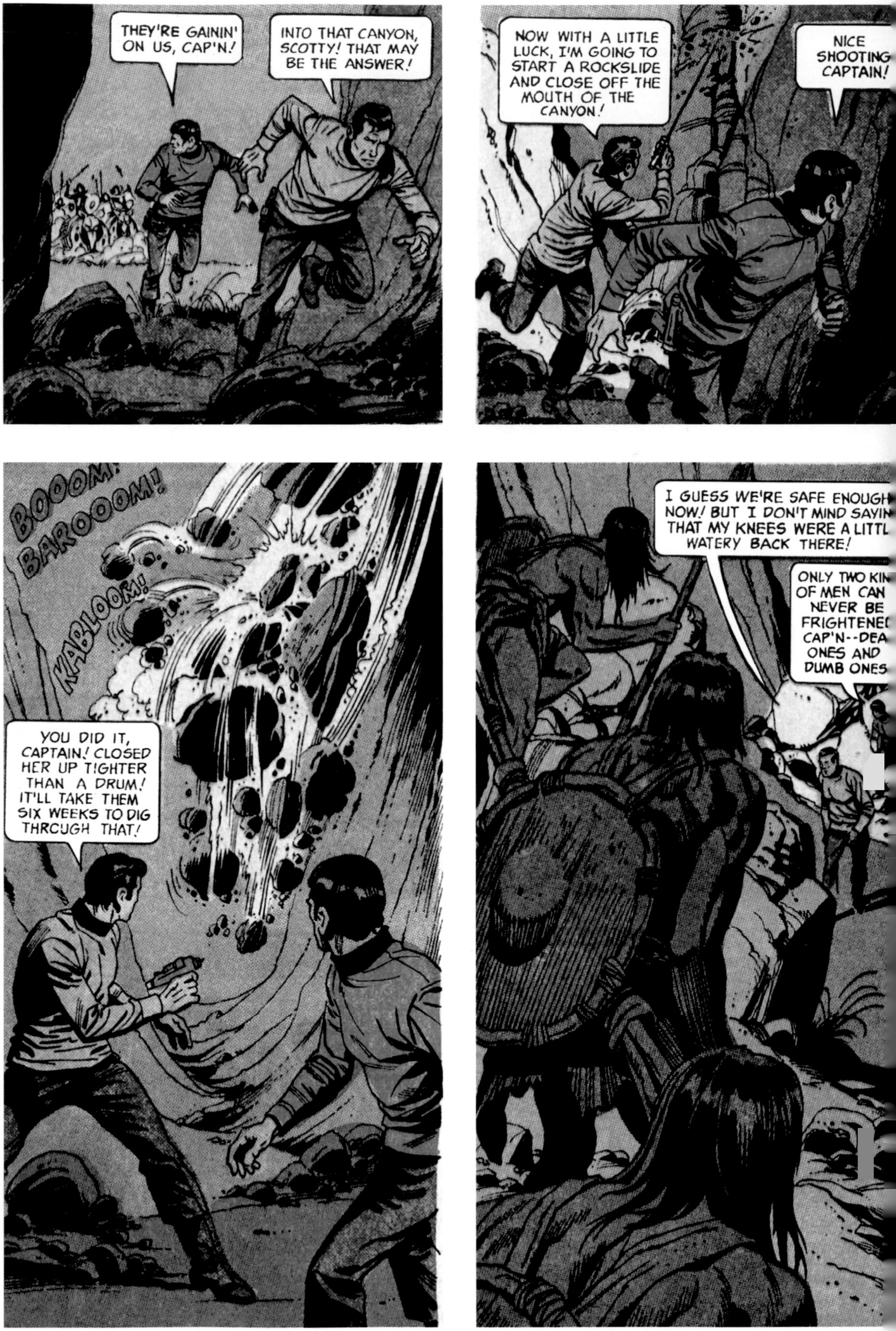
THEY'RE GAININ' ON US, CAP'N!
INTO THAT CANYON, SCOTTY! THAT MAY BE THE ANSWER!
NOW WITH A LITTLE LUCK, I'M GOING TO START A ROCKSLIDE AND CLOSE OFF THE MOUTH OF THE CANYON!
NICE SHOOTING CAPTAIN!
BOOOOM! BAROOOOM!
KABLOOM!
YOU DID IT, CAPTAIN! CLOSED HER UP TIGHTER THAN A DRUM! IT'LL TAKE THEM SIX WEEKS TO DIG THROUGH THAT!
I GUESS WE'RE SAFE ENOUGH NOW! BUT I DON'T MIND SAYIN THAT MY KNEES WERE A LITTL WATERY BACK THERE!
ONLY TWO KIN OF MEN CAN NEVER BE FRIGHTENE CAP'N--DEA ONES AND DUMB ONES

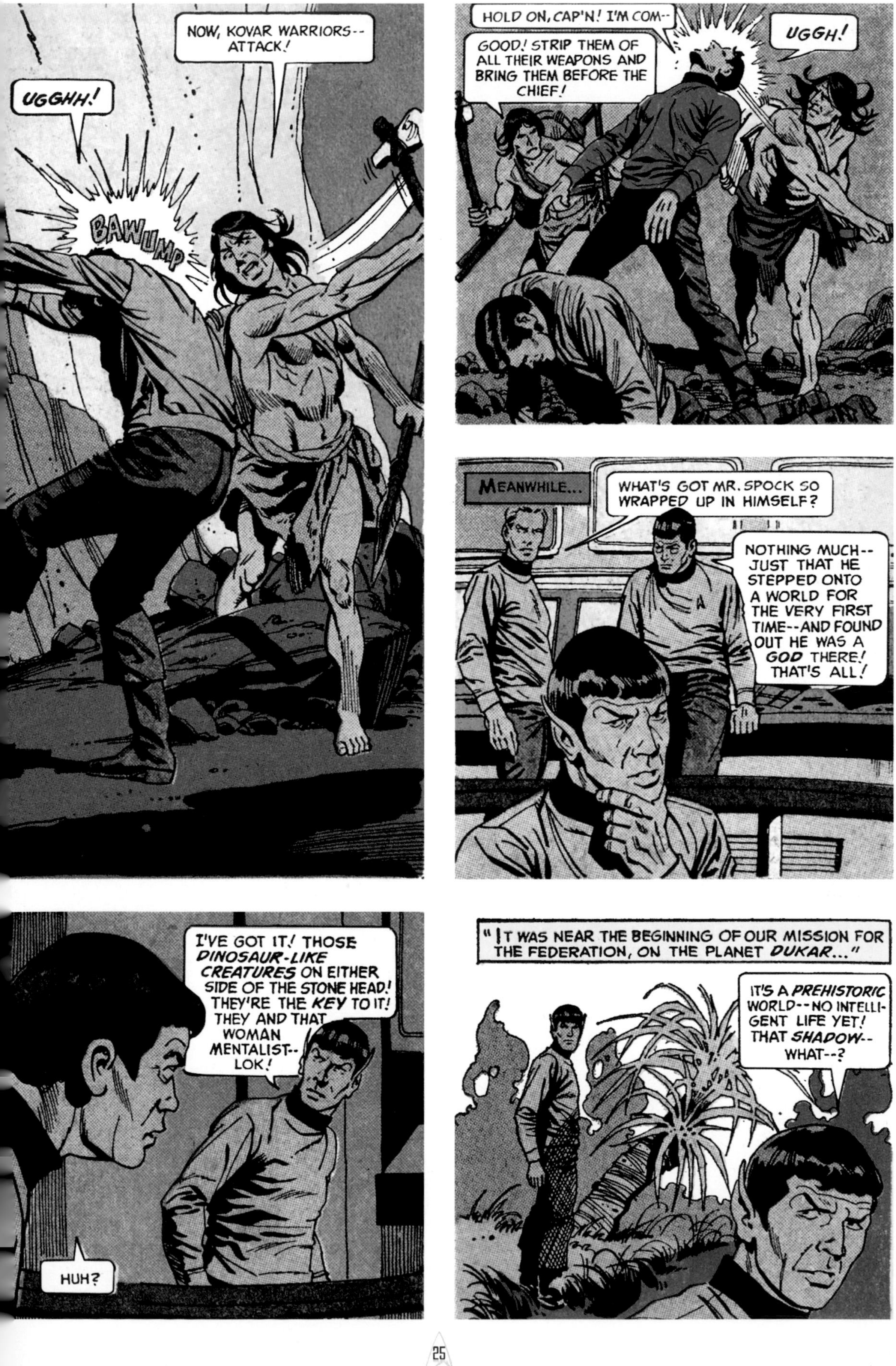
NOW, KOVAR WARRIORS--ATTACK!
UGGHH!
BAWUMP
HOLD ON, CAP'N! I'M COM--
GOOD! STRIP THEM OF ALL THEIR WEAPONS AND BRING THEM BEFORE THE CHIEF!
UGGH!
MEANWHILE...
WHAT'S GOT MR. SPOCK SO WRAPPED UP IN HIMSELF?
NOTHING MUCH--JUST THAT HE STEPPED ONTO A WORLD FOR THE VERY FIRST TIME--AND FOUND OUT HE WAS A GOD THERE! THAT'S ALL!
I'VE GOT IT! THOSE DINOSAUR-LIKE CREATURES ON EITHER SIDE OF THE STONE HEAD! THEY'RE THE KEY TO IT! THEY AND THAT WOMAN MENTALIST--LOK!
HUH?
"IT WAS NEAR THE BEGINNING OF OUR MISSION FOR THE FEDERATION, ON THE PLANET DUKAR..."
IT'S A PREHISTORIC WORLD--NO INTELLIGENT LIFE YET! THAT SHADOW--WHAT--?

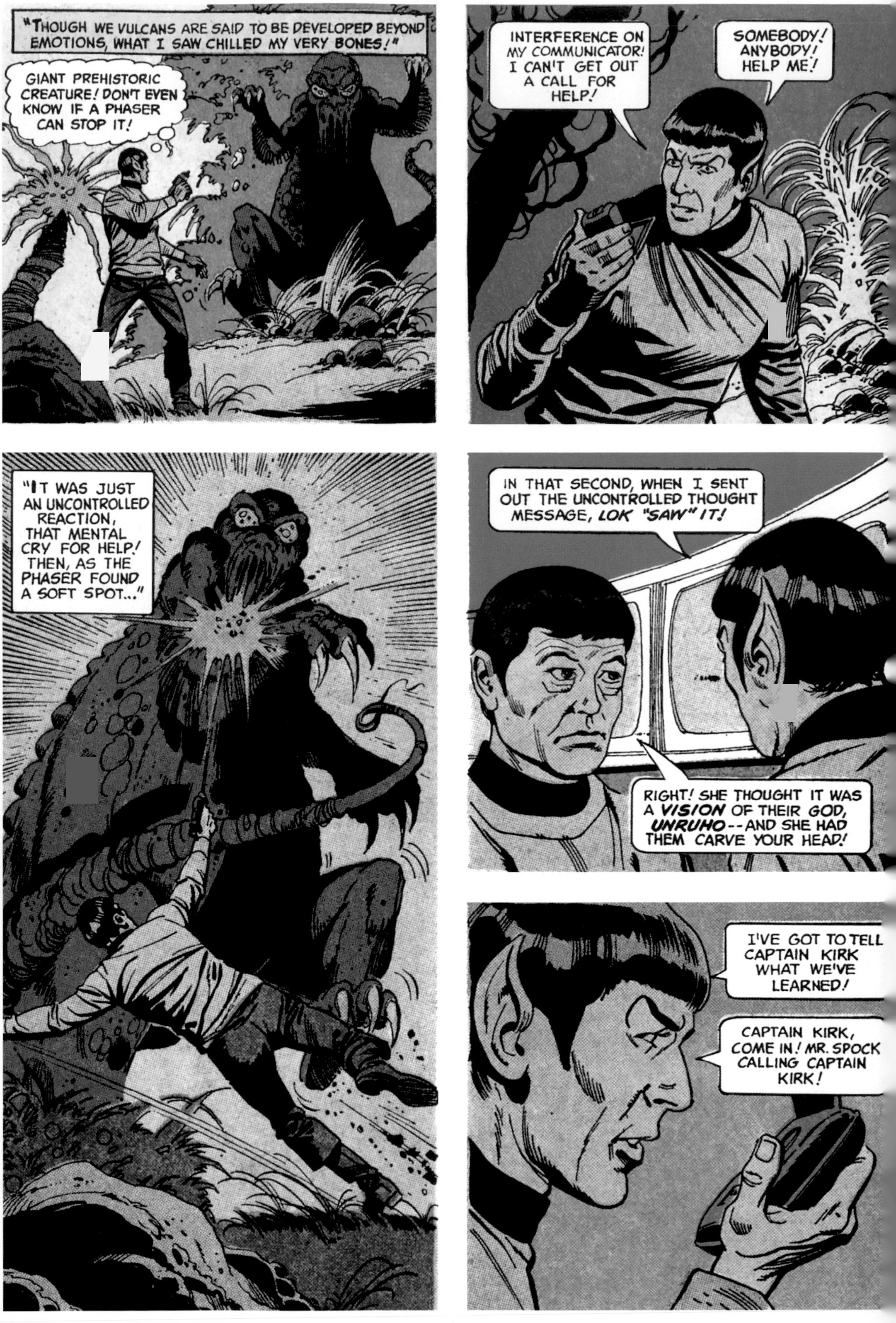
"THOUGH WE VULCANS ARE SAID TO BE DEVELOPED BEYOND EMOTIONS, WHAT I SAW CHILLED MY VERY BONES!"
GIANT PREHISTORIC CREATURE! DON'T EVEN KNOW IF A PHASER CAN STOP IT!
INTERFERENCE ON MY COMMUNICATOR! I CAN'T GET OUT A CALL FOR HELP!
SOMEBODY! ANYBODY! HELP ME!
"IT WAS JUST AN UNCONTROLLED REACTION, THAT MENTAL CRY FOR HELP! THEN, AS THE PHASER FOUND A SOFT SPOT..."
IN THAT SECOND, WHEN I SENT OUT THE UNCONTROLLED THOUGHT MESSAGE, LOK "SAW" IT!
RIGHT! SHE THOUGHT IT WAS A VISION OF THEIR GOD, UNRUHO--AND SHE HAD THEM CARVE YOUR HEAD!
I'VE GOT TO TELL CAPTAIN KIRK WHAT WE'VE LEARNED!
CAPTAIN KIRK, COME IN! MR. SPOCK CALLING CAPTAIN KIRK!

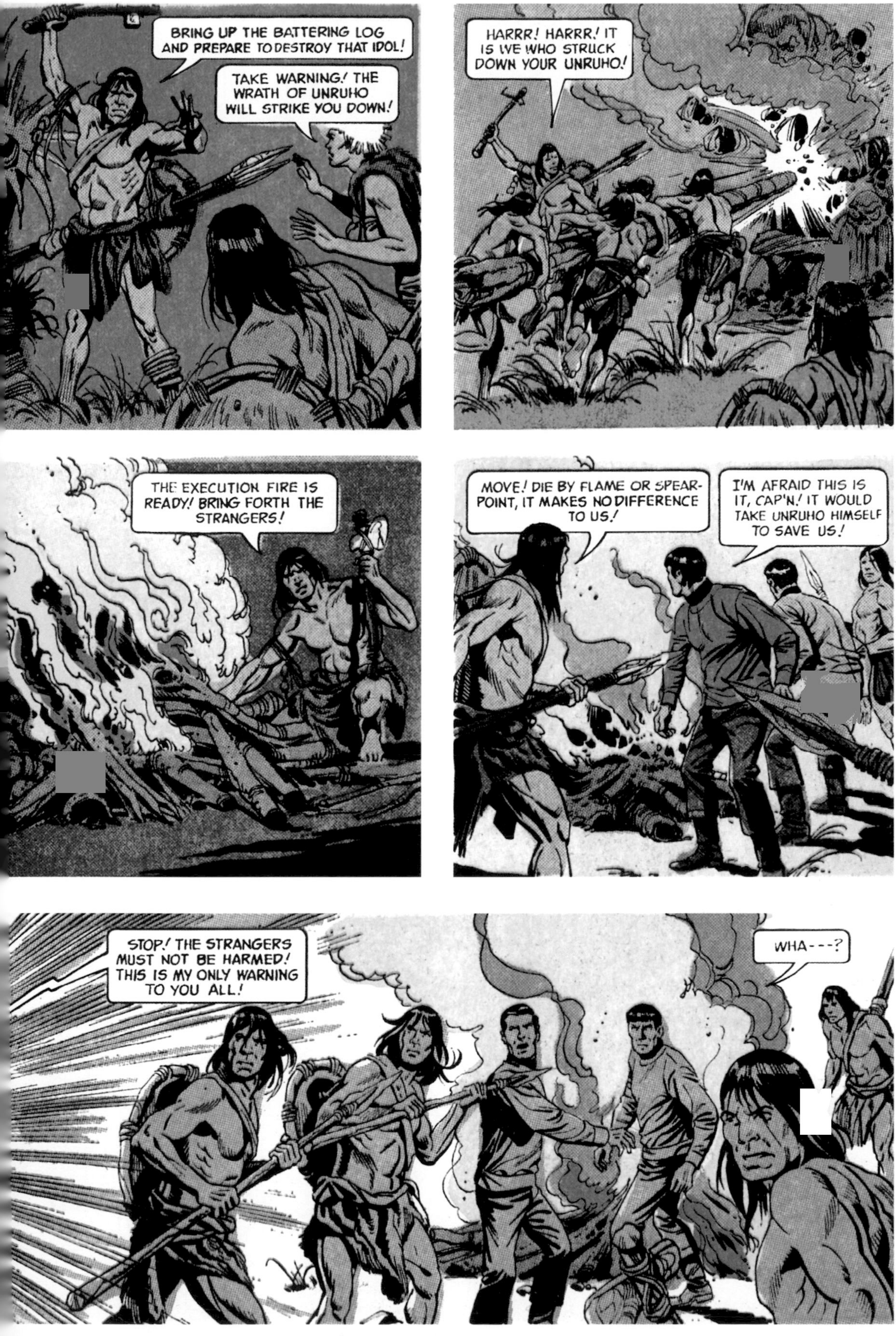
BRING UP THE BATTERING LOG AND PREPARE TO DESTROY THAT IDOL!
TAKE WARNING! THE WRATH OF UNRUHO WILL STRIKE YOU DOWN!
HARRR! HARRR! IT IS WE WHO STRUCK DOWN YOUR UNRUHO!
THE EXECUTION FIRE IS READY! BRING FORTH THE STRANGERS!
MOVE! DIE BY FLAME OR SPEAR-POINT, IT MAKES NO DIFFERENCE TO US!
I'M AFRAID THIS IS IT, CAP'N! IT WOULD TAKE UNRUHO HIMSELF TO SAVE US!
STOP! THE STRANGERS MUST NOT BE HARMED! THIS IS MY ONLY WARNING TO YOU ALL!
WHA---?

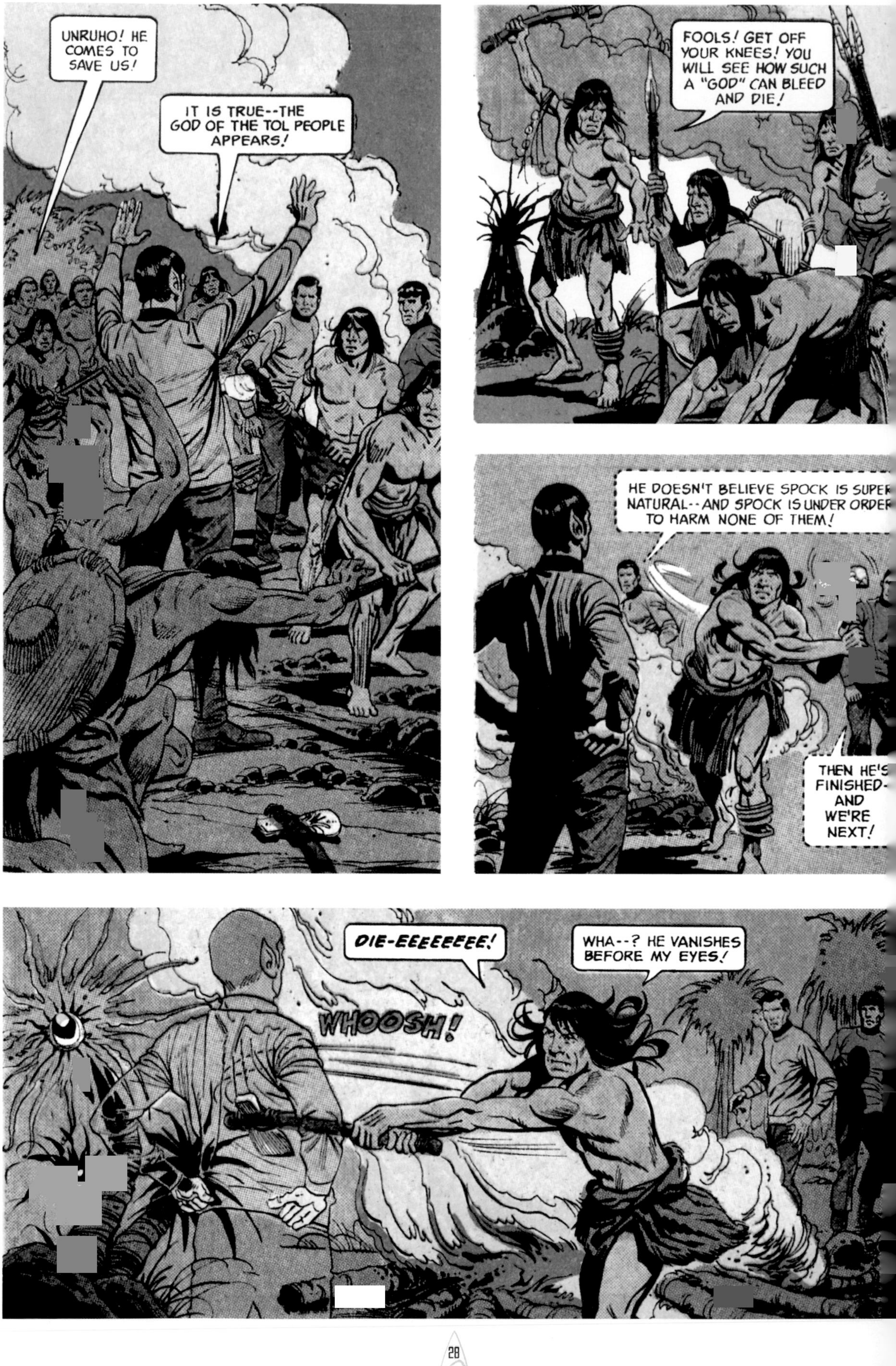
UNRUHO! HE COMES TO SAVE US!
IT IS TRUE--THE GOD OF THE TOL PEOPLE APPEARS!
FOOLS! GET OFF YOUR KNEES! YOU WILL SEE HOW SUCH A "GOD" CAN BLEED AND DIE!
HE DOESN'T BELIEVE SPOCK IS SUPER NATURAL--AND SPOCK IS UNDER ORDER TO HARM NONE OF THEM!
THEN HE'S FINISHED-AND WE'RE NEXT!
DIE-EEEEEEEE!
WHOOSH!
WHA--? HE VANISHES BEFORE MY EYES!

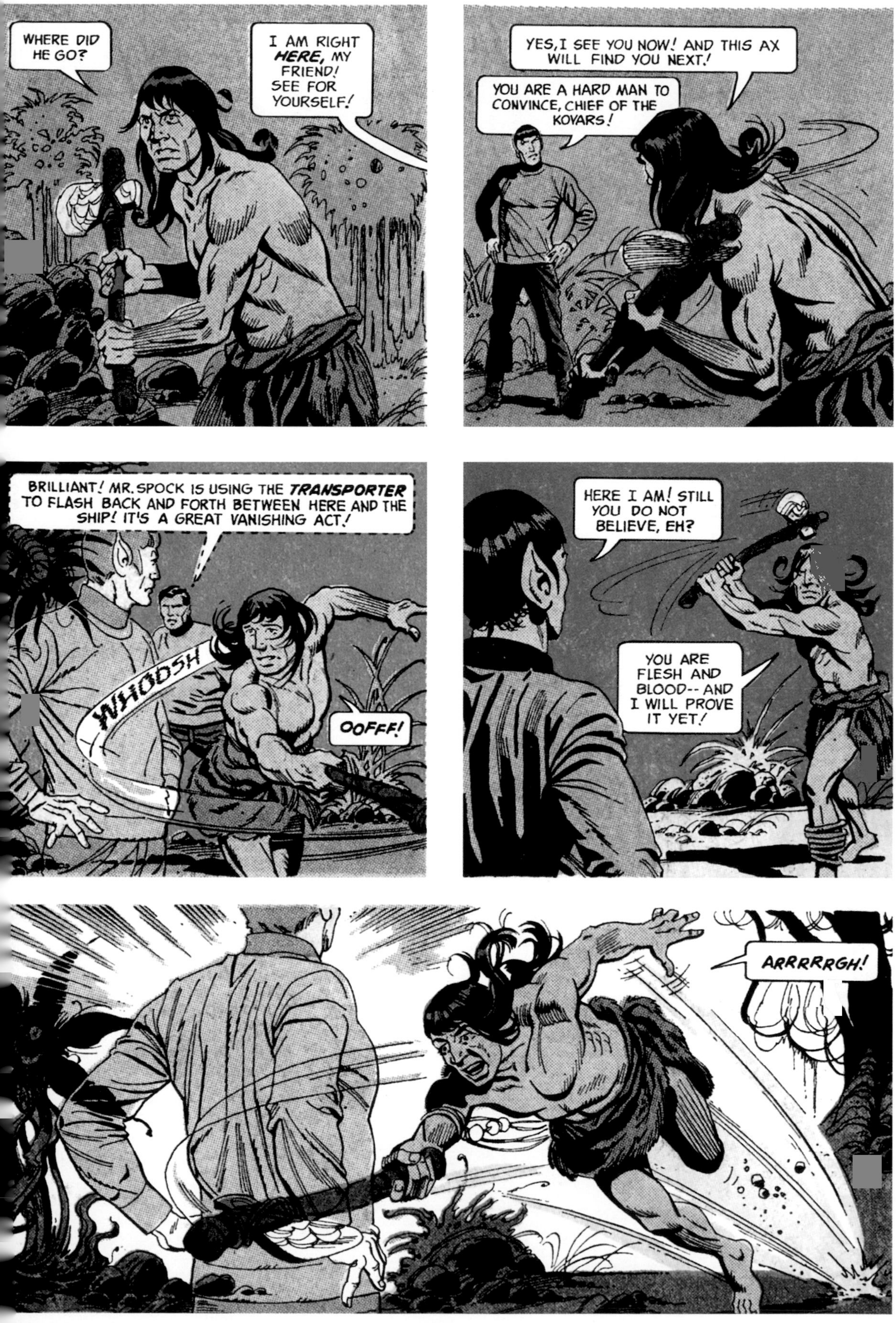
WHERE DID HE GO?
I AM RIGHT **HERE,** MY FRIEND! SEE FOR YOURSELF!
YES, I SEE YOU NOW! AND THIS AX WILL FIND YOU NEXT!
YOU ARE A HARD MAN TO CONVINCE, CHIEF OF THE KOYARS!
BRILLIANT! MR. SPOCK IS USING THE ***TRANSPORTER*** TO FLASH BACK AND FORTH BETWEEN HERE AND THE SHIP! IT'S A GREAT VANISHING ACT!
WHOOSH
OOFFF!
HERE I AM! STILL YOU DO NOT BELIEVE, EH?
YOU ARE FLESH AND BLOOD-- AND I WILL PROVE IT YET!
ARRRRRGH!

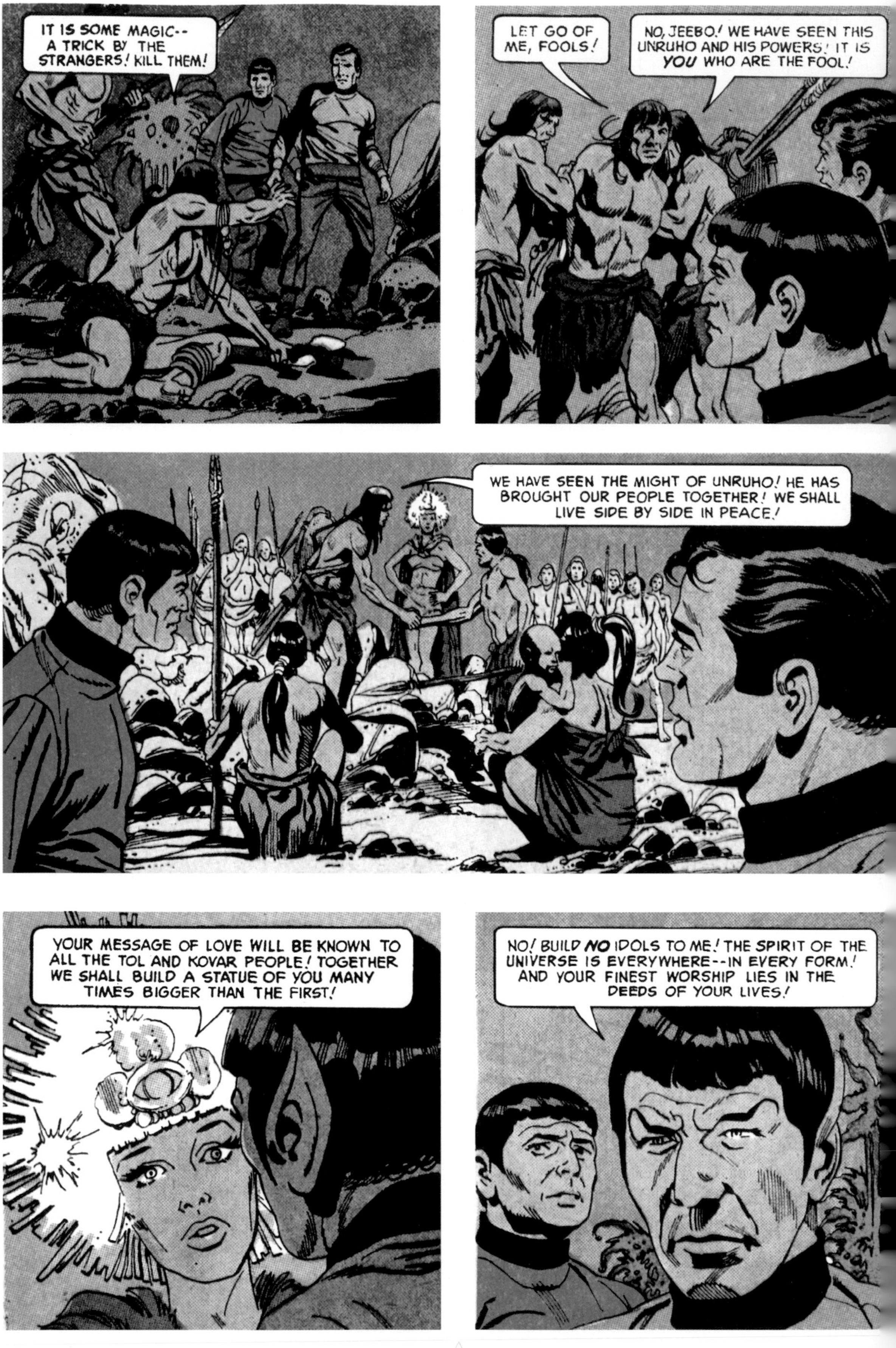
IT IS SOME MAGIC-- A TRICK BY THE STRANGERS! KILL THEM!
LET GO OF ME, FOOLS!
NO, JEEBO! WE HAVE SEEN THIS UNRUHO AND HIS POWERS! IT IS YOU WHO ARE THE FOOL!
WE HAVE SEEN THE MIGHT OF UNRUHO! HE HAS BROUGHT OUR PEOPLE TOGETHER! WE SHALL LIVE SIDE BY SIDE IN PEACE!
YOUR MESSAGE OF LOVE WILL BE KNOWN TO ALL THE TOL AND KOVAR PEOPLE! TOGETHER WE SHALL BUILD A STATUE OF YOU MANY TIMES BIGGER THAN THE FIRST!
NO! BUILD NO IDOLS TO ME! THE SPIRIT OF THE UNIVERSE IS EVERYWHERE--IN EVERY FORM! AND YOUR FINEST WORSHIP LIES IN THE DEEDS OF YOUR LIVES!

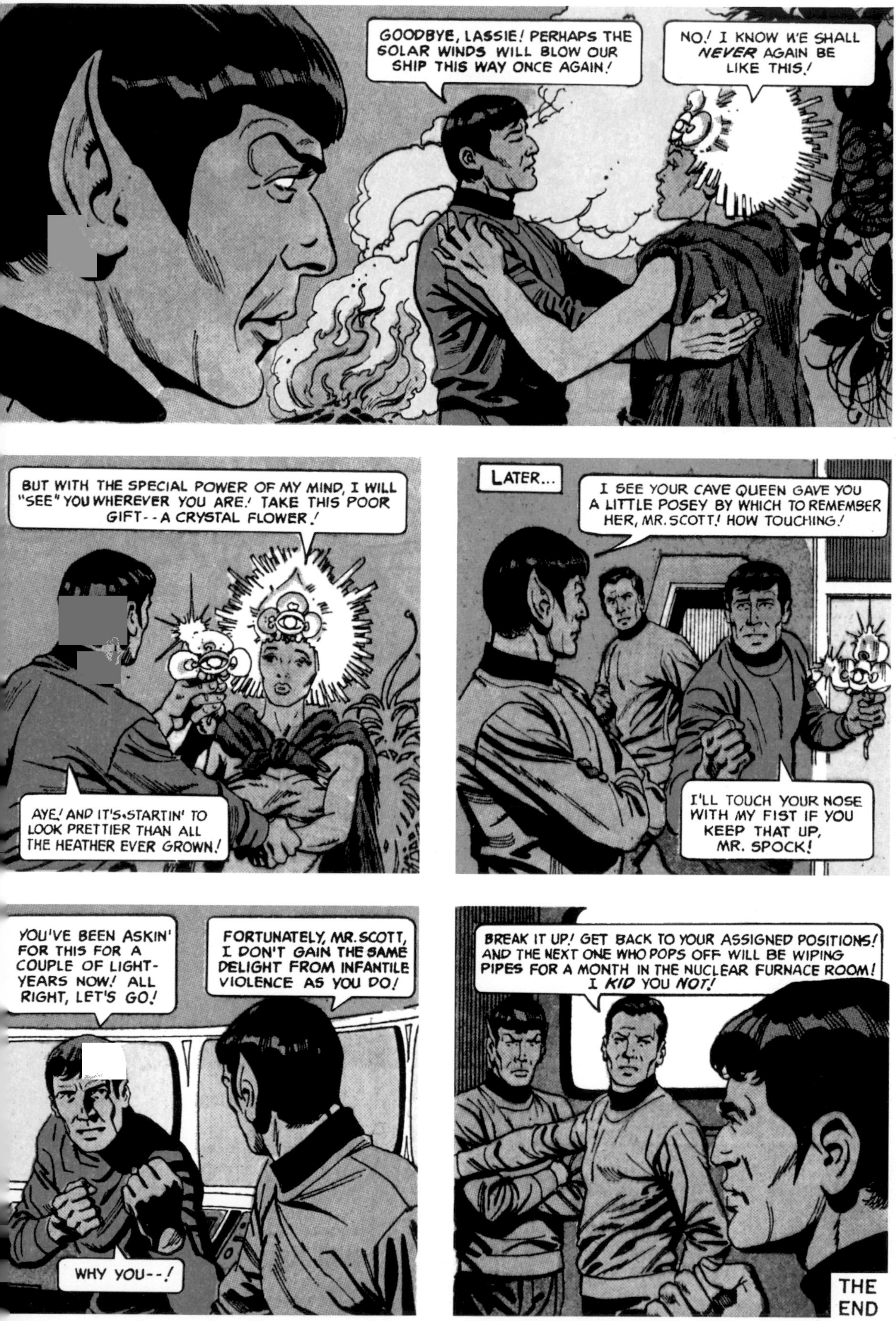
GOODBYE, LASSIE! PERHAPS THE SOLAR WINDS WILL BLOW OUR SHIP THIS WAY ONCE AGAIN!
NO! I KNOW WE SHALL *NEVER* AGAIN BE LIKE THIS!
BUT WITH THE SPECIAL POWER OF MY MIND, I WILL "SEE" YOU WHEREVER YOU ARE! TAKE THIS POOR GIFT--A CRYSTAL FLOWER!
AYE! AND IT'S STARTIN' TO LOOK PRETTIER THAN ALL THE HEATHER EVER GROWN!
LATER...
I SEE YOUR CAVE QUEEN GAVE YOU A LITTLE POSEY BY WHICH TO REMEMBER HER, MR. SCOTT! HOW TOUCHING!
I'LL TOUCH YOUR NOSE WITH MY FIST IF YOU KEEP THAT UP, MR. SPOCK!
YOU'VE BEEN ASKIN' FOR THIS FOR A COUPLE OF LIGHT-YEARS NOW! ALL RIGHT, LET'S GO!
FORTUNATELY, MR. SCOTT, I DON'T GAIN THE SAME DELIGHT FROM INFANTILE VIOLENCE AS YOU DO!
WHY YOU--!
BREAK IT UP! GET BACK TO YOUR ASSIGNED POSITIONS! AND THE NEXT ONE WHO POPS OFF WILL BE WIPING PIPES FOR A MONTH IN THE NUCLEAR FURNACE ROOM! I *KID* YOU *NOT*!
THE END

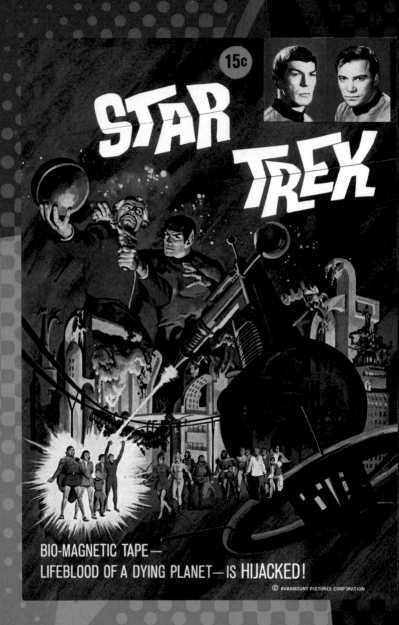

BIO-MAGNETIC TAPE—
LIFEBLOOD OF A DYING PLANET—IS HIJACKED!

© PARAMOUNT PICTURES CORPORATION

Chapter 2
The Hijacked Planet

(Originally Published in 1973)

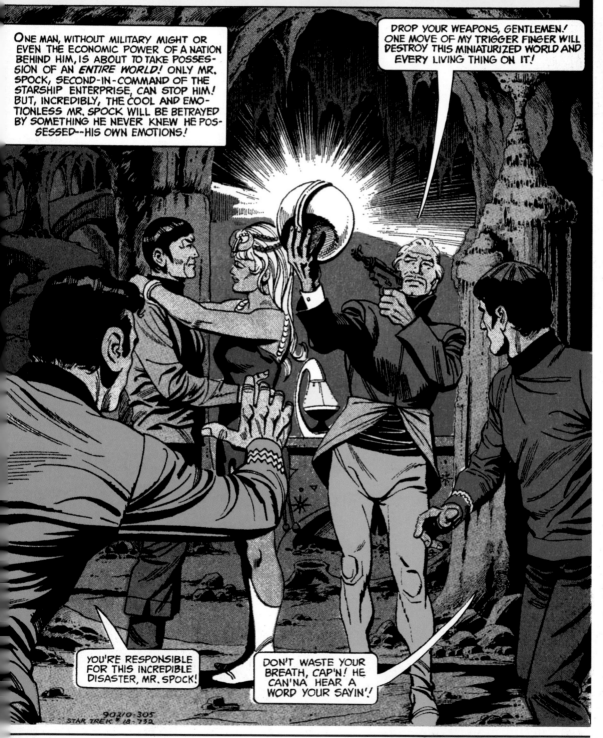

STAR TREK ~~~~ PART I — The HIJACKED PLANET

ONE MAN, WITHOUT MILITARY MIGHT OR EVEN THE ECONOMIC POWER OF A NATION BEHIND HIM, IS ABOUT TO TAKE POSSESSION OF AN *ENTIRE WORLD!* ONLY MR. SPOCK, SECOND-IN-COMMAND OF THE STARSHIP ENTERPRISE, CAN STOP HIM! BUT, INCREDIBLY, THE COOL AND EMOTIONLESS MR. SPOCK WILL BE BETRAYED BY SOMETHING HE NEVER KNEW HE POSSESSED--HIS OWN EMOTIONS!

DROP YOUR WEAPONS, GENTLEMEN! ONE MOVE OF MY TRIGGER FINGER WILL DESTROY THIS MINIATURIZED WORLD AND EVERY LIVING THING ON IT!

YOU'RE RESPONSIBLE FOR THIS INCREDIBLE DISASTER, MR. SPOCK!

DON'T WASTE YOUR BREATH, CAP'N! HE CAN'NA HEAR A WORD YOUR SAYIN'!

90210-305
STAR TREK 18-732

aptain's Log, Stardate 32:48.6 . . DATA REF . . 18.00-18.25

22

CAPTAIN'S LOG SUPPLEMENTAL--IT WAS EARLY IN THE 23RD CENTURY THAT THE FIRST ERRATIC ERUPTIONS OF THE THIRD LARGEST STAR OF STAR SYSTEM 83 BETA WERE RECORDED.

THE AIR WAS THICK WITH CONFLICTING THEORIES AT THE SCIENCE COUNCIL OF THE FEDERATED PLANETS!

THOUGH WE CANNOT AGREE ON THE PRECISE ORIGIN OF THE EXPLOSIONS, THESE PICTURES TAKEN OVER THE PAST THIRTY DAYS PROVE THAT THE DANGER TO PLANET STYRA GROWS IMMEDIATE!

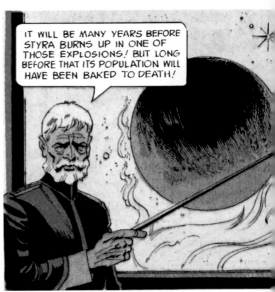

IT WILL BE MANY YEARS BEFORE STYRA BURNS UP IN ONE OF THOSE EXPLOSIONS! BUT LONG BEFORE THAT ITS POPULATION WILL HAVE BEEN BAKED TO DEATH!

THOSE PEOPLE ARE DOOMED! IN THE SHORT TIME REMAINING, IT WOULD BE IMPOSSIBLE TO SUPPLY ENOUGH TRANSPORTA--

--IF I MAY INTERRUPT THE ILLUSTRIOUS DR. KLEEG --THERE IS ONE WAY IN WHICH THAT ENTIRE WORLD CAN BE SAVED!

HOWEVER, FOR REASONS OF SECURITY, I HESITAT TO DISCUSS THIS IN OPEN SESSION! I ASK FOR A TOP-SECRET MEETING OF THE INNER COUNCIL

AND THUS WAS BORN PROJECT ATLAS, THE MOST ASTOUNDING UNDERTAKING IN THE HISTORY OF THE UNIVERSE!

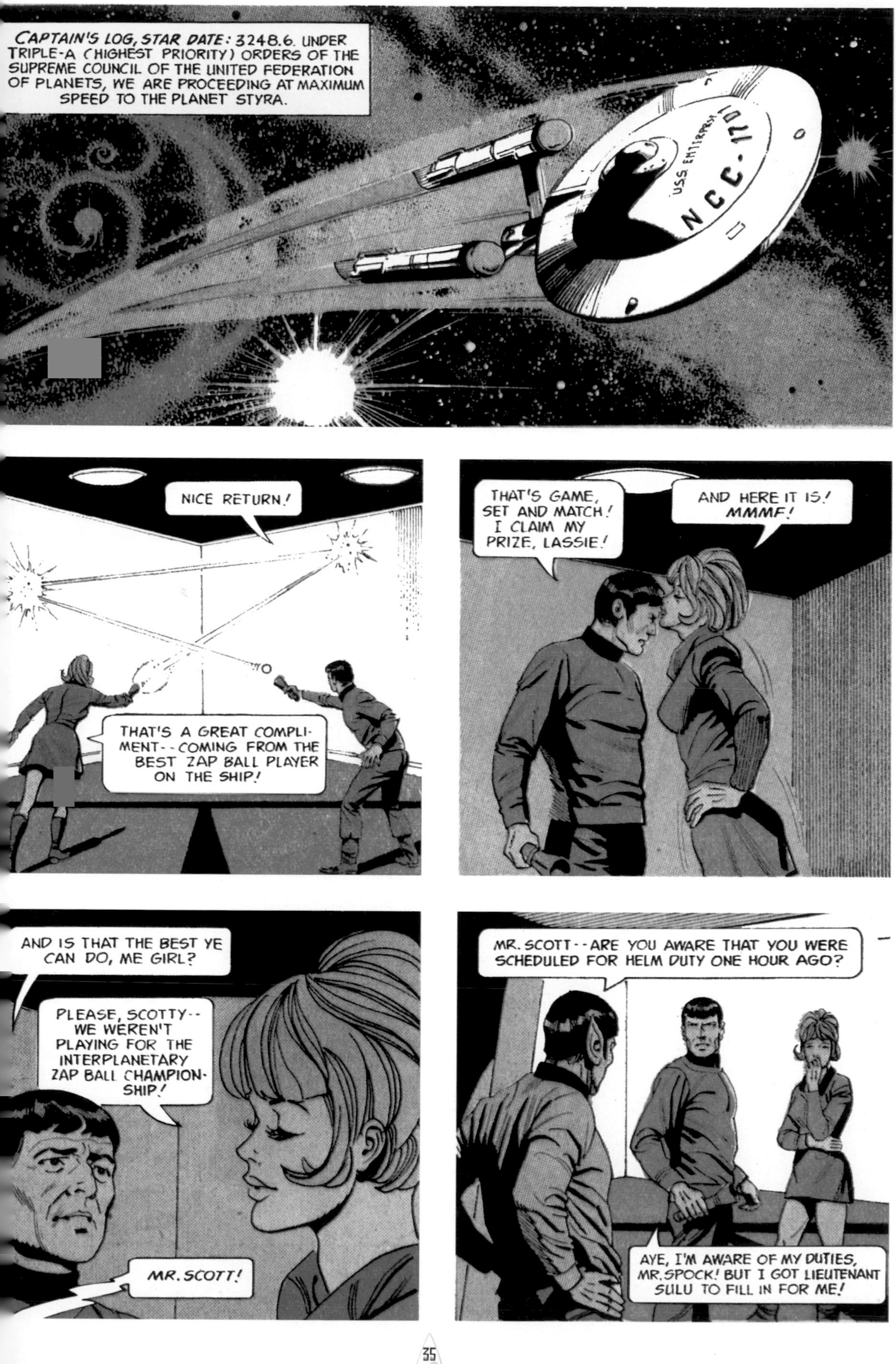
CAPTAIN'S LOG, STAR DATE: 3248.6. UNDER TRIPLE-A (HIGHEST PRIORITY) ORDERS OF THE SUPREME COUNCIL OF THE UNITED FEDERATION OF PLANETS, WE ARE PROCEEDING AT MAXIMUM SPEED TO THE PLANET STYRA.
USS ENTERPRISE
NCC-1701
NICE RETURN!
THAT'S A GREAT COMPLIMENT--COMING FROM THE BEST ZAP BALL PLAYER ON THE SHIP!
THAT'S GAME, SET AND MATCH! I CLAIM MY PRIZE, LASSIE!
AND HERE IT IS! MMMF!
AND IS THAT THE BEST YE CAN DO, ME GIRL?
PLEASE, SCOTTY--WE WEREN'T PLAYING FOR THE INTERPLANETARY ZAP BALL CHAMPIONSHIP!
MR. SCOTT!
MR. SCOTT--ARE YOU AWARE THAT YOU WERE SCHEDULED FOR HELM DUTY ONE HOUR AGO?
AYE, I'M AWARE OF MY DUTIES, MR. SPOCK! BUT I GOT LIEUTENANT SULU TO FILL IN FOR ME!

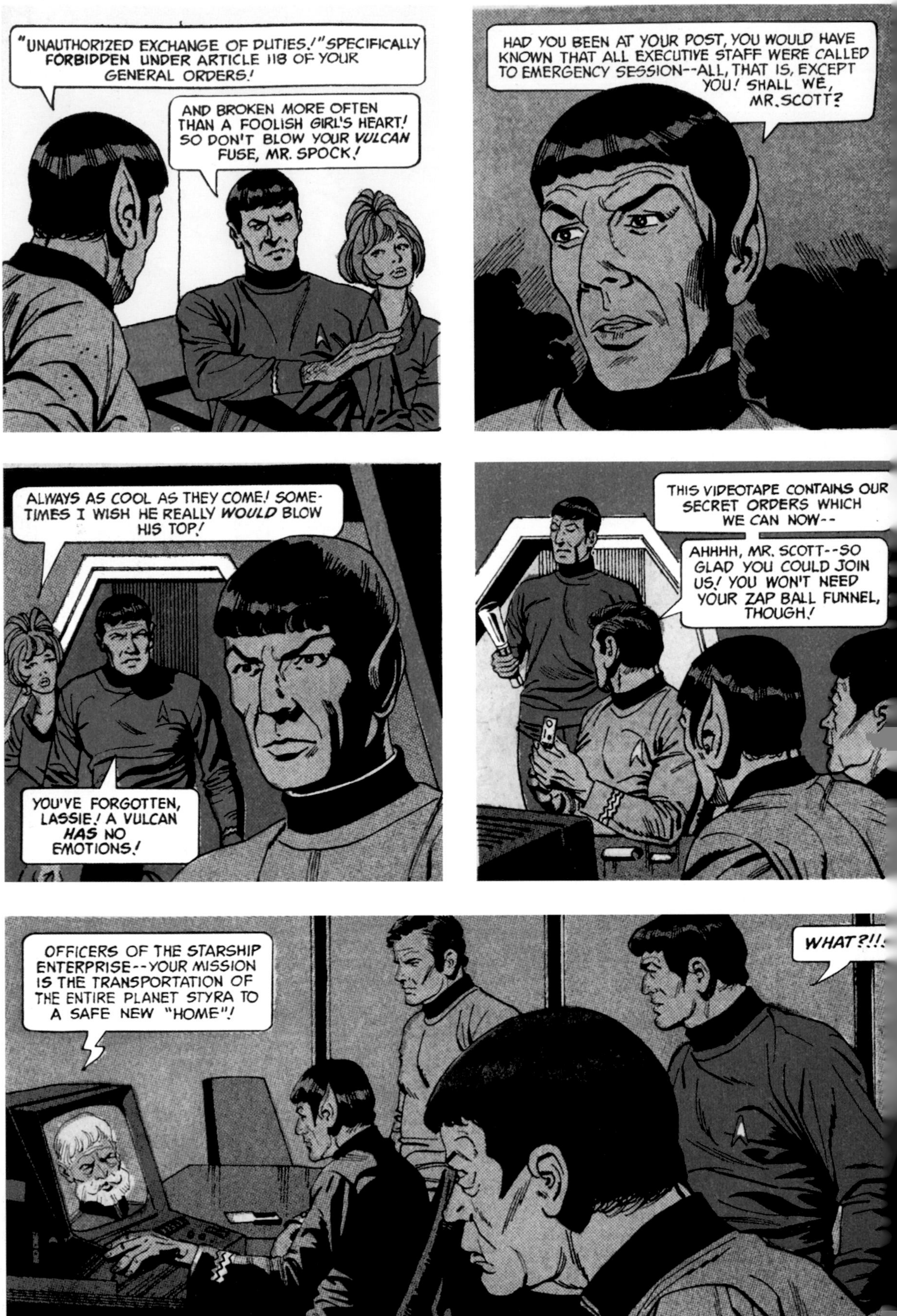
"UNAUTHORIZED EXCHANGE OF DUTIES!" SPECIFICALLY FORBIDDEN UNDER ARTICLE 118 OF YOUR GENERAL ORDERS!
AND BROKEN MORE OFTEN THAN A FOOLISH GIRL'S HEART! SO DON'T BLOW YOUR *VULCAN* FUSE, MR. SPOCK!
HAD YOU BEEN AT YOUR POST, YOU WOULD HAVE KNOWN THAT ALL EXECUTIVE STAFF WERE CALLED TO EMERGENCY SESSION--ALL, THAT IS, EXCEPT YOU! SHALL WE, MR. SCOTT?
ALWAYS AS COOL AS THEY COME! SOME-TIMES I WISH HE REALLY *WOULD* BLOW HIS TOP!
YOU'VE FORGOTTEN, LASSIE! A VULCAN *HAS* NO EMOTIONS!
THIS VIDEOTAPE CONTAINS OUR SECRET ORDERS WHICH WE CAN NOW--
AHHHH, MR. SCOTT--SO GLAD YOU COULD JOIN US! YOU WON'T NEED YOUR ZAP BALL FUNNEL, THOUGH!
OFFICERS OF THE STARSHIP ENTERPRISE--YOUR MISSION IS THE TRANSPORTATION OF THE ENTIRE PLANET STYRA TO A SAFE NEW "HOME"!
WHAT?!!

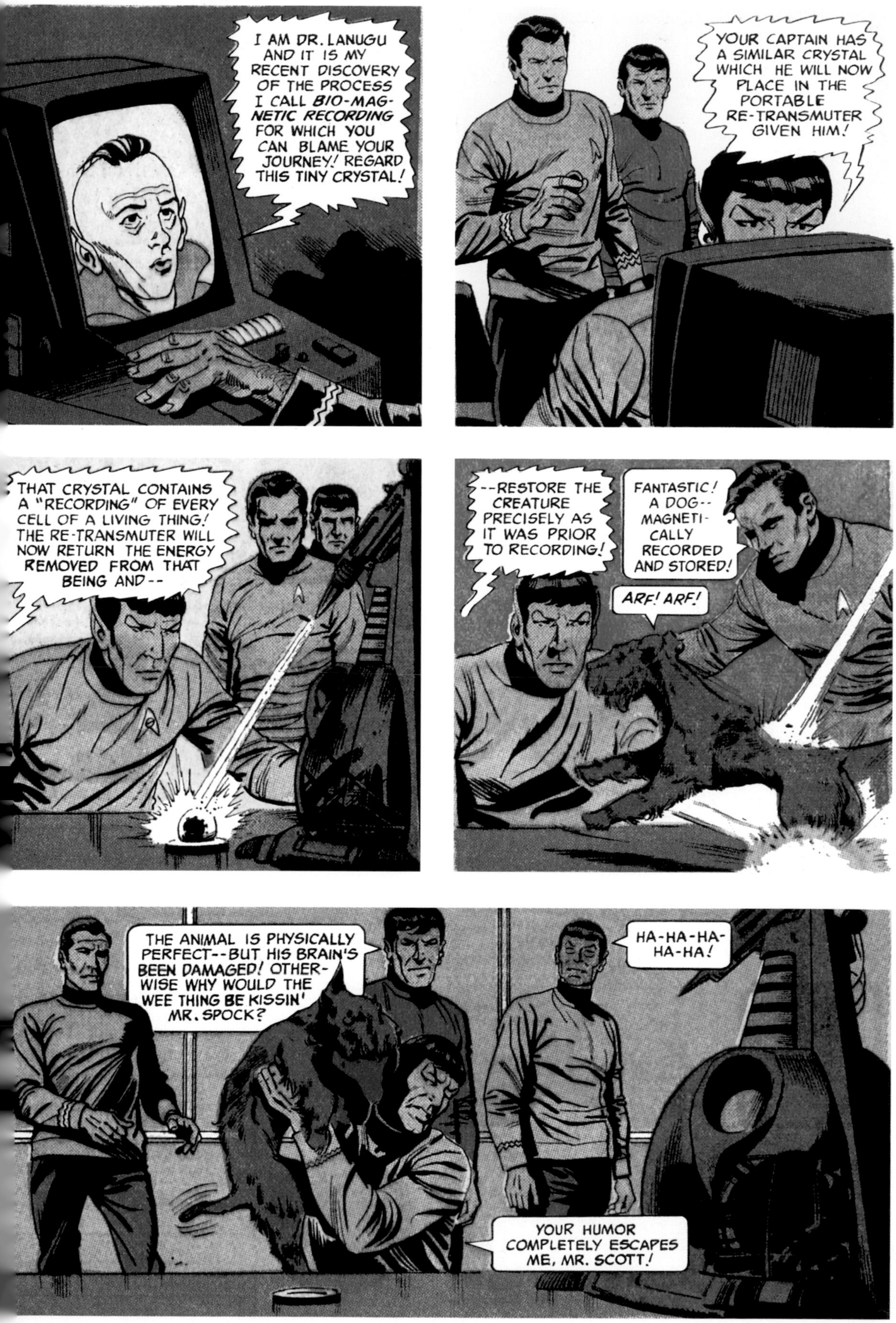
I AM DR. LANUGU AND IT IS MY RECENT DISCOVERY OF THE PROCESS I CALL BIO-MAGNETIC RECORDING FOR WHICH YOU CAN BLAME YOUR JOURNEY! REGARD THIS TINY CRYSTAL!
YOUR CAPTAIN HAS A SIMILAR CRYSTAL WHICH HE WILL NOW PLACE IN THE PORTABLE RE-TRANSMUTER GIVEN HIM!
THAT CRYSTAL CONTAINS A "RECORDING" OF EVERY CELL OF A LIVING THING! THE RE-TRANSMUTER WILL NOW RETURN THE ENERGY REMOVED FROM THAT BEING AND--
--RESTORE THE CREATURE PRECISELY AS IT WAS PRIOR TO RECORDING!
FANTASTIC! A DOG--MAGNETICALLY RECORDED AND STORED!
ARF! ARF!
THE ANIMAL IS PHYSICALLY PERFECT--BUT HIS BRAIN'S BEEN DAMAGED! OTHERWISE WHY WOULD THE WEE THING BE KISSIN' MR. SPOCK?
HA-HA-HA-HA-HA!
YOUR HUMOR COMPLETELY ESCAPES ME, MR. SCOTT!

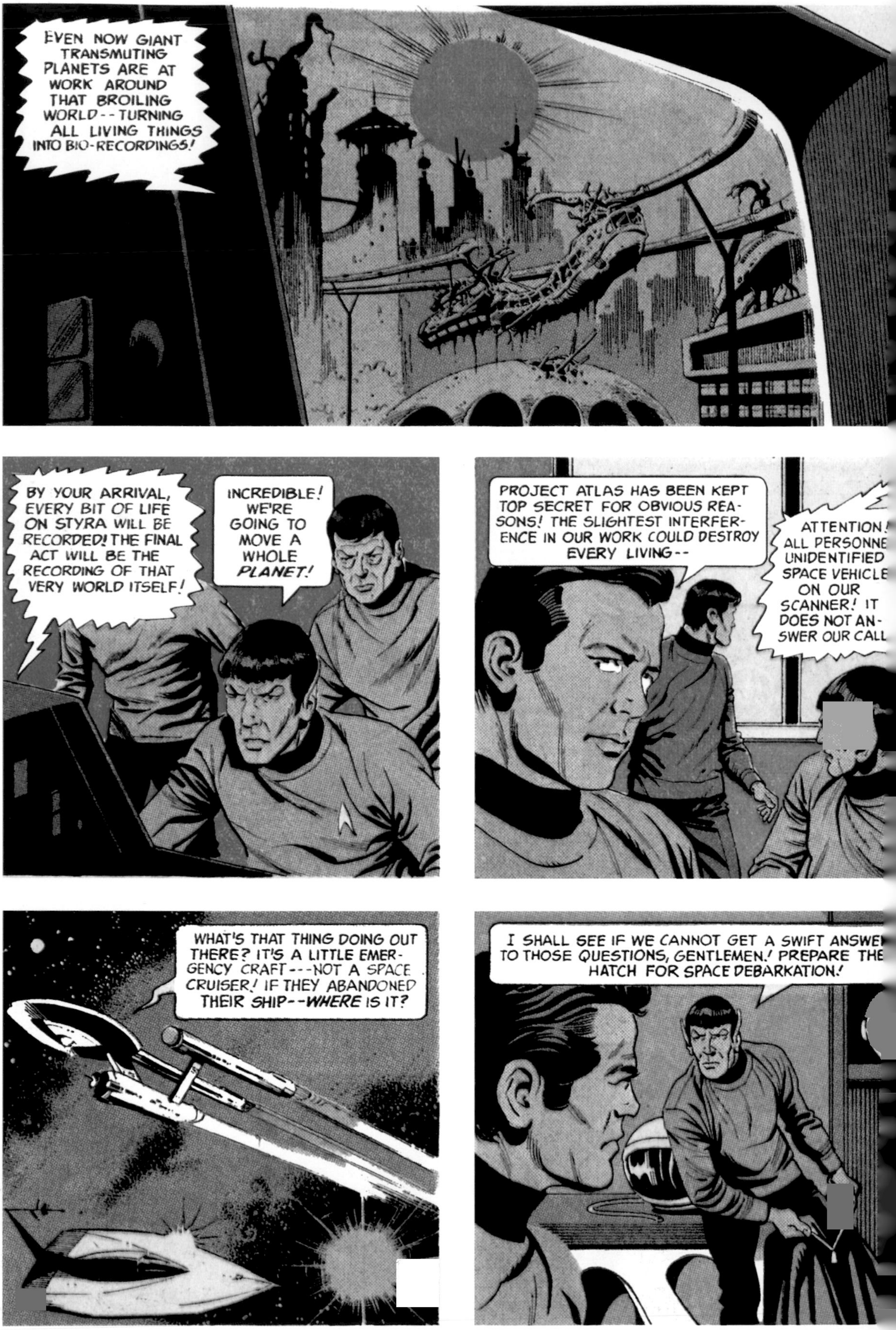
EVEN NOW GIANT TRANSMUTING PLANETS ARE AT WORK AROUND THAT BROILING WORLD--TURNING ALL LIVING THINGS INTO BIO-RECORDINGS!
BY YOUR ARRIVAL, EVERY BIT OF LIFE ON STYRA WILL BE RECORDED! THE FINAL ACT WILL BE THE RECORDING OF THAT VERY WORLD ITSELF!
INCREDIBLE! WE'RE GOING TO MOVE A WHOLE PLANET!
PROJECT ATLAS HAS BEEN KEPT TOP SECRET FOR OBVIOUS REASONS! THE SLIGHTEST INTERFERENCE IN OUR WORK COULD DESTROY EVERY LIVING--
ATTENTION! ALL PERSONNE UNIDENTIFIED SPACE VEHICLE ON OUR SCANNER! IT DOES NOT ANSWER OUR CALL
WHAT'S THAT THING DOING OUT THERE? IT'S A LITTLE EMERGENCY CRAFT---NOT A SPACE CRUISER! IF THEY ABANDONED THEIR SHIP--WHERE IS IT?
I SHALL SEE IF WE CANNOT GET A SWIFT ANSWE TO THOSE QUESTIONS, GENTLEMEN! PREPARE THE HATCH FOR SPACE DEBARKATION!

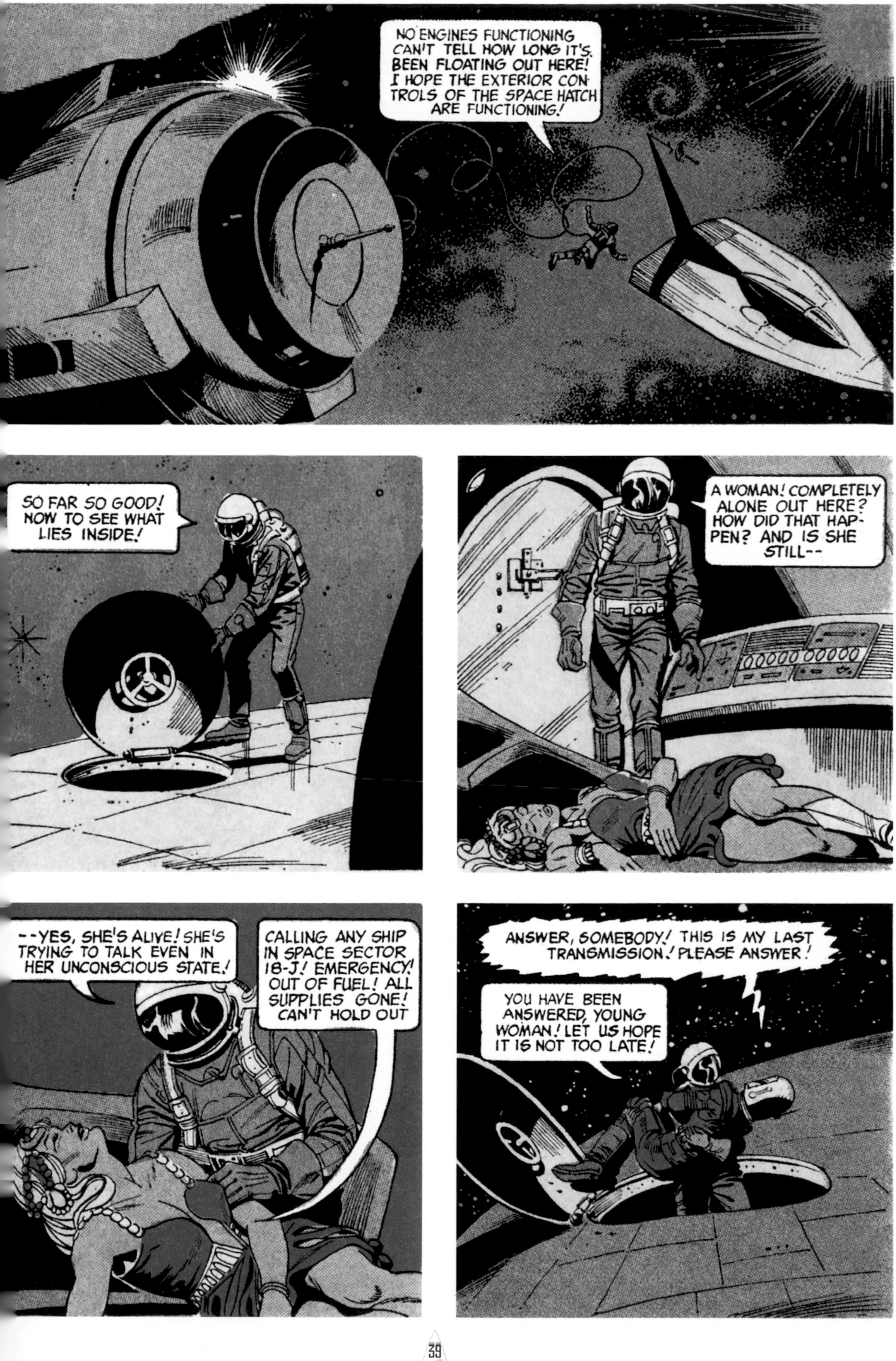
NO ENGINES FUNCTIONING CAN'T TELL HOW LONG IT'S BEEN FLOATING OUT HERE! I HOPE THE EXTERIOR CONTROLS OF THE SPACE HATCH ARE FUNCTIONING!
SO FAR SO GOOD! NOW TO SEE WHAT LIES INSIDE!
A WOMAN! COMPLETELY ALONE OUT HERE? HOW DID THAT HAPPEN? AND IS SHE STILL--
--YES, SHE'S ALIVE! SHE'S TRYING TO TALK EVEN IN HER UNCONSCIOUS STATE!
CALLING ANY SHIP IN SPACE SECTOR 18-J! EMERGENCY! OUT OF FUEL! ALL SUPPLIES GONE! CAN'T HOLD OUT
ANSWER, SOMEBODY! THIS IS MY LAST TRANSMISSION! PLEASE ANSWER!
YOU HAVE BEEN ANSWERED, YOUNG WOMAN! LET US HOPE IT IS NOT TOO LATE!

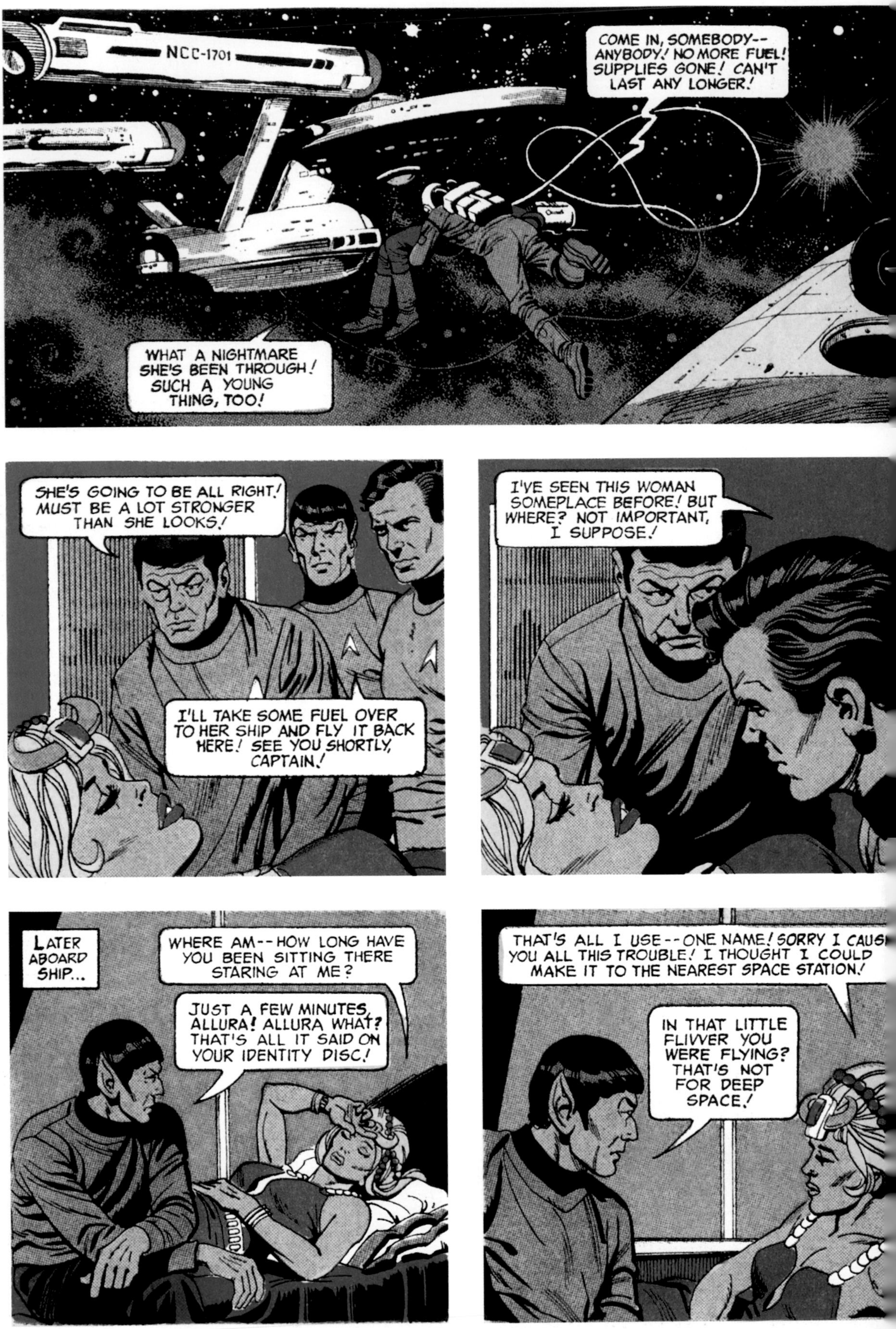

COME IN, SOMEBODY-- ANYBODY! NO MORE FUEL! SUPPLIES GONE! CAN'T LAST ANY LONGER!
WHAT A NIGHTMARE SHE'S BEEN THROUGH! SUCH A YOUNG THING, TOO!
SHE'S GOING TO BE ALL RIGHT! MUST BE A LOT STRONGER THAN SHE LOOKS!
I'LL TAKE SOME FUEL OVER TO HER SHIP AND FLY IT BACK HERE! SEE YOU SHORTLY, CAPTAIN!
I'VE SEEN THIS WOMAN SOMEPLACE BEFORE! BUT WHERE? NOT IMPORTANT, I SUPPOSE!
LATER ABOARD SHIP...
WHERE AM--HOW LONG HAVE YOU BEEN SITTING THERE STARING AT ME?
JUST A FEW MINUTES, ALLURA! ALLURA WHAT? THAT'S ALL IT SAID ON YOUR IDENTITY DISC!
THAT'S ALL I USE--ONE NAME! SORRY I CAUS YOU ALL THIS TROUBLE! I THOUGHT I COULD MAKE IT TO THE NEAREST SPACE STATION!
IN THAT LITTLE FLIVVER YOU WERE FLYING? THAT'S NOT FOR DEEP SPACE!

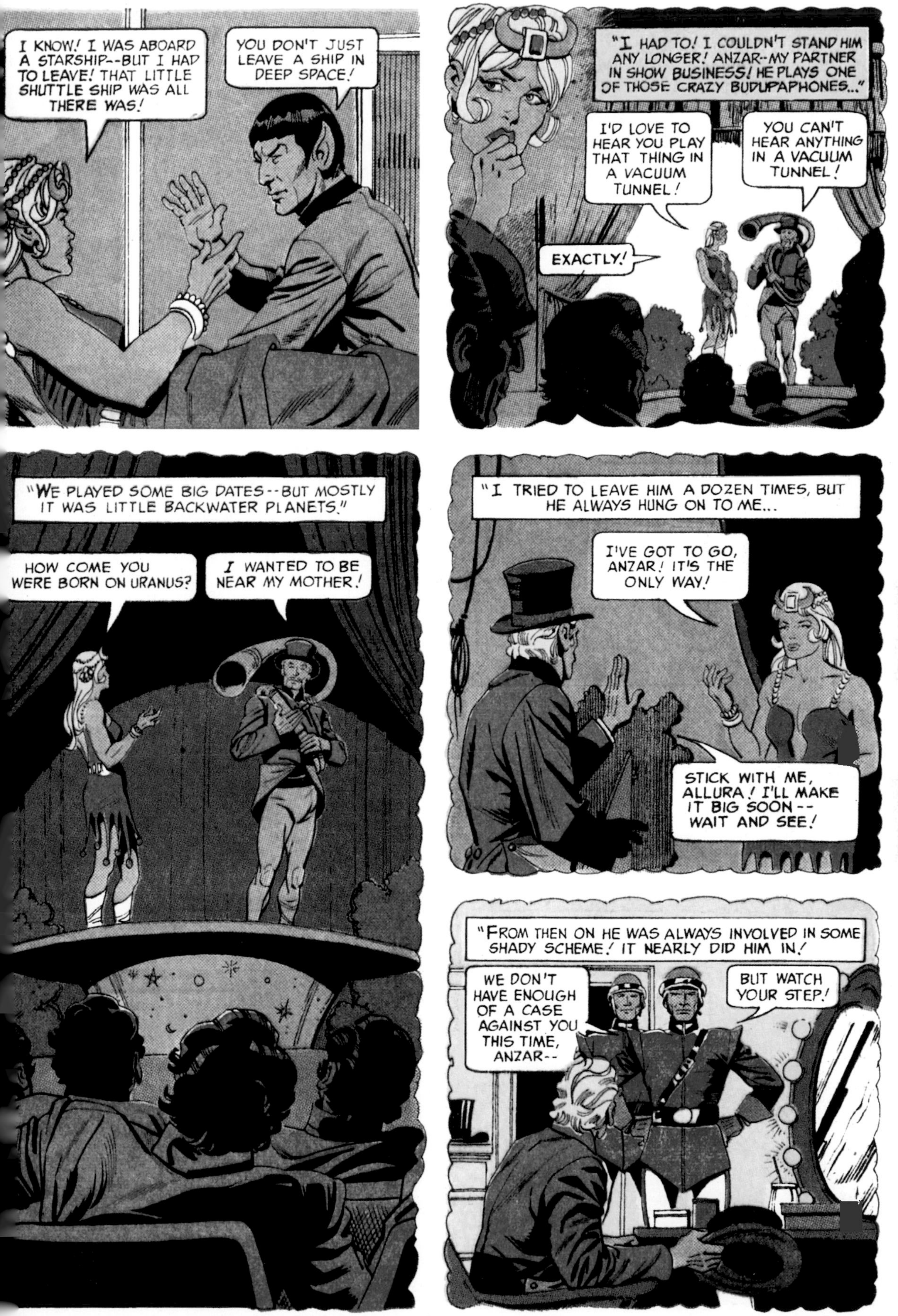
I KNOW! I WAS ABOARD A STARSHIP--BUT I HAD TO LEAVE! THAT LITTLE SHUTTLE SHIP WAS ALL THERE WAS!
YOU DON'T JUST LEAVE A SHIP IN DEEP SPACE!
"I HAD TO! I COULDN'T STAND HIM ANY LONGER! ANZAR--MY PARTNER IN SHOW BUSINESS! HE PLAYS ONE OF THOSE CRAZY BUDUPAPHONES..."
I'D LOVE TO HEAR YOU PLAY THAT THING IN A VACUUM TUNNEL!
YOU CAN'T HEAR ANYTHING IN A VACUUM TUNNEL!
EXACTLY!
"WE PLAYED SOME BIG DATES--BUT MOSTLY IT WAS LITTLE BACKWATER PLANETS."
HOW COME YOU WERE BORN ON URANUS?
I WANTED TO BE NEAR MY MOTHER!
"I TRIED TO LEAVE HIM A DOZEN TIMES, BUT HE ALWAYS HUNG ON TO ME...
I'VE GOT TO GO, ANZAR! IT'S THE ONLY WAY!
STICK WITH ME, ALLURA! I'LL MAKE IT BIG SOON--WAIT AND SEE!
"FROM THEN ON HE WAS ALWAYS INVOLVED IN SOME SHADY SCHEME! IT NEARLY DID HIM IN!
WE DON'T HAVE ENOUGH OF A CASE AGAINST YOU THIS TIME, ANZAR--
BUT WATCH YOUR STEP!

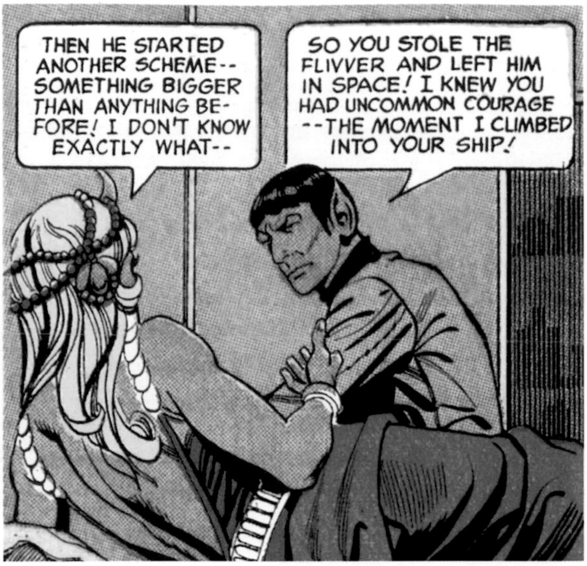
THEN HE STARTED ANOTHER SCHEME-- SOMETHING BIGGER THAN ANYTHING BE-FORE! I DON'T KNOW EXACTLY WHAT--
SO YOU STOLE THE FLIVVER AND LEFT HIM IN SPACE! I KNEW YOU HAD UNCOMMON COURAGE --THE MOMENT I CLIMBED INTO YOUR SHIP!

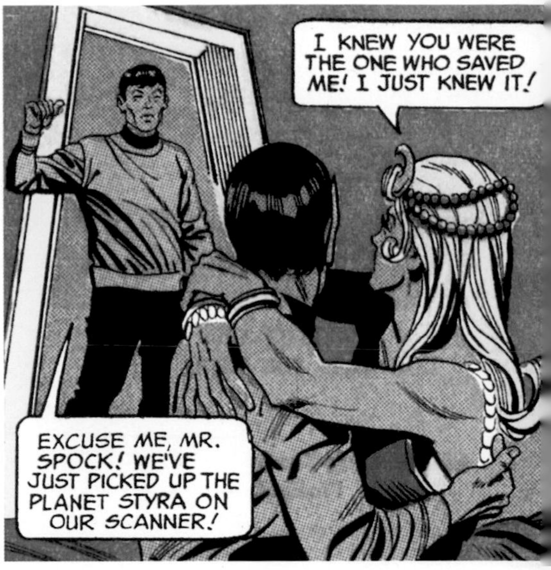
I KNEW YOU WERE THE ONE WHO SAVED ME! I JUST KNEW IT!
EXCUSE ME, MR. SPOCK! WE'VE JUST PICKED UP THE PLANET STYRA ON OUR SCANNER!

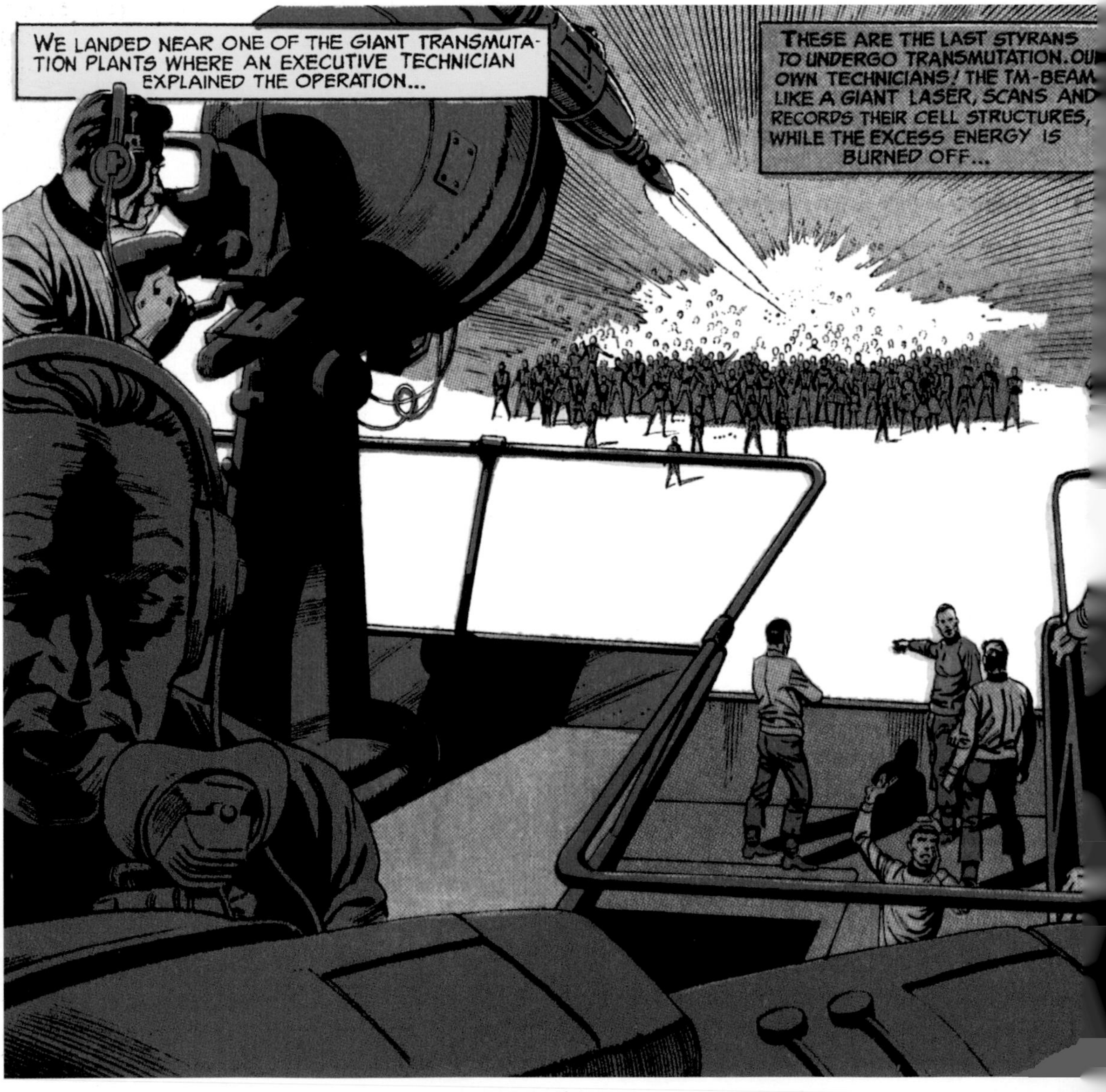
WE LANDED NEAR ONE OF THE GIANT TRANSMUTATION PLANTS WHERE AN EXECUTIVE TECHNICIAN EXPLAINED THE OPERATION...
THESE ARE THE LAST STYRANS TO UNDERGO TRANSMUTATION. OU
OWN TECHNICIANS! THE TM-BEAM LIKE A GIANT LASER, SCANS AND RECORDS THEIR CELL STRUCTURES, WHILE THE EXCESS ENERGY IS BURNED OFF...

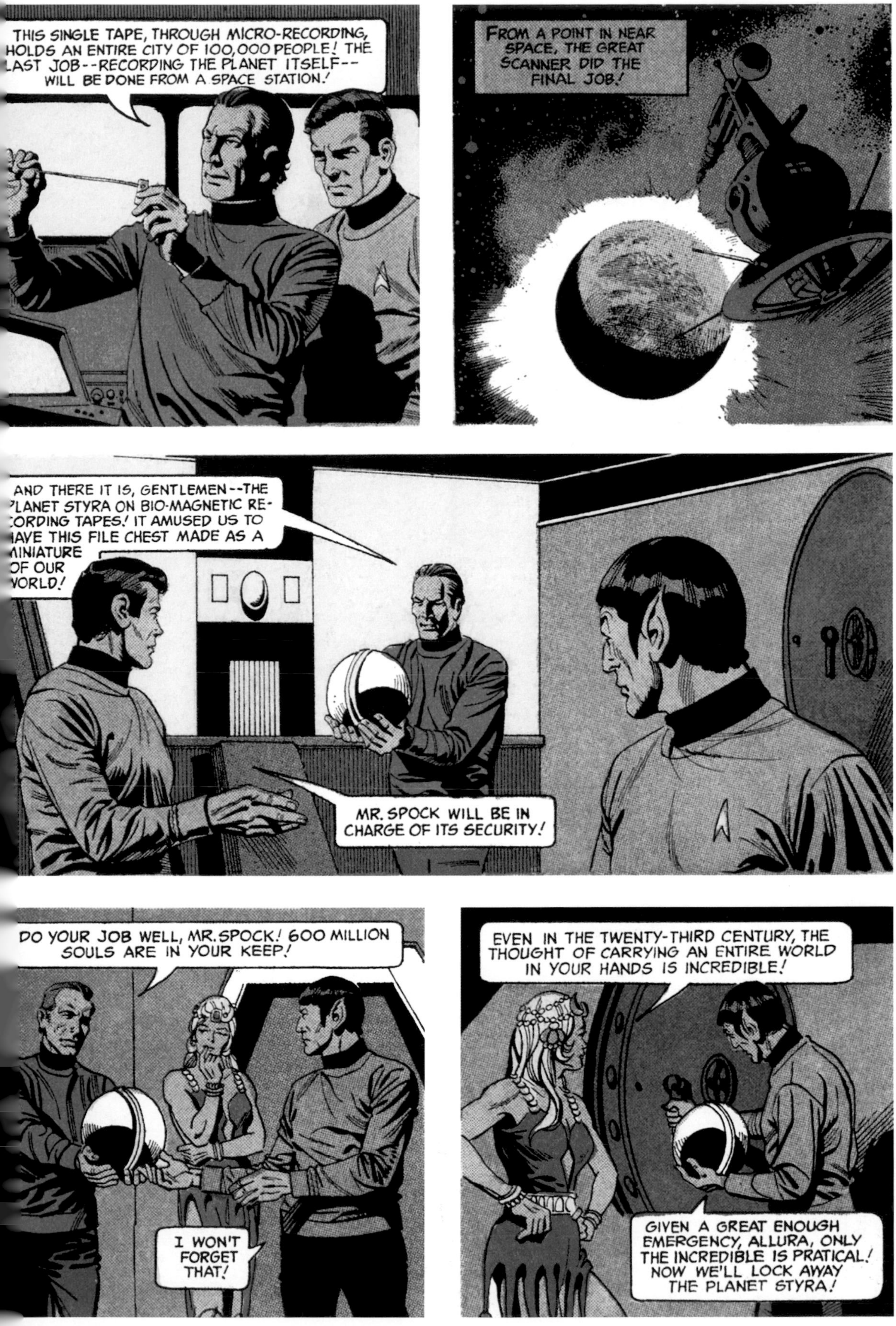
THIS SINGLE TAPE, THROUGH MICRO-RECORDING, HOLDS AN ENTIRE CITY OF 100,000 PEOPLE! THE LAST JOB--RECORDING THE PLANET ITSELF--WILL BE DONE FROM A SPACE STATION!
FROM A POINT IN NEAR SPACE, THE GREAT SCANNER DID THE FINAL JOB!
AND THERE IT IS, GENTLEMEN--THE PLANET STYRA ON BIO-MAGNETIC RECORDING TAPES! IT AMUSED US TO HAVE THIS FILE CHEST MADE AS A MINIATURE OF OUR WORLD!
MR. SPOCK WILL BE IN CHARGE OF ITS SECURITY!
DO YOUR JOB WELL, MR. SPOCK! 600 MILLION SOULS ARE IN YOUR KEEP!
I WON'T FORGET THAT!
EVEN IN THE TWENTY-THIRD CENTURY, THE THOUGHT OF CARRYING AN ENTIRE WORLD IN YOUR HANDS IS INCREDIBLE!
GIVEN A GREAT ENOUGH EMERGENCY, ALLURA, ONLY THE INCREDIBLE IS PRATICAL! NOW WE'LL LOCK AWAY THE PLANET STYRA!

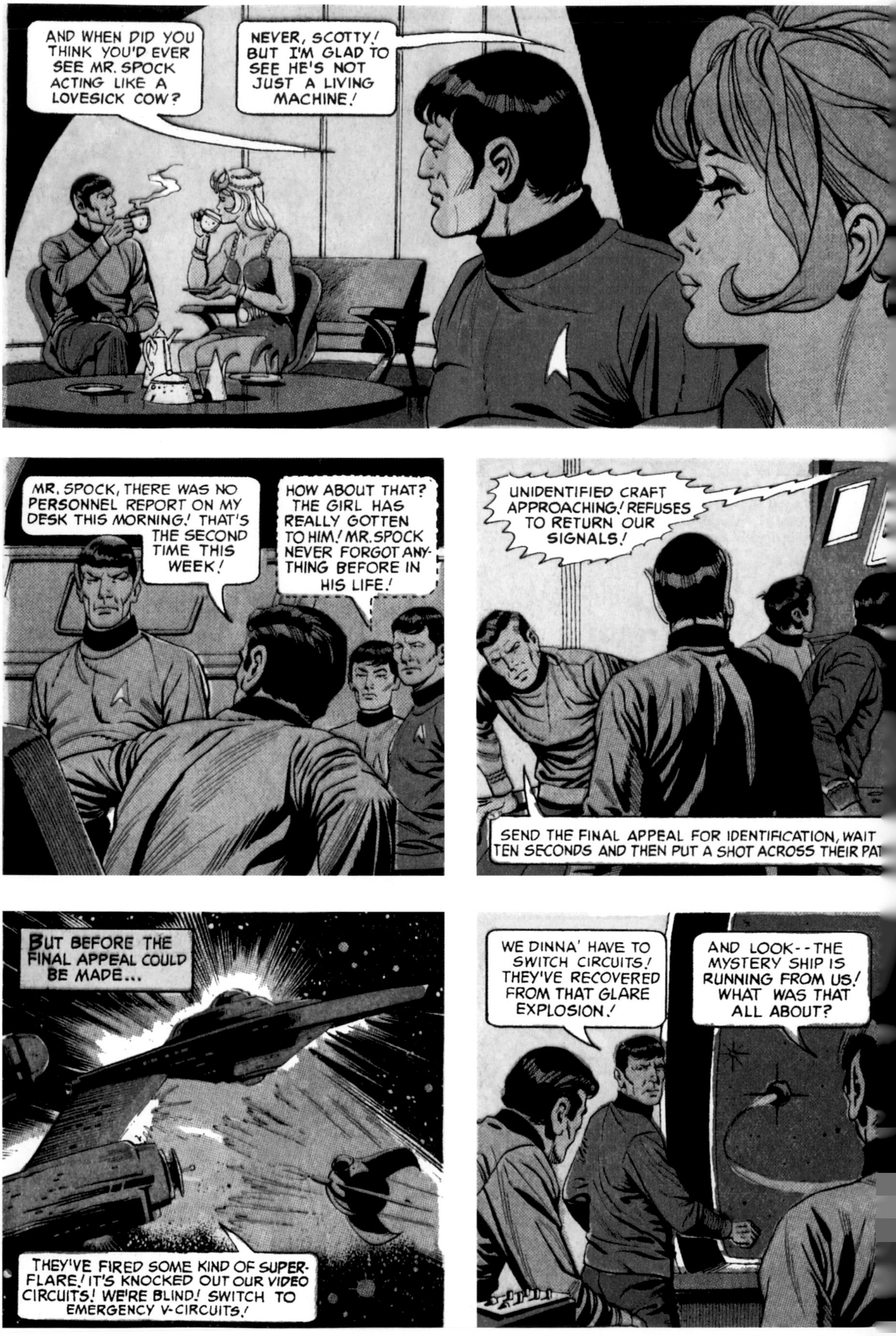
AND WHEN DID YOU THINK YOU'D EVER SEE MR. SPOCK ACTING LIKE A LOVESICK COW?
NEVER, SCOTTY! BUT I'M GLAD TO SEE HE'S NOT JUST A LIVING MACHINE!
MR. SPOCK, THERE WAS NO PERSONNEL REPORT ON MY DESK THIS MORNING! THAT'S THE SECOND TIME THIS WEEK!
HOW ABOUT THAT? THE GIRL HAS REALLY GOTTEN TO HIM! MR. SPOCK NEVER FORGOT ANYTHING BEFORE IN HIS LIFE!
UNIDENTIFIED CRAFT APPROACHING! REFUSES TO RETURN OUR SIGNALS!
SEND THE FINAL APPEAL FOR IDENTIFICATION, WAIT TEN SECONDS AND THEN PUT A SHOT ACROSS THEIR PAT
BUT BEFORE THE FINAL APPEAL COULD BE MADE...
THEY'VE FIRED SOME KIND OF SUPER-FLARE! IT'S KNOCKED OUT OUR VIDEO CIRCUITS! WE'RE BLIND! SWITCH TO EMERGENCY V-CIRCUITS!
WE DINNA' HAVE TO SWITCH CIRCUITS! THEY'VE RECOVERED FROM THAT GLARE EXPLOSION!
AND LOOK--THE MYSTERY SHIP IS RUNNING FROM US! WHAT WAS THAT ALL ABOUT?

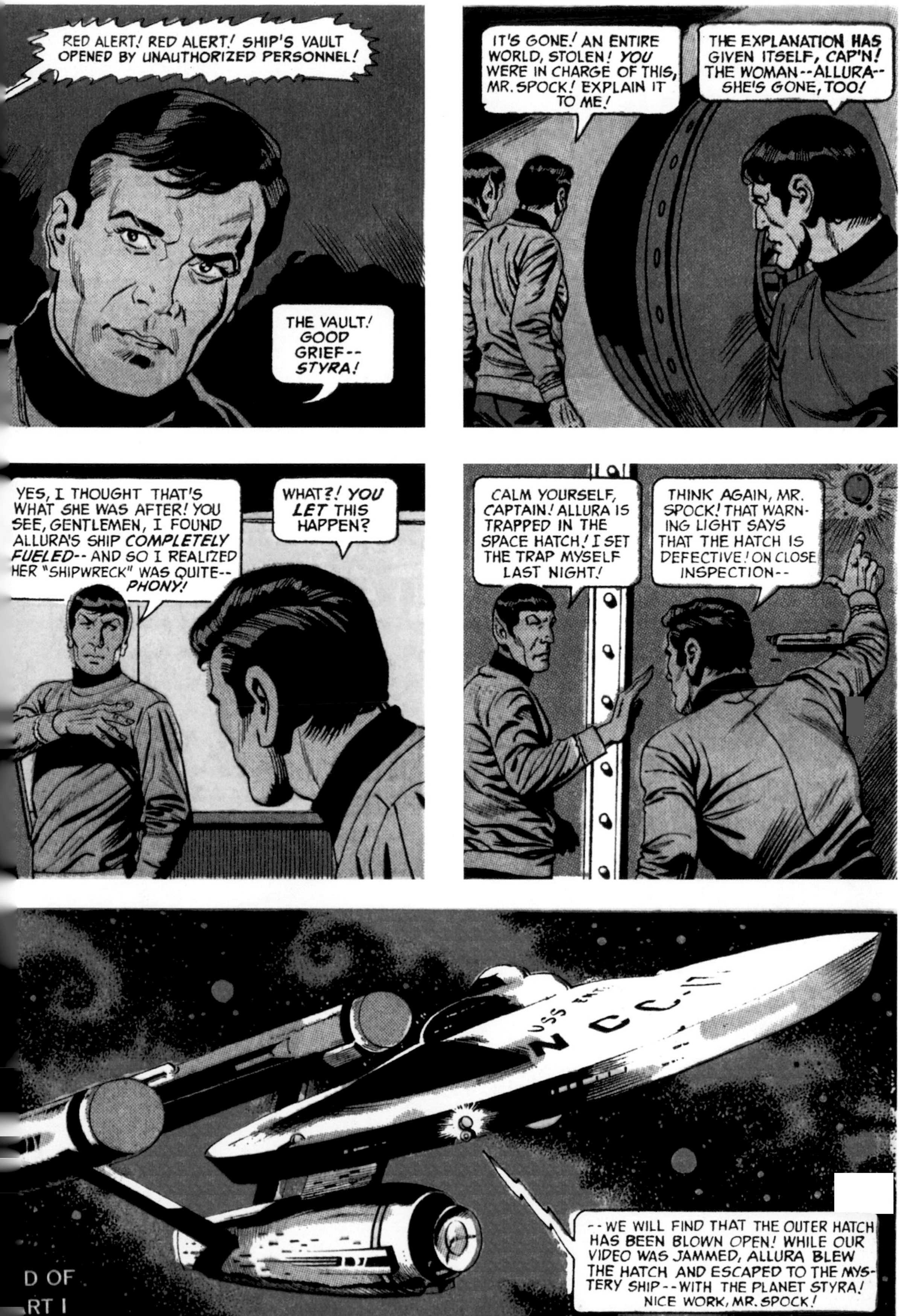
RED ALERT! RED ALERT! SHIP'S VAULT OPENED BY UNAUTHORIZED PERSONNEL!
THE VAULT! GOOD GRIEF-- STYRA!
IT'S GONE! AN ENTIRE WORLD, STOLEN! YOU WERE IN CHARGE OF THIS, MR. SPOCK! EXPLAIN IT TO ME!
THE EXPLANATION HAS GIVEN ITSELF, CAP'N! THE WOMAN--ALLURA--SHE'S GONE, TOO!
YES, I THOUGHT THAT'S WHAT SHE WAS AFTER! YOU SEE, GENTLEMEN, I FOUND ALLURA'S SHIP COMPLETELY FUELED-- AND SO I REALIZED HER "SHIPWRECK" WAS QUITE-- PHONY!
WHAT?! YOU LET THIS HAPPEN?
CALM YOURSELF, CAPTAIN! ALLURA IS TRAPPED IN THE SPACE HATCH! I SET THE TRAP MYSELF LAST NIGHT!
THINK AGAIN, MR. SPOCK! THAT WARNING LIGHT SAYS THAT THE HATCH IS DEFECTIVE! ON CLOSE INSPECTION--
--WE WILL FIND THAT THE OUTER HATCH HAS BEEN BLOWN OPEN! WHILE OUR VIDEO WAS JAMMED, ALLURA BLEW THE HATCH AND ESCAPED TO THE MYSTERY SHIP--WITH THE PLANET STYRA! NICE WORK, MR. SPOCK!
D OF
RT I

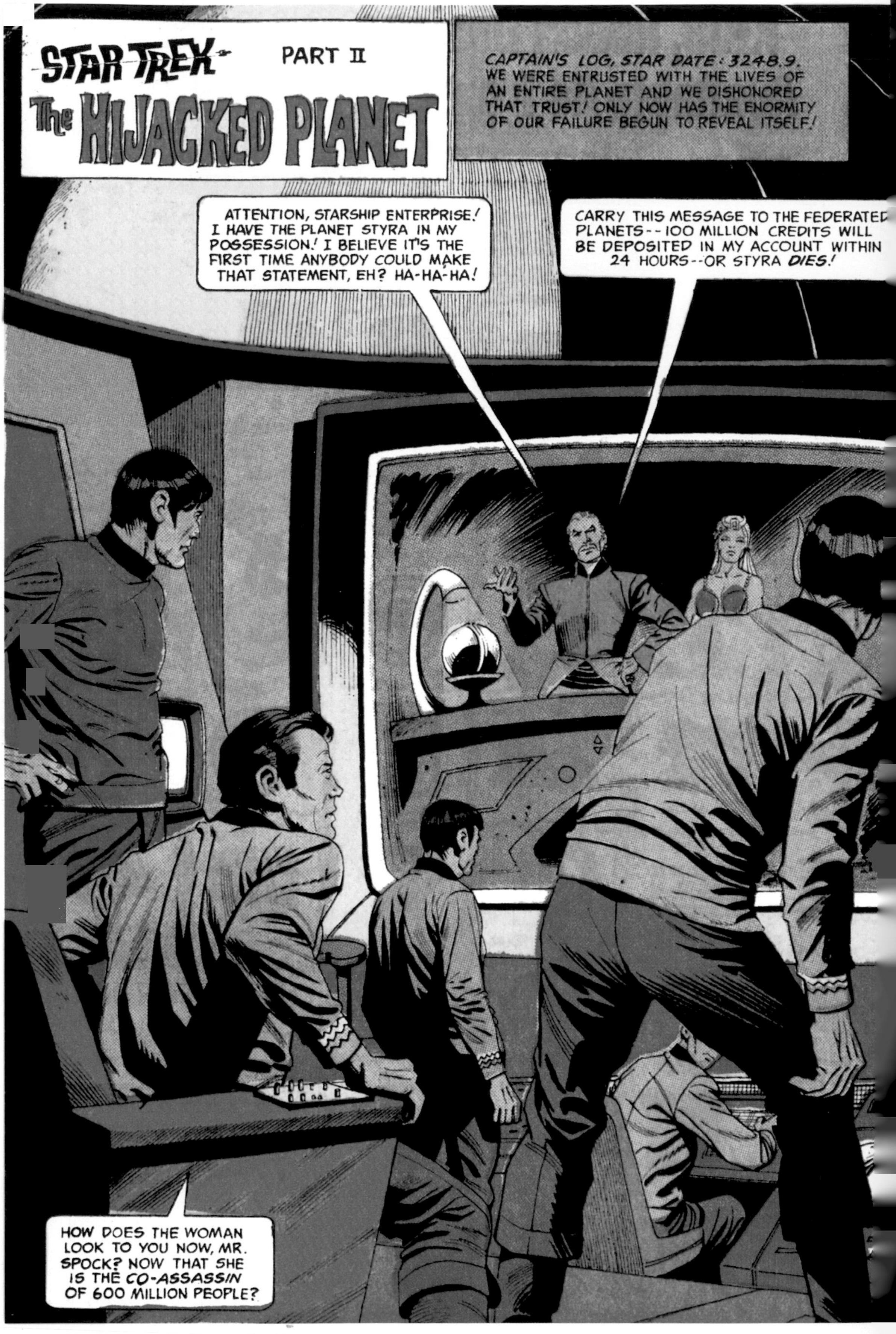
STAR TREK PART II
The HIJACKED PLANET
CAPTAIN'S LOG, STAR DATE: 3248.9. WE WERE ENTRUSTED WITH THE LIVES OF AN ENTIRE PLANET AND WE DISHONORED THAT TRUST! ONLY NOW HAS THE ENORMITY OF OUR FAILURE BEGUN TO REVEAL ITSELF!
ATTENTION, STARSHIP ENTERPRISE! I HAVE THE PLANET STYRA IN MY POSSESSION! I BELIEVE IT'S THE FIRST TIME ANYBODY COULD MAKE THAT STATEMENT, EH? HA-HA-HA!
CARRY THIS MESSAGE TO THE FEDERATED PLANETS--100 MILLION CREDITS WILL BE DEPOSITED IN MY ACCOUNT WITHIN 24 HOURS--OR STYRA DIES!
HOW DOES THE WOMAN LOOK TO YOU NOW, MR. SPOCK? NOW THAT SHE IS THE CO-ASSASSIN OF 600 MILLION PEOPLE?

WITH A SCRAMBLING DEVICE TO SECURE TRANSMISSION, WE IMMEDIATELY CONVEYED THE MESSAGE TO THE *COUNCIL*...

--LEAVING US NO CHOICE! WE CANNOT PERMIT THE LIVES, THE HISTORY, THE CULTURE OF AN ENTIRE WORLD TO DIE FOR WANT OF MONEY!

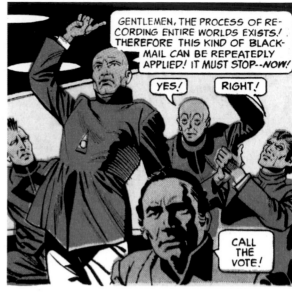

GENTLEMEN, THE PROCESS OF RE-CORDING ENTIRE WORLDS EXISTS! THEREFORE THIS KIND OF BLACK-MAIL CAN BE REPEATEDLY APPLIED! IT MUST STOP--*NOW!*

YES!

RIGHT!

CALL THE VOTE!

THE VOTE HAS BEEN CARRIED! WE SHALL DO EVERYTHING--SHORT OF PAYING BLACKMAIL-- TO SAVE STYRA! THIS DECISION REMAINS-- *TOP SECRET!*

THIS DECISION SHALL NOT BE MADE PUBLIC IMMEDIATELY, SO THAT YOU MAY BE FREE TO ACT, CAPTAIN KIRK!

I UNDERSTAND, SIR --WE'LL NEED ALL THE MANEUVERING ROOM WE CAN GET! THIS ANZAR MEANS *BUSINESS!*

YOUR BASIC TERMS ARE ACCEPTABLE TO THE COUNCIL! BUT CERTAIN DETAILS NEED TO BE WORKED OUT!

WHY, CAPTAIN--YOU'RE BARGAINING! FINE-- I'M AN. OLD TRADER MYSELF! I'LL MEET YOU IN THE GREAT CAVE OF LUROTA AT NOON TOMORROW!

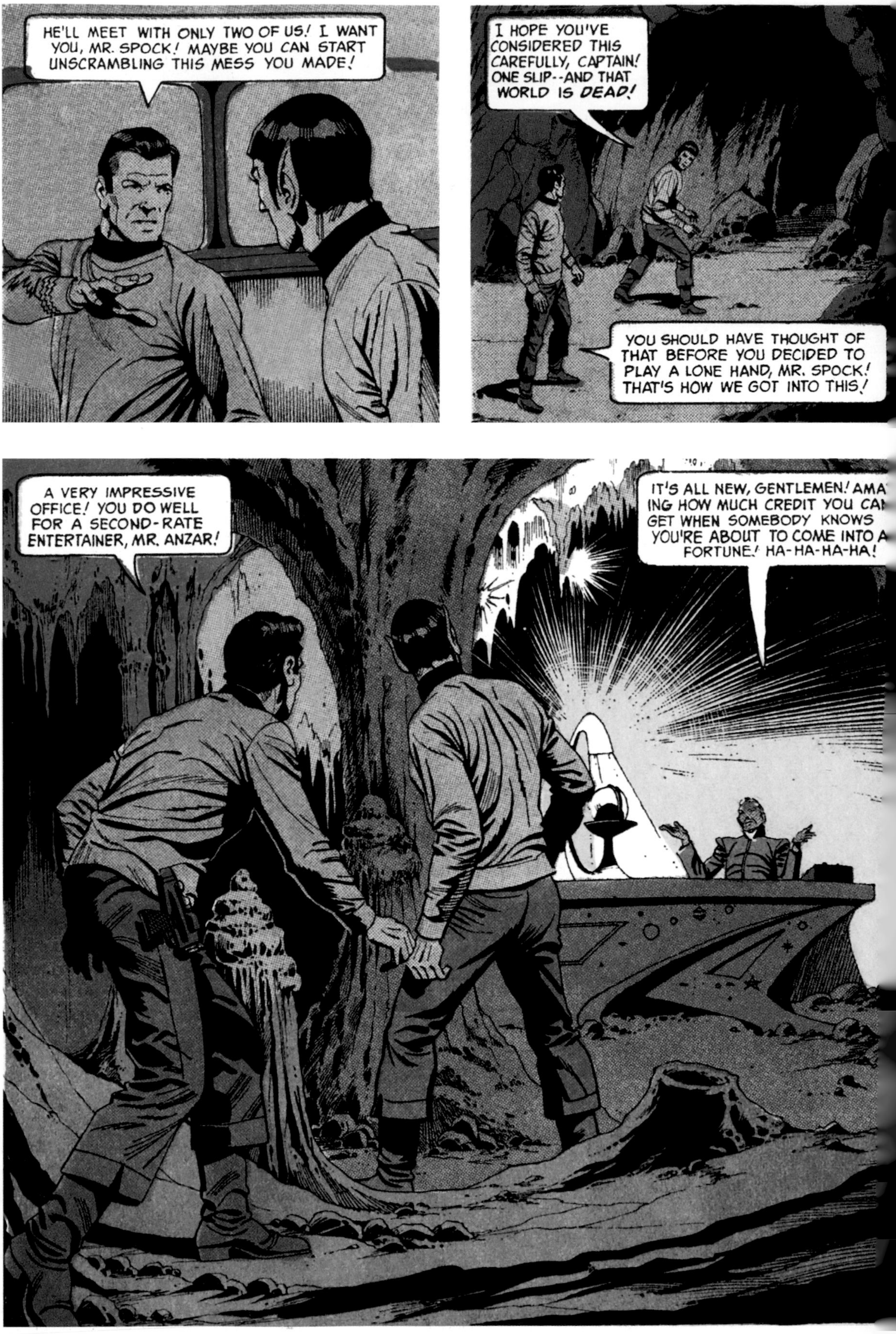

HE'LL MEET WITH ONLY TWO OF US! I WANT YOU, MR. SPOCK! MAYBE YOU CAN START UNSCRAMBLING THIS MESS YOU MADE!
I HOPE YOU'VE CONSIDERED THIS CAREFULLY, CAPTAIN! ONE SLIP--AND THAT WORLD IS *DEAD!*
YOU SHOULD HAVE THOUGHT OF THAT BEFORE YOU DECIDED TO PLAY A LONE HAND, MR. SPOCK! THAT'S HOW WE GOT INTO THIS!
A VERY IMPRESSIVE OFFICE! YOU DO WELL FOR A SECOND-RATE ENTERTAINER, MR. ANZAR!
IT'S ALL NEW, GENTLEMEN! AMA ING HOW MUCH CREDIT YOU CA GET WHEN SOMEBODY KNOWS YOU'RE ABOUT TO COME INTO A FORTUNE! HA-HA-HA-HA!

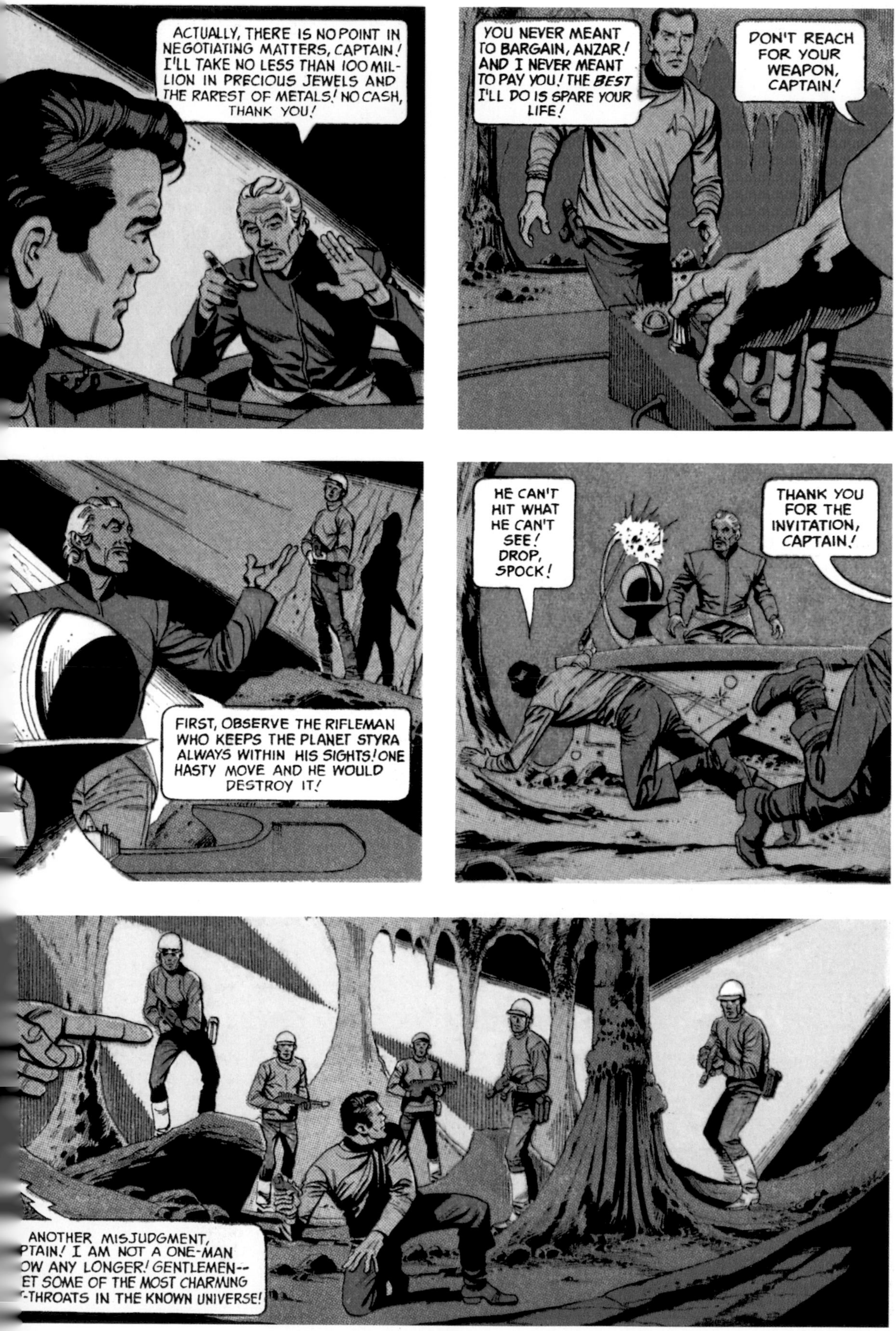
ACTUALLY, THERE IS NO POINT IN NEGOTIATING MATTERS, CAPTAIN! I'LL TAKE NO LESS THAN 100 MILLION IN PRECIOUS JEWELS AND THE RAREST OF METALS! NO CASH, THANK YOU!
YOU NEVER MEANT TO BARGAIN, ANZAR! AND I NEVER MEANT TO PAY YOU! THE BEST I'LL DO IS SPARE YOUR LIFE!
DON'T REACH FOR YOUR WEAPON, CAPTAIN!
FIRST, OBSERVE THE RIFLEMAN WHO KEEPS THE PLANET STYRA ALWAYS WITHIN HIS SIGHTS! ONE HASTY MOVE AND HE WOULD DESTROY IT!
HE CAN'T HIT WHAT HE CAN'T SEE! DROP, SPOCK!
THANK YOU FOR THE INVITATION, CAPTAIN!
ANOTHER MISJUDGMENT, PTAIN! I AM NOT A ONE-MAN OW ANY LONGER! GENTLEMEN-- ET SOME OF THE MOST CHARMING -THROATS IN THE KNOWN UNIVERSE!

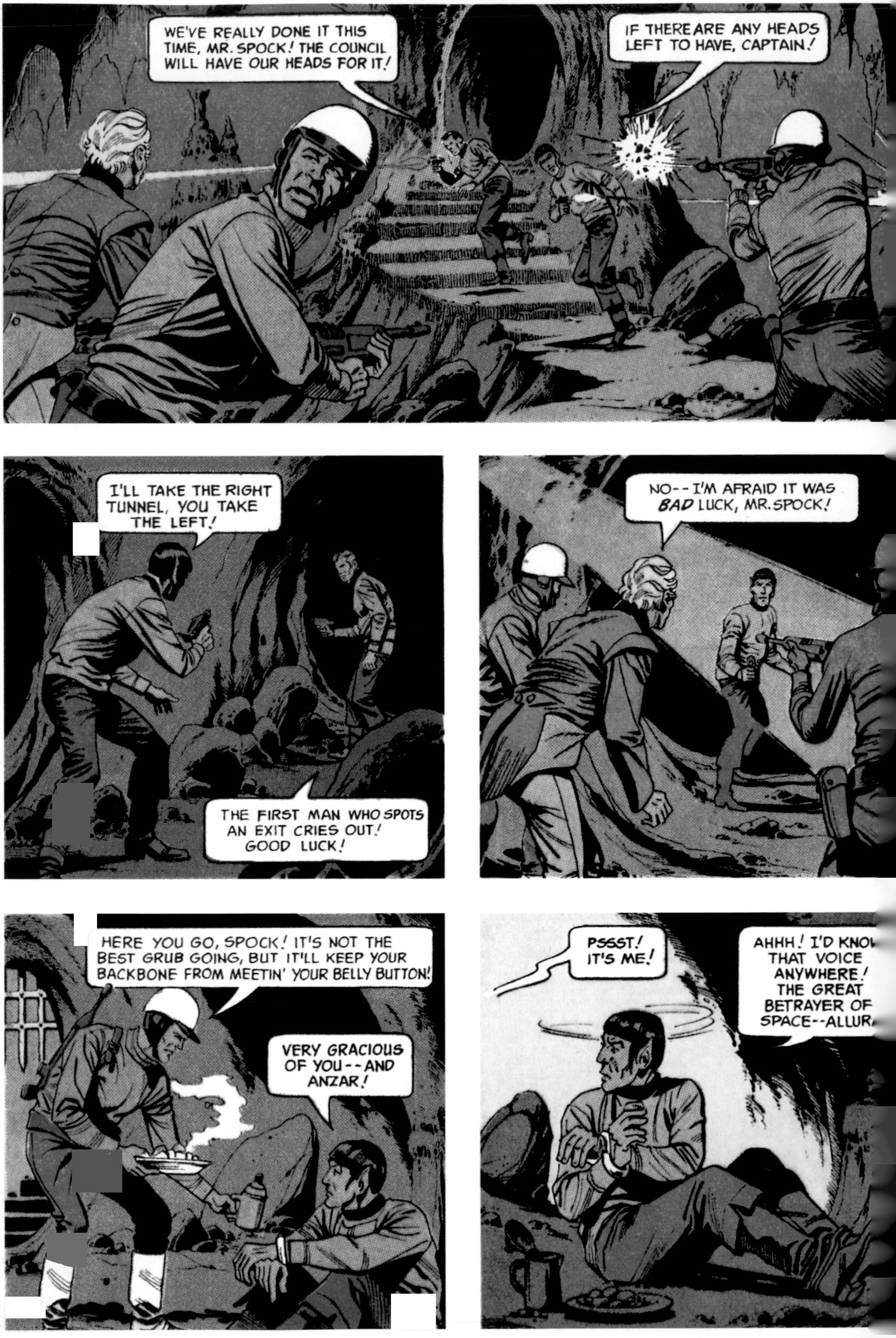
WE'VE REALLY DONE IT THIS TIME, MR. SPOCK! THE COUNCIL WILL HAVE OUR HEADS FOR IT!
IF THERE ARE ANY HEADS LEFT TO HAVE, CAPTAIN!
I'LL TAKE THE RIGHT TUNNEL, YOU TAKE THE LEFT!
THE FIRST MAN WHO SPOTS AN EXIT CRIES OUT! GOOD LUCK!
NO-- I'M AFRAID IT WAS *BAD* LUCK, MR. SPOCK!
HERE YOU GO, SPOCK! IT'S NOT THE BEST GRUB GOING, BUT IT'LL KEEP YOUR BACKBONE FROM MEETIN' YOUR BELLY BUTTON!
VERY GRACIOUS OF YOU--AND ANZAR!
PSSST! IT'S ME!
AHHH! I'D KNOW THAT VOICE ANYWHERE! THE GREAT BETRAYER OF SPACE--ALLUR

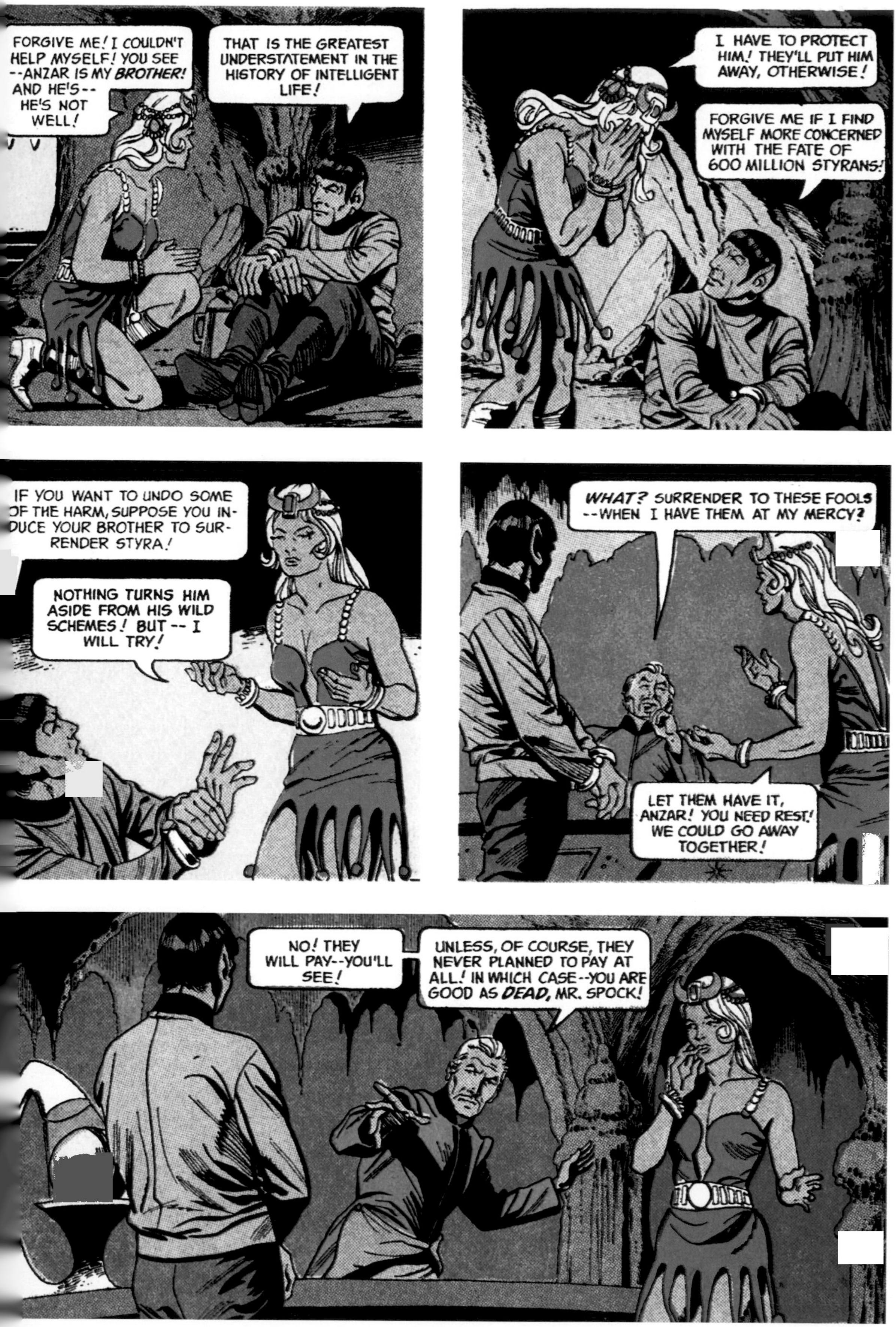
FORGIVE ME! I COULDN'T HELP MYSELF! YOU SEE --ANZAR IS MY BROTHER! AND HE'S-- HE'S NOT WELL!
THAT IS THE GREATEST UNDERSTATEMENT IN THE HISTORY OF INTELLIGENT LIFE!
I HAVE TO PROTECT HIM! THEY'LL PUT HIM AWAY, OTHERWISE!
FORGIVE ME IF I FIND MYSELF MORE CONCERNED WITH THE FATE OF 600 MILLION STYRANS!
IF YOU WANT TO UNDO SOME OF THE HARM, SUPPOSE YOU INDUCE YOUR BROTHER TO SURRENDER STYRA!
NOTHING TURNS HIM ASIDE FROM HIS WILD SCHEMES! BUT -- I WILL TRY!
WHAT? SURRENDER TO THESE FOOLS --WHEN I HAVE THEM AT MY MERCY?
LET THEM HAVE IT, ANZAR! YOU NEED REST! WE COULD GO AWAY TOGETHER!
NO! THEY WILL PAY--YOU'LL SEE!
UNLESS, OF COURSE, THEY NEVER PLANNED TO PAY AT ALL! IN WHICH CASE--YOU ARE GOOD AS DEAD, MR. SPOCK!

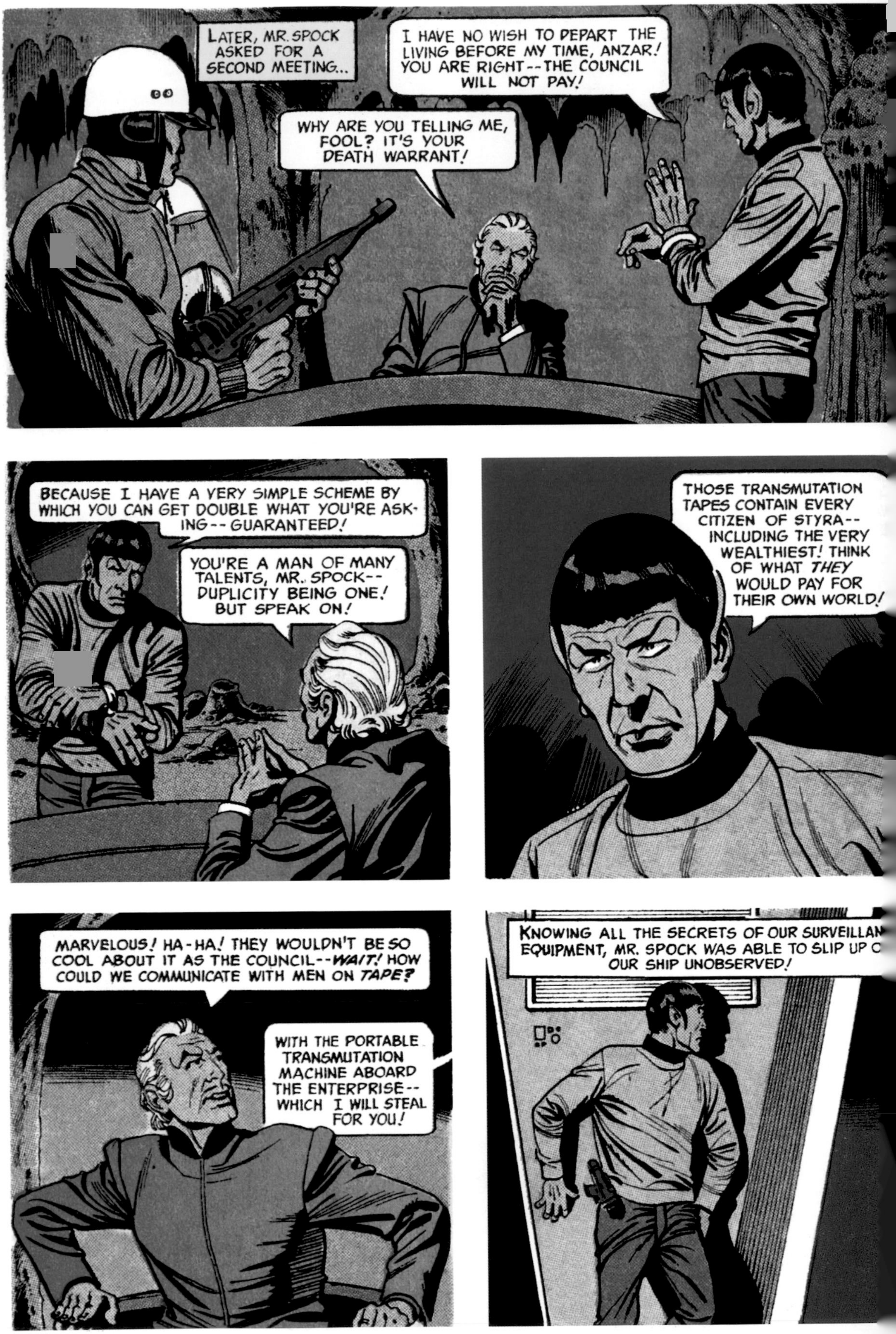
LATER, MR. SPOCK ASKED FOR A SECOND MEETING...
I HAVE NO WISH TO DEPART THE LIVING BEFORE MY TIME, ANZAR! YOU ARE RIGHT--THE COUNCIL WILL NOT PAY!
WHY ARE YOU TELLING ME, FOOL? IT'S YOUR DEATH WARRANT!
BECAUSE I HAVE A VERY SIMPLE SCHEME BY WHICH YOU CAN GET DOUBLE WHAT YOU'RE ASKING--GUARANTEED!
YOU'RE A MAN OF MANY TALENTS, MR. SPOCK--DUPLICITY BEING ONE! BUT SPEAK ON!
THOSE TRANSMUTATION TAPES CONTAIN EVERY CITIZEN OF STYRA--INCLUDING THE VERY WEALTHIEST! THINK OF WHAT *THEY* WOULD PAY FOR THEIR OWN WORLD!
MARVELOUS! HA-HA! THEY WOULDN'T BE SO COOL ABOUT IT AS THE COUNCIL--*WAIT!* HOW COULD WE COMMUNICATE WITH MEN ON *TAPE?*
WITH THE PORTABLE TRANSMUTATION MACHINE ABOARD THE ENTERPRISE--WHICH I WILL STEAL FOR YOU!
KNOWING ALL THE SECRETS OF OUR SURVEILLAN
EQUIPMENT, MR. SPOCK WAS ABLE TO SLIP UP O
OUR SHIP UNOBSERVED!

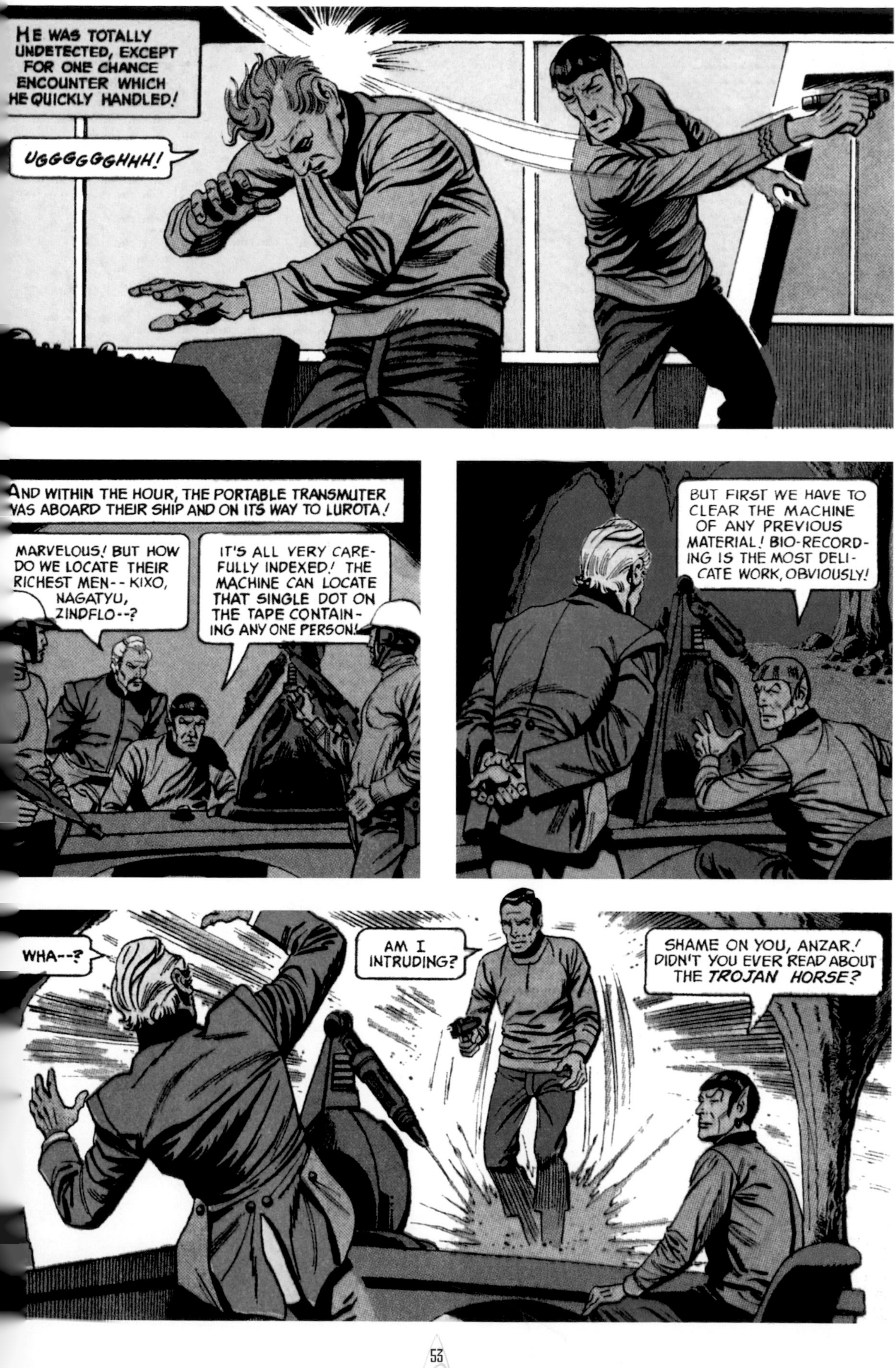
HE WAS TOTALLY UNDETECTED, EXCEPT FOR ONE CHANCE ENCOUNTER WHICH HE QUICKLY HANDLED!
UGGGGGGHHH!
AND WITHIN THE HOUR, THE PORTABLE TRANSMUTER WAS ABOARD THEIR SHIP AND ON ITS WAY TO LUROTA!
MARVELOUS! BUT HOW DO WE LOCATE THEIR RICHEST MEN-- KIXO, NAGATYU, ZINDFLO--?
IT'S ALL VERY CAREFULLY INDEXED! THE MACHINE CAN LOCATE THAT SINGLE DOT ON THE TAPE CONTAINING ANY ONE PERSON!
BUT FIRST WE HAVE TO CLEAR THE MACHINE OF ANY PREVIOUS MATERIAL! BIO-RECORDING IS THE MOST DELICATE WORK, OBVIOUSLY!
WHA--?
AM I INTRUDING?
SHAME ON YOU, ANZAR! DIDN'T YOU EVER READ ABOUT THE TROJAN HORSE?

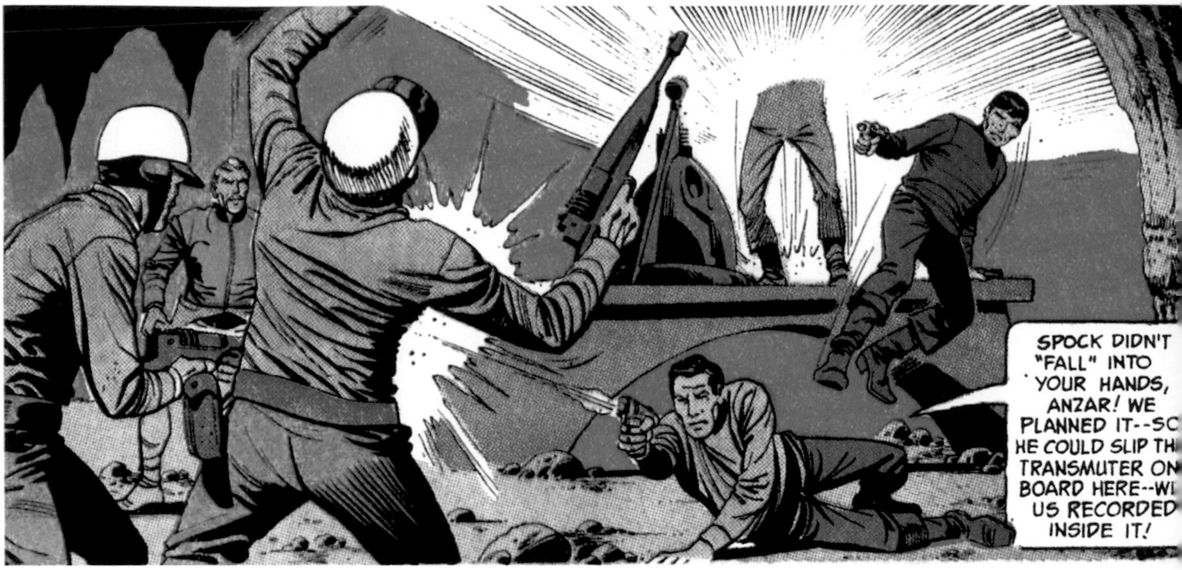
SPOCK DIDN'T "FALL" INTO YOUR HANDS, ANZAR! WE PLANNED IT--SC
HE COULD SLIP TH
TRANSMUTER ON
BOARD HERE--WI
US RECORDED INSIDE IT!

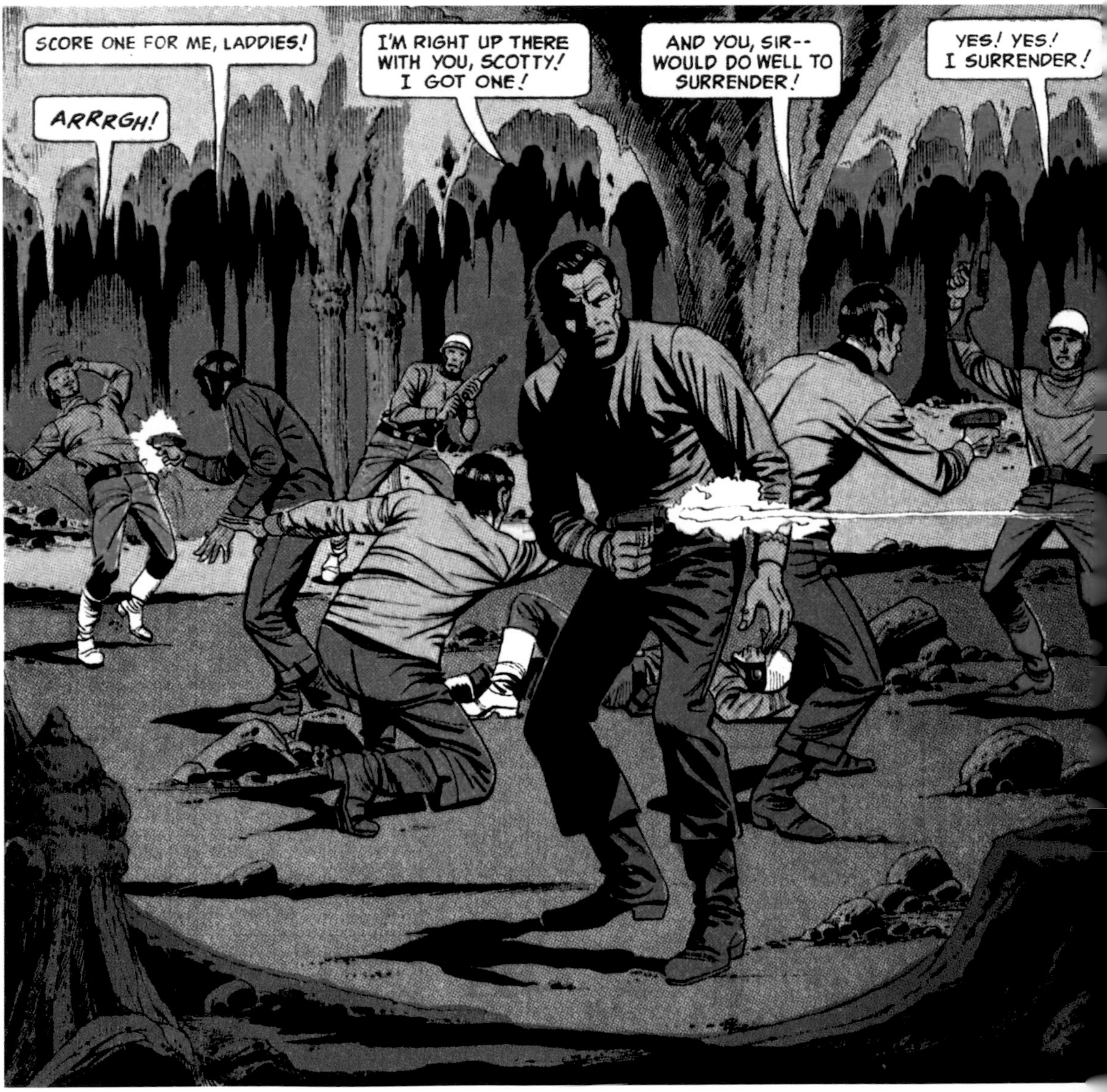
SCORE ONE FOR ME, LADDIES!
ARRRGH!
I'M RIGHT UP THERE WITH YOU, SCOTTY! I GOT ONE!
AND YOU, SIR-- WOULD DO WELL TO SURRENDER!
YES! YES! I SURRENDER!

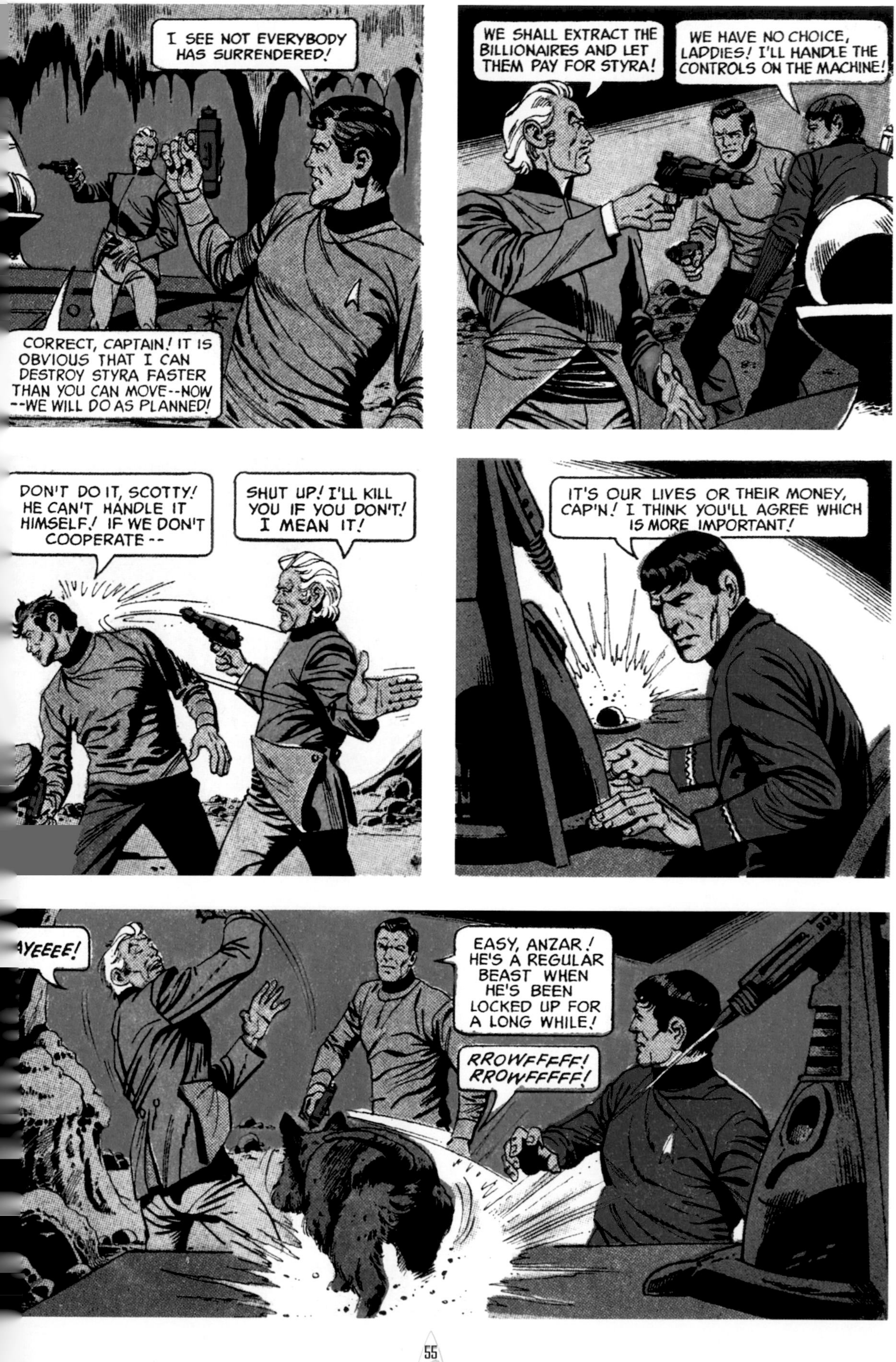
I SEE NOT EVERYBODY HAS SURRENDERED!
CORRECT, CAPTAIN! IT IS OBVIOUS THAT I CAN DESTROY STYRA FASTER THAN YOU CAN MOVE--NOW --WE WILL DO AS PLANNED!
WE SHALL EXTRACT THE BILLIONAIRES AND LET THEM PAY FOR STYRA!
WE HAVE NO CHOICE, LADDIES! I'LL HANDLE THE CONTROLS ON THE MACHINE!
DON'T DO IT, SCOTTY! HE CAN'T HANDLE IT HIMSELF! IF WE DON'T COOPERATE --
SHUT UP! I'LL KILL YOU IF YOU DON'T! I MEAN IT!
IT'S OUR LIVES OR THEIR MONEY, CAP'N! I THINK YOU'LL AGREE WHICH IS MORE IMPORTANT!
AYEEEE!
EASY, ANZAR! HE'S A REGULAR BEAST WHEN HE'S BEEN LOCKED UP FOR A LONG WHILE!
RROWFFFFF! RROWFFFFF!

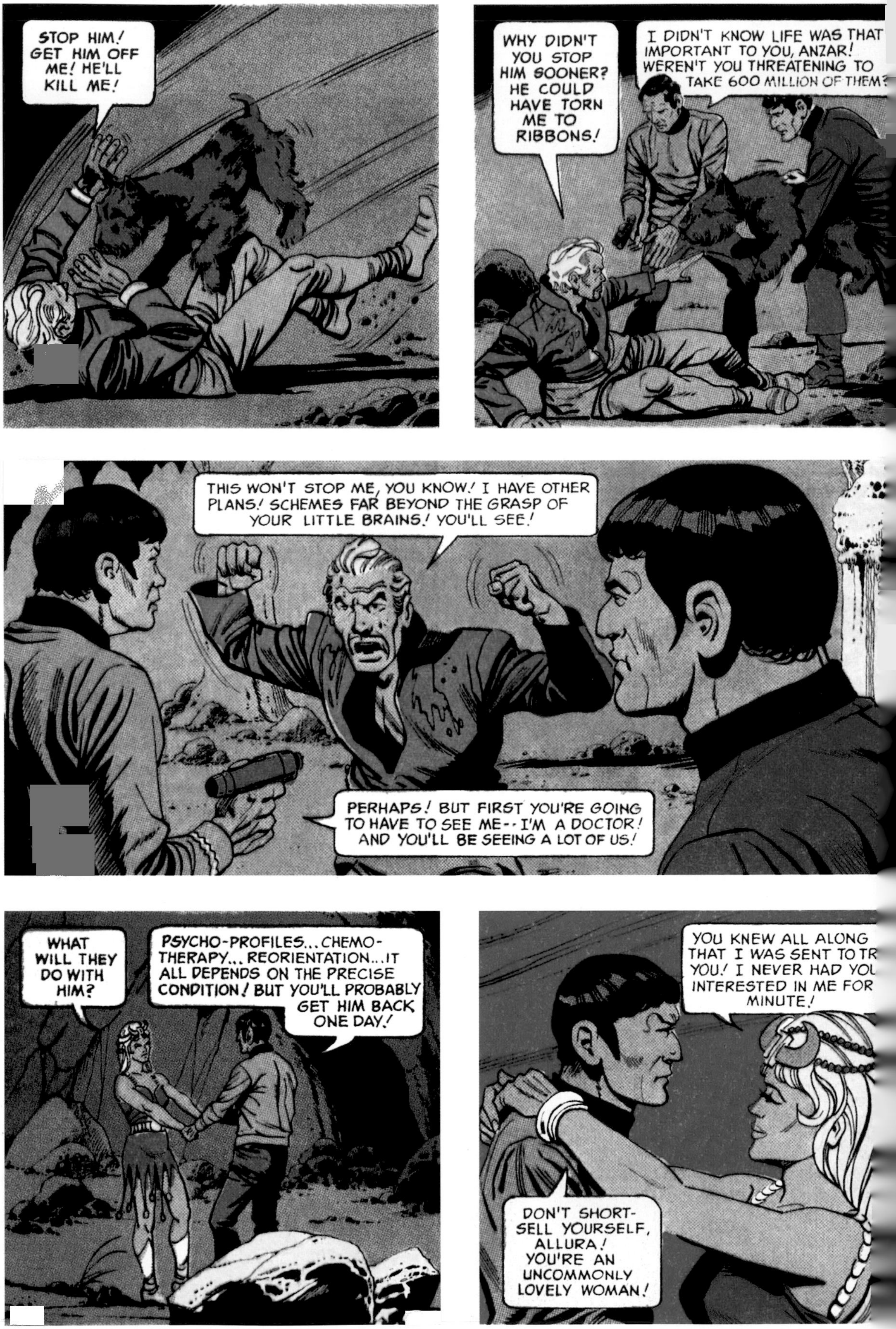
STOP HIM! GET HIM OFF ME! HE'LL KILL ME!
WHY DIDN'T YOU STOP HIM SOONER? HE COULD HAVE TORN ME TO RIBBONS!
I DIDN'T KNOW LIFE WAS THAT IMPORTANT TO YOU, ANZAR! WEREN'T YOU THREATENING TO TAKE 600 MILLION OF THEM?
THIS WON'T STOP ME, YOU KNOW! I HAVE OTHER PLANS! SCHEMES FAR BEYOND THE GRASP OF YOUR LITTLE BRAINS! YOU'LL SEE!
PERHAPS! BUT FIRST YOU'RE GOING TO HAVE TO SEE ME--I'M A DOCTOR! AND YOU'LL BE SEEING A LOT OF US!
WHAT WILL THEY DO WITH HIM?
PSYCHO-PROFILES... CHEMO-THERAPY... REORIENTATION... IT ALL DEPENDS ON THE PRECISE CONDITION! BUT YOU'LL PROBABLY GET HIM BACK ONE DAY!
YOU KNEW ALL ALONG THAT I WAS SENT TO TR YOU! I NEVER HAD YO INTERESTED IN ME FOR MINUTE!
DON'T SHORT-SELL YOURSELF, ALLURA! YOU'RE AN UNCOMMONLY LOVELY WOMAN!

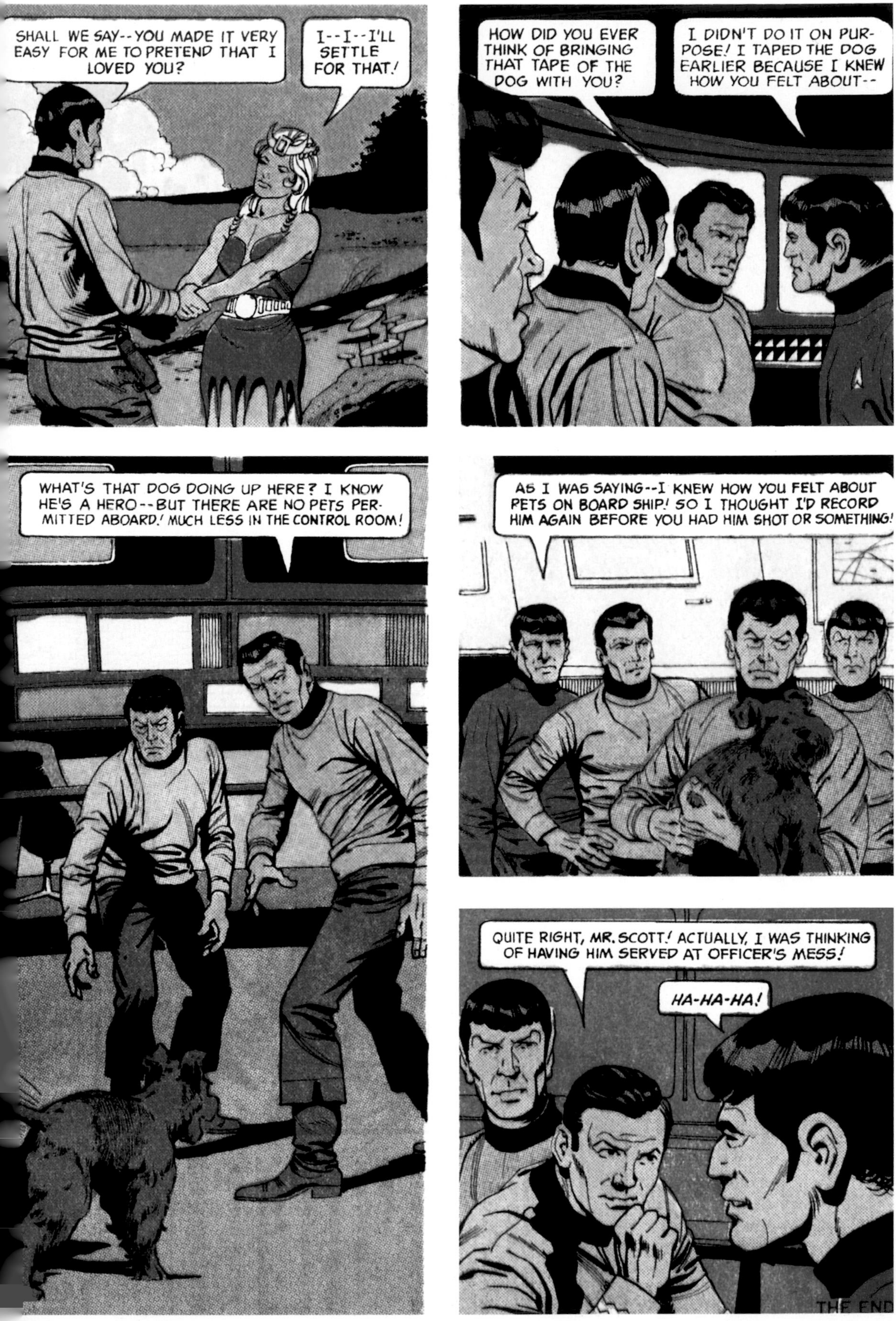
SHALL WE SAY--YOU MADE IT VERY EASY FOR ME TO PRETEND THAT I LOVED YOU?
I--I--I'LL SETTLE FOR THAT!
HOW DID YOU EVER THINK OF BRINGING THAT TAPE OF THE DOG WITH YOU?
I DIDN'T DO IT ON PURPOSE! I TAPED THE DOG EARLIER BECAUSE I KNEW HOW YOU FELT ABOUT--
WHAT'S THAT DOG DOING UP HERE? I KNOW HE'S A HERO--BUT THERE ARE NO PETS PERMITTED ABOARD! MUCH LESS IN THE CONTROL ROOM!
AS I WAS SAYING--I KNEW HOW YOU FELT ABOUT PETS ON BOARD SHIP! SO I THOUGHT I'D RECORD HIM AGAIN BEFORE YOU HAD HIM SHOT OR SOMETHING!
QUITE RIGHT, MR. SCOTT! ACTUALLY, I WAS THINKING OF HAVING HIM SERVED AT OFFICER'S MESS!
HA-HA-HA!
THE END

STAR TREK

20c

"Turn back or die"—But the Enterprise crew is determined to explore the HAUNTED ASTEROID

© PARAMOUNT PICTURES CORPORATION

Chapter 3
The Haunted Asteroid

[Originally Published in July, 1973]

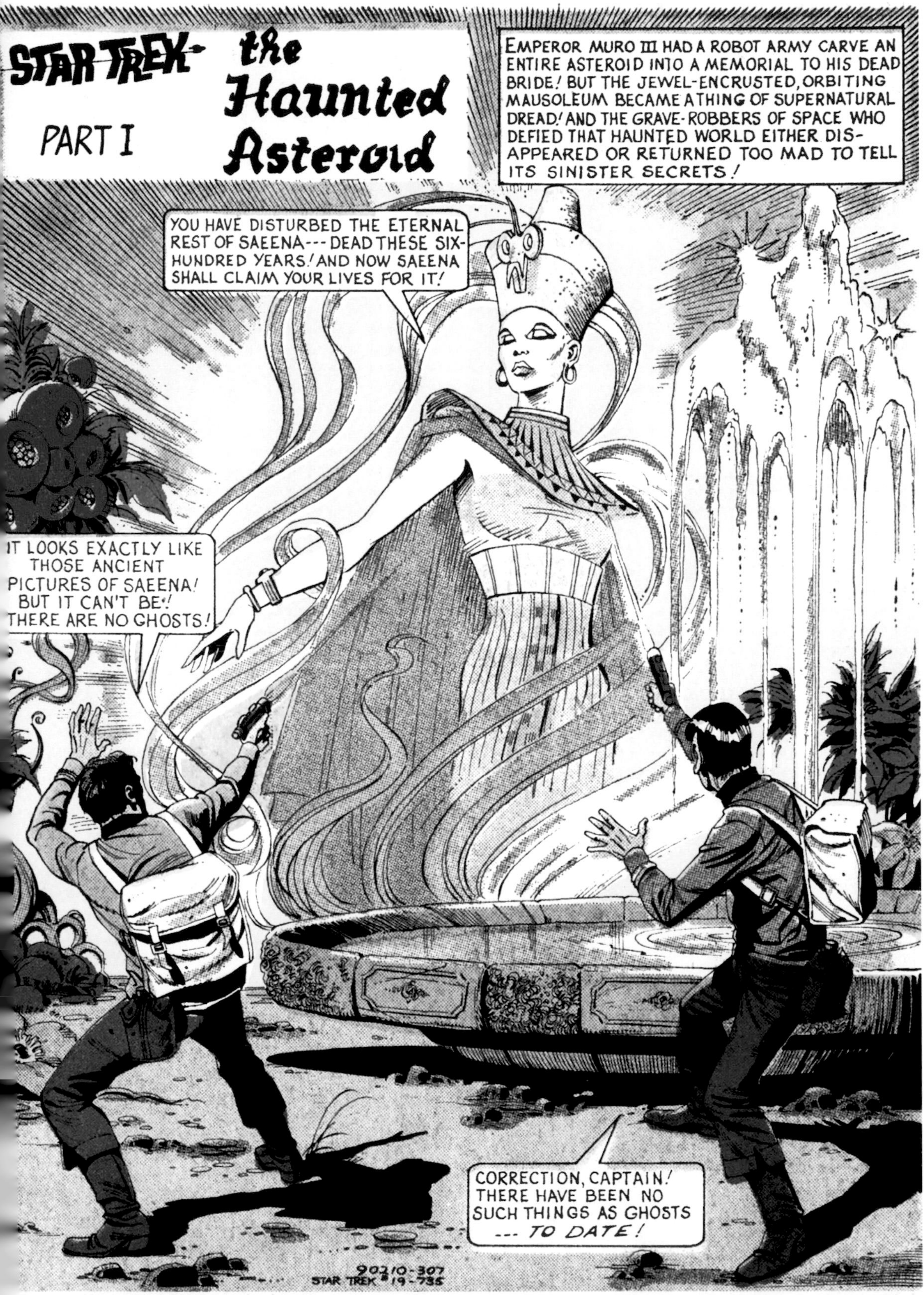
STAR TREK
PART I
the Haunted Asteroid
EMPEROR MURO III HAD A ROBOT ARMY CARVE AN ENTIRE ASTEROID INTO A MEMORIAL TO HIS DEAD BRIDE! BUT THE JEWEL-ENCRUSTED, ORBITING MAUSOLEUM BECAME A THING OF SUPERNATURAL DREAD! AND THE GRAVE-ROBBERS OF SPACE WHO DEFIED THAT HAUNTED WORLD EITHER DISAPPEARED OR RETURNED TOO MAD TO TELL ITS SINISTER SECRETS!
YOU HAVE DISTURBED THE ETERNAL REST OF SAEENA--- DEAD THESE SIX-HUNDRED YEARS! AND NOW SAEENA SHALL CLAIM YOUR LIVES FOR IT!
IT LOOKS EXACTLY LIKE THOSE ANCIENT PICTURES OF SAEENA! BUT IT CAN'T BE! THERE ARE NO GHOSTS!
CORRECTION, CAPTAIN! THERE HAVE BEEN NO SUCH THINGS AS GHOSTS --- TO DATE!
90210-307
STAR TREK #19-735

aptain's Log, Stardate 24:92.5 . . DATA REF . . 19.00-19.23

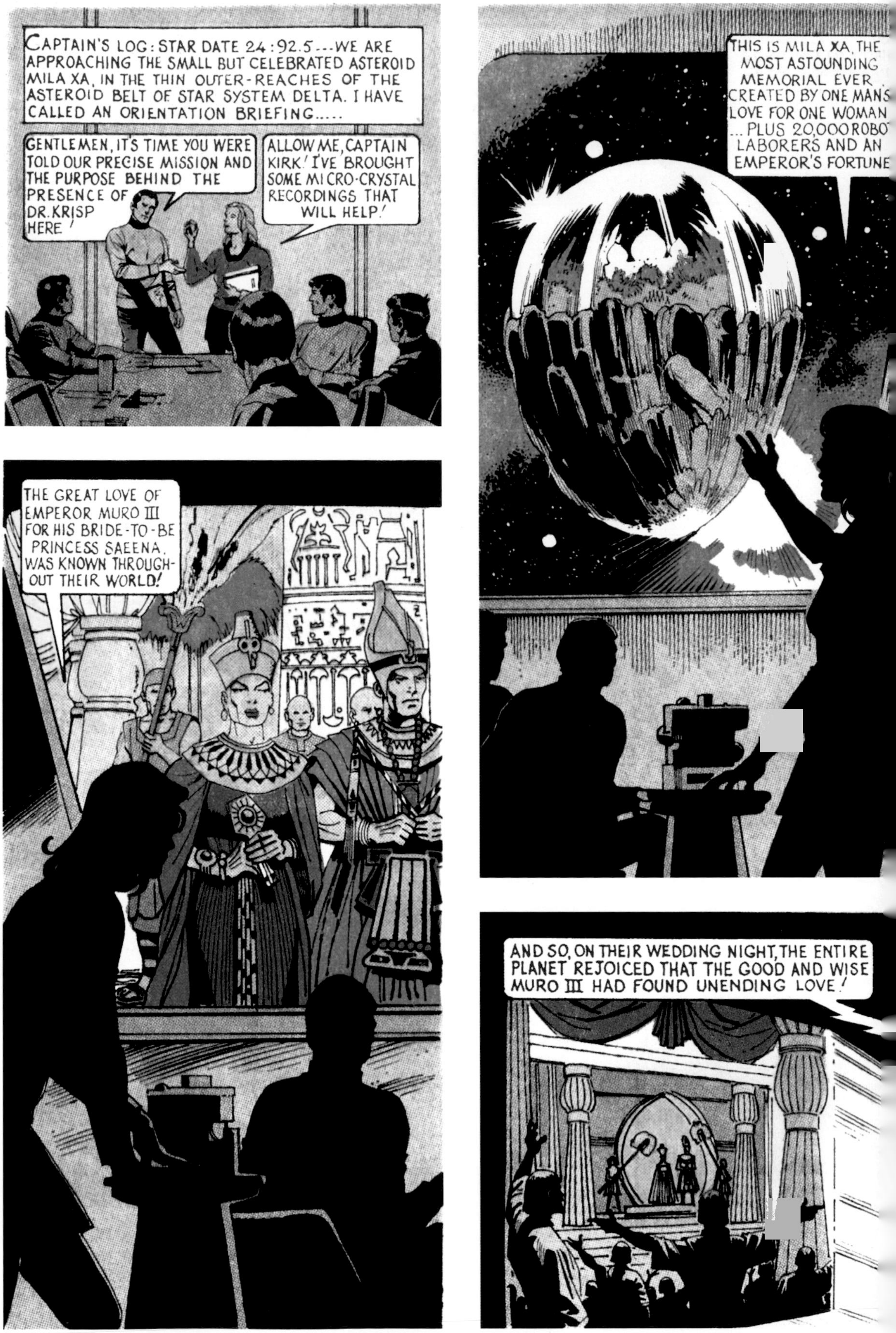
CAPTAIN'S LOG: STAR DATE 24:92.5---WE ARE APPROACHING THE SMALL BUT CELEBRATED ASTEROID MILA XA, IN THE THIN OUTER-REACHES OF THE ASTEROID BELT OF STAR SYSTEM DELTA. I HAVE CALLED AN ORIENTATION BRIEFING.....
GENTLEMEN, IT'S TIME YOU WERE TOLD OUR PRECISE MISSION AND THE PURPOSE BEHIND THE PRESENCE OF DR. KRISP HERE!
ALLOW ME, CAPTAIN KIRK! I'VE BROUGHT SOME MICRO-CRYSTAL RECORDINGS THAT WILL HELP!
THIS IS MILA XA, THE MOST ASTOUNDING MEMORIAL EVER CREATED BY ONE MAN'S LOVE FOR ONE WOMAN ...PLUS 20,000 ROBOT LABORERS AND AN EMPEROR'S FORTUNE
THE GREAT LOVE OF EMPEROR MURO III FOR HIS BRIDE-TO-BE PRINCESS SAEENA, WAS KNOWN THROUGH-OUT THEIR WORLD!
AND SO, ON THEIR WEDDING NIGHT, THE ENTIRE PLANET REJOICED THAT THE GOOD AND WISE MURO III HAD FOUND UNENDING LOVE!

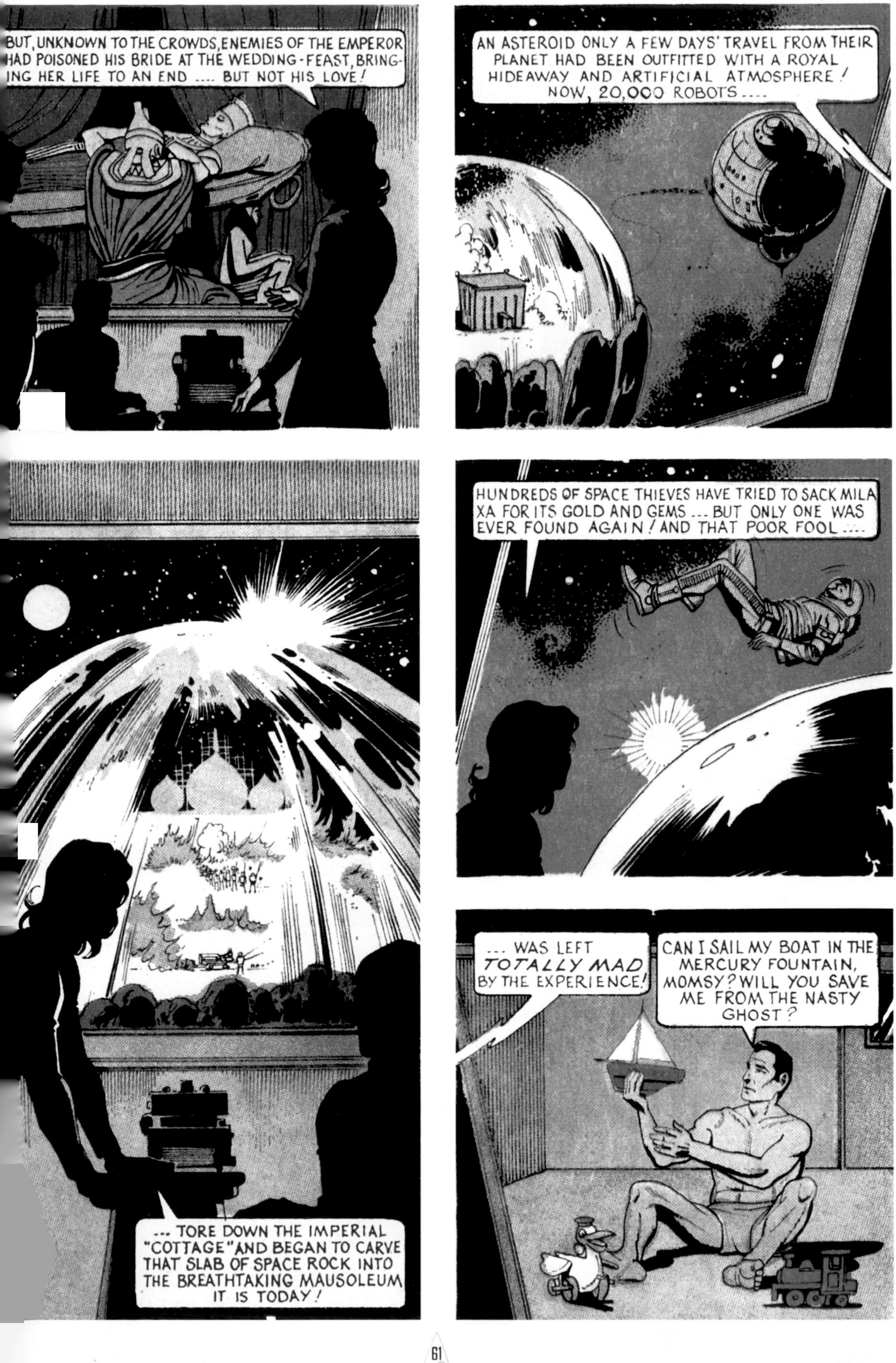
BUT, UNKNOWN TO THE CROWDS, ENEMIES OF THE EMPEROR HAD POISONED HIS BRIDE AT THE WEDDING-FEAST, BRINGING HER LIFE TO AN END .... BUT NOT HIS LOVE!
AN ASTEROID ONLY A FEW DAYS' TRAVEL FROM THEIR PLANET HAD BEEN OUTFITTED WITH A ROYAL HIDEAWAY AND ARTIFICIAL ATMOSPHERE! NOW, 20,000 ROBOTS ....
--- TORE DOWN THE IMPERIAL "COTTAGE" AND BEGAN TO CARVE THAT SLAB OF SPACE ROCK INTO THE BREATHTAKING MAUSOLEUM IT IS TODAY!
HUNDREDS OF SPACE THIEVES HAVE TRIED TO SACK MILAXA FOR ITS GOLD AND GEMS ... BUT ONLY ONE WAS EVER FOUND AGAIN! AND THAT POOR FOOL ....
... WAS LEFT TOTALLY MAD BY THE EXPERIENCE!
CAN I SAIL MY BOAT IN THE MERCURY FOUNTAIN, MOMSY? WILL YOU SAVE ME FROM THE NASTY GHOST?

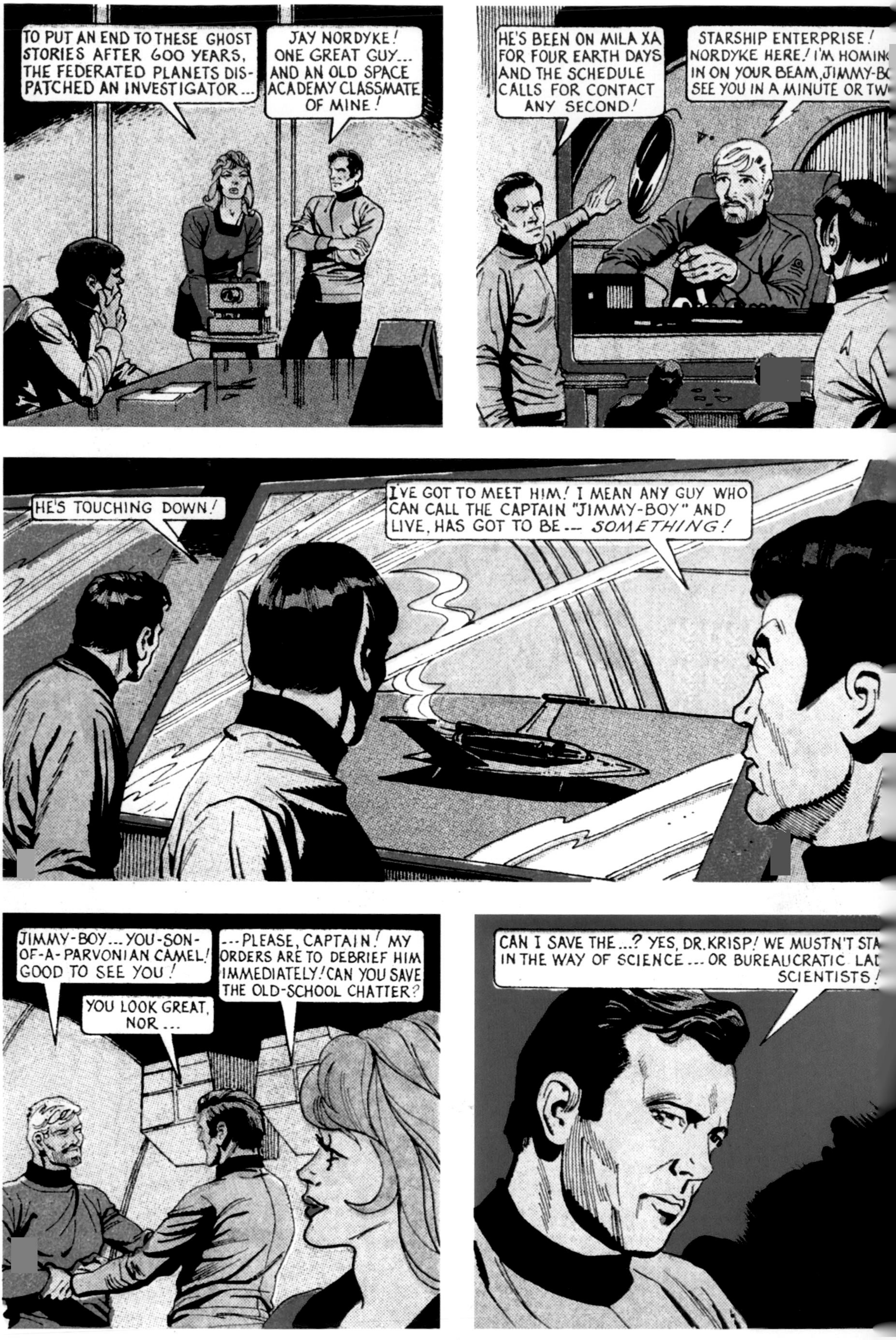
TO PUT AN END TO THESE GHOST STORIES AFTER 600 YEARS, THE FEDERATED PLANETS DIS-PATCHED AN INVESTIGATOR...
JAY NORDYKE! ONE GREAT GUY... AND AN OLD SPACE ACADEMY CLASSMATE OF MINE!
HE'S BEEN ON MILA XA FOR FOUR EARTH DAYS AND THE SCHEDULE CALLS FOR CONTACT ANY SECOND!
STARSHIP ENTERPRISE! NORDYKE HERE! I'M HOMIN IN ON YOUR BEAM, JIMMY-BO SEE YOU IN A MINUTE OR TW
HE'S TOUCHING DOWN!
I'VE GOT TO MEET HIM! I MEAN ANY GUY WHO CAN CALL THE CAPTAIN "JIMMY-BOY" AND LIVE, HAS GOT TO BE --- SOMETHING!
JIMMY-BOY... YOU-SON-OF-A-PARVONIAN CAMEL! GOOD TO SEE YOU!
YOU LOOK GREAT, NOR...
---PLEASE, CAPTAIN! MY ORDERS ARE TO DEBRIEF HIM IMMEDIATELY! CAN YOU SAVE THE OLD-SCHOOL CHATTER?
CAN I SAVE THE...? YES, DR. KRISP! WE MUSTN'T STA IN THE WAY OF SCIENCE... OR BUREAUCRATIC LAD SCIENTISTS!

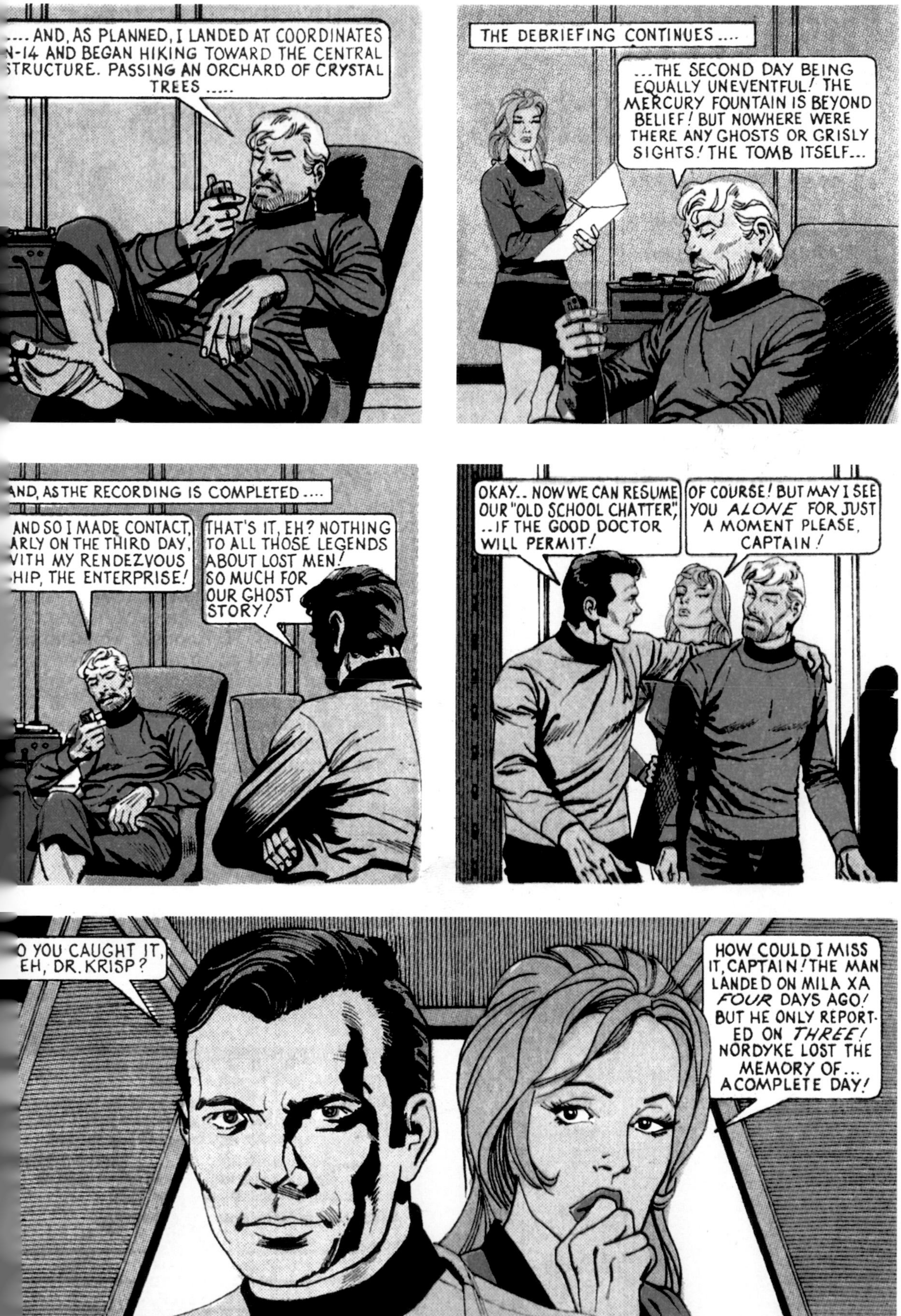
.... AND, AS PLANNED, I LANDED AT COORDINATES N-14 AND BEGAN HIKING TOWARD THE CENTRAL STRUCTURE. PASSING AN ORCHARD OF CRYSTAL TREES .....
THE DEBRIEFING CONTINUES ....
...THE SECOND DAY BEING EQUALLY UNEVENTFUL! THE MERCURY FOUNTAIN IS BEYOND BELIEF! BUT NOWHERE WERE THERE ANY GHOSTS OR GRISLY SIGHTS! THE TOMB ITSELF...
AND, AS THE RECORDING IS COMPLETED ....
AND SO I MADE CONTACT, ARLY ON THE THIRD DAY, WITH MY RENDEZVOUS HIP, THE ENTERPRISE!
THAT'S IT, EH? NOTHING TO ALL THOSE LEGENDS ABOUT LOST MEN! SO MUCH FOR OUR GHOST STORY!
OKAY.. NOW WE CAN RESUME OUR "OLD SCHOOL CHATTER", ..IF THE GOOD DOCTOR WILL PERMIT!
OF COURSE! BUT MAY I SEE YOU ALONE FOR JUST A MOMENT PLEASE, CAPTAIN!
O YOU CAUGHT IT, EH, DR. KRISP?
HOW COULD I MISS IT, CAPTAIN! THE MAN LANDED ON MILA XA FOUR DAYS AGO! BUT HE ONLY REPORTED ON THREE! NORDYKE LOST THE MEMORY OF... A COMPLETE DAY!

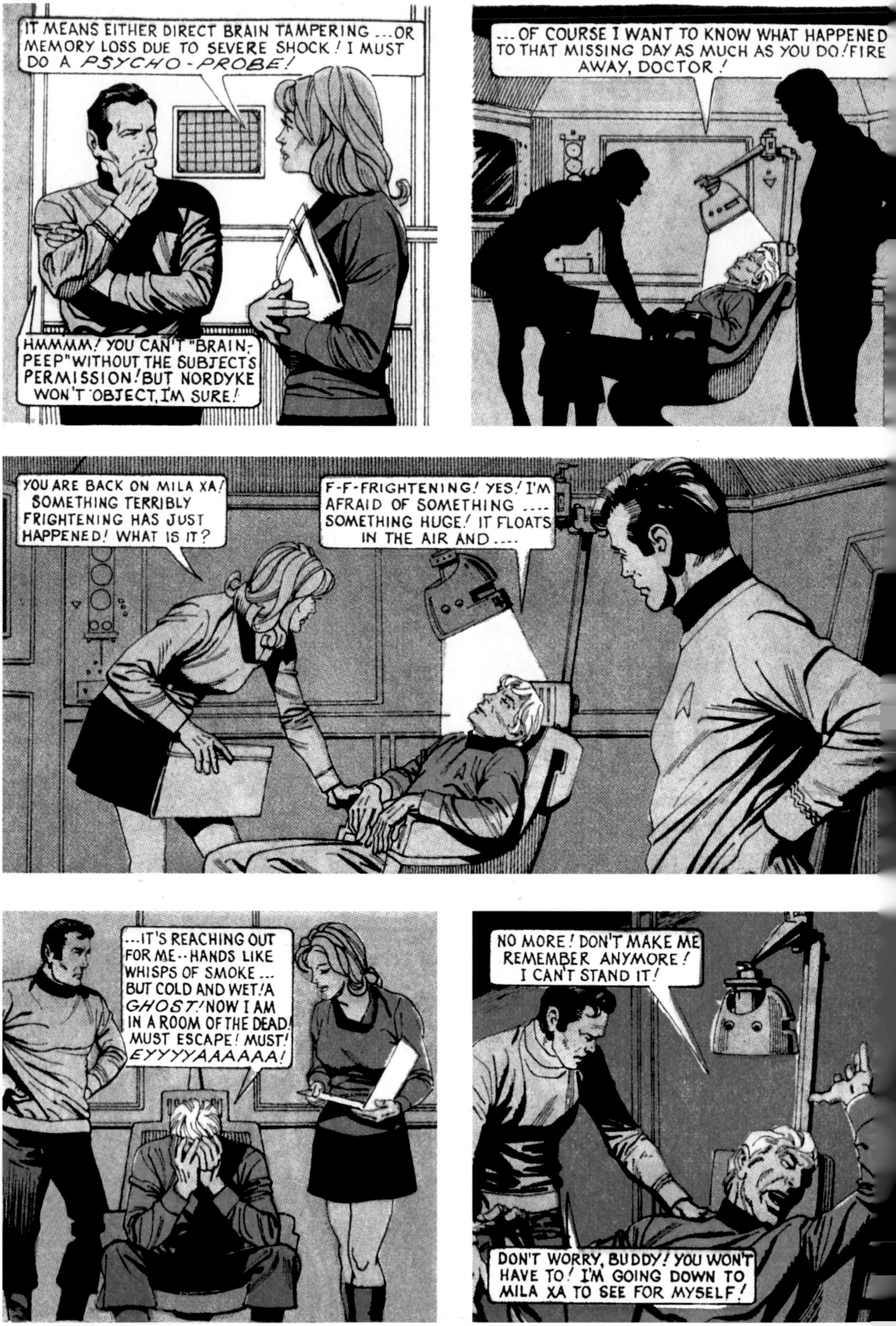
IT MEANS EITHER DIRECT BRAIN TAMPERING ...OR MEMORY LOSS DUE TO SEVERE SHOCK! I MUST DO A PSYCHO-PROBE!
HMMMM! YOU CAN'T "BRAIN-PEEP" WITHOUT THE SUBJECTS PERMISSION! BUT NORDYKE WON'T OBJECT, I'M SURE!
...OF COURSE I WANT TO KNOW WHAT HAPPENED TO THAT MISSING DAY AS MUCH AS YOU DO! FIRE AWAY, DOCTOR!
YOU ARE BACK ON MILA XA! SOMETHING TERRIBLY FRIGHTENING HAS JUST HAPPENED! WHAT IS IT?
F-F-FRIGHTENING! YES! I'M AFRAID OF SOMETHING .... SOMETHING HUGE! IT FLOATS IN THE AIR AND ....
...IT'S REACHING OUT FOR ME--HANDS LIKE WHISPS OF SMOKE ... BUT COLD AND WET! A GHOST! NOW I AM IN A ROOM OF THE DEAD! MUST ESCAPE! MUST! EYYYYAAAAAA!
NO MORE! DON'T MAKE ME REMEMBER ANYMORE! I CAN'T STAND IT!
DON'T WORRY, BUDDY! YOU WON'T HAVE TO! I'M GOING DOWN TO MILA XA TO SEE FOR MYSELF!

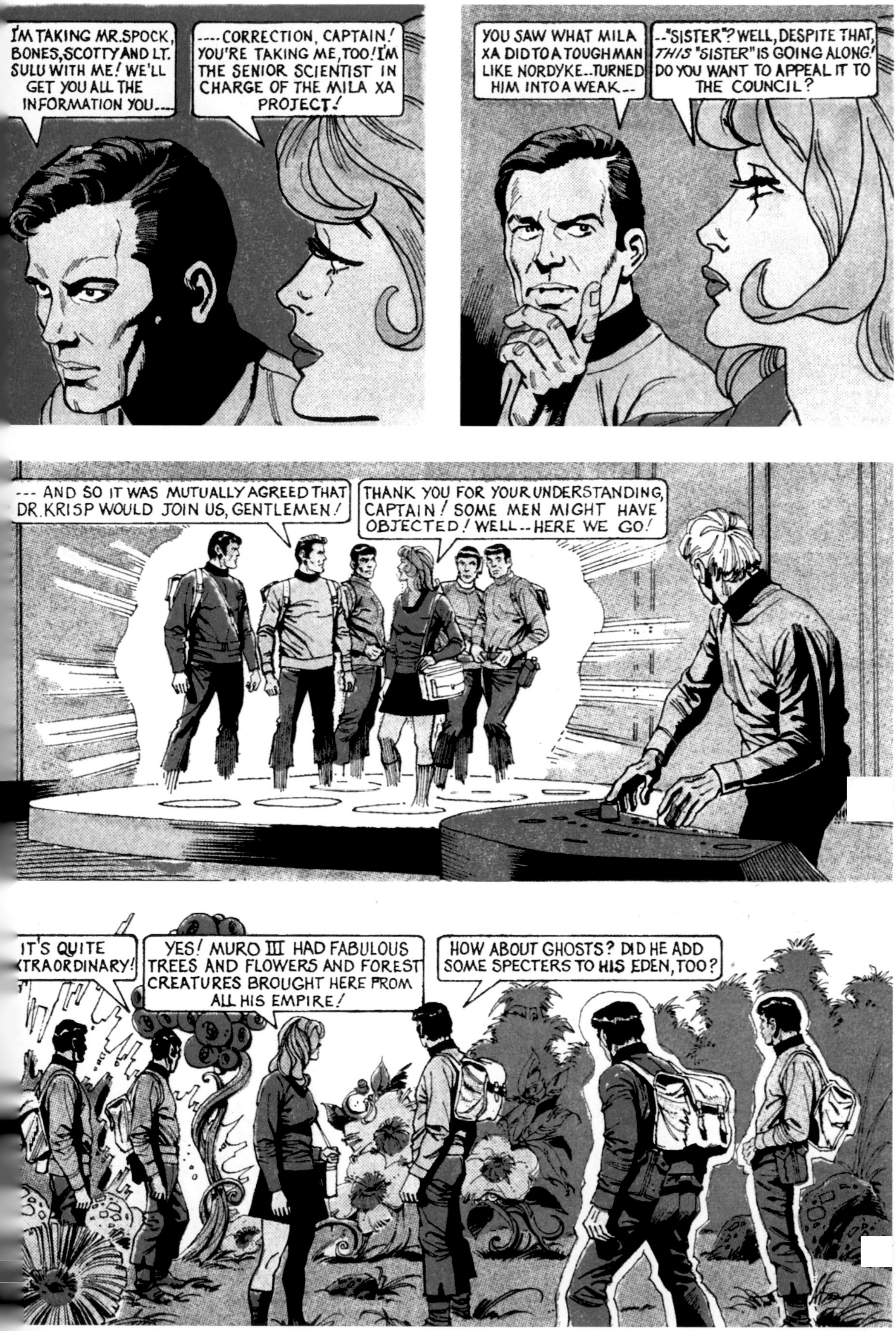
I'M TAKING MR. SPOCK, BONES, SCOTTY AND LT. SULU WITH ME! WE'LL GET YOU ALL THE INFORMATION YOU---
----CORRECTION, CAPTAIN! YOU'RE TAKING ME, TOO! I'M THE SENIOR SCIENTIST IN CHARGE OF THE MILA XA PROJECT!
YOU SAW WHAT MILA XA DID TO A TOUGH MAN LIKE NORDYKE--TURNED HIM INTO A WEAK--
--"SISTER"? WELL, DESPITE THAT, THIS "SISTER" IS GOING ALONG! DO YOU WANT TO APPEAL IT TO THE COUNCIL?
--- AND SO IT WAS MUTUALLY AGREED THAT DR. KRISP WOULD JOIN US, GENTLEMEN!
THANK YOU FOR YOUR UNDERSTANDING, CAPTAIN! SOME MEN MIGHT HAVE OBJECTED! WELL--HERE WE GO!
IT'S QUITE XTRAORDINARY!
YES! MURO III HAD FABULOUS TREES AND FLOWERS AND FOREST CREATURES BROUGHT HERE FROM ALL HIS EMPIRE!
HOW ABOUT GHOSTS? DID HE ADD SOME SPECTERS TO HIS EDEN, TOO?

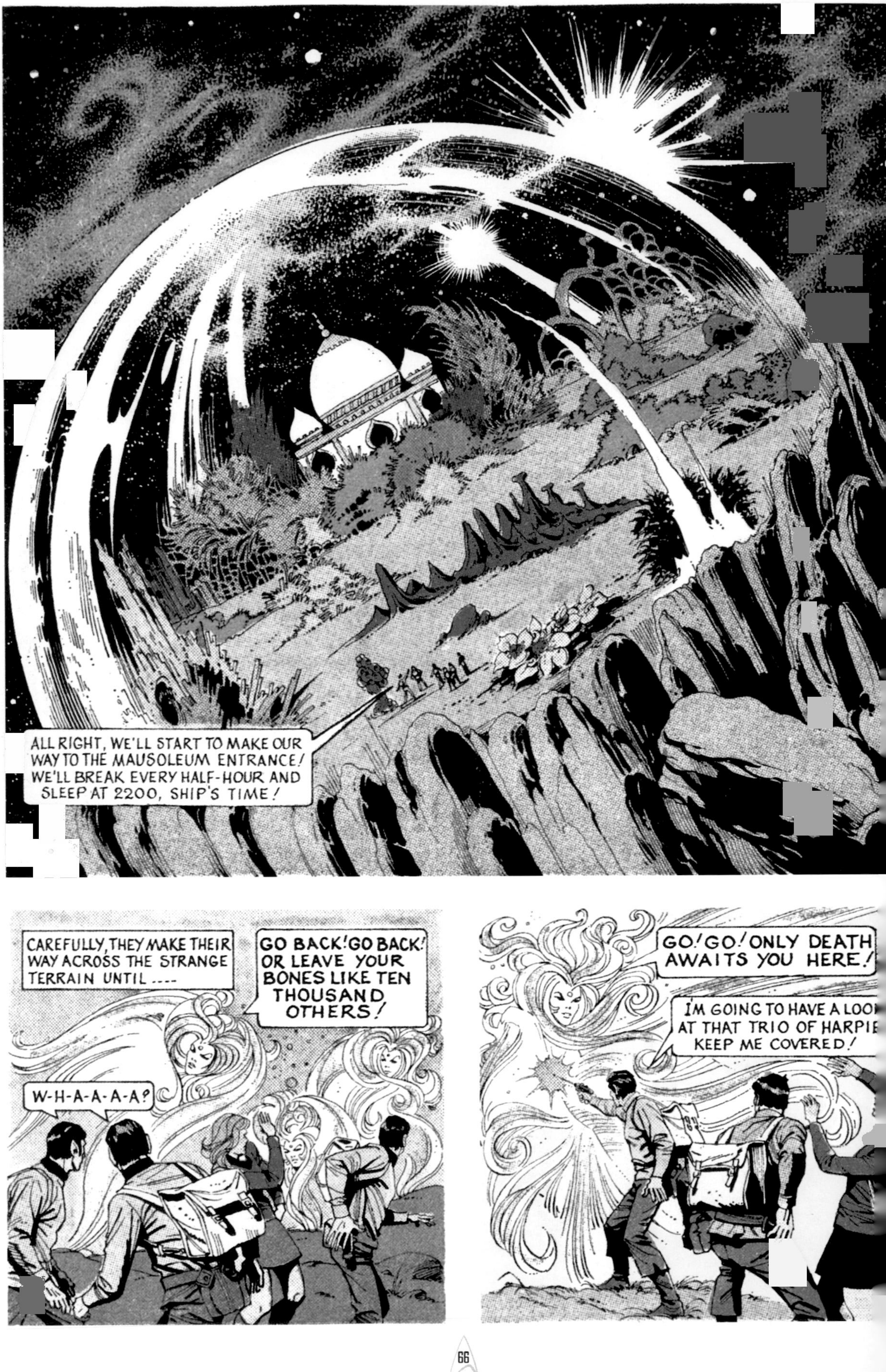
ALL RIGHT, WE'LL START TO MAKE OUR WAY TO THE MAUSOLEUM ENTRANCE! WE'LL BREAK EVERY HALF-HOUR AND SLEEP AT 2200, SHIP'S TIME!
CAREFULLY, THEY MAKE THEIR WAY ACROSS THE STRANGE TERRAIN UNTIL ----
GO BACK! GO BACK! OR LEAVE YOUR BONES LIKE TEN THOUSAND OTHERS!
W-H-A-A-A-A?
GO! GO! ONLY DEATH AWAITS YOU HERE!
I'M GOING TO HAVE A LOOK AT THAT TRIO OF HARPIE KEEP ME COVERED!

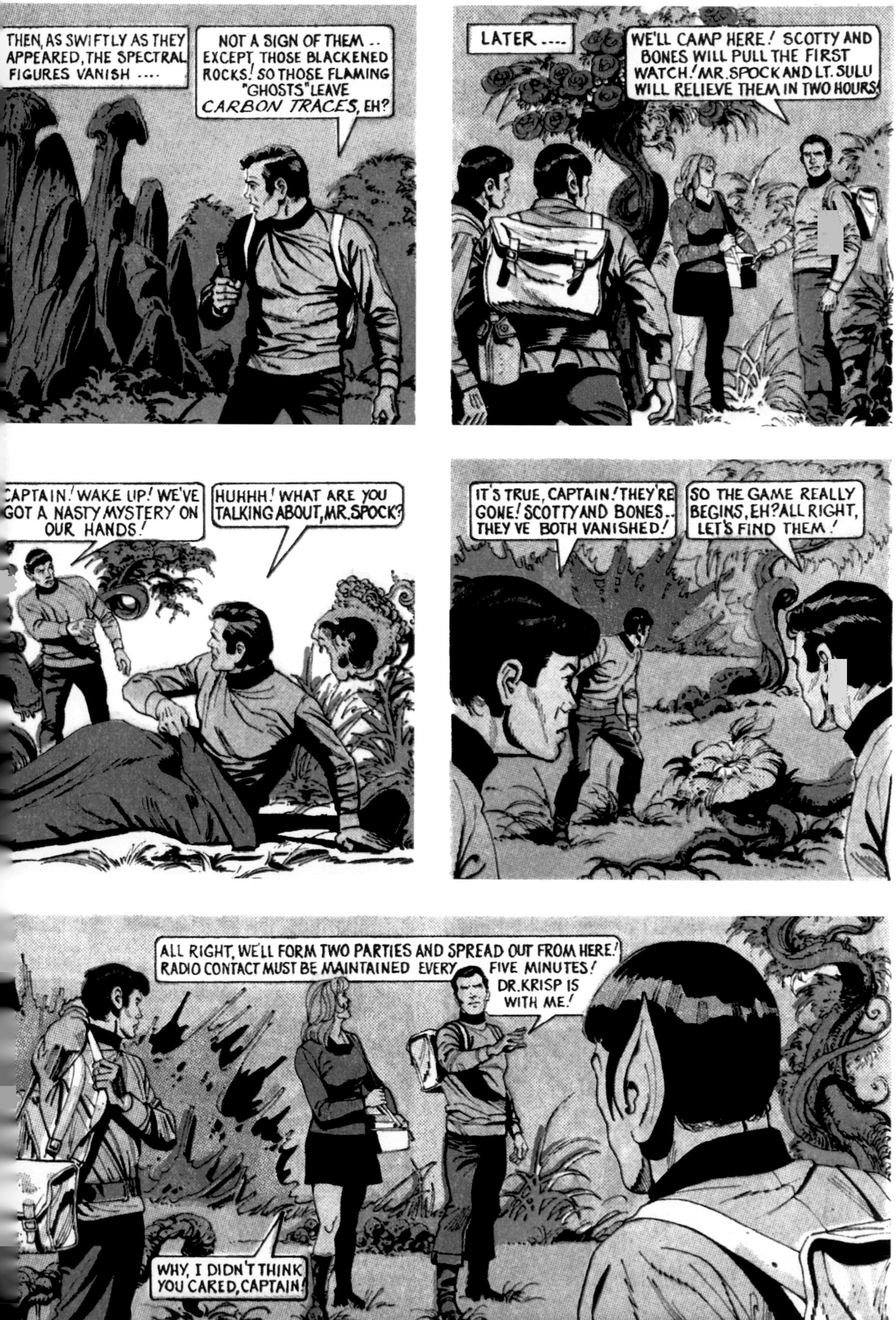
THEN, AS SWIFTLY AS THEY APPEARED, THE SPECTRAL FIGURES VANISH ....
NOT A SIGN OF THEM .. EXCEPT THOSE BLACKENED ROCKS! SO THOSE FLAMING "GHOSTS" LEAVE CARBON TRACES, EH?
LATER ....
WE'LL CAMP HERE! SCOTTY AND BONES WILL PULL THE FIRST WATCH! MR. SPOCK AND LT. SULU WILL RELIEVE THEM IN TWO HOURS!
CAPTAIN! WAKE UP! WE'VE GOT A NASTY MYSTERY ON OUR HANDS!
HUHHH! WHAT ARE YOU TALKING ABOUT, MR. SPOCK?
IT'S TRUE, CAPTAIN! THEY'RE GONE! SCOTTY AND BONES .. THEY'VE BOTH VANISHED!
SO THE GAME REALLY BEGINS, EH? ALL RIGHT, LET'S FIND THEM!
ALL RIGHT, WE'LL FORM TWO PARTIES AND SPREAD OUT FROM HERE! RADIO CONTACT MUST BE MAINTAINED EVERY FIVE MINUTES! DR. KRISP IS WITH ME!
WHY, I DIDN'T THINK YOU CARED, CAPTAIN!

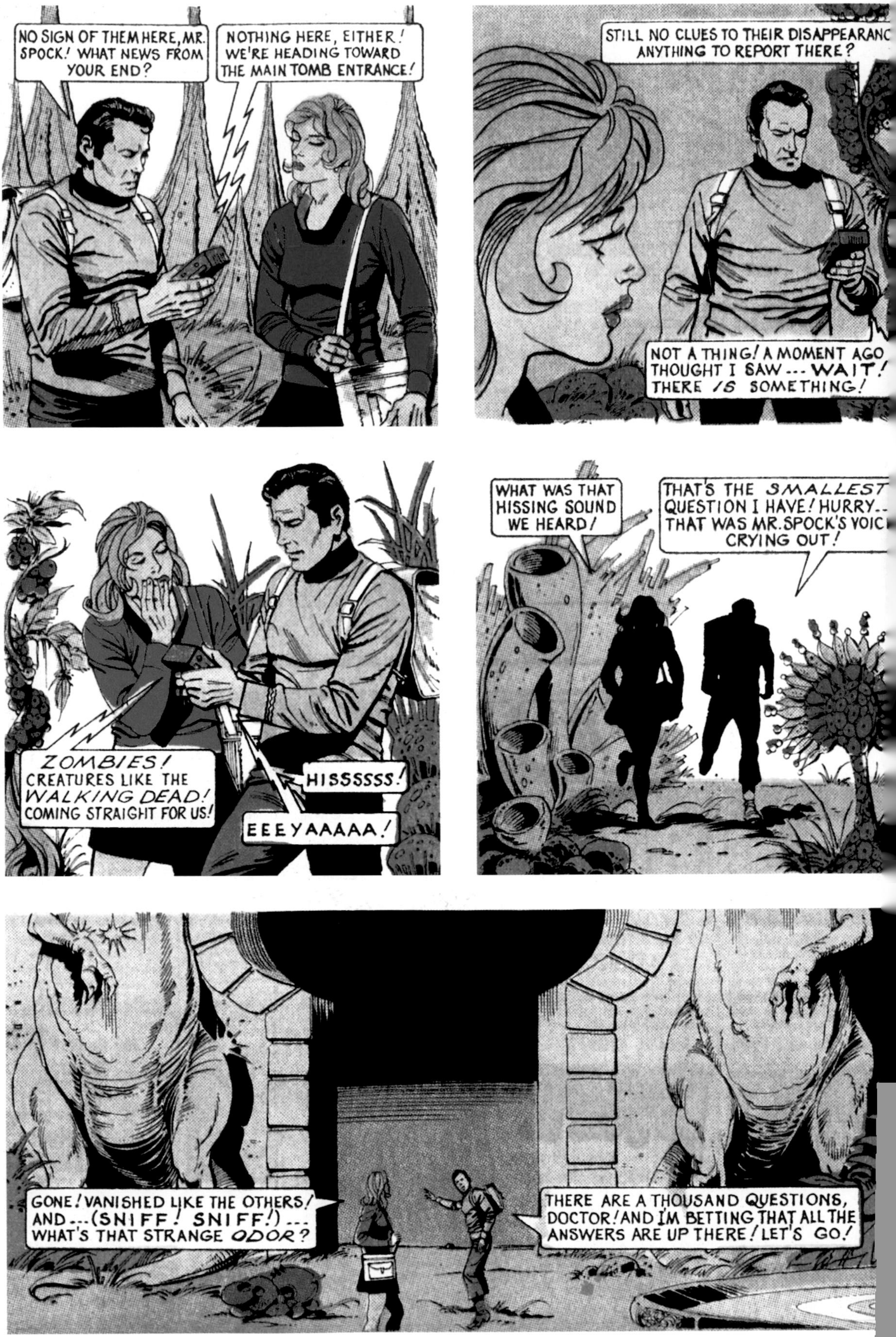
NO SIGN OF THEM HERE, MR. SPOCK! WHAT NEWS FROM YOUR END?
NOTHING HERE, EITHER! WE'RE HEADING TOWARD THE MAIN TOMB ENTRANCE!
STILL NO CLUES TO THEIR DISAPPEARANC ANYTHING TO REPORT THERE?
NOT A THING! A MOMENT AGO THOUGHT I SAW --- WAIT! THERE IS SOMETHING!
ZOMBIES! CREATURES LIKE THE WALKING DEAD! COMING STRAIGHT FOR US!
HISSSSSS!
EEEYAAAAA!
WHAT WAS THAT HISSING SOUND WE HEARD!
THAT'S THE SMALLEST QUESTION I HAVE! HURRY-- THAT WAS MR. SPOCK'S VOIC CRYING OUT!
GONE! VANISHED LIKE THE OTHERS! AND ---(SNIFF! SNIFF!) --- WHAT'S THAT STRANGE ODOR?
THERE ARE A THOUSAND QUESTIONS, DOCTOR! AND I'M BETTING THAT ALL THE ANSWERS ARE UP THERE! LET'S GO!

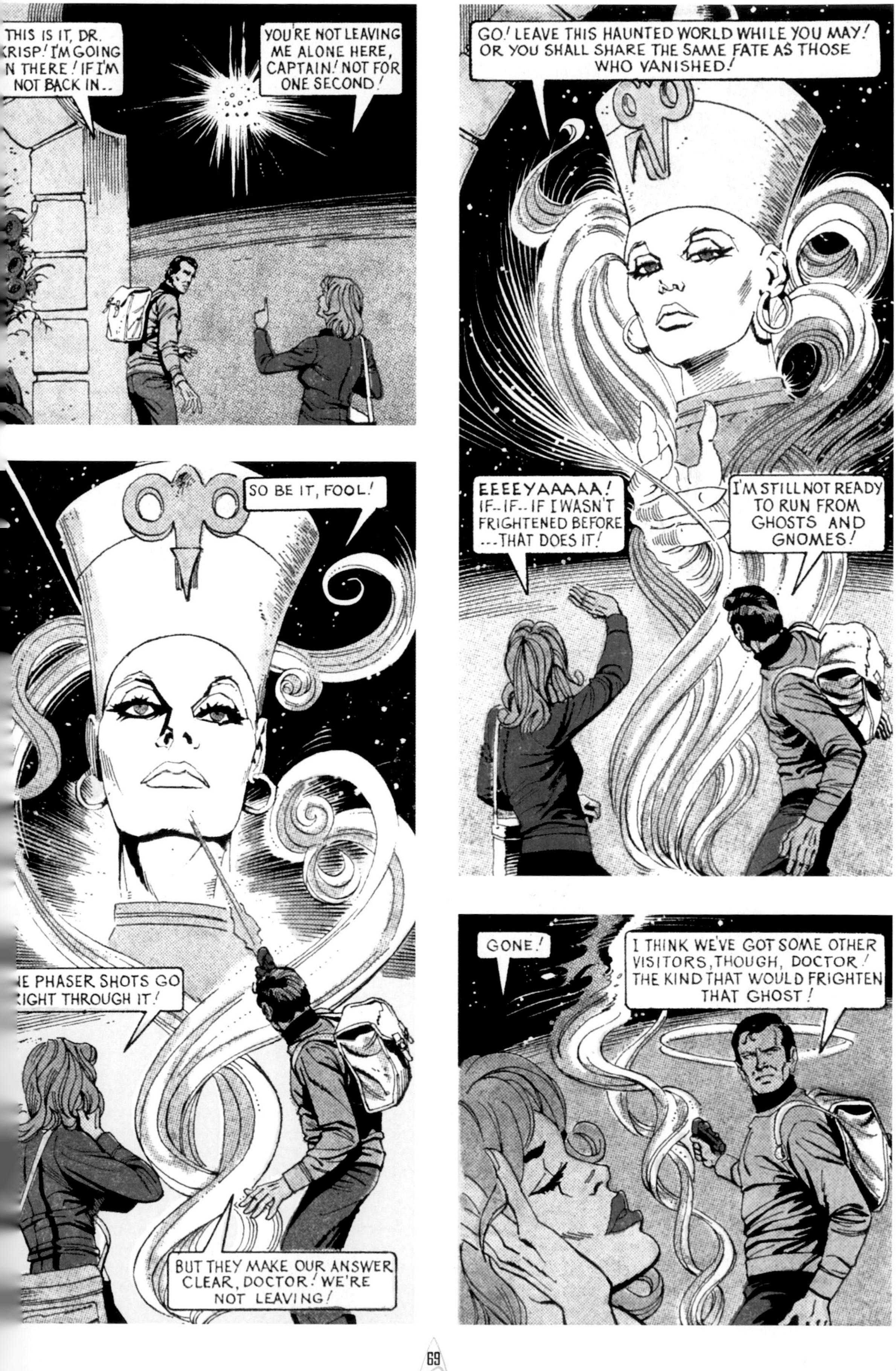
THIS IS IT, DR. RISP! I'M GOING N THERE! IF I'M NOT BACK IN..
YOU'RE NOT LEAVING ME ALONE HERE, CAPTAIN! NOT FOR ONE SECOND!
GO! LEAVE THIS HAUNTED WORLD WHILE YOU MAY! OR YOU SHALL SHARE THE SAME FATE AS THOSE WHO VANISHED!
EEEEYAAAAA! IF-- IF-- IF I WASN'T FRIGHTENED BEFORE --- THAT DOES IT!
I'M STILL NOT READY TO RUN FROM GHOSTS AND GNOMES!
SO BE IT, FOOL!
E PHASER SHOTS GO IGHT THROUGH IT!
BUT THEY MAKE OUR ANSWER CLEAR, DOCTOR! WE'RE NOT LEAVING!
GONE!
I THINK WE'VE GOT SOME OTHER VISITORS, THOUGH, DOCTOR! THE KIND THAT WOULD FRIGHTEN THAT GHOST!

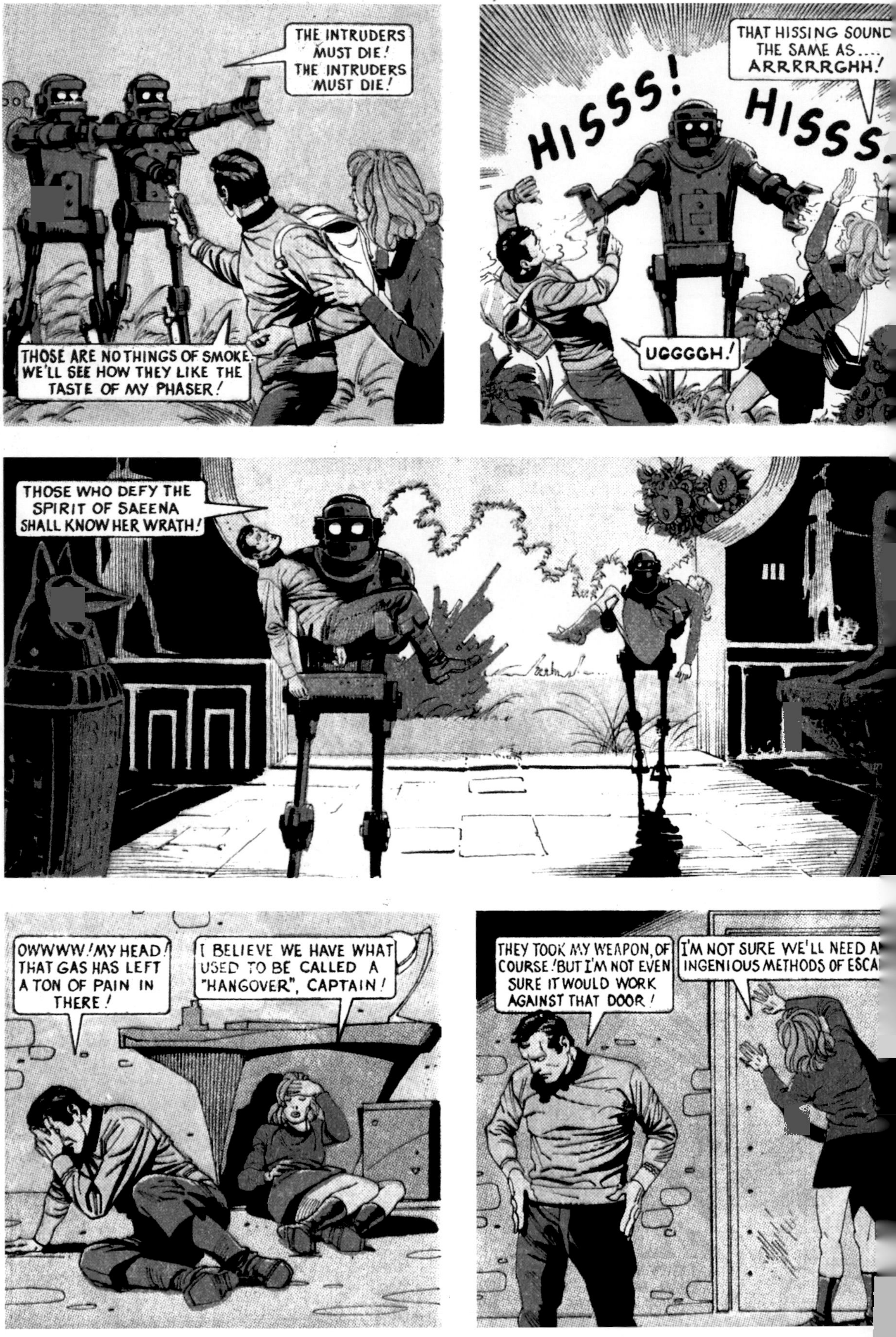
THE INTRUDERS MUST DIE! THE INTRUDERS MUST DIE!
THOSE ARE NO THINGS OF SMOKE. WE'LL SEE HOW THEY LIKE THE TASTE OF MY PHASER!
THAT HISSING SOUND THE SAME AS.... ARRRRRGHH!
HISSS!
HISSS.
UGGGGH!
THOSE WHO DEFY THE SPIRIT OF SAEENA SHALL KNOW HER WRATH!
OWWWW! MY HEAD! THAT GAS HAS LEFT A TON OF PAIN IN THERE!
I BELIEVE WE HAVE WHAT USED TO BE CALLED A "HANGOVER", CAPTAIN!
THEY TOOK MY WEAPON, OF COURSE! BUT I'M NOT EVEN SURE IT WOULD WORK AGAINST THAT DOOR!
I'M NOT SURE WE'LL NEED A INGENIOUS METHODS OF ESCA

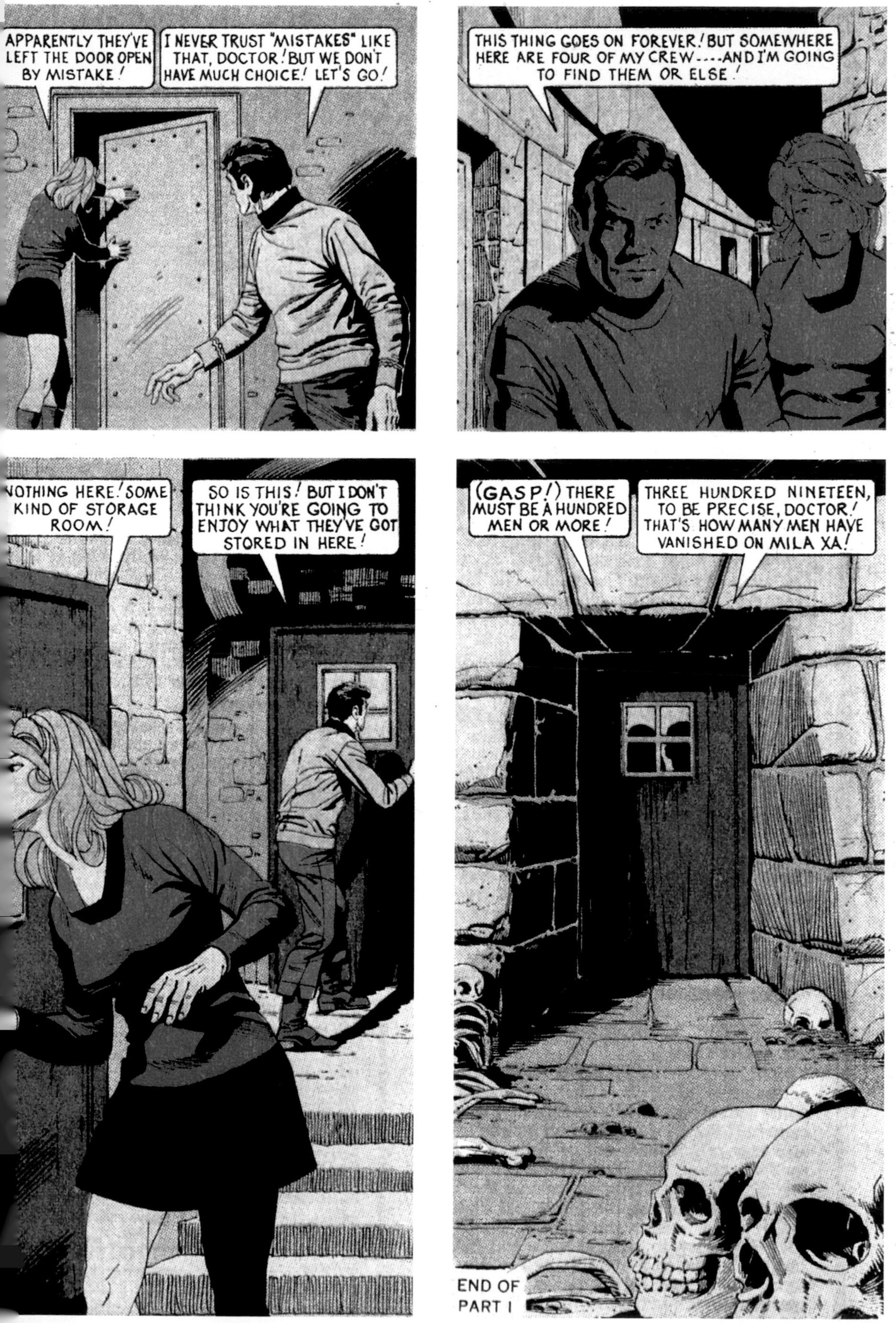
APPARENTLY THEY'VE LEFT THE DOOR OPEN BY MISTAKE!
I NEVER TRUST "MISTAKES" LIKE THAT, DOCTOR! BUT WE DON'T HAVE MUCH CHOICE! LET'S GO!
THIS THING GOES ON FOREVER! BUT SOMEWHERE HERE ARE FOUR OF MY CREW----AND I'M GOING TO FIND THEM OR ELSE!
NOTHING HERE! SOME KIND OF STORAGE ROOM!
SO IS THIS! BUT I DON'T THINK YOU'RE GOING TO ENJOY WHAT THEY'VE GOT STORED IN HERE!
(GASP!) THERE MUST BE A HUNDRED MEN OR MORE!
THREE HUNDRED NINETEEN, TO BE PRECISE, DOCTOR! THAT'S HOW MANY MEN HAVE VANISHED ON MILA XA!
END OF PART I

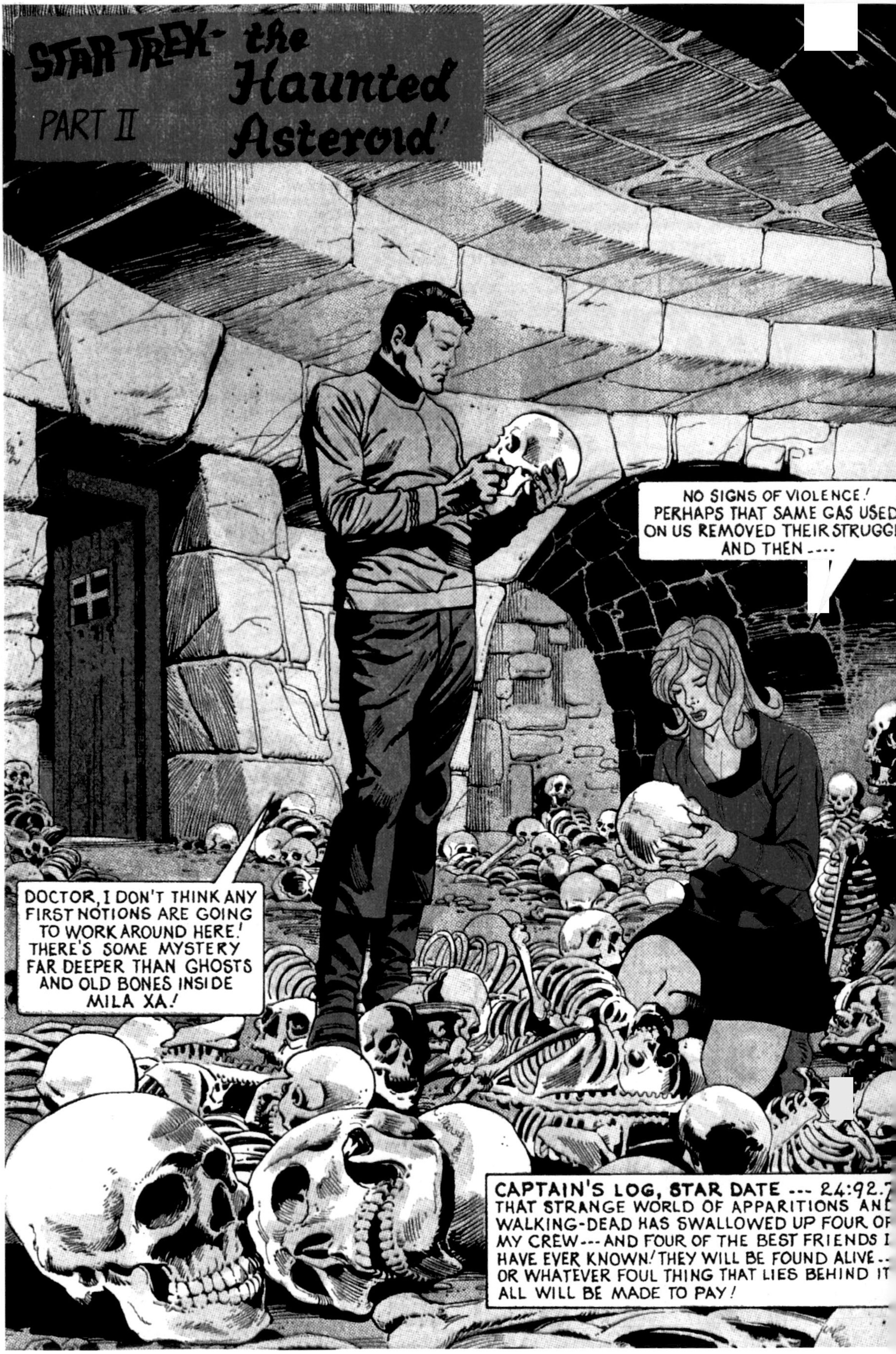
STAR TREK
the Haunted Asteroid!
PART II
NO SIGNS OF VIOLENCE! PERHAPS THAT SAME GAS USED ON US REMOVED THEIR STRUGGL AND THEN ----
DOCTOR, I DON'T THINK ANY FIRST NOTIONS ARE GOING TO WORK AROUND HERE! THERE'S SOME MYSTERY FAR DEEPER THAN GHOSTS AND OLD BONES INSIDE MILA XA!
CAPTAIN'S LOG, STAR DATE --- 24:92.7
THAT STRANGE WORLD OF APPARITIONS AND WALKING-DEAD HAS SWALLOWED UP FOUR OF MY CREW --- AND FOUR OF THE BEST FRIENDS I HAVE EVER KNOWN! THEY WILL BE FOUND ALIVE -- OR WHATEVER FOUL THING THAT LIES BEHIND IT ALL WILL BE MADE TO PAY!

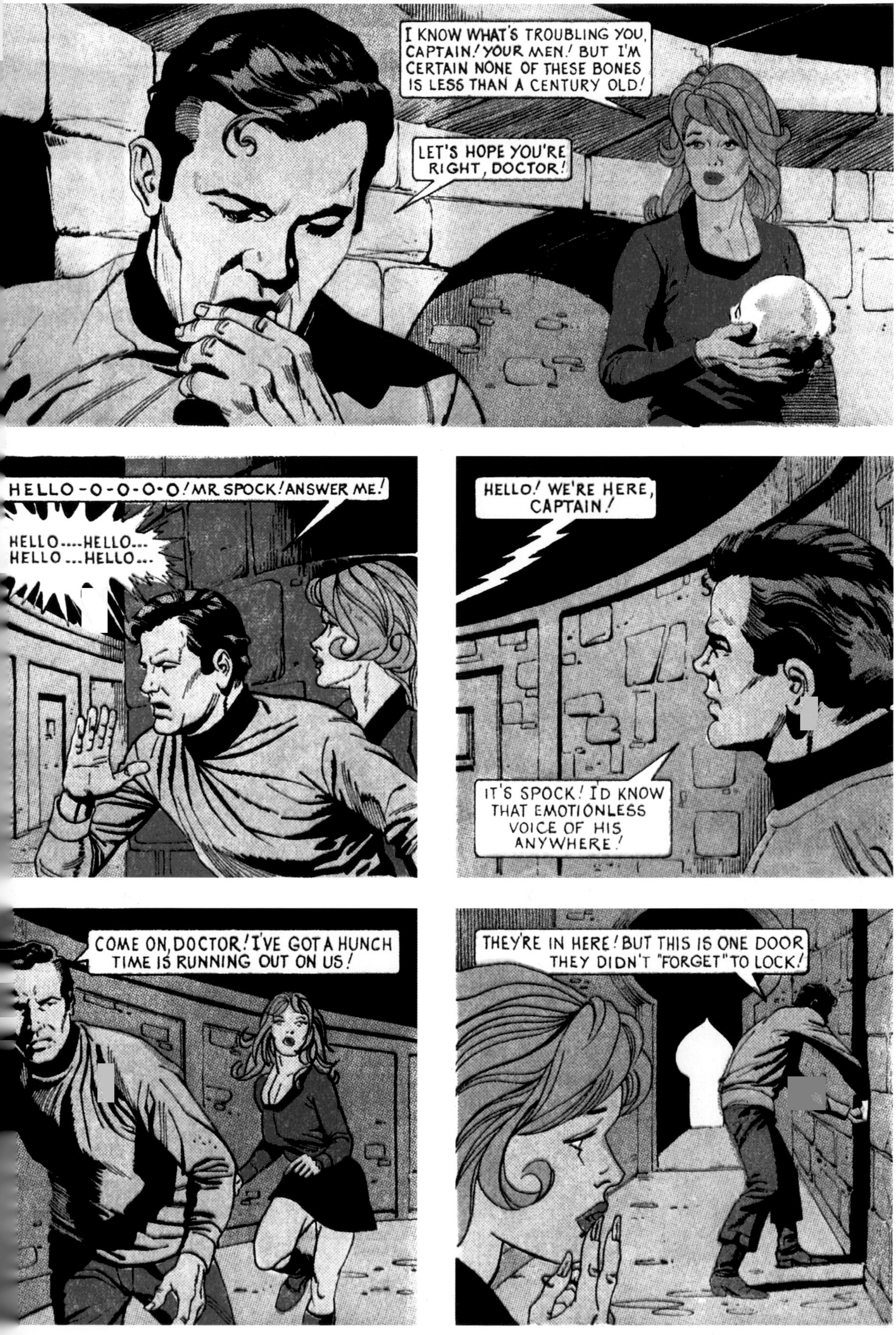
I KNOW WHAT'S TROUBLING YOU, CAPTAIN! YOUR MEN! BUT I'M CERTAIN NONE OF THESE BONES IS LESS THAN A CENTURY OLD!
LET'S HOPE YOU'RE RIGHT, DOCTOR!
HELLO-O-O-O-O! MR SPOCK! ANSWER ME!
HELLO....HELLO... HELLO...HELLO...
HELLO! WE'RE HERE, CAPTAIN!
IT'S SPOCK! I'D KNOW THAT EMOTIONLESS VOICE OF HIS ANYWHERE!
COME ON, DOCTOR! I'VE GOT A HUNCH TIME IS RUNNING OUT ON US!
THEY'RE IN HERE! BUT THIS IS ONE DOOR THEY DIDN'T "FORGET" TO LOCK!

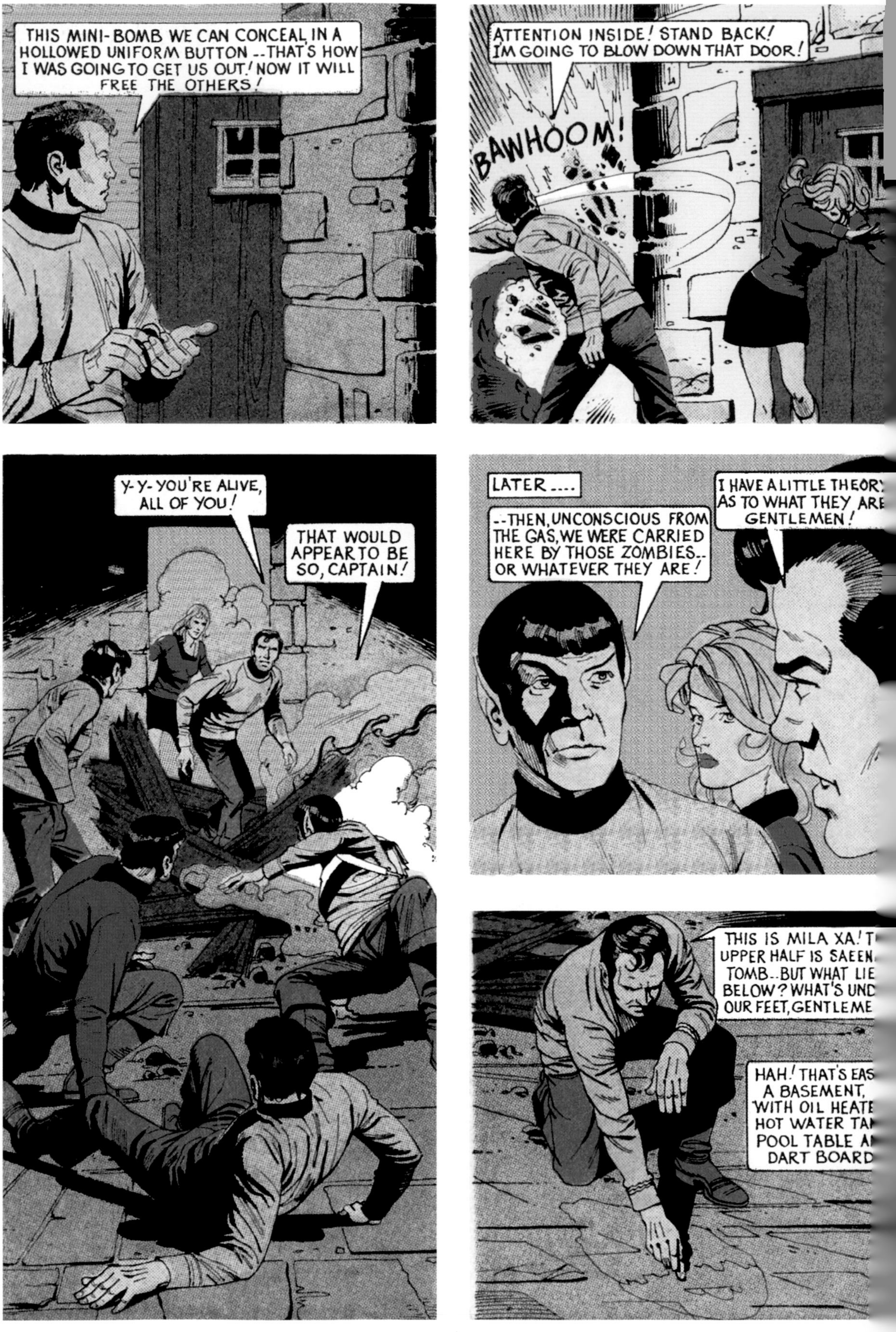

THIS MINI-BOMB WE CAN CONCEAL IN A HOLLOWED UNIFORM BUTTON --THAT'S HOW I WAS GOING TO GET US OUT! NOW IT WILL FREE THE OTHERS!
ATTENTION INSIDE! STAND BACK! I'M GOING TO BLOW DOWN THAT DOOR!
BAWHOOM!
Y-Y-YOU'RE ALIVE, ALL OF YOU!
THAT WOULD APPEAR TO BE SO, CAPTAIN!
LATER....
--THEN, UNCONSCIOUS FROM THE GAS, WE WERE CARRIED HERE BY THOSE ZOMBIES.. OR WHATEVER THEY ARE!
I HAVE A LITTLE THEOR AS TO WHAT THEY AR GENTLEMEN!
THIS IS MILA XA! T UPPER HALF IS SAEEN TOMB--BUT WHAT LIE BELOW? WHAT'S UND OUR FEET, GENTLEME
HAH! THAT'S EAS A BASEMENT, WITH OIL HEATE HOT WATER TA POOL TABLE A DART BOARD

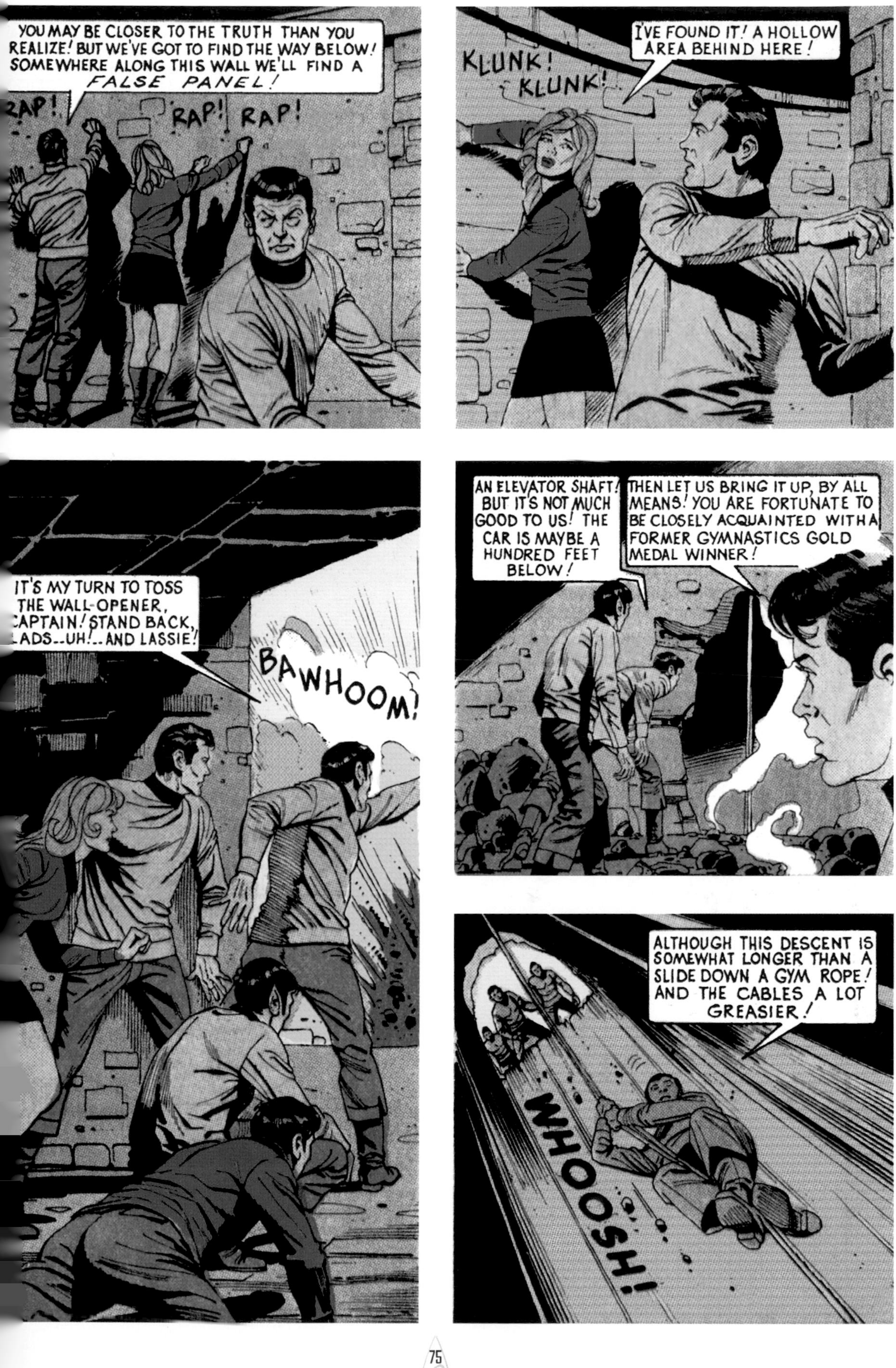
YOU MAY BE CLOSER TO THE TRUTH THAN YOU REALIZE! BUT WE'VE GOT TO FIND THE WAY BELOW! SOMEWHERE ALONG THIS WALL WE'LL FIND A FALSE PANEL!
RAP! RAP! RAP!
KLUNK! KLUNK!
I'VE FOUND IT! A HOLLOW AREA BEHIND HERE!
IT'S MY TURN TO TOSS THE WALL-OPENER, CAPTAIN! STAND BACK, LADS...UH!...AND LASSIE!
BAWHOOM!
AN ELEVATOR SHAFT! BUT IT'S NOT MUCH GOOD TO US! THE CAR IS MAYBE A HUNDRED FEET BELOW!
THEN LET US BRING IT UP, BY ALL MEANS! YOU ARE FORTUNATE TO BE CLOSELY ACQUAINTED WITH A FORMER GYMNASTICS GOLD MEDAL WINNER!
ALTHOUGH THIS DESCENT IS SOMEWHAT LONGER THAN A SLIDE DOWN A GYM ROPE! AND THE CABLES A LOT GREASIER!
WHOOSH!

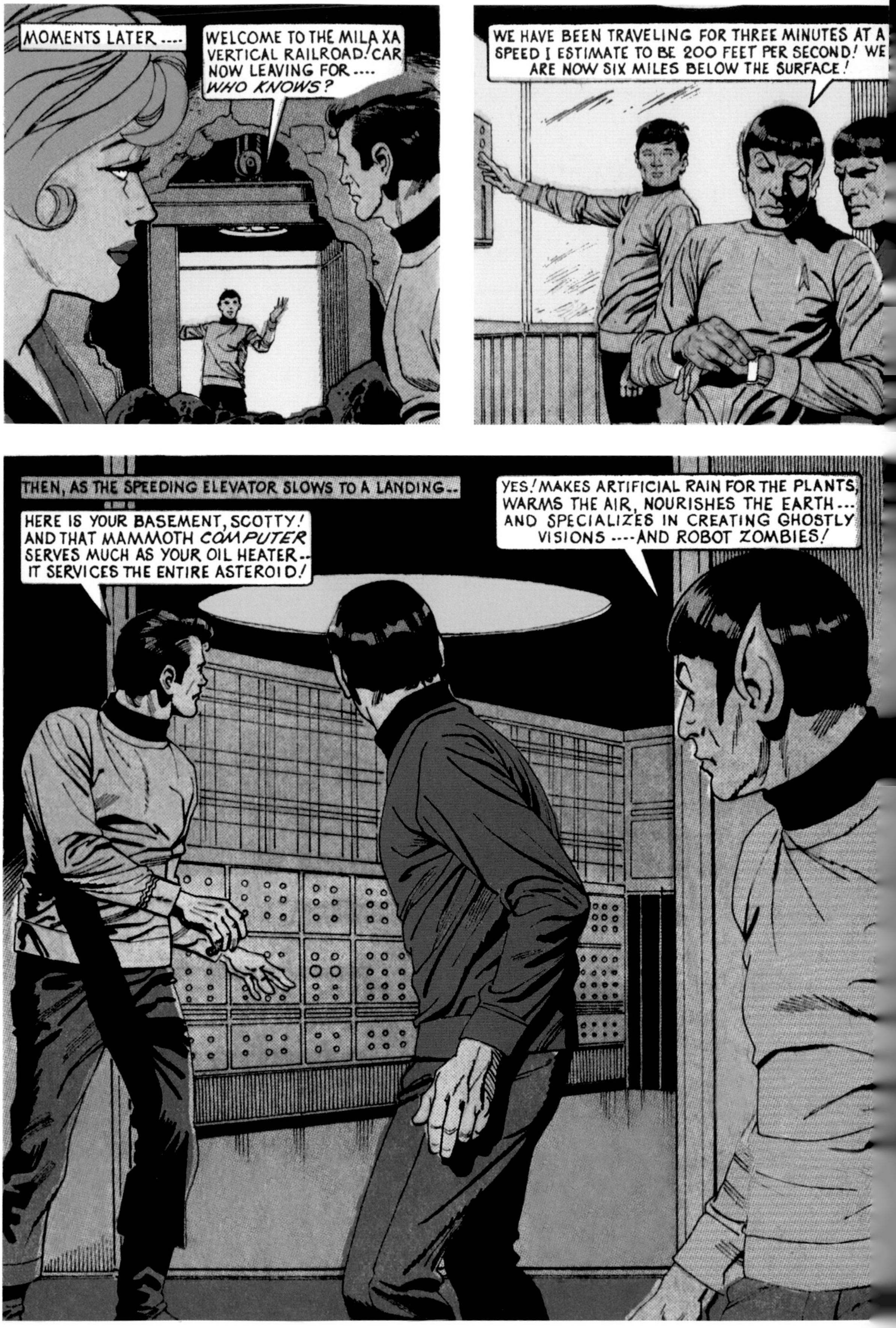
MOMENTS LATER ....
WELCOME TO THE MILA XA VERTICAL RAILROAD! CAR NOW LEAVING FOR .... WHO KNOWS?
WE HAVE BEEN TRAVELING FOR THREE MINUTES AT A SPEED I ESTIMATE TO BE 200 FEET PER SECOND! WE ARE NOW SIX MILES BELOW THE SURFACE!
THEN, AS THE SPEEDING ELEVATOR SLOWS TO A LANDING..
HERE IS YOUR BASEMENT, SCOTTY! AND THAT MAMMOTH COMPUTER SERVES MUCH AS YOUR OIL HEATER.. IT SERVICES THE ENTIRE ASTEROID!
YES! MAKES ARTIFICIAL RAIN FOR THE PLANTS, WARMS THE AIR, NOURISHES THE EARTH... AND SPECIALIZES IN CREATING GHOSTLY VISIONS ----AND ROBOT ZOMBIES!

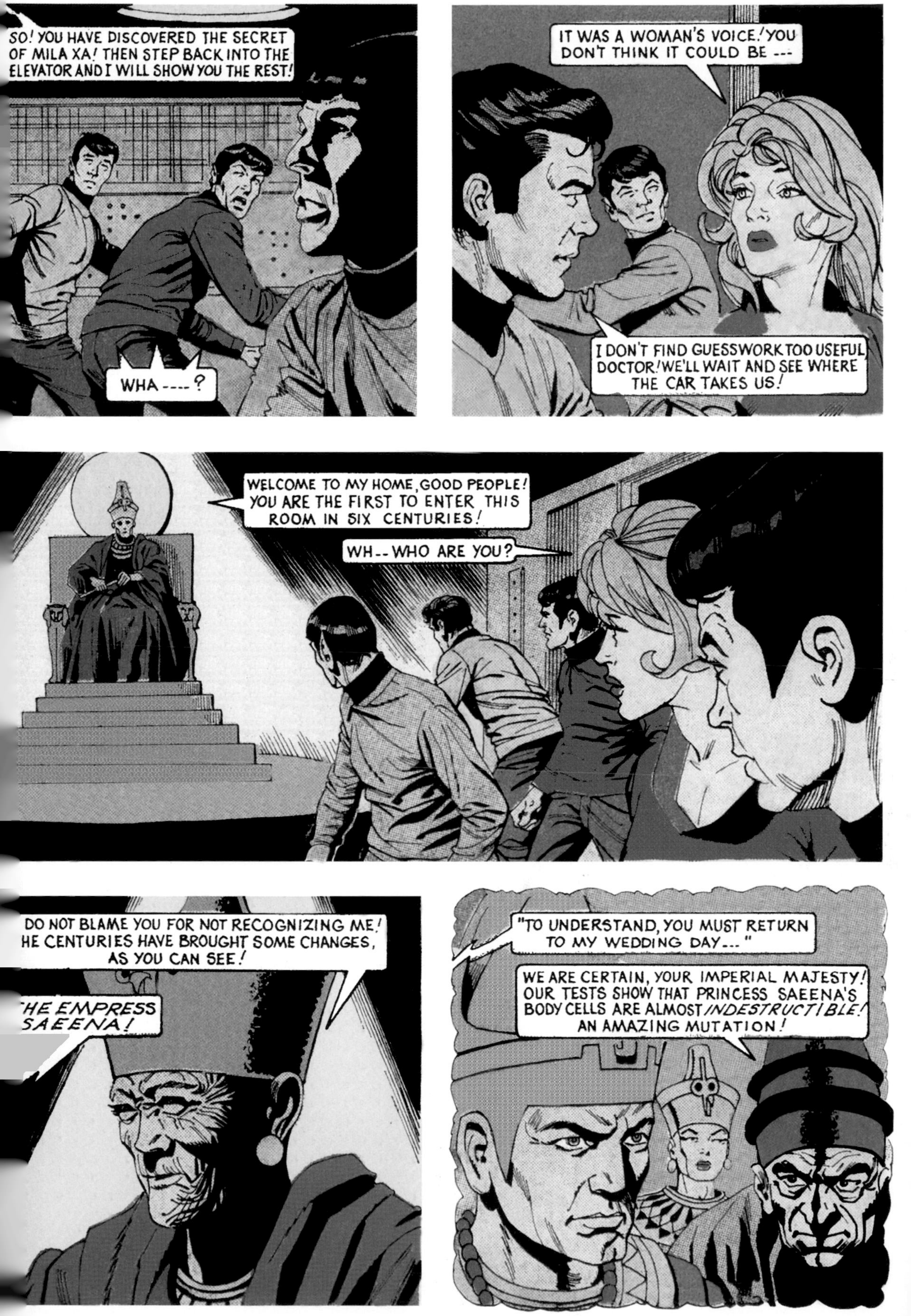
SO! YOU HAVE DISCOVERED THE SECRET OF MILA XA! THEN STEP BACK INTO THE ELEVATOR AND I WILL SHOW YOU THE REST!
WHA ----?
IT WAS A WOMAN'S VOICE! YOU DON'T THINK IT COULD BE ---
I DON'T FIND GUESSWORK TOO USEFUL DOCTOR! WE'LL WAIT AND SEE WHERE THE CAR TAKES US!
WELCOME TO MY HOME, GOOD PEOPLE! YOU ARE THE FIRST TO ENTER THIS ROOM IN SIX CENTURIES!
WH--WHO ARE YOU?
DO NOT BLAME YOU FOR NOT RECOGNIZING ME! HE CENTURIES HAVE BROUGHT SOME CHANGES, AS YOU CAN SEE!
HE EMPRESS SAEENA!
"TO UNDERSTAND, YOU MUST RETURN TO MY WEDDING DAY---"
WE ARE CERTAIN, YOUR IMPERIAL MAJESTY! OUR TESTS SHOW THAT PRINCESS SAEENA'S BODY CELLS ARE ALMOST INDESTRUCTIBLE! AN AMAZING MUTATION!

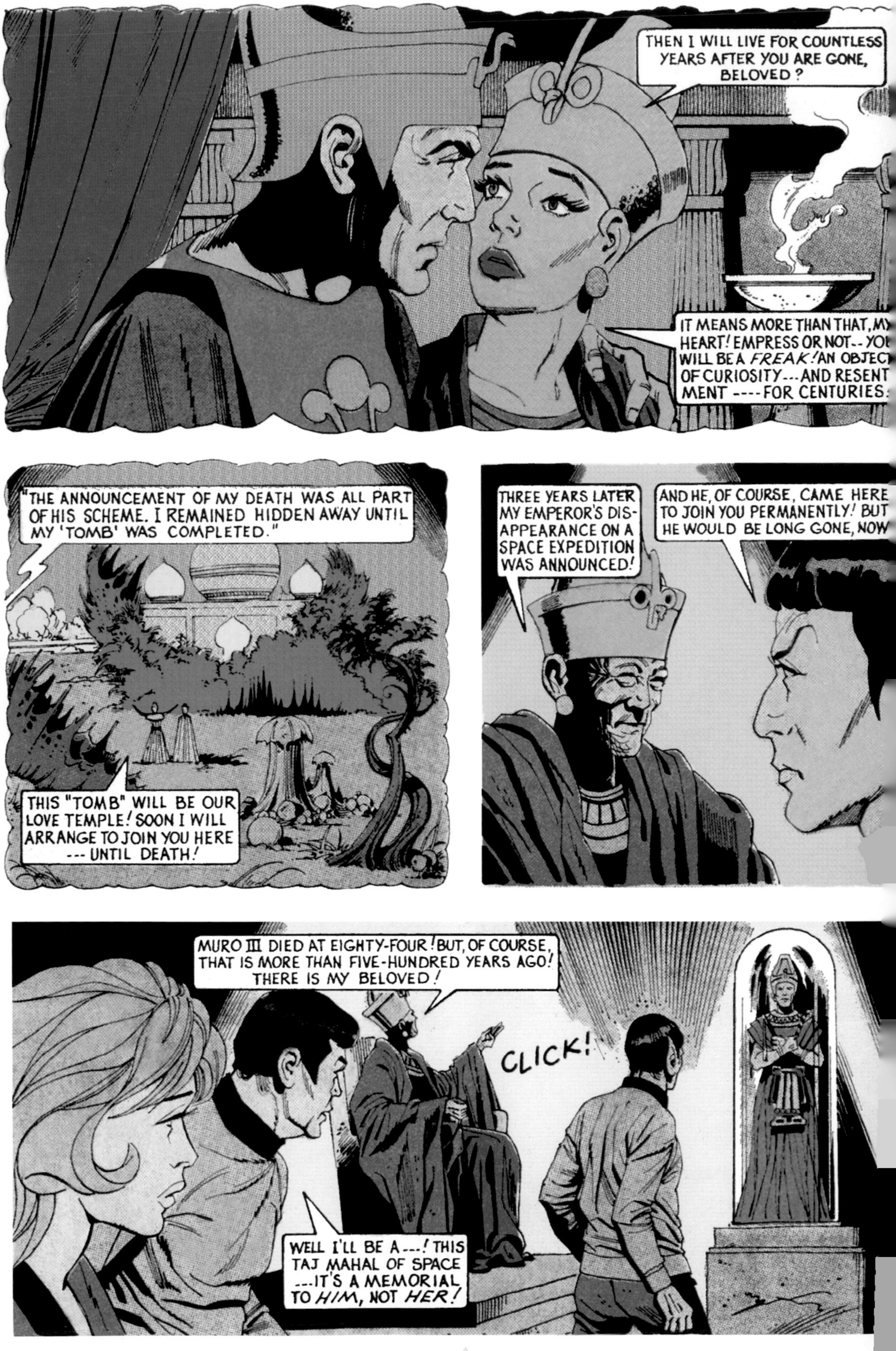
THEN I WILL LIVE FOR COUNTLESS YEARS AFTER YOU ARE GONE, BELOVED?
IT MEANS MORE THAN THAT, MY HEART! EMPRESS OR NOT-- YOU WILL BE A FREAK! AN OBJECT OF CURIOSITY--- AND RESENTMENT ----FOR CENTURIES.
"THE ANNOUNCEMENT OF MY DEATH WAS ALL PART OF HIS SCHEME. I REMAINED HIDDEN AWAY UNTIL MY 'TOMB' WAS COMPLETED."
THIS "TOMB" WILL BE OUR LOVE TEMPLE! SOON I WILL ARRANGE TO JOIN YOU HERE --- UNTIL DEATH!
THREE YEARS LATER MY EMPEROR'S DISAPPEARANCE ON A SPACE EXPEDITION WAS ANNOUNCED!
AND HE, OF COURSE, CAME HERE TO JOIN YOU PERMANENTLY! BUT HE WOULD BE LONG GONE, NOW
MURO III DIED AT EIGHTY-FOUR! BUT, OF COURSE, THAT IS MORE THAN FIVE-HUNDRED YEARS AGO! THERE IS MY BELOVED!
CLICK!
WELL I'LL BE A---! THIS TAJ MAHAL OF SPACE ---IT'S A MEMORIAL TO HIM, NOT HER!

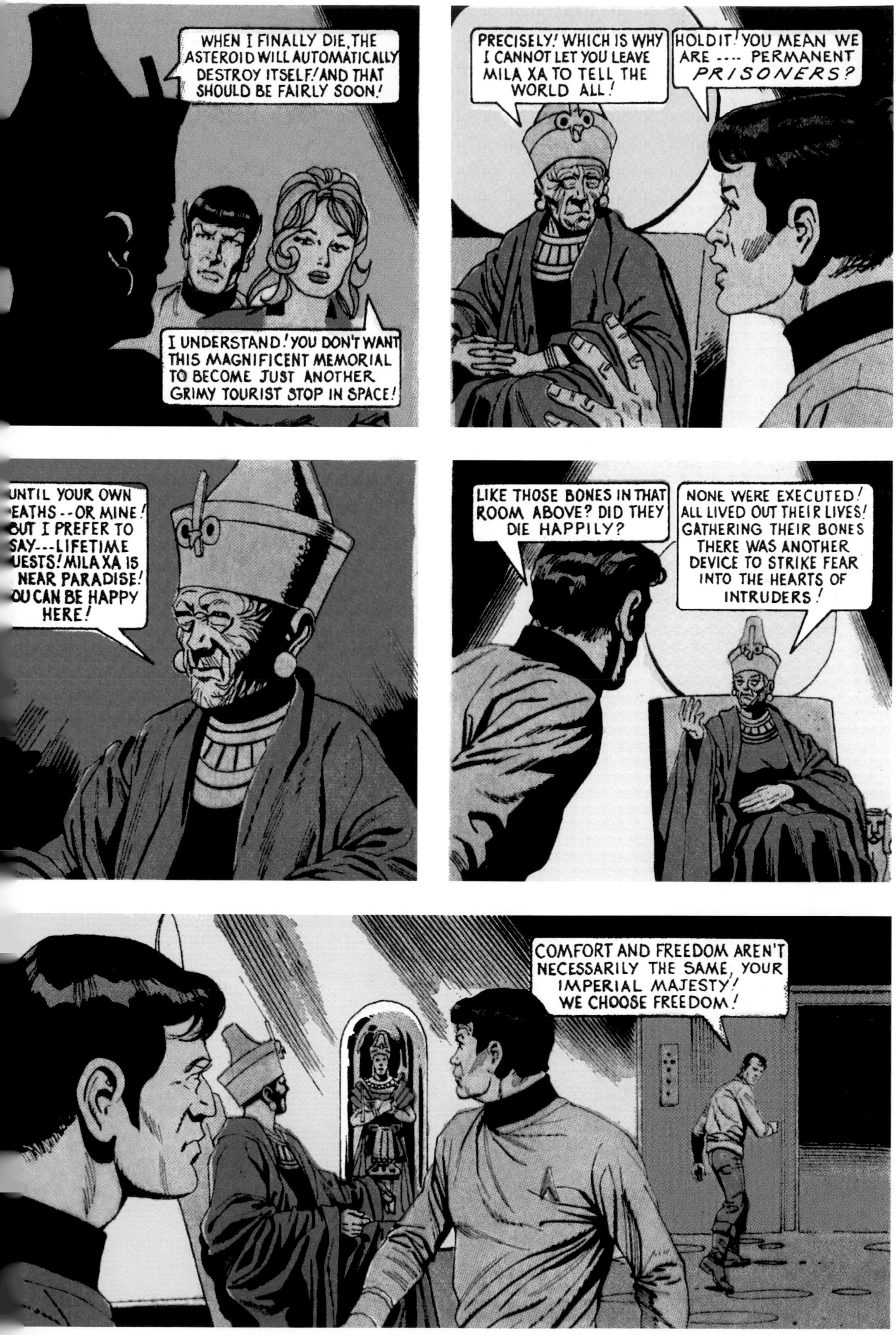
WHEN I FINALLY DIE, THE ASTEROID WILL AUTOMATICALLY DESTROY ITSELF! AND THAT SHOULD BE FAIRLY SOON!
I UNDERSTAND! YOU DON'T WANT THIS MAGNIFICENT MEMORIAL TO BECOME JUST ANOTHER GRIMY TOURIST STOP IN SPACE!
PRECISELY! WHICH IS WHY I CANNOT LET YOU LEAVE MILA XA TO TELL THE WORLD ALL!
HOLD IT! YOU MEAN WE ARE ---- PERMANENT PRISONERS?
UNTIL YOUR OWN DEATHS--OR MINE! BUT I PREFER TO SAY---LIFETIME GUESTS! MILA XA IS NEAR PARADISE! YOU CAN BE HAPPY HERE!
LIKE THOSE BONES IN THAT ROOM ABOVE? DID THEY DIE HAPPILY?
NONE WERE EXECUTED! ALL LIVED OUT THEIR LIVES! GATHERING THEIR BONES THERE WAS ANOTHER DEVICE TO STRIKE FEAR INTO THE HEARTS OF INTRUDERS!
COMFORT AND FREEDOM AREN'T NECESSARILY THE SAME, YOUR IMPERIAL MAJESTY! WE CHOOSE FREEDOM!

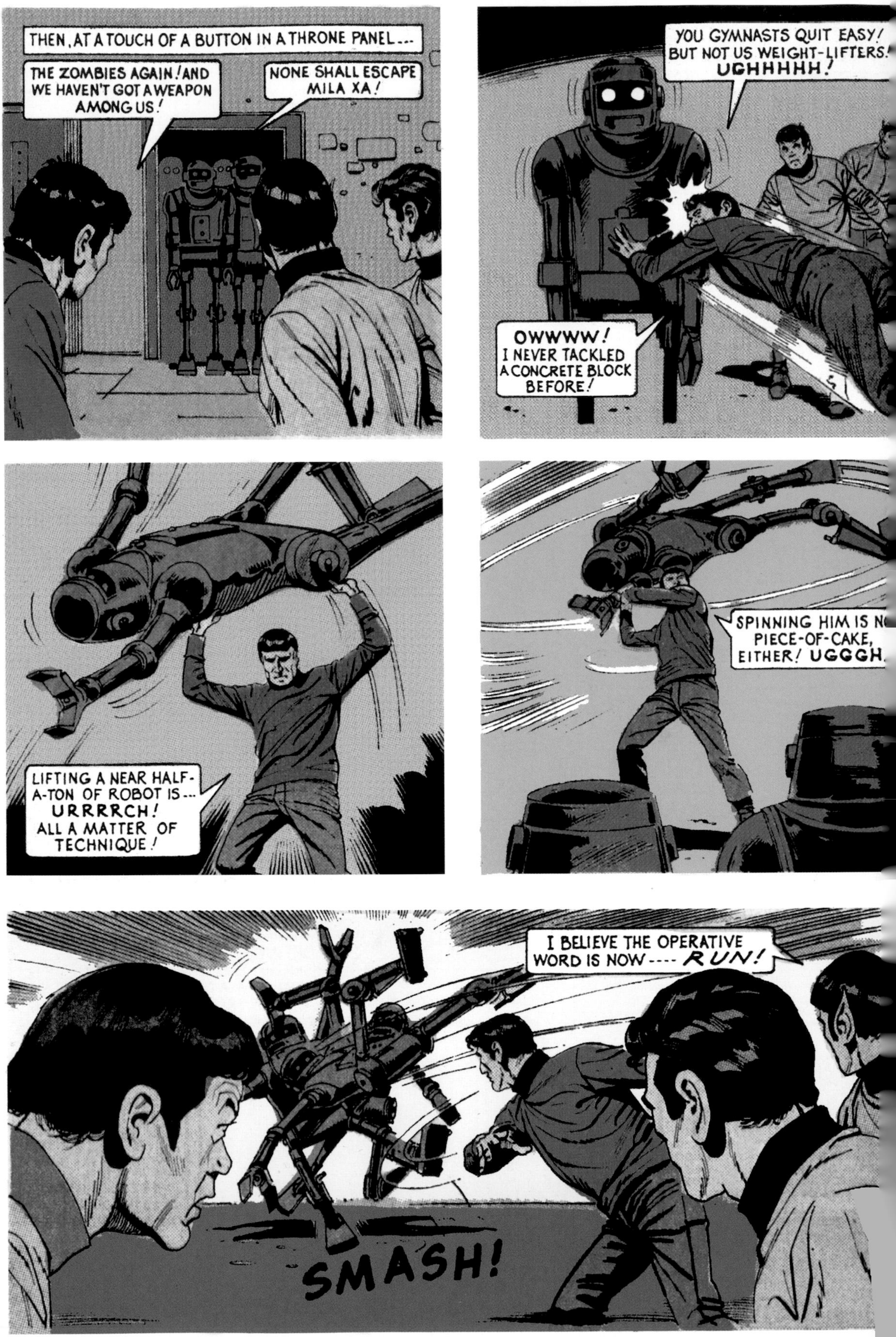
THEN, AT A TOUCH OF A BUTTON IN A THRONE PANEL...
THE ZOMBIES AGAIN! AND WE HAVEN'T GOT A WEAPON AMONG US!
NONE SHALL ESCAPE MILA XA!
YOU GYMNASTS QUIT EASY! BUT NOT US WEIGHT-LIFTERS! UGHHHHH!
OWWWW! I NEVER TACKLED A CONCRETE BLOCK BEFORE!
LIFTING A NEAR HALF-A-TON OF ROBOT IS... URRRRCH! ALL A MATTER OF TECHNIQUE!
SPINNING HIM IS N PIECE-OF-CAKE, EITHER! UGGGH
I BELIEVE THE OPERATIVE WORD IS NOW---- RUN!
SMASH!

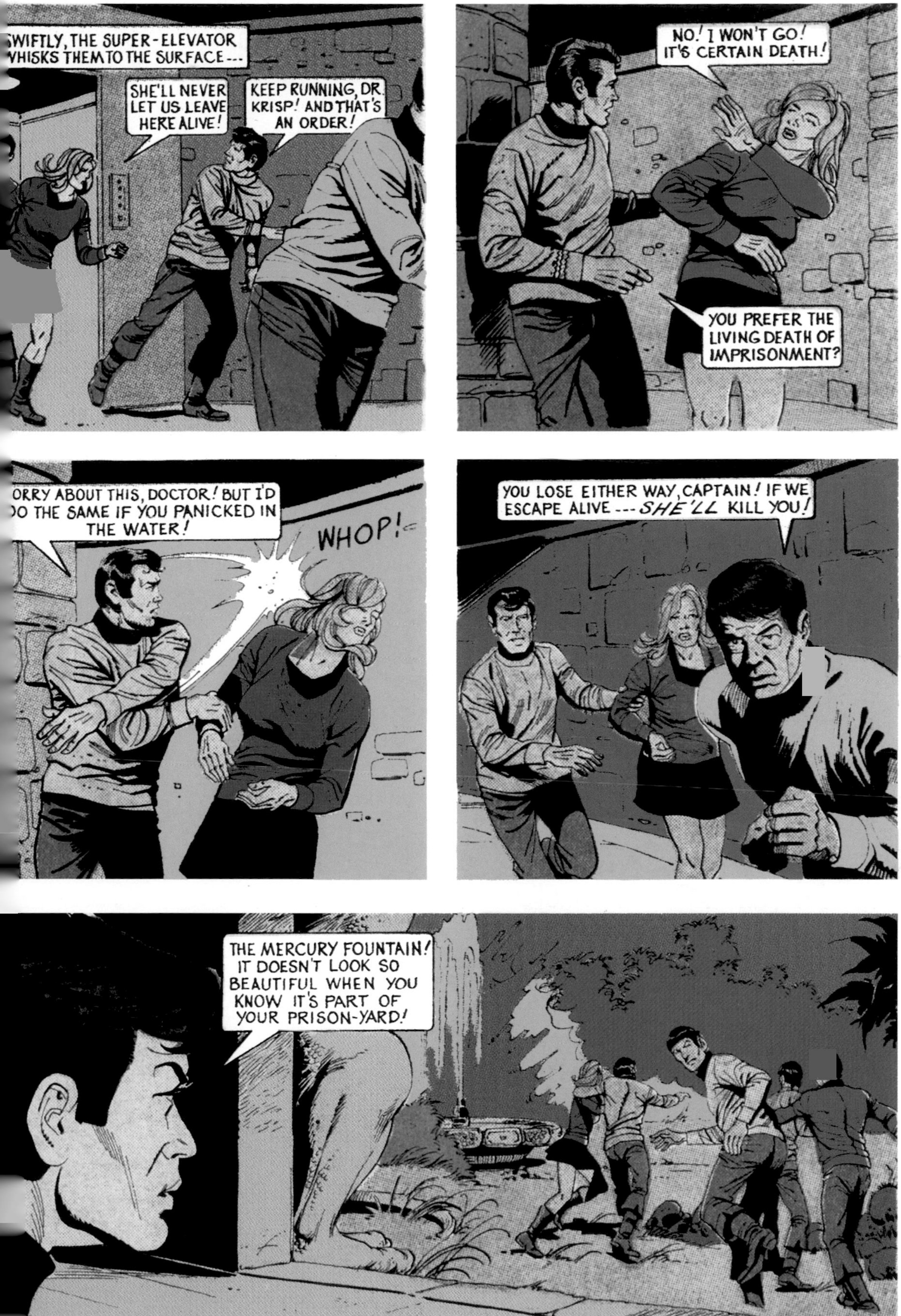
WIFTLY, THE SUPER-ELEVATOR
WHISKS THEM TO THE SURFACE---
SHE'LL NEVER LET US LEAVE HERE ALIVE!
KEEP RUNNING, DR. KRISP! AND THAT'S AN ORDER!
NO! I WON'T GO! IT'S CERTAIN DEATH!
YOU PREFER THE LIVING DEATH OF IMPRISONMENT?
ORRY ABOUT THIS, DOCTOR! BUT I'D
O THE SAME IF YOU PANICKED IN
THE WATER!
WHOP!
YOU LOSE EITHER WAY, CAPTAIN! IF WE ESCAPE ALIVE --- SHE'LL KILL YOU!
THE MERCURY FOUNTAIN! IT DOESN'T LOOK SO BEAUTIFUL WHEN YOU KNOW IT'S PART OF YOUR PRISON-YARD!

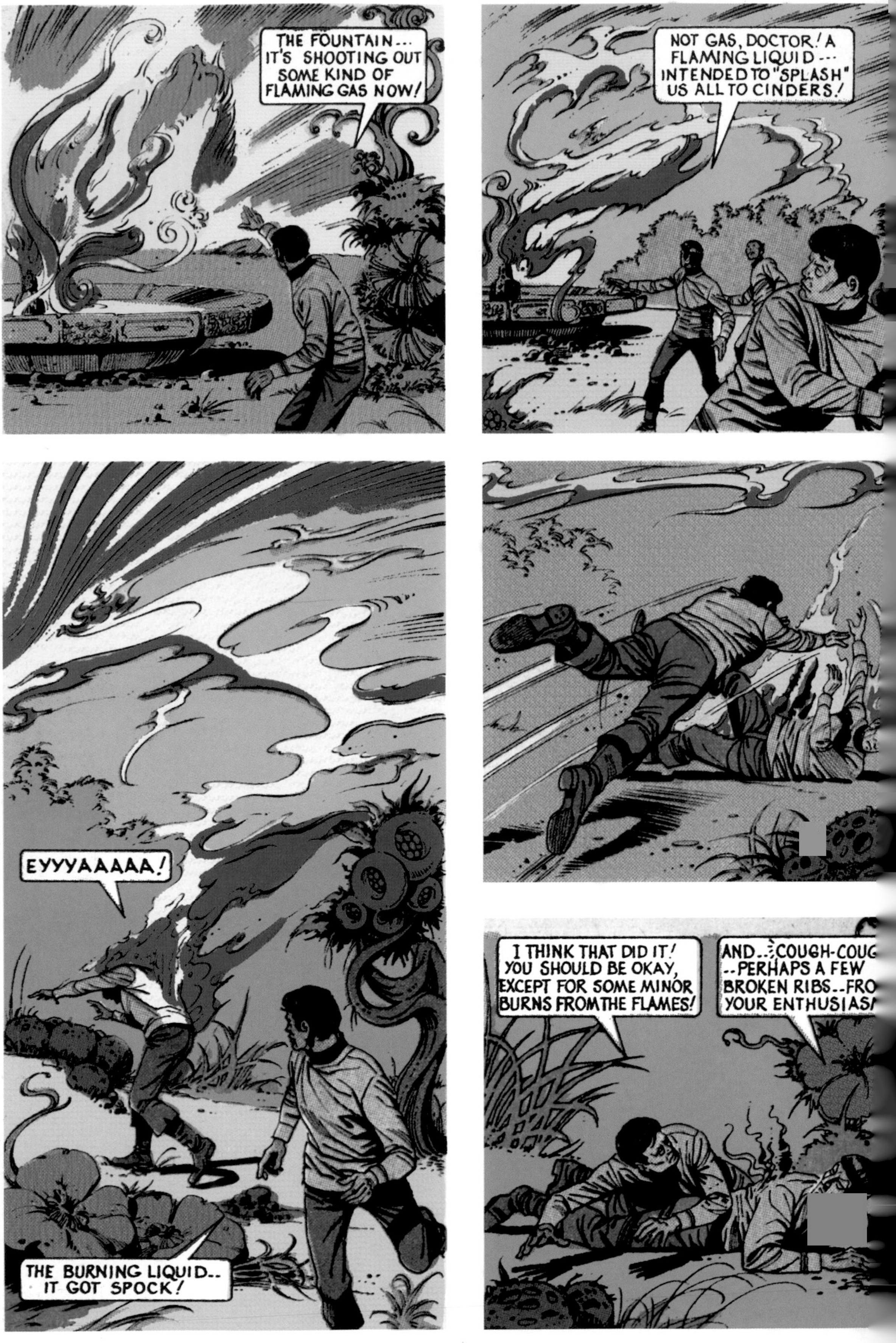
THE FOUNTAIN... IT'S SHOOTING OUT SOME KIND OF FLAMING GAS NOW!
NOT GAS, DOCTOR! A FLAMING LIQUID--- INTENDED TO "SPLASH" US ALL TO CINDERS!
EYYYAAAAA!
THE BURNING LIQUID.. IT GOT SPOCK!
I THINK THAT DID IT! YOU SHOULD BE OKAY, EXCEPT FOR SOME MINOR BURNS FROM THE FLAMES!
AND..COUGH-COUG --PERHAPS A FEW BROKEN RIBS..FRO YOUR ENTHUSIAS

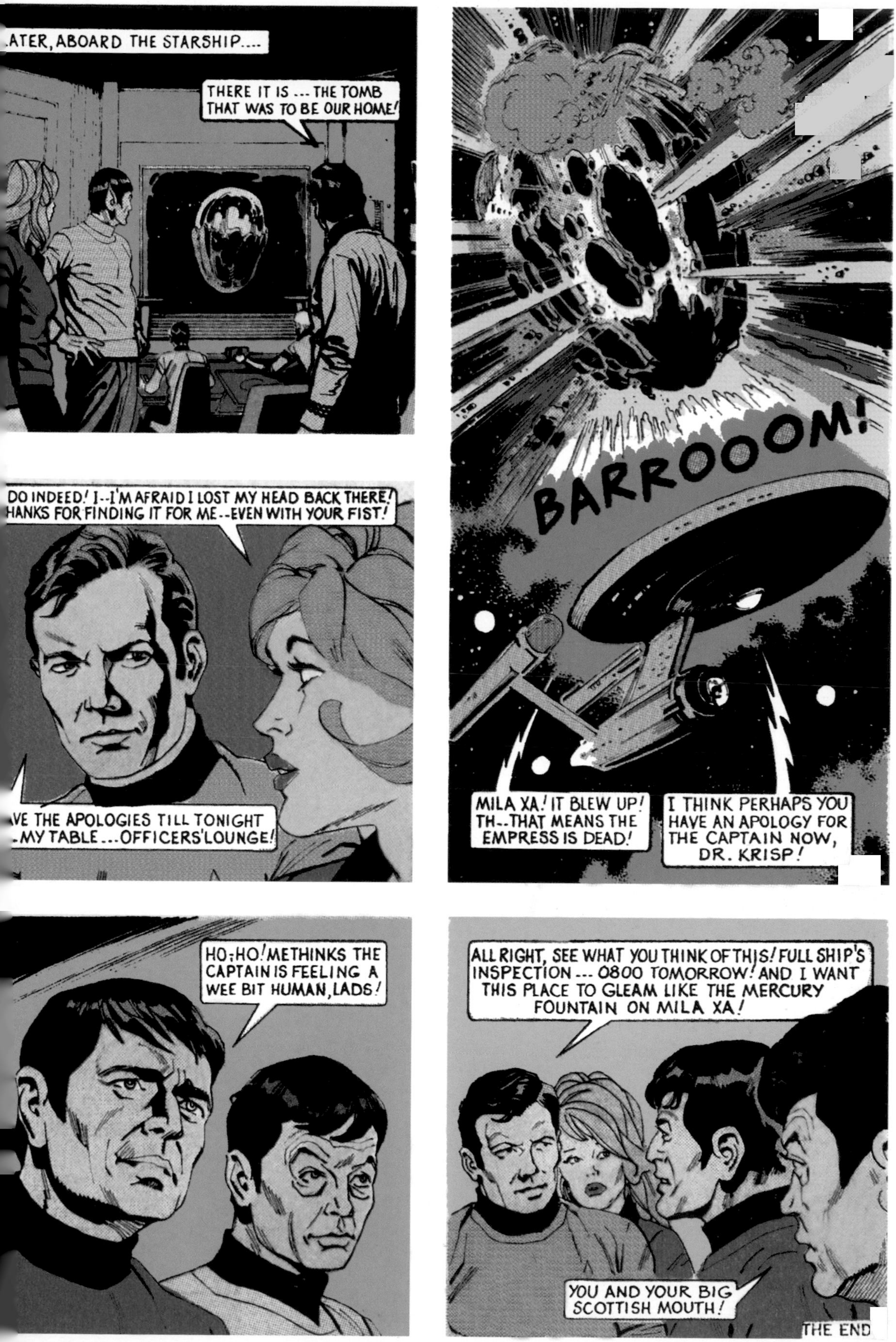

ATER, ABOARD THE STARSHIP....
THERE IT IS ... THE TOMB THAT WAS TO BE OUR HOME!
BARROOOM!
MILA XA! IT BLEW UP! TH--THAT MEANS THE EMPRESS IS DEAD!
I THINK PERHAPS YOU HAVE AN APOLOGY FOR THE CAPTAIN NOW, DR. KRISP!
DO INDEED! I--I'M AFRAID I LOST MY HEAD BACK THERE! HANKS FOR FINDING IT FOR ME--EVEN WITH YOUR FIST!
VE THE APOLOGIES TILL TONIGHT .MY TABLE... OFFICERS' LOUNGE!
HO-HO! METHINKS THE CAPTAIN IS FEELING A WEE BIT HUMAN, LADS!
ALL RIGHT, SEE WHAT YOU THINK OF THIS! FULL SHIP'S INSPECTION --- 0800 TOMORROW! AND I WANT THIS PLACE TO GLEAM LIKE THE MERCURY FOUNTAIN ON MILA XA!
YOU AND YOUR BIG SCOTTISH MOUTH!
THE END

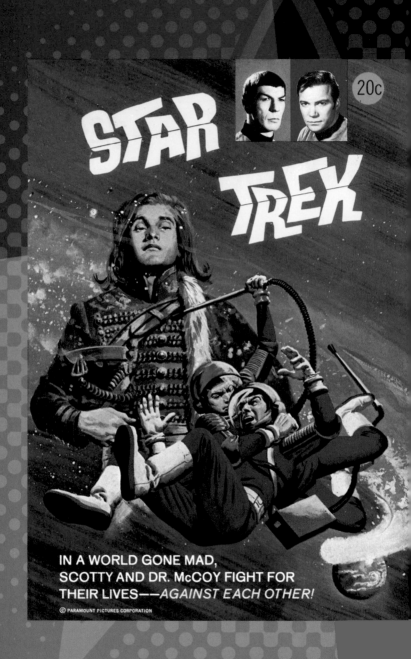

IN A WORLD GONE MAD,
SCOTTY AND DR. McCOY FIGHT FOR
THEIR LIVES——*AGAINST EACH OTHER!*

© PARAMOUNT PICTURES CORPORATION

Chapter 4
A World Gone Mad

(Originally Published in September, 1973)

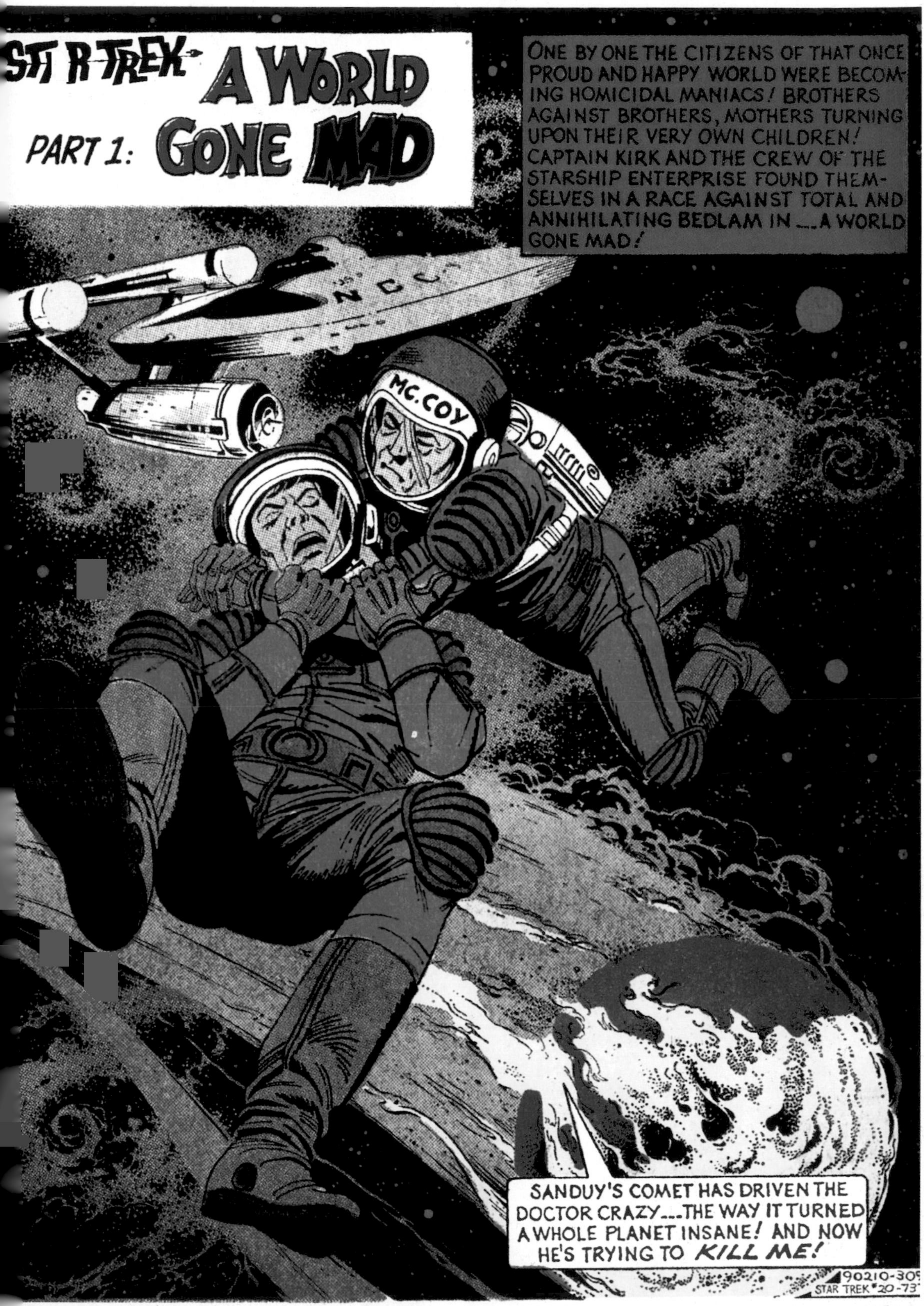

A WORLD
PART 1: GONE MAD
ONE BY ONE THE CITIZENS OF THAT ONCE PROUD AND HAPPY WORLD WERE BECOMING HOMICIDAL MANIACS! BROTHERS AGAINST BROTHERS, MOTHERS TURNING UPON THEIR VERY OWN CHILDREN! CAPTAIN KIRK AND THE CREW OF THE STARSHIP ENTERPRISE FOUND THEMSELVES IN A RACE AGAINST TOTAL AND ANNIHILATING BEDLAM IN ... A WORLD GONE MAD!
MC.COY
SANDUY'S COMET HAS DRIVEN THE DOCTOR CRAZY... THE WAY IT TURNED A WHOLE PLANET INSANE! AND NOW HE'S TRYING TO *KILL ME!*

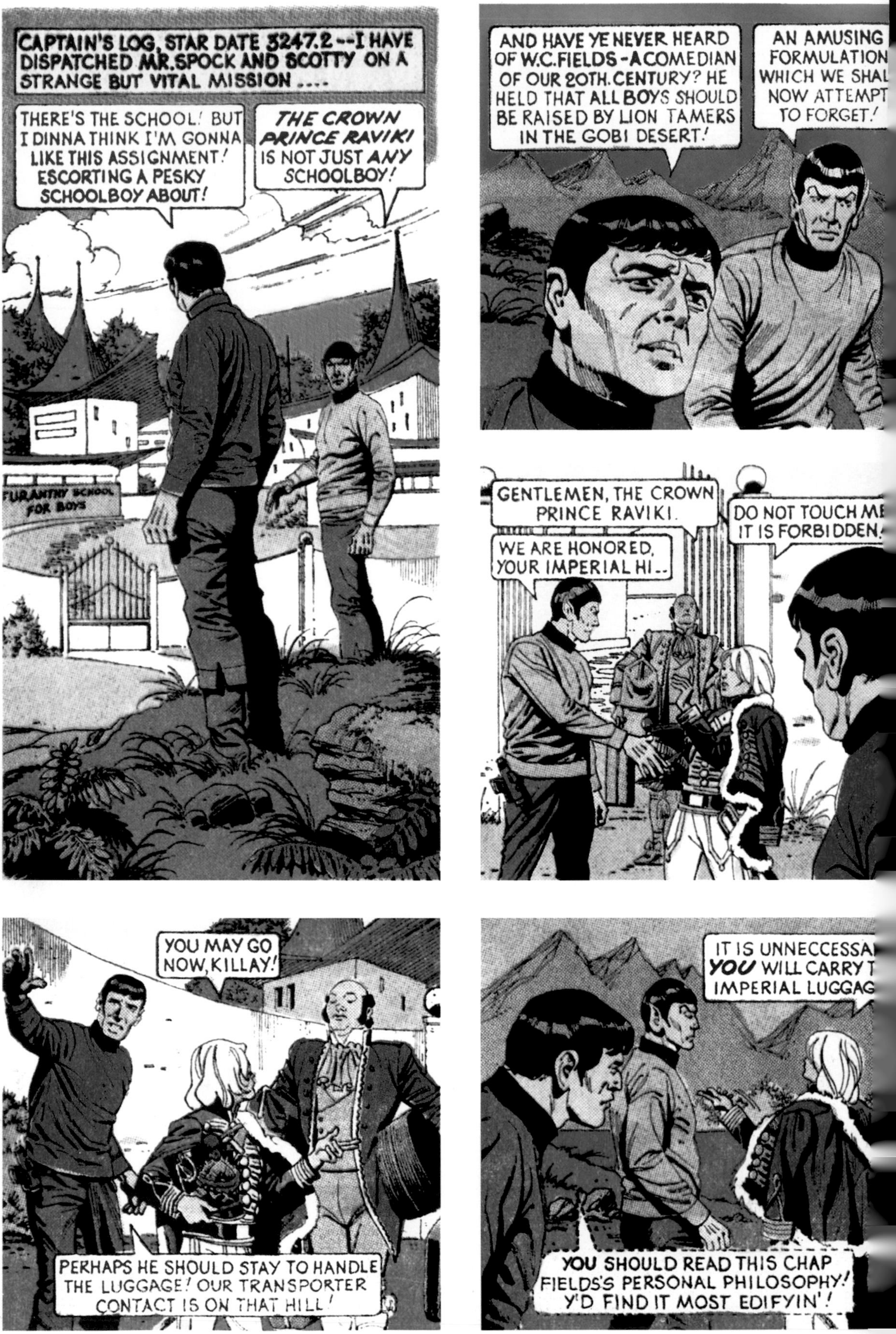

CAPTAIN'S LOG, STAR DATE 3247.2 --I HAVE DISPATCHED MR.SPOCK AND SCOTTY ON A STRANGE BUT VITAL MISSION ....
THERE'S THE SCHOOL! BUT I DINNA THINK I'M GONNA LIKE THIS ASSIGNMENT! ESCORTING A PESKY SCHOOLBOY ABOUT!
THE CROWN PRINCE RAVIKI IS NOT JUST ANY SCHOOLBOY!
FURANTHY SCHOOL FOR BOYS
AND HAVE YE NEVER HEARD OF W.C.FIELDS-A COMEDIAN OF OUR 20TH.CENTURY? HE HELD THAT ALL BOYS SHOULD BE RAISED BY LION TAMERS IN THE GOBI DESERT!
AN AMUSING FORMULATION WHICH WE SHAL NOW ATTEMPT TO FORGET!
GENTLEMEN, THE CROWN PRINCE RAVIKI.
WE ARE HONORED, YOUR IMPERIAL HI..
DO NOT TOUCH ME IT IS FORBIDDEN!
YOU MAY GO NOW, KILLAY!
PERHAPS HE SHOULD STAY TO HANDLE THE LUGGAGE! OUR TRANSPORTER CONTACT IS ON THAT HILL!
IT IS UNNECCESSA YOU WILL CARRY T IMPERIAL LUGGAG
YOU SHOULD READ THIS CHAP FIELDS'S PERSONAL PHILOSOPHY! Y'D FIND IT MOST EDIFYIN'!

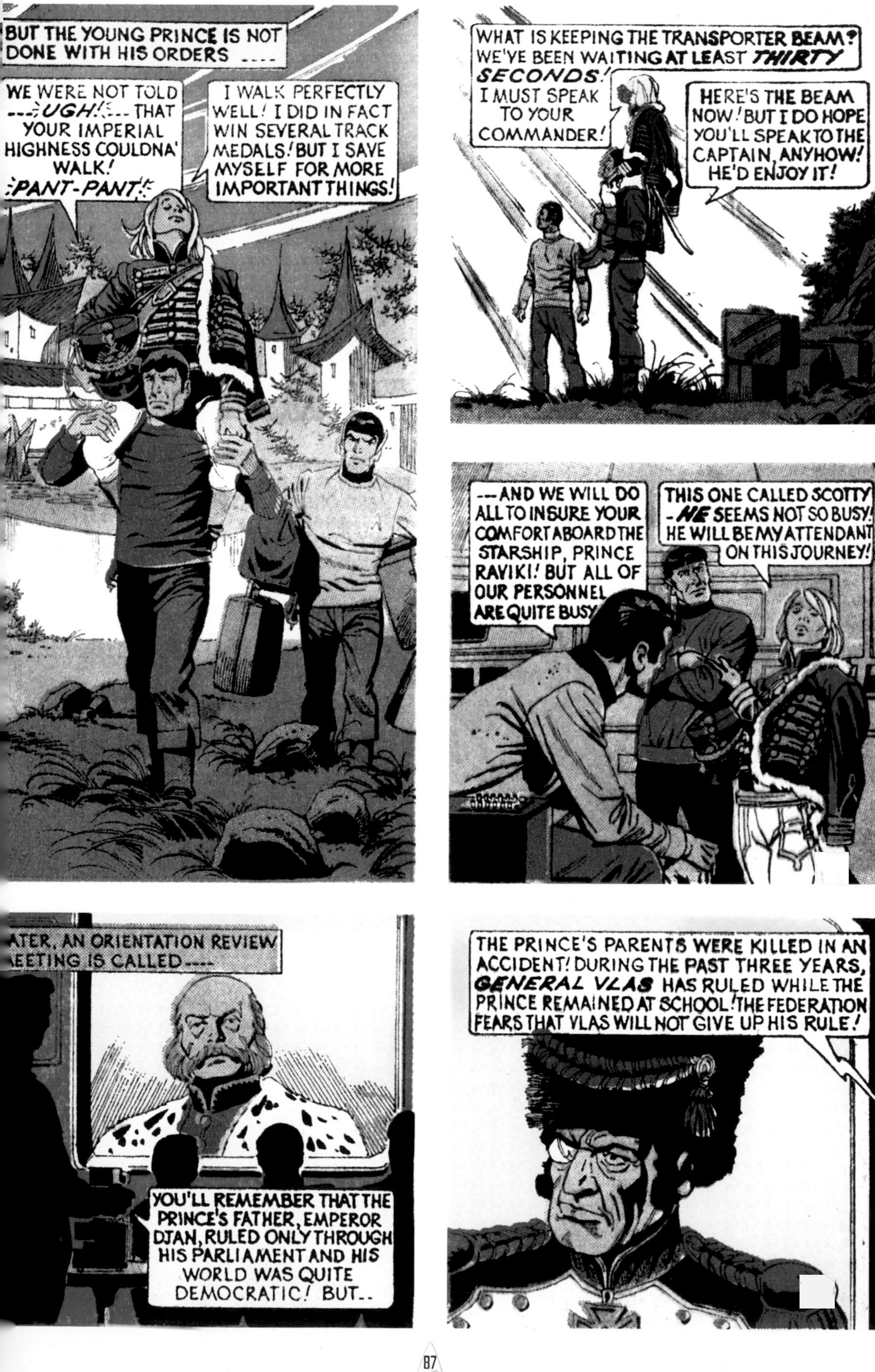
BUT THE YOUNG PRINCE IS NOT DONE WITH HIS ORDERS ....
WE WERE NOT TOLD ---UGH!---THAT YOUR IMPERIAL HIGHNESS COULDNA' WALK! PANT-PANT!
I WALK PERFECTLY WELL! I DID IN FACT WIN SEVERAL TRACK MEDALS! BUT I SAVE MYSELF FOR MORE IMPORTANT THINGS!
WHAT IS KEEPING THE TRANSPORTER BEAM? WE'VE BEEN WAITING AT LEAST THIRTY SECONDS! I MUST SPEAK TO YOUR COMMANDER!
HERE'S THE BEAM NOW! BUT I DO HOPE YOU'LL SPEAK TO THE CAPTAIN, ANYHOW! HE'D ENJOY IT!
---AND WE WILL DO ALL TO INSURE YOUR COMFORT ABOARD THE STARSHIP, PRINCE RAVIKI! BUT ALL OF OUR PERSONNEL ARE QUITE BUSY
THIS ONE CALLED SCOTTY - HE SEEMS NOT SO BUSY! HE WILL BE MY ATTENDANT ON THIS JOURNEY!
ATER, AN ORIENTATION REVIEW EETING IS CALLED ----
YOU'LL REMEMBER THAT THE PRINCE'S FATHER, EMPEROR DJAN, RULED ONLY THROUGH HIS PARLIAMENT AND HIS WORLD WAS QUITE DEMOCRATIC! BUT..
THE PRINCE'S PARENTS WERE KILLED IN AN ACCIDENT! DURING THE PAST THREE YEARS, GENERAL VLAS HAS RULED WHILE THE PRINCE REMAINED AT SCHOOL! THE FEDERATION FEARS THAT VLAS WILL NOT GIVE UP HIS RULE!

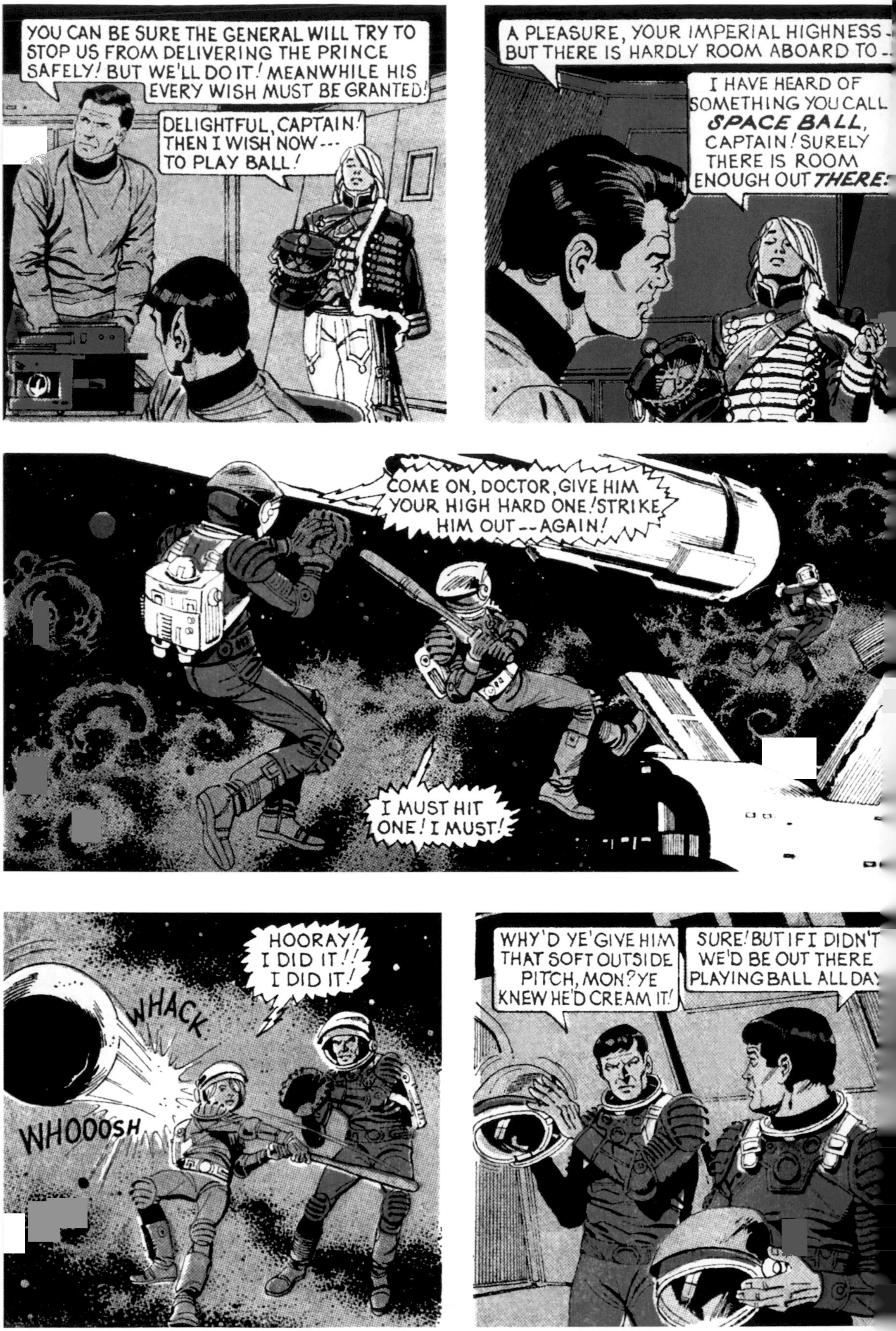
YOU CAN BE SURE THE GENERAL WILL TRY TO STOP US FROM DELIVERING THE PRINCE SAFELY! BUT WE'LL DO IT! MEANWHILE HIS EVERY WISH MUST BE GRANTED!
DELIGHTFUL, CAPTAIN! THEN I WISH NOW--- TO PLAY BALL!
A PLEASURE, YOUR IMPERIAL HIGHNESS - BUT THERE IS HARDLY ROOM ABOARD TO --
I HAVE HEARD OF SOMETHING YOU CALL SPACE BALL, CAPTAIN! SURELY THERE IS ROOM ENOUGH OUT THERE!
COME ON, DOCTOR, GIVE HIM YOUR HIGH HARD ONE! STRIKE HIM OUT -- AGAIN!
I MUST HIT ONE! I MUST!
HOORAY! I DID IT!! I DID IT!
WHACK
WHOOOSH
WHY'D YE GIVE HIM THAT SOFT OUTSIDE PITCH, MON? YE KNEW HE'D CREAM IT!
SURE! BUT IF I DIDN'T WE'D BE OUT THERE PLAYING BALL ALL DA

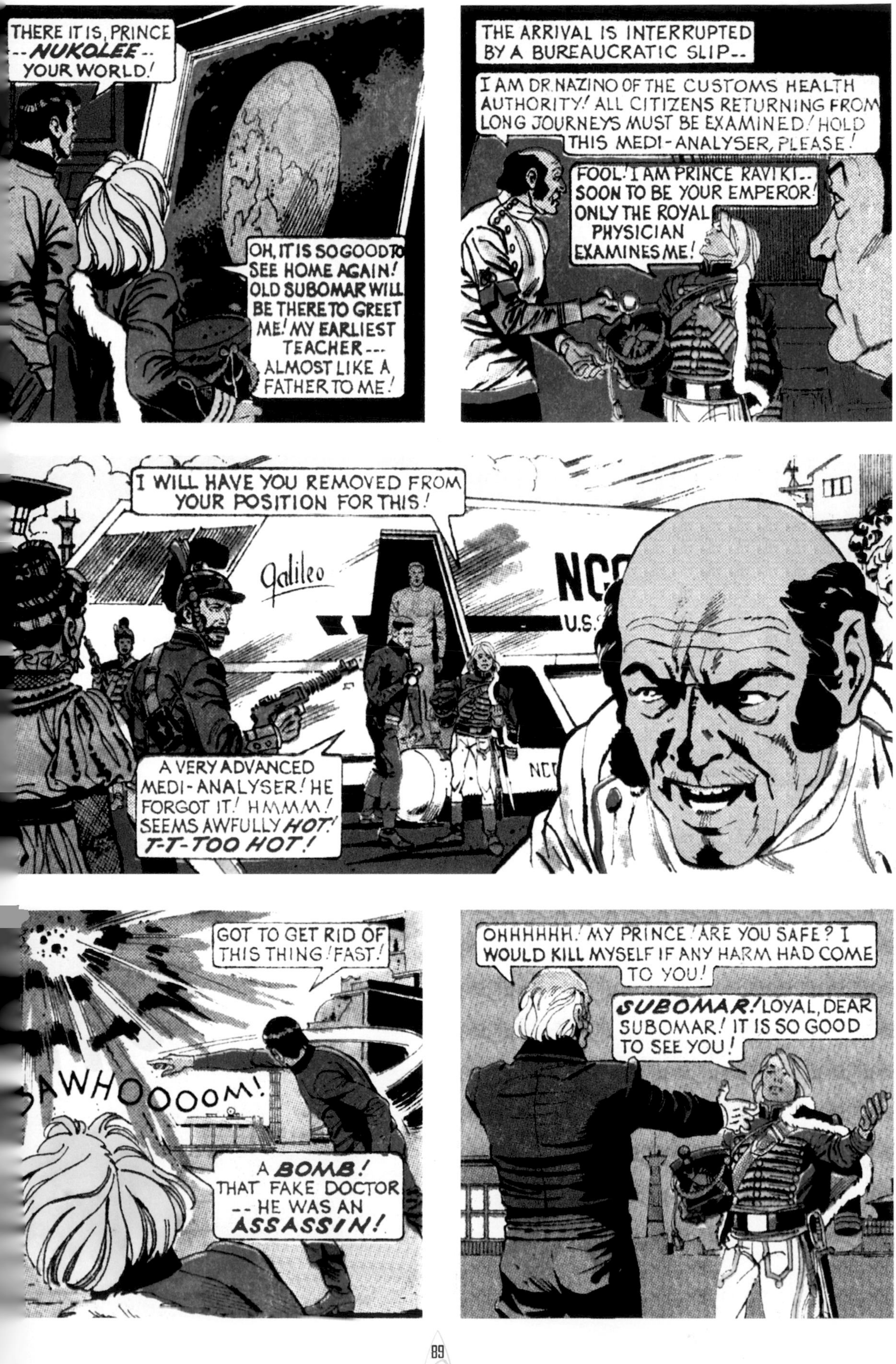
THERE IT IS, PRINCE --NUKOLEE-- YOUR WORLD!
OH, IT IS SO GOOD TO SEE HOME AGAIN! OLD SUBOMAR WILL BE THERE TO GREET ME! MY EARLIEST TEACHER--- ALMOST LIKE A FATHER TO ME!
THE ARRIVAL IS INTERRUPTED BY A BUREAUCRATIC SLIP--
I AM DR. NAZINO OF THE CUSTOMS HEALTH AUTHORITY! ALL CITIZENS RETURNING FROM LONG JOURNEYS MUST BE EXAMINED! HOLD THIS MEDI-ANALYSER, PLEASE!
FOOL! I AM PRINCE RAVIKI.. SOON TO BE YOUR EMPEROR! ONLY THE ROYAL PHYSICIAN EXAMINES ME!
I WILL HAVE YOU REMOVED FROM YOUR POSITION FOR THIS!
Galileo
NCC
U.S.
A VERY ADVANCED MEDI-ANALYSER! HE FORGOT IT! HMMM! SEEMS AWFULLY HOT! T-T-TOO HOT!
GOT TO GET RID OF THIS THING! FAST!
AWHOOOOM!
A BOMB! THAT FAKE DOCTOR -- HE WAS AN ASSASSIN!
OHHHHHH! MY PRINCE! ARE YOU SAFE? I WOULD KILL MYSELF IF ANY HARM HAD COME TO YOU!
SUBOMAR! LOYAL, DEAR SUBOMAR! IT IS SO GOOD TO SEE YOU!

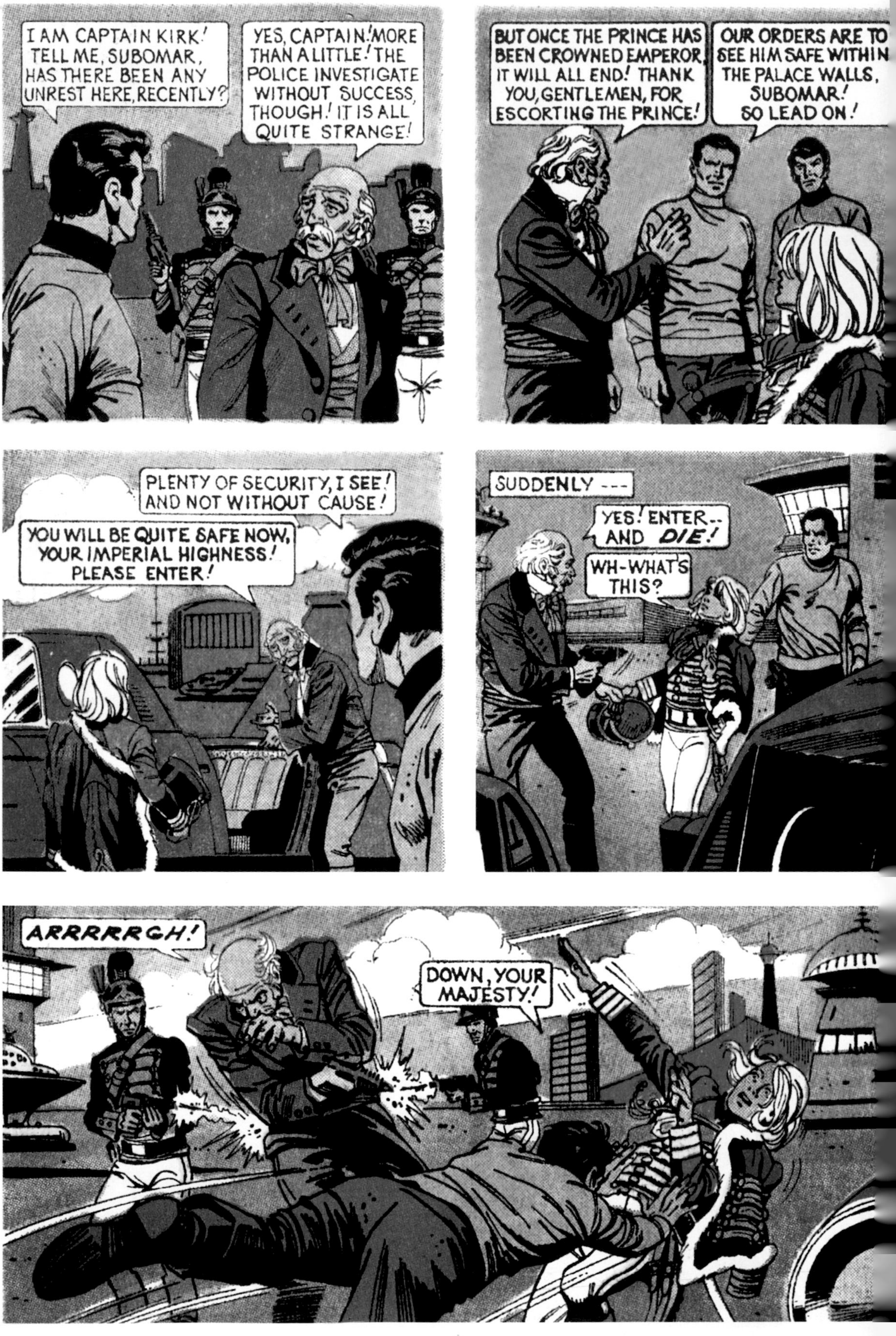
I AM CAPTAIN KIRK! TELL ME, SUBOMAR, HAS THERE BEEN ANY UNREST HERE, RECENTLY?
YES, CAPTAIN! MORE THAN A LITTLE! THE POLICE INVESTIGATE WITHOUT SUCCESS, THOUGH! IT IS ALL QUITE STRANGE!
BUT ONCE THE PRINCE HAS BEEN CROWNED EMPEROR, IT WILL ALL END! THANK YOU, GENTLEMEN, FOR ESCORTING THE PRINCE!
OUR ORDERS ARE TO SEE HIM SAFE WITHIN THE PALACE WALLS, SUBOMAR! SO LEAD ON!
PLENTY OF SECURITY, I SEE! AND NOT WITHOUT CAUSE!
YOU WILL BE QUITE SAFE NOW, YOUR IMPERIAL HIGHNESS! PLEASE ENTER!
SUDDENLY ---
YES! ENTER-- AND DIE!
WH-WHAT'S THIS?
ARRRRRGH!
DOWN, YOUR MAJESTY!

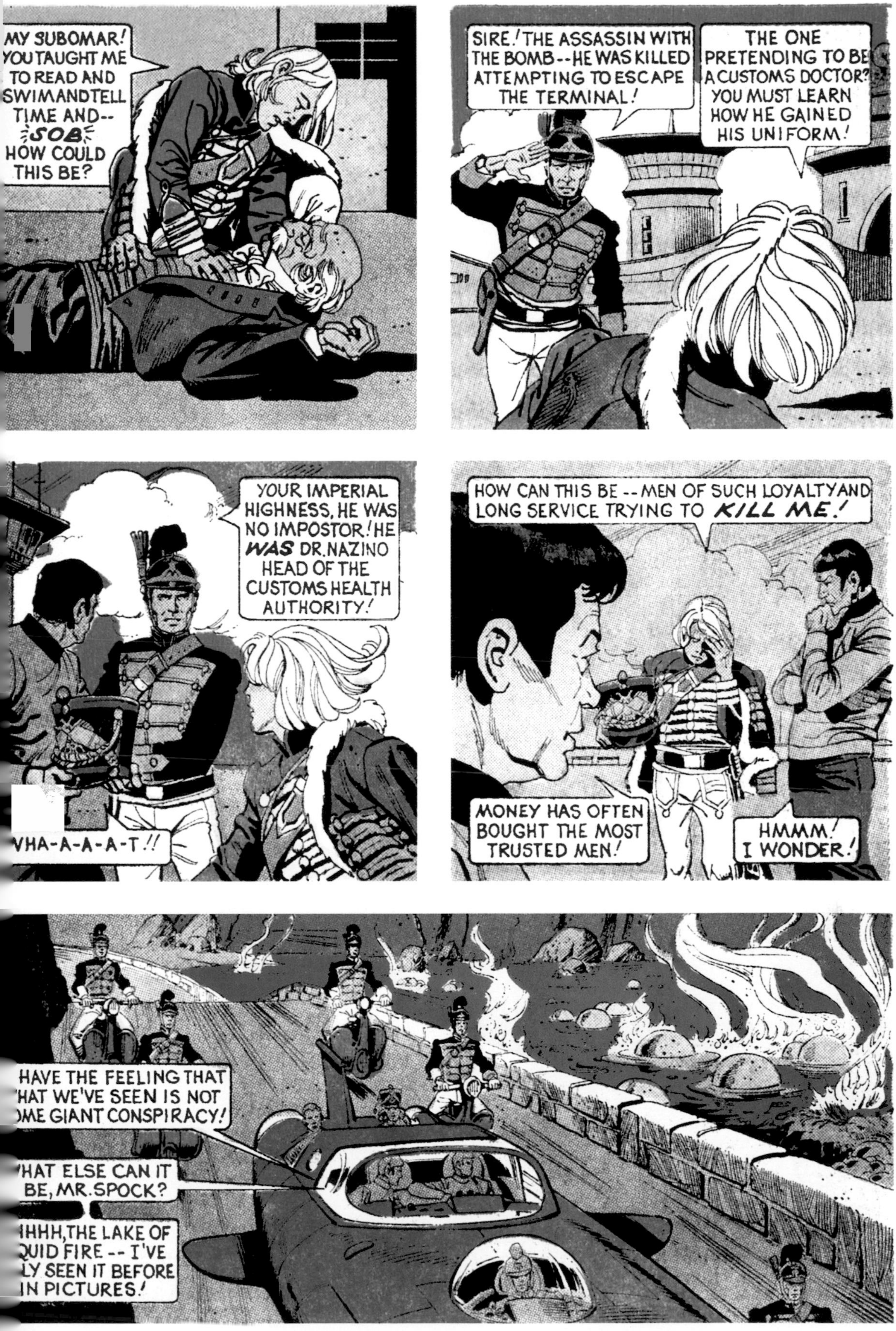
MY SUBOMAR! YOU TAUGHT ME TO READ AND SWIM AND TELL TIME AND-- SOB HOW COULD THIS BE?
SIRE! THE ASSASSIN WITH THE BOMB--HE WAS KILLED ATTEMPTING TO ESCAPE THE TERMINAL!
THE ONE PRETENDING TO BE A CUSTOMS DOCTOR? YOU MUST LEARN HOW HE GAINED HIS UNIFORM!
YOUR IMPERIAL HIGHNESS, HE WAS NO IMPOSTOR! HE WAS DR. NAZINO HEAD OF THE CUSTOMS HEALTH AUTHORITY!
WHA-A-A-A-T!!
HOW CAN THIS BE -- MEN OF SUCH LOYALTY AND LONG SERVICE TRYING TO KILL ME!
MONEY HAS OFTEN BOUGHT THE MOST TRUSTED MEN!
HMMM! I WONDER!
HAVE THE FEELING THAT HAT WE'VE SEEN IS NOT OME GIANT CONSPIRACY!
HAT ELSE CAN IT BE, MR. SPOCK?
HHHH, THE LAKE OF QUID FIRE -- I'VE LY SEEN IT BEFORE IN PICTURES!

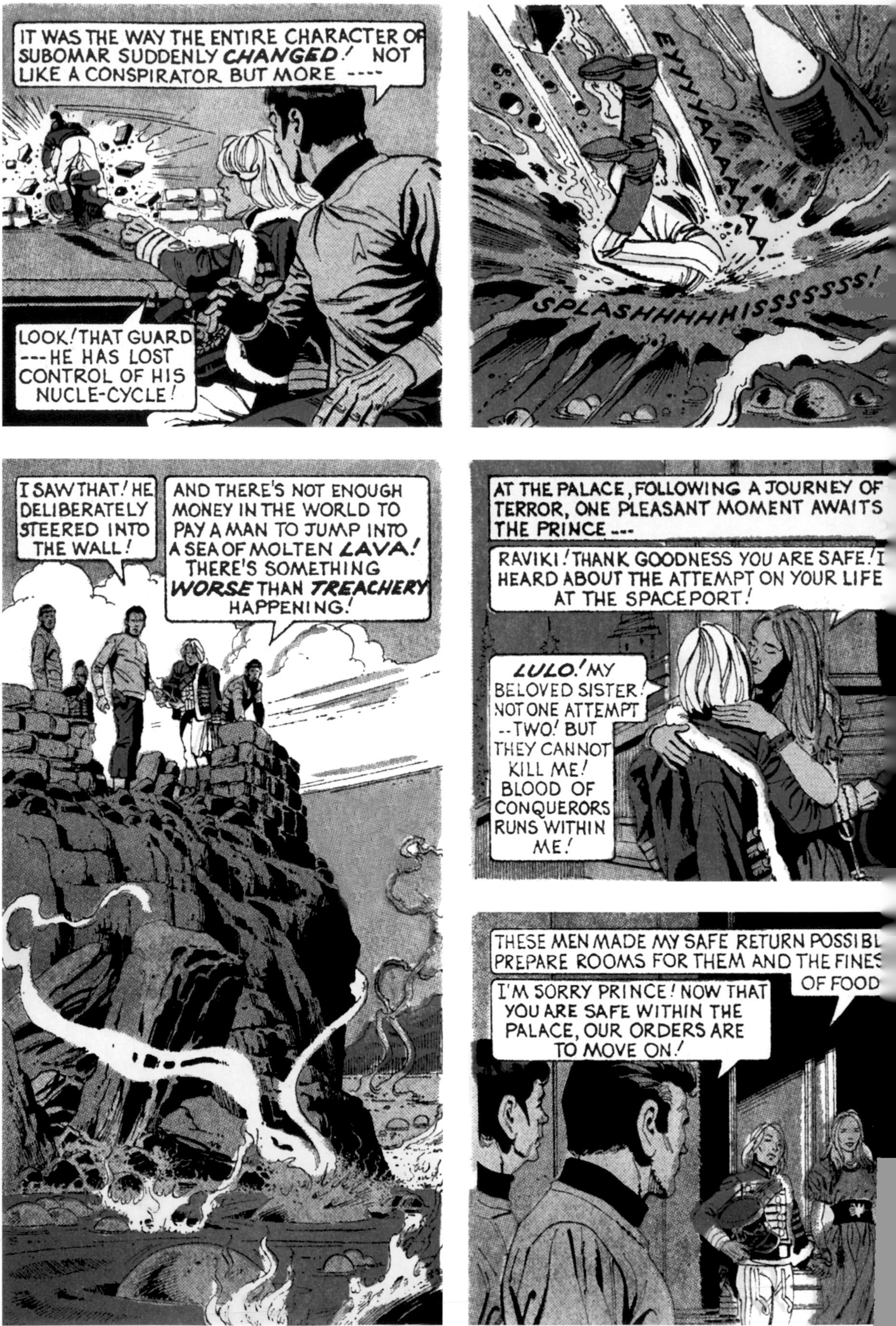
IT WAS THE WAY THE ENTIRE CHARACTER OF SUBOMAR SUDDENLY CHANGED! NOT LIKE A CONSPIRATOR BUT MORE ----
LOOK! THAT GUARD ---HE HAS LOST CONTROL OF HIS NUCLE-CYCLE!
EYYYAAAAAAA---
SPLASHHHHHISSSSSSSS!
I SAW THAT! HE DELIBERATELY STEERED INTO THE WALL!
AND THERE'S NOT ENOUGH MONEY IN THE WORLD TO PAY A MAN TO JUMP INTO A SEA OF MOLTEN LAVA! THERE'S SOMETHING WORSE THAN TREACHERY HAPPENING!
AT THE PALACE, FOLLOWING A JOURNEY OF TERROR, ONE PLEASANT MOMENT AWAITS THE PRINCE ---
RAVIKI! THANK GOODNESS YOU ARE SAFE! I HEARD ABOUT THE ATTEMPT ON YOUR LIFE AT THE SPACEPORT!
LULO! MY BELOVED SISTER! NOT ONE ATTEMPT --TWO! BUT THEY CANNOT KILL ME! BLOOD OF CONQUERORS RUNS WITHIN ME!
THESE MEN MADE MY SAFE RETURN POSSIBL PREPARE ROOMS FOR THEM AND THE FINES OF FOOD
I'M SORRY PRINCE! NOW THAT YOU ARE SAFE WITHIN THE PALACE, OUR ORDERS ARE TO MOVE ON!

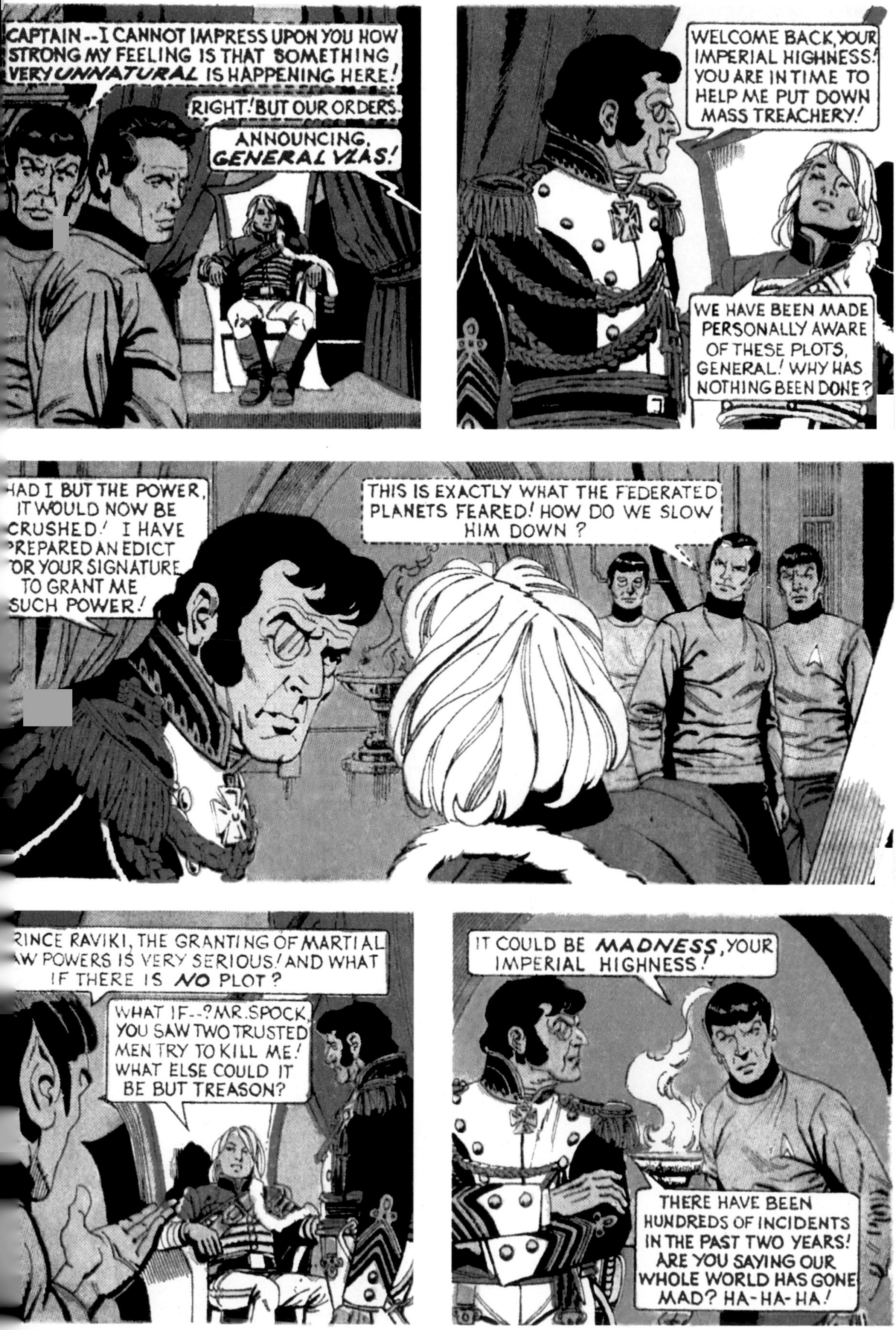
CAPTAIN--I CANNOT IMPRESS UPON YOU HOW STRONG MY FEELING IS THAT SOMETHING VERY *UNNATURAL* IS HAPPENING HERE!
RIGHT! BUT OUR ORDERS.
ANNOUNCING, *GENERAL VLAS!*
WELCOME BACK, YOUR IMPERIAL HIGHNESS! YOU ARE IN TIME TO HELP ME PUT DOWN MASS TREACHERY!
WE HAVE BEEN MADE PERSONALLY AWARE OF THESE PLOTS, GENERAL! WHY HAS NOTHING BEEN DONE?
HAD I BUT THE POWER, IT WOULD NOW BE CRUSHED! I HAVE PREPARED AN EDICT FOR YOUR SIGNATURE TO GRANT ME SUCH POWER!
THIS IS EXACTLY WHAT THE FEDERATED PLANETS FEARED! HOW DO WE SLOW HIM DOWN?
RINCE RAVIKI, THE GRANTING OF MARTIAL AW POWERS IS VERY SERIOUS! AND WHAT IF THERE IS *NO* PLOT?
WHAT IF--? MR. SPOCK, YOU SAW TWO TRUSTED MEN TRY TO KILL ME! WHAT ELSE COULD IT BE BUT TREASON?
IT COULD BE *MADNESS*, YOUR IMPERIAL HIGHNESS!
THERE HAVE BEEN HUNDREDS OF INCIDENTS IN THE PAST TWO YEARS! ARE YOU SAYING OUR WHOLE WORLD HAS GONE MAD? HA-HA-HA!

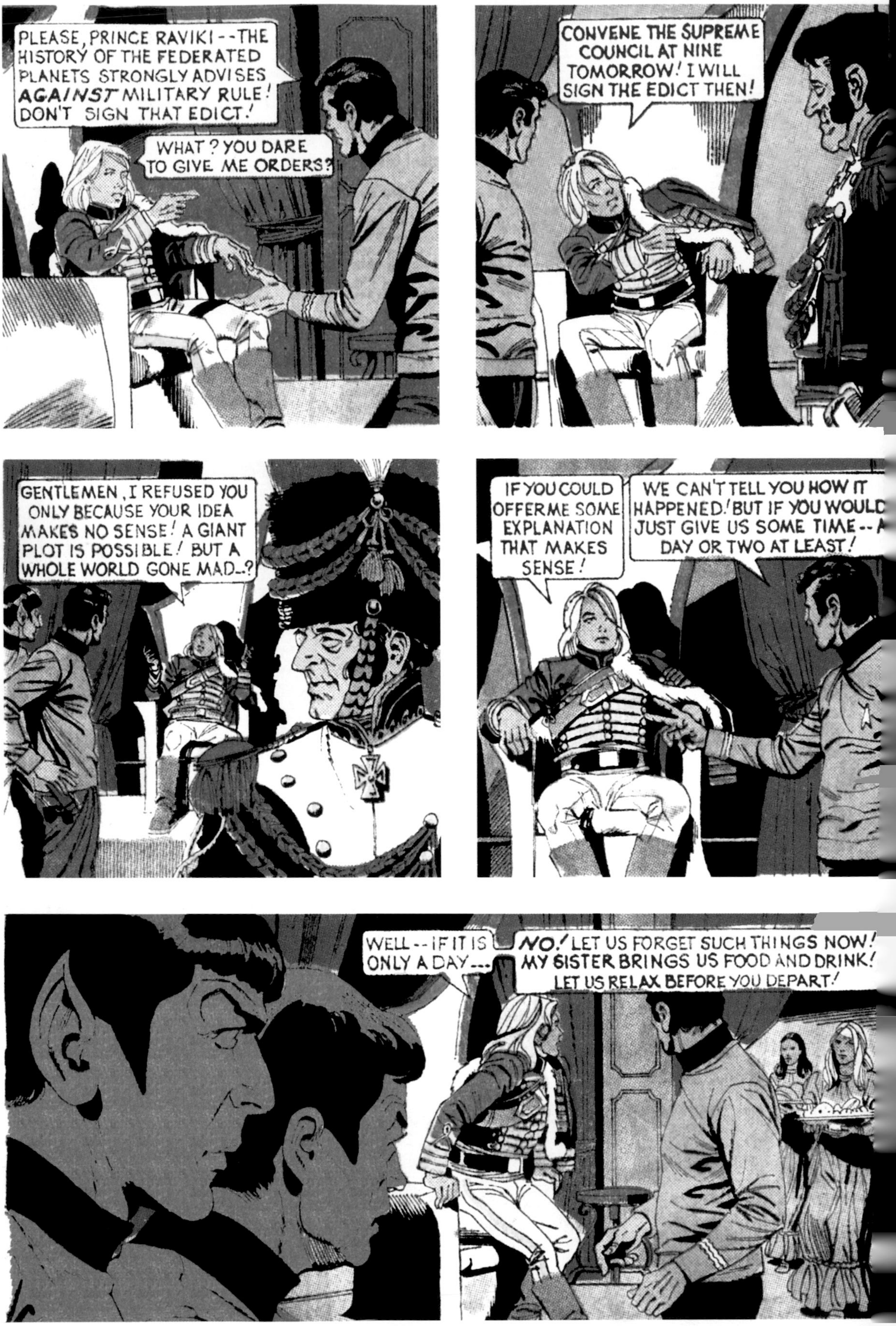
PLEASE, PRINCE RAVIKI -- THE HISTORY OF THE FEDERATED PLANETS STRONGLY ADVISES AGAINST MILITARY RULE! DON'T SIGN THAT EDICT!
WHAT? YOU DARE TO GIVE ME ORDERS?
CONVENE THE SUPREME COUNCIL AT NINE TOMORROW! I WILL SIGN THE EDICT THEN!
GENTLEMEN, I REFUSED YOU ONLY BECAUSE YOUR IDEA MAKES NO SENSE! A GIANT PLOT IS POSSIBLE! BUT A WHOLE WORLD GONE MAD--?
IF YOU COULD OFFER ME SOME EXPLANATION THAT MAKES SENSE!
WE CAN'T TELL YOU HOW IT HAPPENED! BUT IF YOU WOULD JUST GIVE US SOME TIME -- A DAY OR TWO AT LEAST!
WELL -- IF IT IS ONLY A DAY---
NO! LET US FORGET SUCH THINGS NOW! MY SISTER BRINGS US FOOD AND DRINK! LET US RELAX BEFORE YOU DEPART!

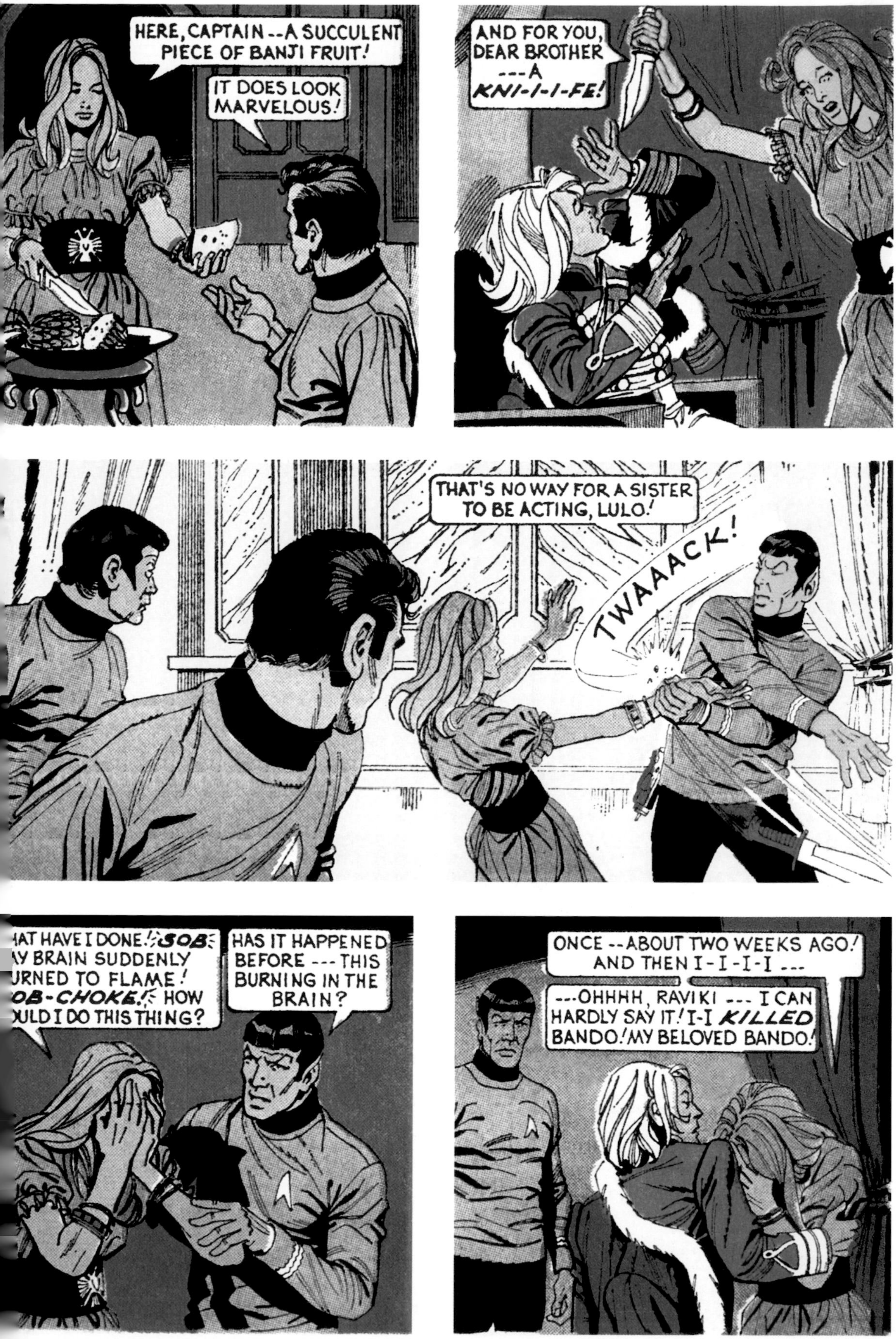
HERE, CAPTAIN --A SUCCULENT PIECE OF BANJI FRUIT!
IT DOES LOOK MARVELOUS!
AND FOR YOU, DEAR BROTHER ---A KNI-I-I-FE!
THAT'S NO WAY FOR A SISTER TO BE ACTING, LULO!
TWAAACK!
HAT HAVE I DONE! SOB! Y BRAIN SUDDENLY URNED TO FLAME! OB-CHOKE! HOW ULD I DO THIS THING?
HAS IT HAPPENED BEFORE --- THIS BURNING IN THE BRAIN?
ONCE --ABOUT TWO WEEKS AGO! AND THEN I-I-I-I ---
---OHHHH, RAVIKI --- I CAN HARDLY SAY IT! I-I KILLED BANDO! MY BELOVED BANDO!

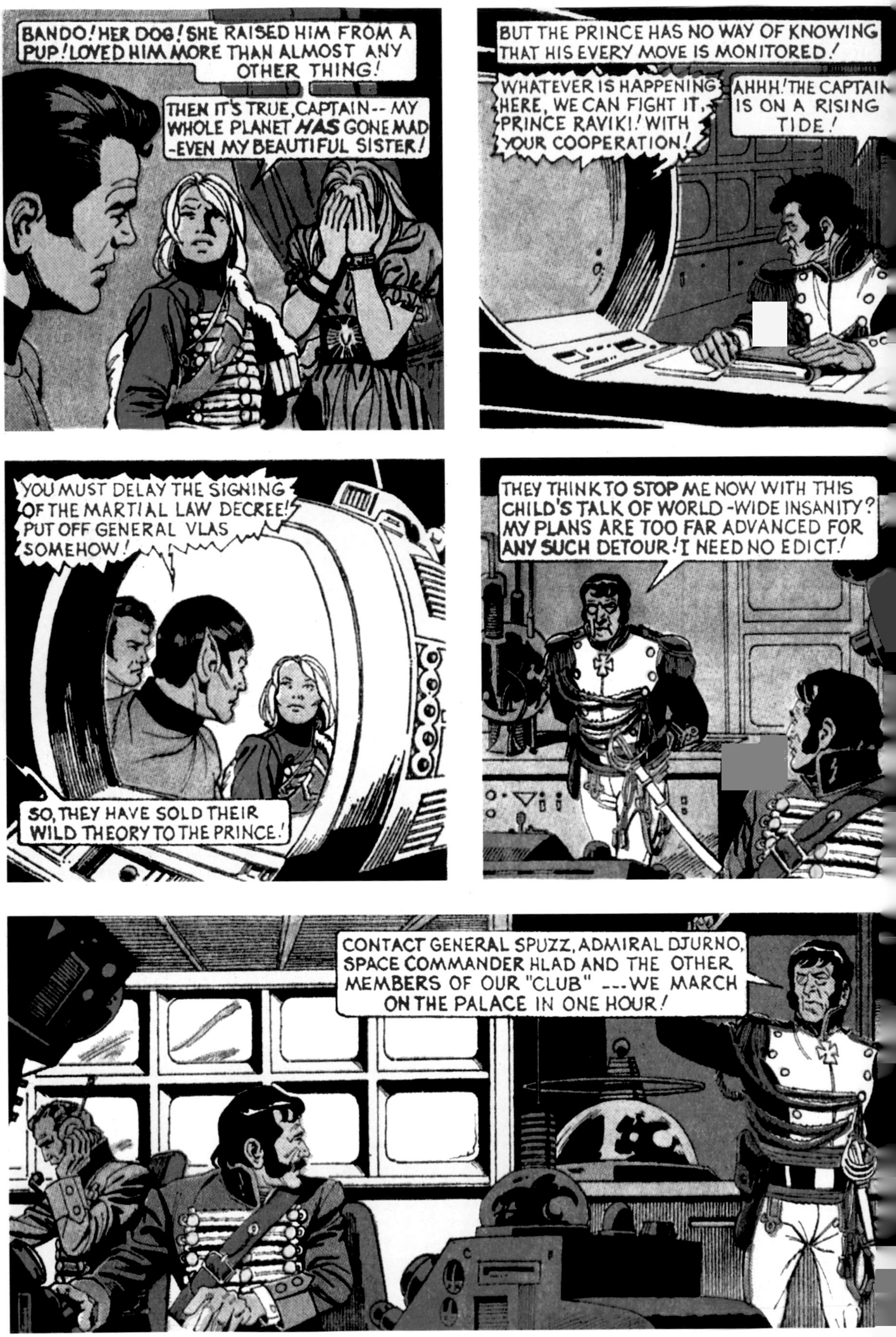
BANDO! HER DOG! SHE RAISED HIM FROM A PUP! LOVED HIM MORE THAN ALMOST ANY OTHER THING!
THEN IT'S TRUE, CAPTAIN-- MY WHOLE PLANET HAS GONE MAD -EVEN MY BEAUTIFUL SISTER!
BUT THE PRINCE HAS NO WAY OF KNOWING THAT HIS EVERY MOVE IS MONITORED!
WHATEVER IS HAPPENING HERE, WE CAN FIGHT IT, PRINCE RAVIKI! WITH YOUR COOPERATION!
AHHH! THE CAPTAIN IS ON A RISING TIDE!
YOU MUST DELAY THE SIGNING OF THE MARTIAL LAW DECREE! PUT OFF GENERAL VLAS SOMEHOW!
SO, THEY HAVE SOLD THEIR WILD THEORY TO THE PRINCE!
THEY THINK TO STOP ME NOW WITH THIS CHILD'S TALK OF WORLD-WIDE INSANITY? MY PLANS ARE TOO FAR ADVANCED FOR ANY SUCH DETOUR! I NEED NO EDICT!
CONTACT GENERAL SPUZZ, ADMIRAL DJURNO, SPACE COMMANDER HLAD AND THE OTHER MEMBERS OF OUR "CLUB" ---WE MARCH ON THE PALACE IN ONE HOUR!

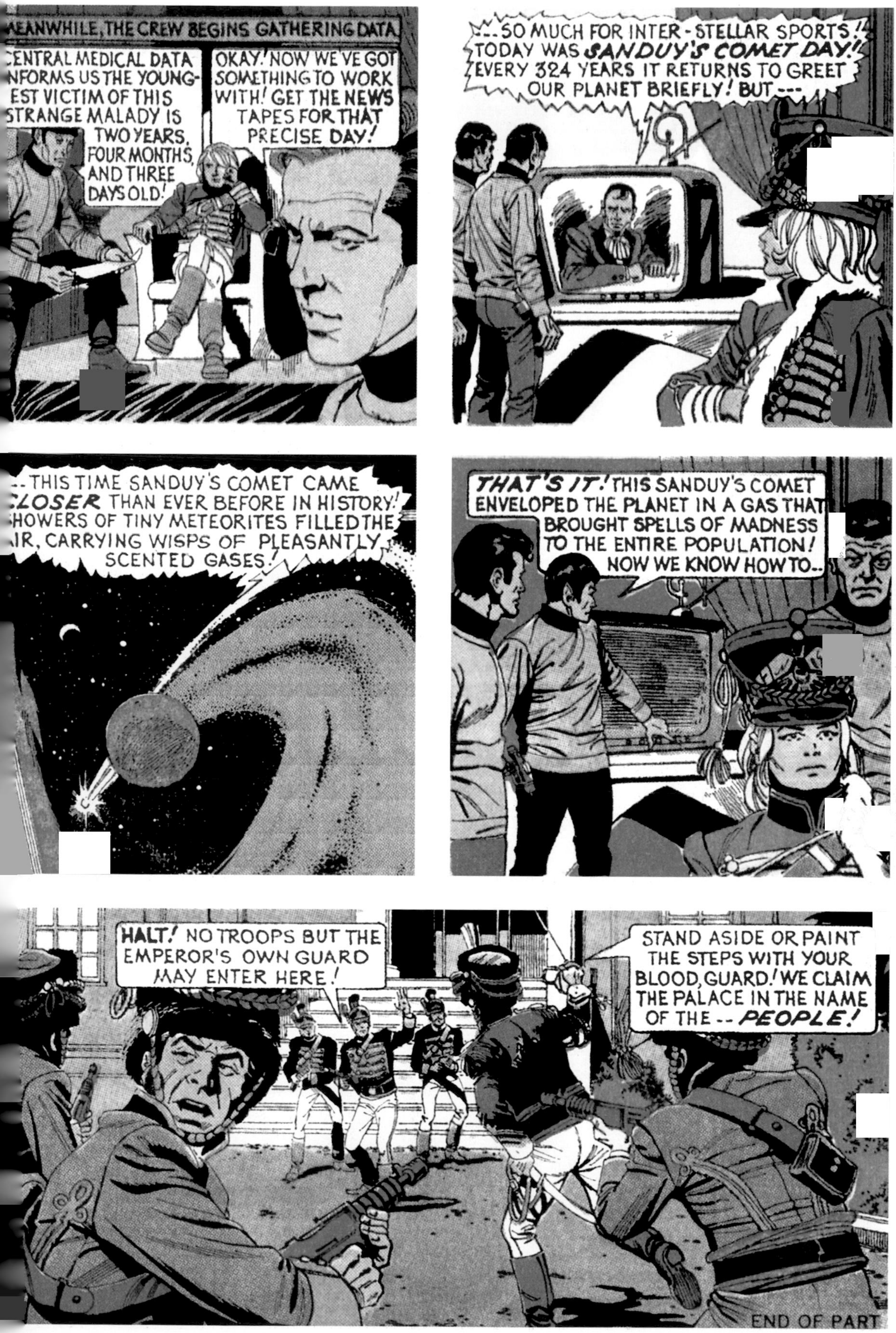

MEANWHILE, THE CREW BEGINS GATHERING DATA
CENTRAL MEDICAL DATA INFORMS US THE YOUNGEST VICTIM OF THIS STRANGE MALADY IS TWO YEARS, FOUR MONTHS, AND THREE DAYS OLD!
OKAY! NOW WE'VE GOT SOMETHING TO WORK WITH! GET THE NEWS TAPES FOR THAT PRECISE DAY!
--SO MUCH FOR INTER-STELLAR SPORTS! TODAY WAS SANDUY'S COMET DAY! EVERY 324 YEARS IT RETURNS TO GREET OUR PLANET BRIEFLY! BUT---
--THIS TIME SANDUY'S COMET CAME CLOSER THAN EVER BEFORE IN HISTORY! SHOWERS OF TINY METEORITES FILLED THE AIR, CARRYING WISPS OF PLEASANTLY SCENTED GASES!
THAT'S IT! THIS SANDUY'S COMET ENVELOPED THE PLANET IN A GAS THAT BROUGHT SPELLS OF MADNESS TO THE ENTIRE POPULATION! NOW WE KNOW HOW TO..
HALT! NO TROOPS BUT THE EMPEROR'S OWN GUARD MAY ENTER HERE!
STAND ASIDE OR PAINT THE STEPS WITH YOUR BLOOD, GUARD! WE CLAIM THE PALACE IN THE NAME OF THE--PEOPLE!
END OF PART

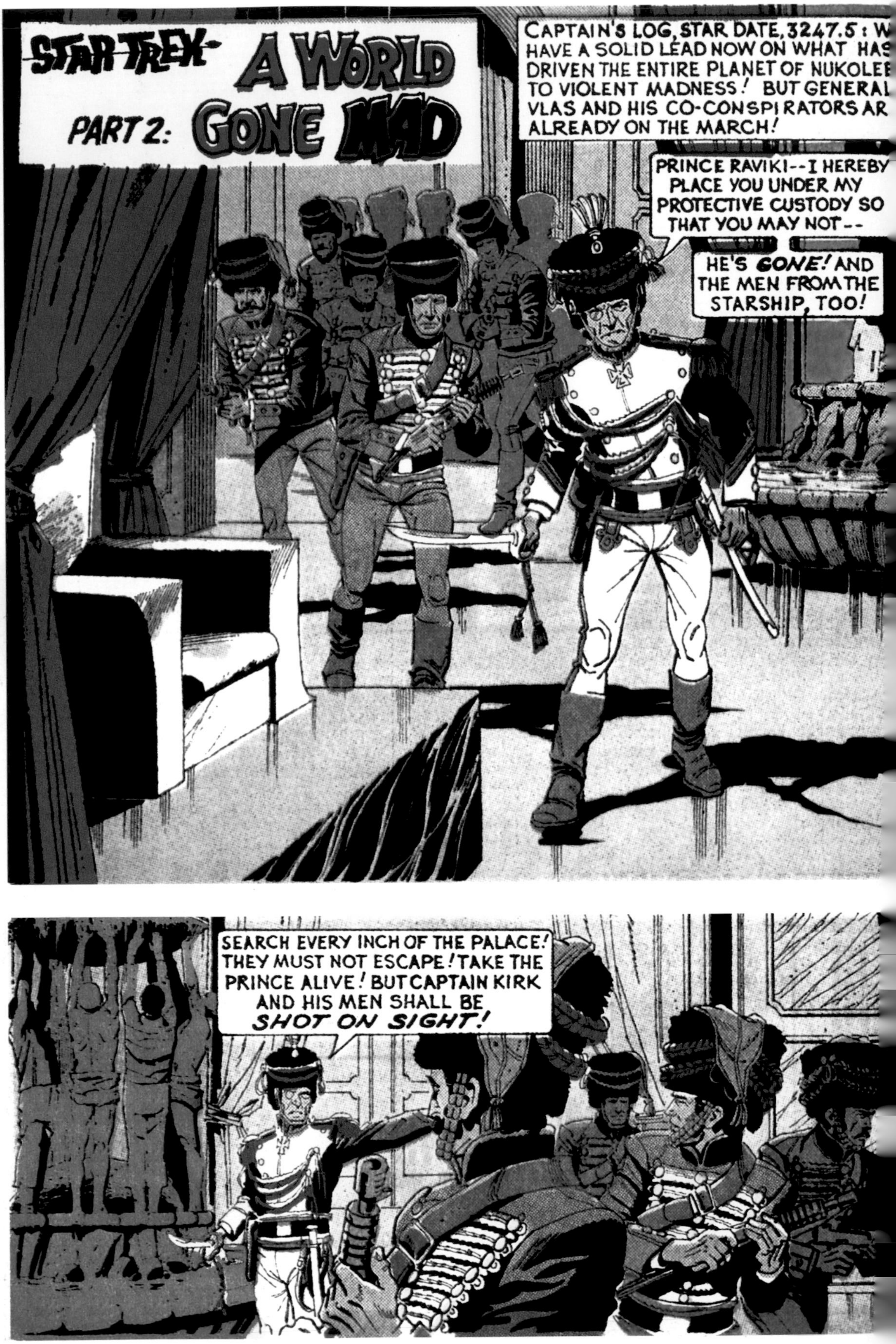
STAR TREK - A WORLD GONE MAD
PART 2:
CAPTAIN'S LOG, STAR DATE, 3247.5 : W HAVE A SOLID LEAD NOW ON WHAT HAS DRIVEN THE ENTIRE PLANET OF NUKOLEE TO VIOLENT MADNESS! BUT GENERAL VLAS AND HIS CO-CONSPIRATORS AR ALREADY ON THE MARCH!
PRINCE RAVIKI--I HEREBY PLACE YOU UNDER MY PROTECTIVE CUSTODY SO THAT YOU MAY NOT--
HE'S GONE! AND THE MEN FROM THE STARSHIP, TOO!
SEARCH EVERY INCH OF THE PALACE! THEY MUST NOT ESCAPE! TAKE THE PRINCE ALIVE! BUT CAPTAIN KIRK AND HIS MEN SHALL BE SHOT ON SIGHT!

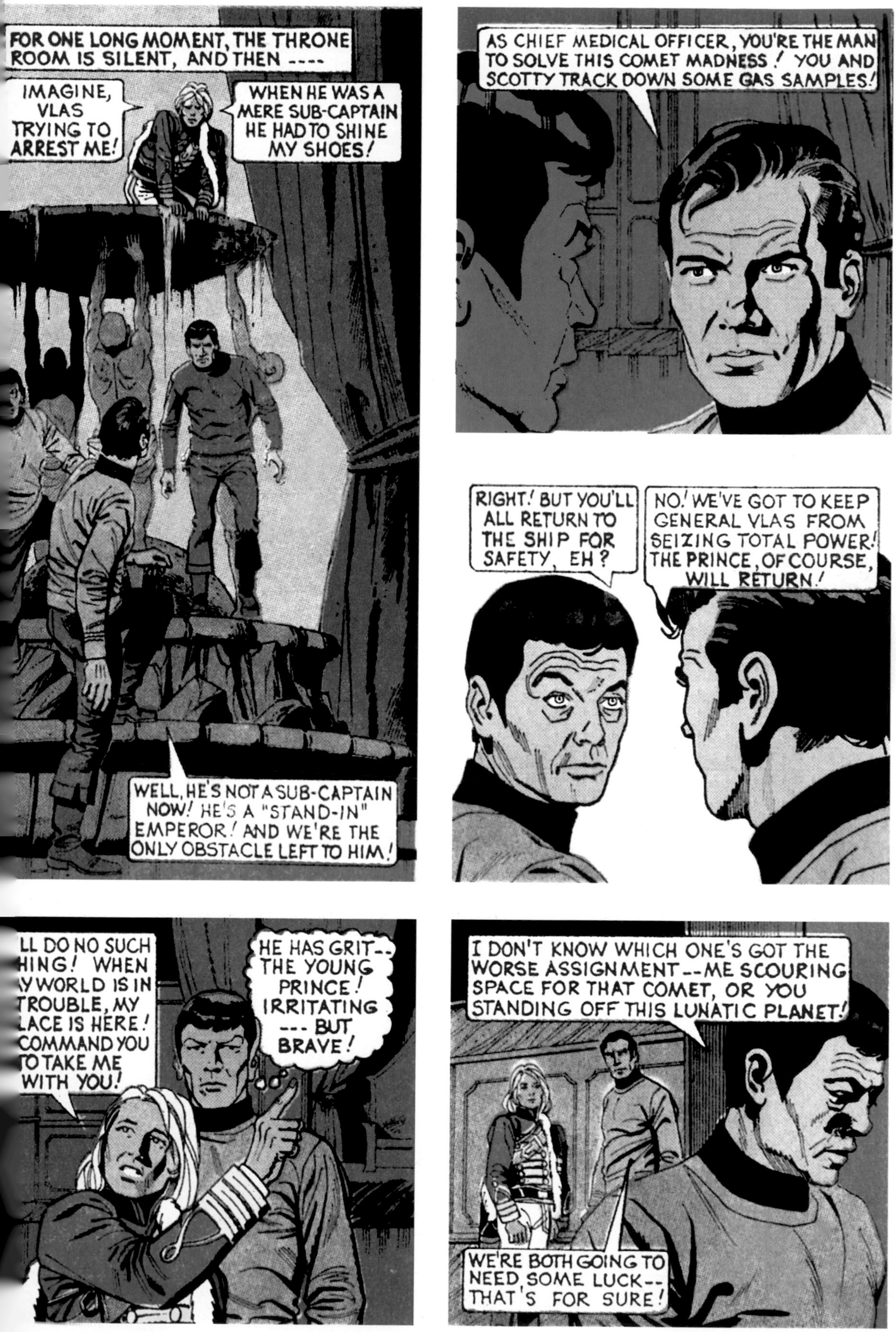
FOR ONE LONG MOMENT, THE THRONE ROOM IS SILENT, AND THEN ----
IMAGINE, VLAS TRYING TO ARREST ME!
WHEN HE WAS A MERE SUB-CAPTAIN HE HAD TO SHINE MY SHOES!
WELL, HE'S NOT A SUB-CAPTAIN NOW! HE'S A "STAND-IN" EMPEROR! AND WE'RE THE ONLY OBSTACLE LEFT TO HIM!
AS CHIEF MEDICAL OFFICER, YOU'RE THE MAN TO SOLVE THIS COMET MADNESS! YOU AND SCOTTY TRACK DOWN SOME GAS SAMPLES!
RIGHT! BUT YOU'LL ALL RETURN TO THE SHIP FOR SAFETY, EH?
NO! WE'VE GOT TO KEEP GENERAL VLAS FROM SEIZING TOTAL POWER! THE PRINCE, OF COURSE, WILL RETURN!
LL DO NO SUCH HING! WHEN Y WORLD IS IN TROUBLE, MY LACE IS HERE! COMMAND YOU TO TAKE ME WITH YOU!
HE HAS GRIT-- THE YOUNG PRINCE! IRRITATING --- BUT BRAVE!
I DON'T KNOW WHICH ONE'S GOT THE WORSE ASSIGNMENT --ME SCOURING SPACE FOR THAT COMET, OR YOU STANDING OFF THIS LUNATIC PLANET!
WE'RE BOTH GOING TO NEED SOME LUCK-- THAT'S FOR SURE!

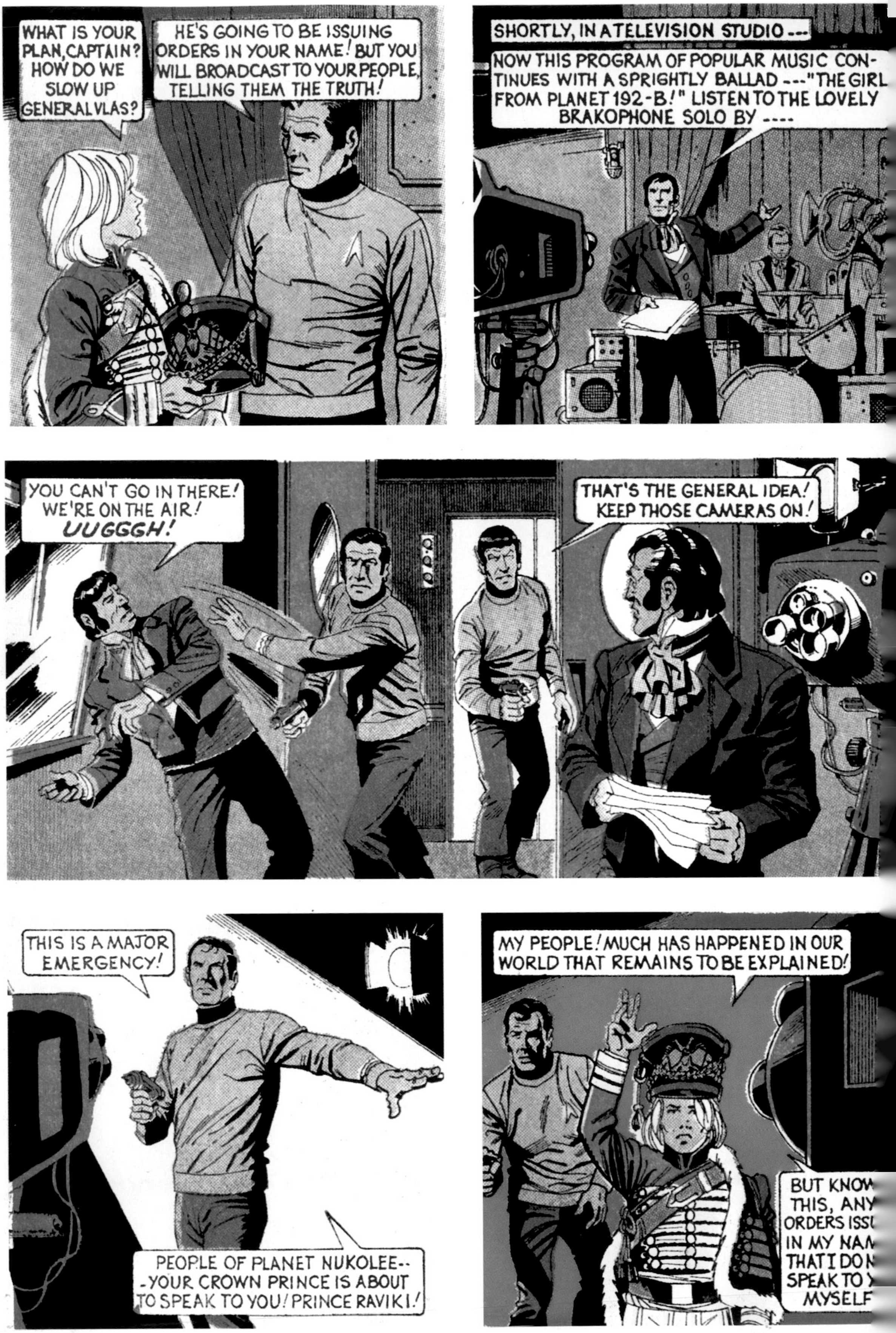

WHAT IS YOUR PLAN, CAPTAIN? HOW DO WE SLOW UP GENERAL VLAS?
HE'S GOING TO BE ISSUING ORDERS IN YOUR NAME! BUT YOU WILL BROADCAST TO YOUR PEOPLE, TELLING THEM THE TRUTH!
SHORTLY, IN A TELEVISION STUDIO ---
NOW THIS PROGRAM OF POPULAR MUSIC CONTINUES WITH A SPRIGHTLY BALLAD ---"THE GIRL FROM PLANET 192-B!" LISTEN TO THE LOVELY BRAKOPHONE SOLO BY ----
YOU CAN'T GO IN THERE! WE'RE ON THE AIR! UUGGGH!
THAT'S THE GENERAL IDEA! KEEP THOSE CAMERAS ON!
THIS IS A MAJOR EMERGENCY!
PEOPLE OF PLANET NUKOLEE-- -YOUR CROWN PRINCE IS ABOUT TO SPEAK TO YOU! PRINCE RAVIKI!
MY PEOPLE! MUCH HAS HAPPENED IN OUR WORLD THAT REMAINS TO BE EXPLAINED!
BUT KNOW THIS, ANY ORDERS ISSU IN MY NAM THAT I DON SPEAK TO Y MYSELF

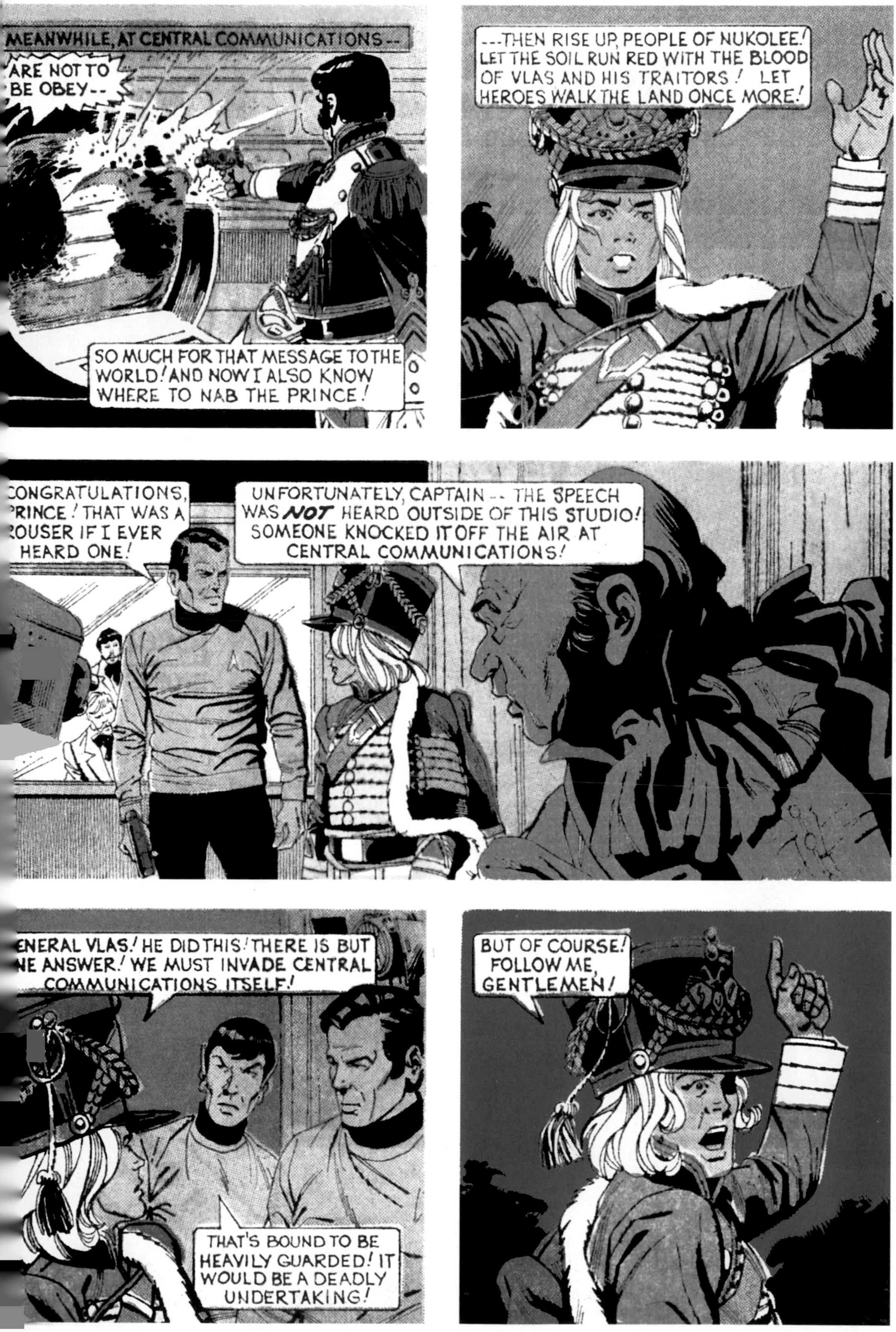
MEANWHILE, AT CENTRAL COMMUNICATIONS --
ARE NOT TO BE OBEY--
SO MUCH FOR THAT MESSAGE TO THE WORLD! AND NOW I ALSO KNOW WHERE TO NAB THE PRINCE!
---THEN RISE UP, PEOPLE OF NUKOLEE! LET THE SOIL RUN RED WITH THE BLOOD OF VLAS AND HIS TRAITORS! LET HEROES WALK THE LAND ONCE MORE!
CONGRATULATIONS, PRINCE! THAT WAS A ROUSER IF I EVER HEARD ONE!
UNFORTUNATELY, CAPTAIN -- THE SPEECH WAS NOT HEARD OUTSIDE OF THIS STUDIO! SOMEONE KNOCKED IT OFF THE AIR AT CENTRAL COMMUNICATIONS!
ENERAL VLAS! HE DID THIS! THERE IS BUT NE ANSWER! WE MUST INVADE CENTRAL COMMUNICATIONS ITSELF!
THAT'S BOUND TO BE HEAVILY GUARDED! IT WOULD BE A DEADLY UNDERTAKING!
BUT OF COURSE! FOLLOW ME, GENTLEMEN!

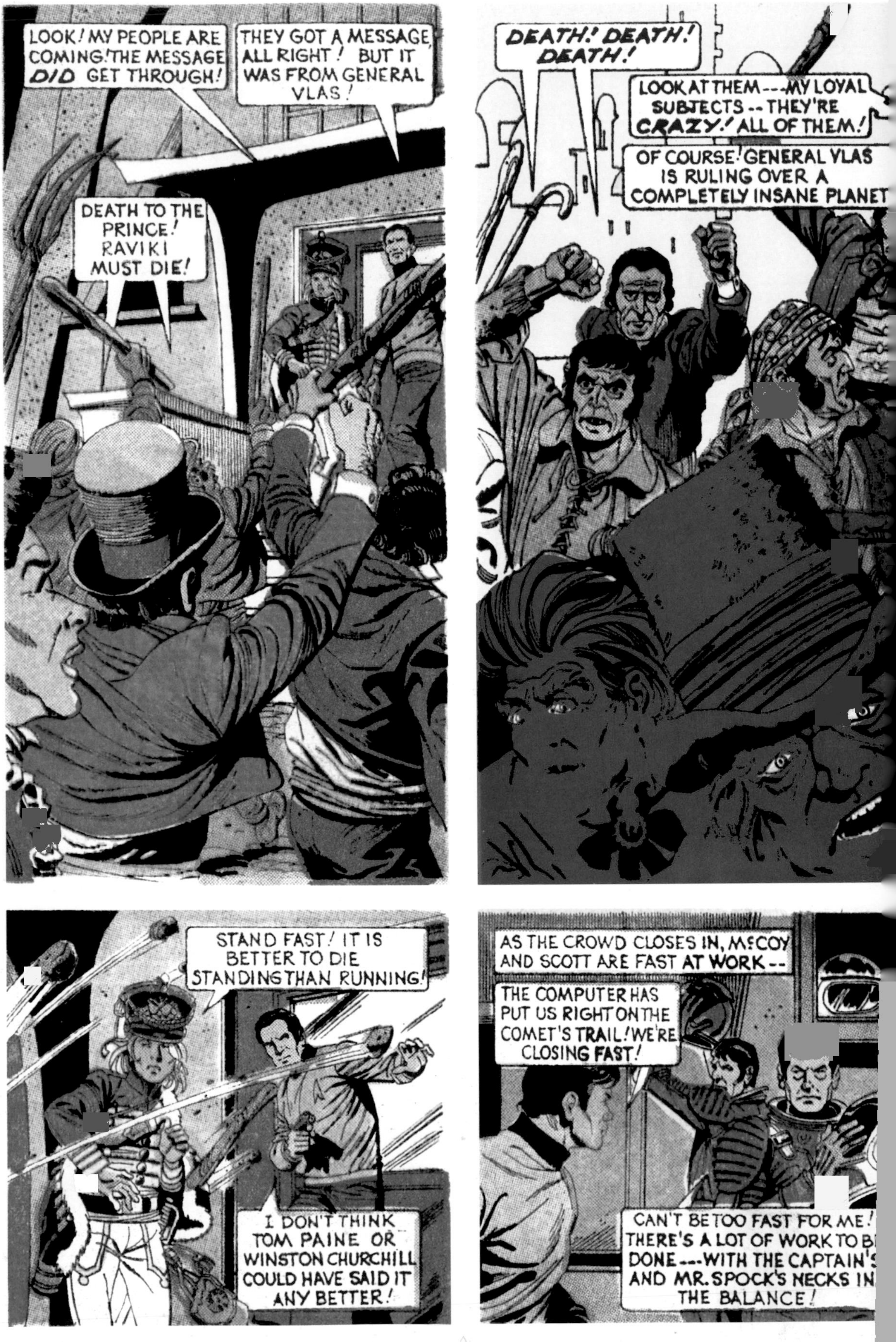
LOOK! MY PEOPLE ARE COMING! THE MESSAGE DID GET THROUGH!
THEY GOT A MESSAGE, ALL RIGHT! BUT IT WAS FROM GENERAL VLAS!
DEATH TO THE PRINCE! RAVIKI MUST DIE!
DEATH! DEATH! DEATH!
LOOK AT THEM---MY LOYAL SUBJECTS -- THEY'RE CRAZY! ALL OF THEM!
OF COURSE! GENERAL VLAS IS RULING OVER A COMPLETELY INSANE PLANET
STAND FAST! IT IS BETTER TO DIE STANDING THAN RUNNING!
I DON'T THINK TOM PAINE OR WINSTON CHURCHILL COULD HAVE SAID IT ANY BETTER!
AS THE CROWD CLOSES IN, McCOY AND SCOTT ARE FAST AT WORK--
THE COMPUTER HAS PUT US RIGHT ON THE COMET'S TRAIL! WE'RE CLOSING FAST!
CAN'T BE TOO FAST FOR ME! THERE'S A LOT OF WORK TO B
DONE---WITH THE CAPTAIN'S AND MR. SPOCK'S NECKS IN THE BALANCE!

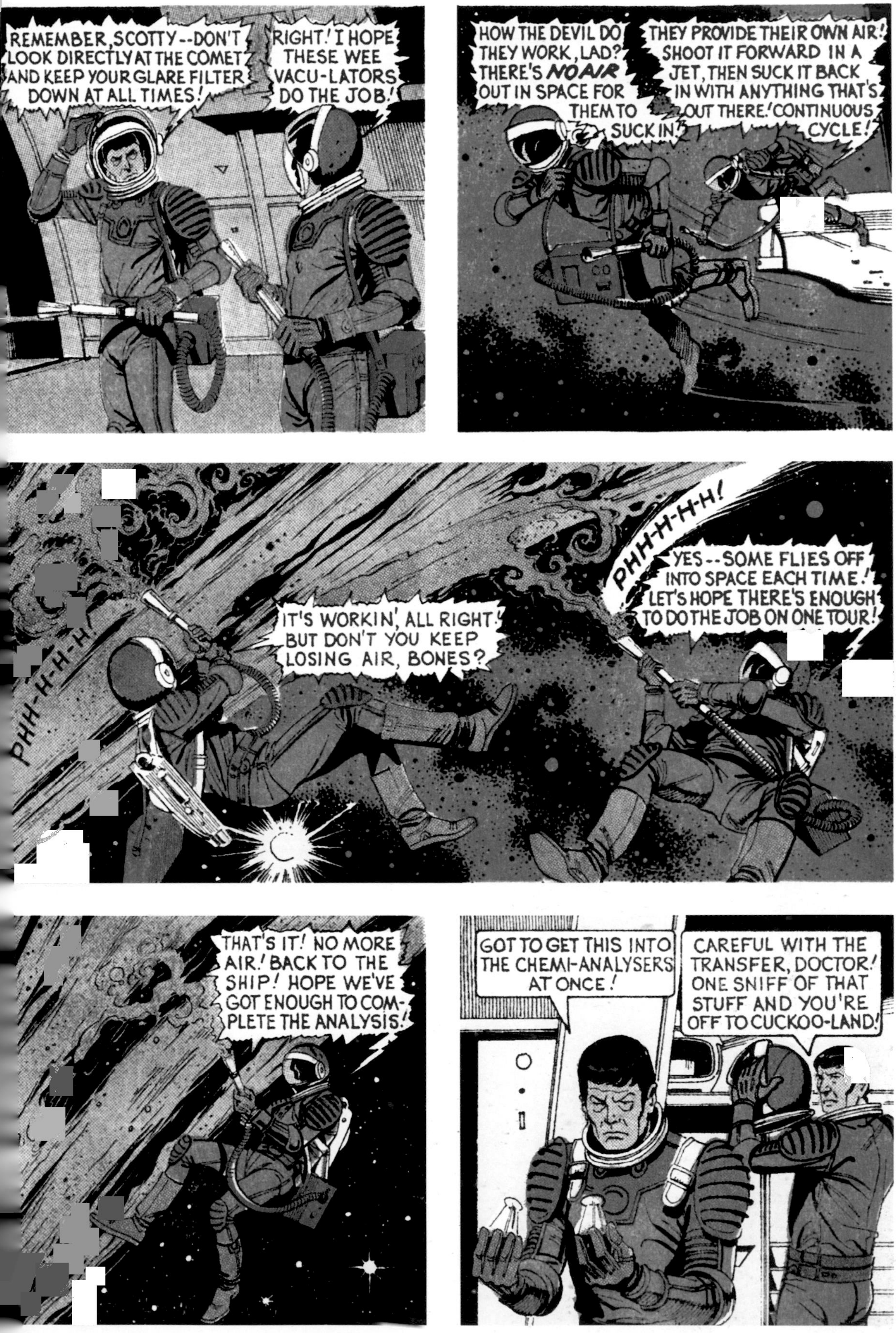
REMEMBER, SCOTTY--DON'T LOOK DIRECTLY AT THE COMET AND KEEP YOUR GLARE FILTER DOWN AT ALL TIMES!
RIGHT! I HOPE THESE WEE VACU-LATORS DO THE JOB!
HOW THE DEVIL DO THEY WORK, LAD? THERE'S NO AIR OUT IN SPACE FOR THEM TO SUCK IN!
THEY PROVIDE THEIR OWN AIR! SHOOT IT FORWARD IN A JET, THEN SUCK IT BACK IN WITH ANYTHING THAT'S OUT THERE! CONTINUOUS CYCLE!
PHH-H-H-H
IT'S WORKIN', ALL RIGHT! BUT DON'T YOU KEEP LOSING AIR, BONES?
PHH-H-H-H!
YES--SOME FLIES OFF INTO SPACE EACH TIME! LET'S HOPE THERE'S ENOUGH TO DO THE JOB ON ONE TOUR!
THAT'S IT! NO MORE AIR! BACK TO THE SHIP! HOPE WE'VE GOT ENOUGH TO COMPLETE THE ANALYSIS!
GOT TO GET THIS INTO THE CHEMI-ANALYSERS AT ONCE!
CAREFUL WITH THE TRANSFER, DOCTOR! ONE SNIFF OF THAT STUFF AND YOU'RE OFF TO CUCKOO-LAND!

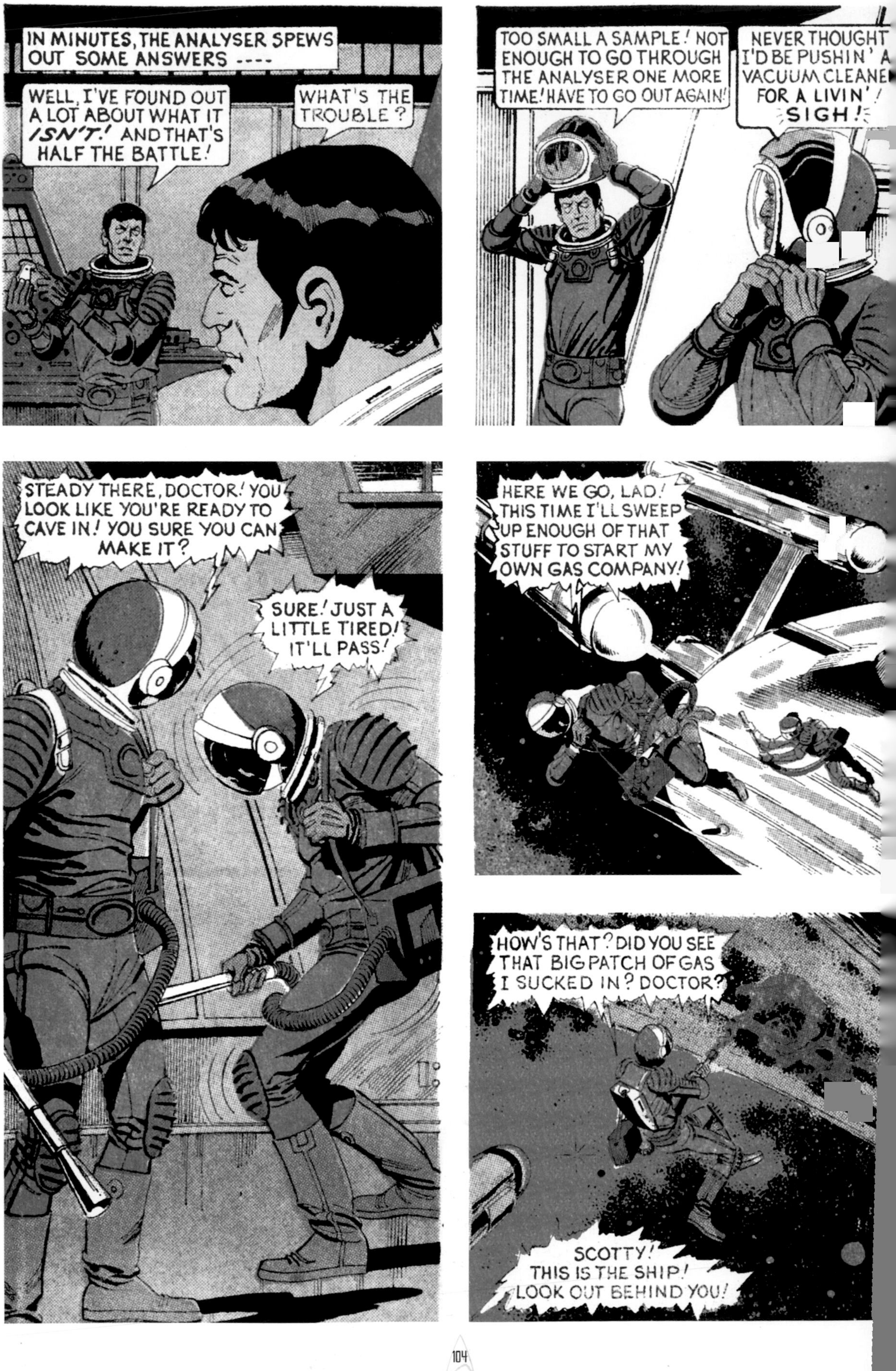
IN MINUTES, THE ANALYSER SPEWS OUT SOME ANSWERS ----
WELL, I'VE FOUND OUT A LOT ABOUT WHAT IT ISN'T! AND THAT'S HALF THE BATTLE!
WHAT'S THE TROUBLE?
TOO SMALL A SAMPLE! NOT ENOUGH TO GO THROUGH THE ANALYSER ONE MORE TIME! HAVE TO GO OUT AGAIN!
NEVER THOUGHT I'D BE PUSHIN' A VACUUM CLEANE FOR A LIVIN'! SIGH!
STEADY THERE, DOCTOR! YOU LOOK LIKE YOU'RE READY TO CAVE IN! YOU SURE YOU CAN MAKE IT?
SURE! JUST A LITTLE TIRED! IT'LL PASS!
HERE WE GO, LAD! THIS TIME I'LL SWEEP UP ENOUGH OF THAT STUFF TO START MY OWN GAS COMPANY!
HOW'S THAT? DID YOU SEE THAT BIG PATCH OF GAS I SUCKED IN? DOCTOR?
SCOTTY! THIS IS THE SHIP! LOOK OUT BEHIND YOU!

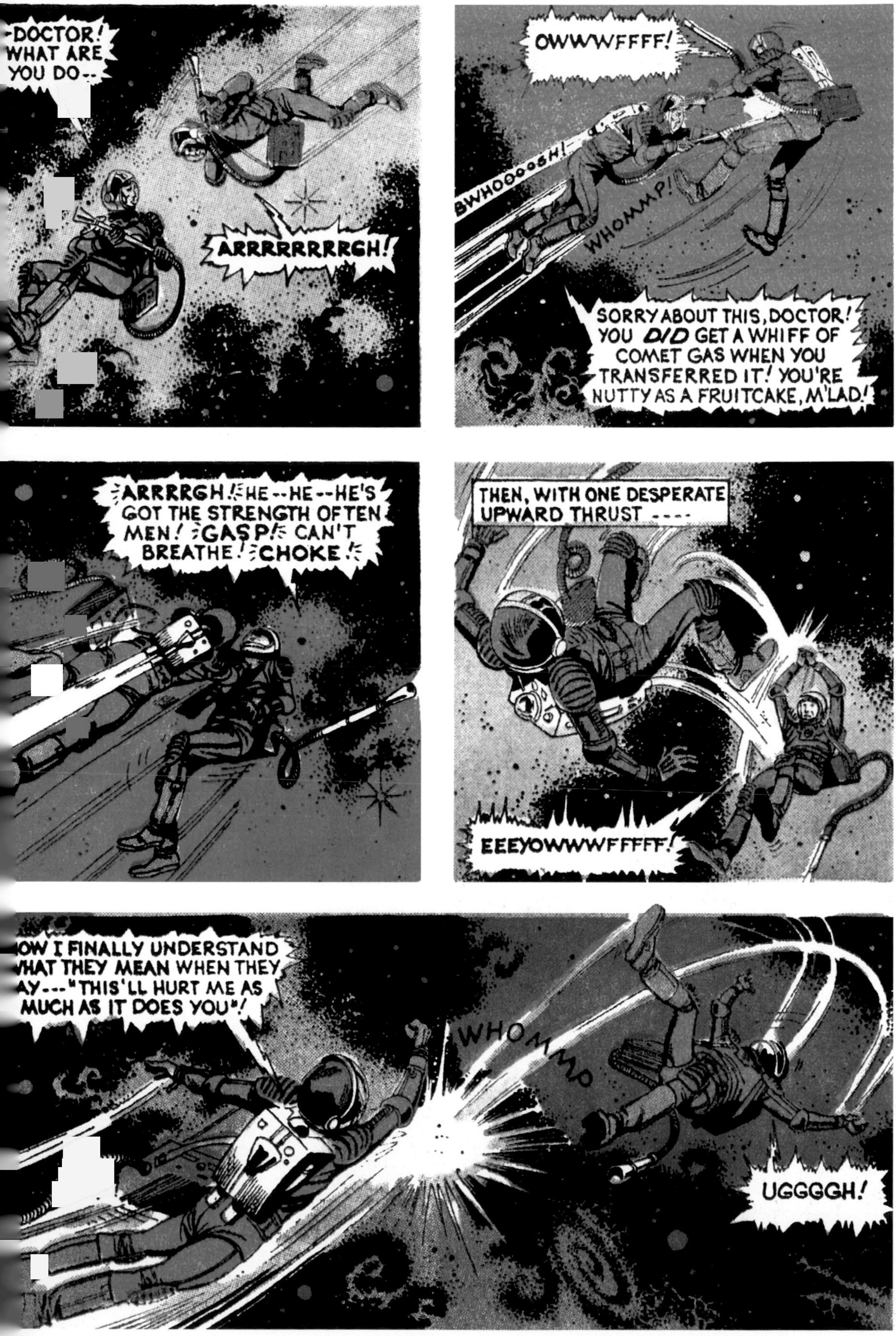
-DOCTOR! WHAT ARE YOU DO--
ARRRRRRRRGH!
OWWWFFFF!
BWHOOOOOSH!
WHOMMP!
SORRY ABOUT THIS, DOCTOR! YOU DID GET A WHIFF OF COMET GAS WHEN YOU TRANSFERRED IT! YOU'RE NUTTY AS A FRUITCAKE, M'LAD!
ARRRRGH! HE--HE--HE'S GOT THE STRENGTH OF TEN MEN! GASP! CAN'T BREATHE! CHOKE!
THEN, WITH ONE DESPERATE UPWARD THRUST ----
EEEYOWWWFFFFF!
OW I FINALLY UNDERSTAND WHAT THEY MEAN WHEN THEY AY---"THIS'LL HURT ME AS MUCH AS IT DOES YOU"!
WHOMMP
UGGGGH!

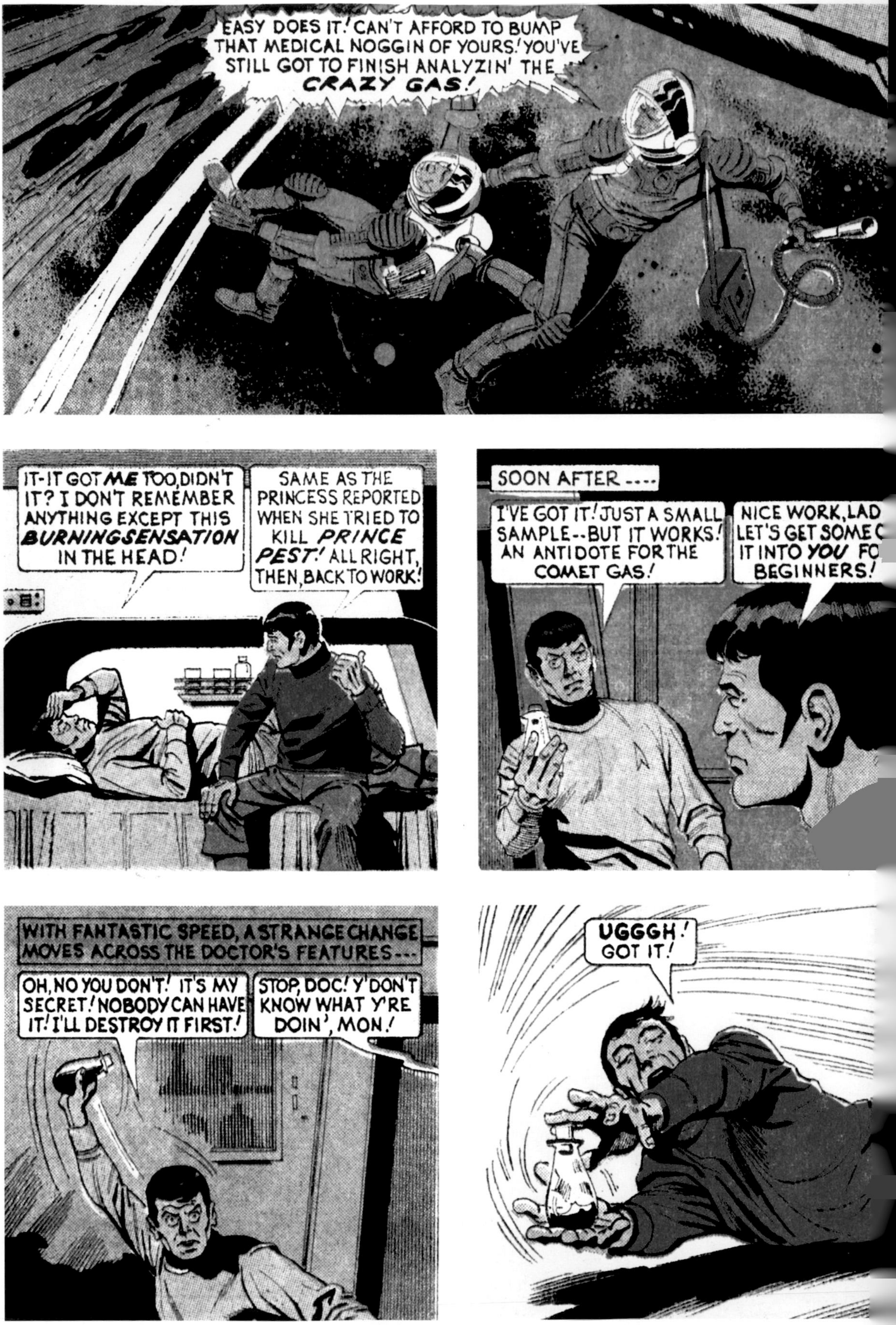
EASY DOES IT! CAN'T AFFORD TO BUMP THAT MEDICAL NOGGIN OF YOURS! YOU'VE STILL GOT TO FINISH ANALYZIN' THE CRAZY GAS!
IT-IT GOT ME TOO, DIDN'T IT? I DON'T REMEMBER ANYTHING EXCEPT THIS BURNING SENSATION IN THE HEAD!
SAME AS THE PRINCESS REPORTED WHEN SHE TRIED TO KILL PRINCE PEST! ALL RIGHT, THEN, BACK TO WORK!
SOON AFTER ----
I'VE GOT IT! JUST A SMALL SAMPLE--BUT IT WORKS! AN ANTIDOTE FOR THE COMET GAS!
NICE WORK, LAD LET'S GET SOME C IT INTO YOU FO BEGINNERS!
WITH FANTASTIC SPEED, A STRANGE CHANGE MOVES ACROSS THE DOCTOR'S FEATURES---
OH, NO YOU DON'T! IT'S MY SECRET! NOBODY CAN HAVE IT! I'LL DESTROY IT FIRST!
STOP, DOC! Y'DON'T KNOW WHAT Y'RE DOIN', MON!
UGGGH! GOT IT!

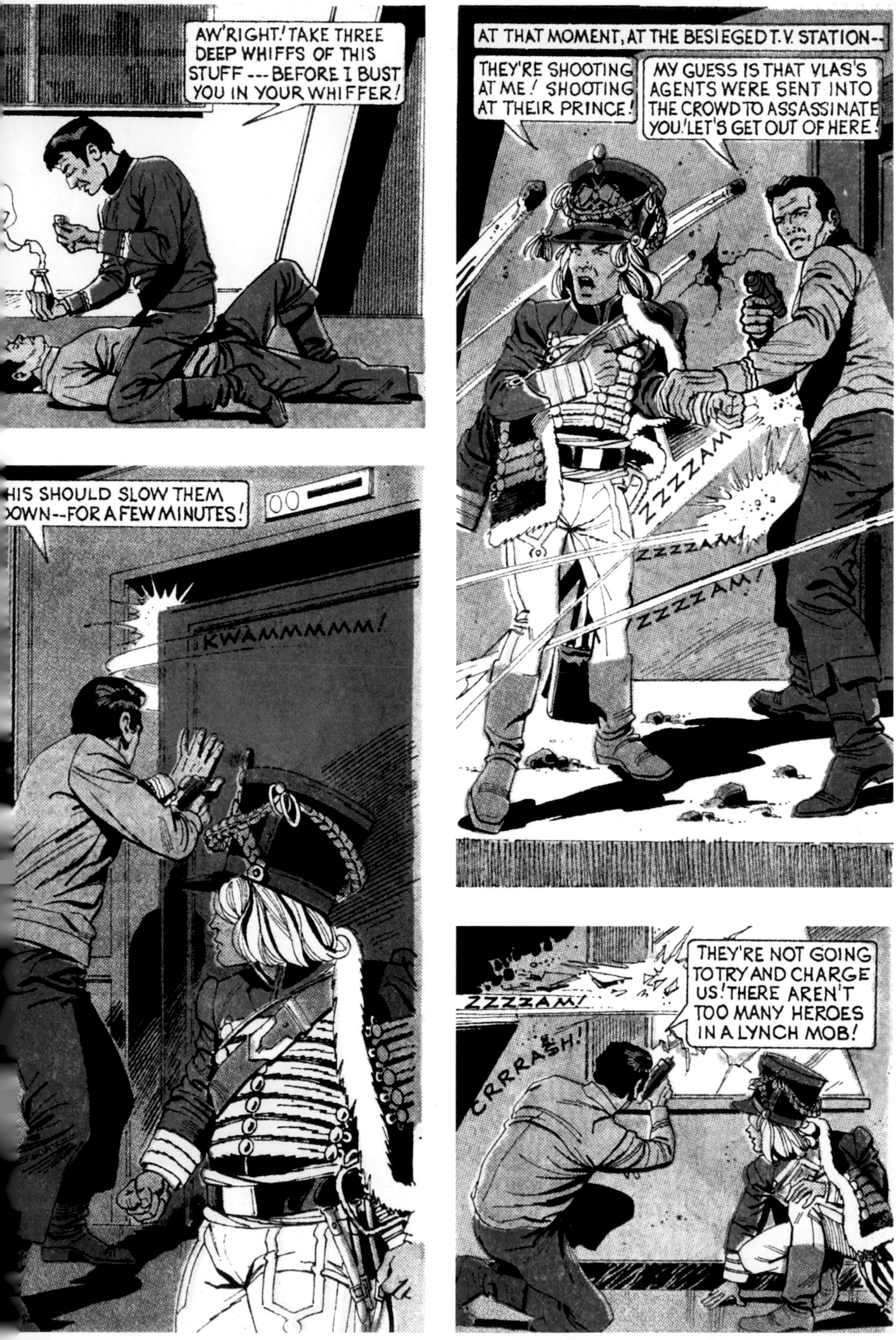
AW'RIGHT! TAKE THREE DEEP WHIFFS OF THIS STUFF --- BEFORE I BUST YOU IN YOUR WHIFFER!
AT THAT MOMENT, AT THE BESIEGED T.V. STATION--
THEY'RE SHOOTING AT ME! SHOOTING AT THEIR PRINCE!
MY GUESS IS THAT VLAS'S AGENTS WERE SENT INTO THE CROWD TO ASSASSINATE YOU! LET'S GET OUT OF HERE!
ZZZZAM
ZZZZAM!
ZZZZAM!
HIS SHOULD SLOW THEM OWN--FOR A FEW MINUTES!
KWAMMMMMM!
ZZZZAM!
CRRRASH!
THEY'RE NOT GOING TO TRY AND CHARGE US! THERE AREN'T TOO MANY HEROES IN A LYNCH MOB!

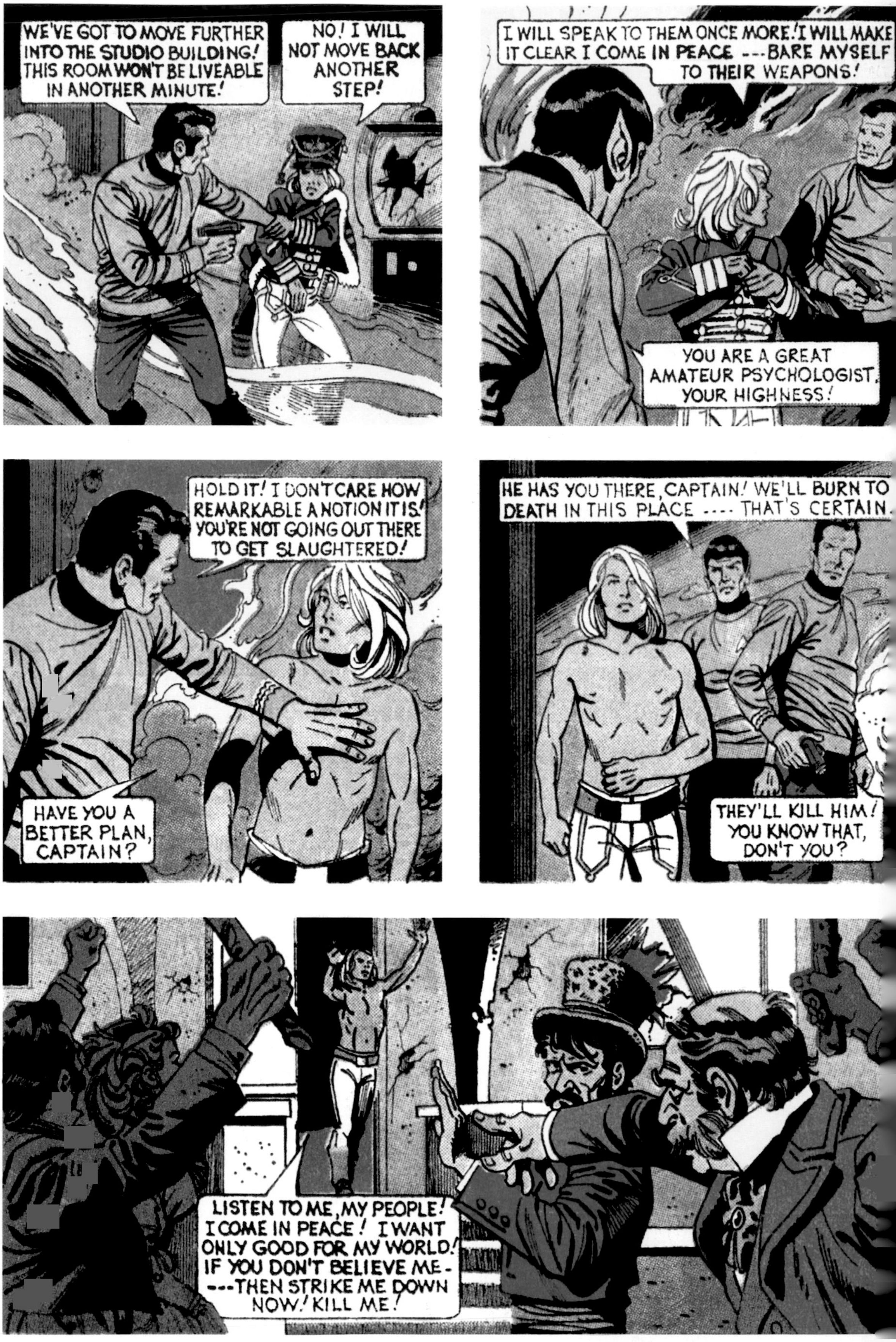
WE'VE GOT TO MOVE FURTHER INTO THE STUDIO BUILDING! THIS ROOM WON'T BE LIVEABLE IN ANOTHER MINUTE!
NO! I WILL NOT MOVE BACK ANOTHER STEP!
I WILL SPEAK TO THEM ONCE MORE! I WILL MAKE IT CLEAR I COME IN PEACE ---BARE MYSELF TO THEIR WEAPONS!
YOU ARE A GREAT AMATEUR PSYCHOLOGIST, YOUR HIGHNESS!
HOLD IT! I DON'T CARE HOW REMARKABLE A NOTION IT IS! YOU'RE NOT GOING OUT THERE TO GET SLAUGHTERED!
HAVE YOU A BETTER PLAN, CAPTAIN?
HE HAS YOU THERE, CAPTAIN! WE'LL BURN TO DEATH IN THIS PLACE ---- THAT'S CERTAIN.
THEY'LL KILL HIM! YOU KNOW THAT, DON'T YOU?
LISTEN TO ME, MY PEOPLE! I COME IN PEACE! I WANT ONLY GOOD FOR MY WORLD! IF YOU DON'T BELIEVE ME- ---THEN STRIKE ME DOWN NOW! KILL ME!

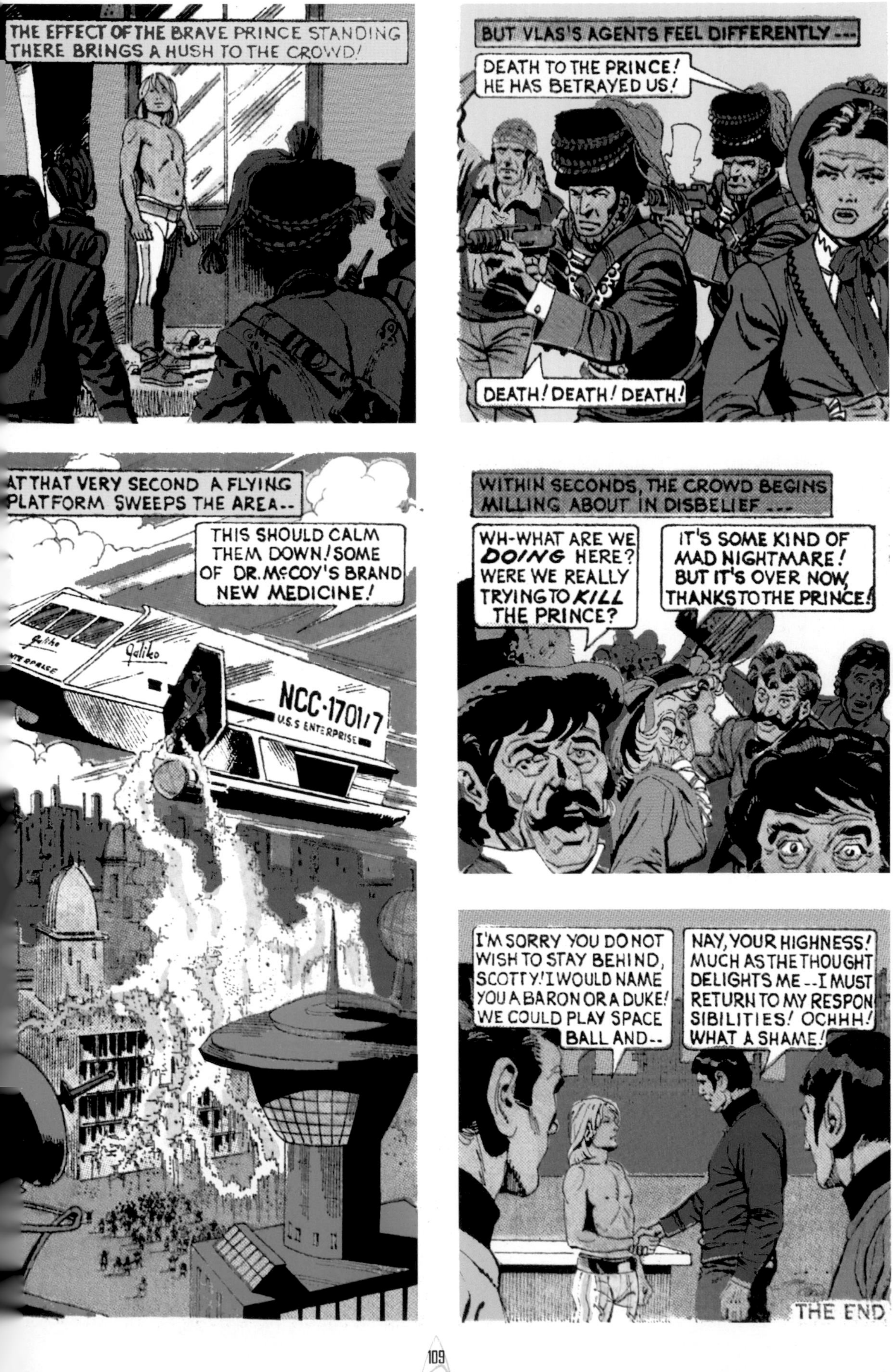
THE EFFECT OF THE BRAVE PRINCE STANDING THERE BRINGS A HUSH TO THE CROWD!
BUT VLAS'S AGENTS FEEL DIFFERENTLY ---
DEATH TO THE PRINCE! HE HAS BETRAYED US!
DEATH! DEATH! DEATH!
AT THAT VERY SECOND A FLYING PLATFORM SWEEPS THE AREA--
THIS SHOULD CALM THEM DOWN! SOME OF DR. McCOY'S BRAND NEW MEDICINE!
NCC-1701/7
U.S.S ENTERPRISE
WITHIN SECONDS, THE CROWD BEGINS MILLING ABOUT IN DISBELIEF ---
WH-WHAT ARE WE DOING HERE? WERE WE REALLY TRYING TO KILL THE PRINCE?
IT'S SOME KIND OF MAD NIGHTMARE! BUT IT'S OVER NOW, THANKS TO THE PRINCE!
I'M SORRY YOU DO NOT WISH TO STAY BEHIND, SCOTTY! I WOULD NAME YOU A BARON OR A DUKE! WE COULD PLAY SPACE BALL AND--
NAY, YOUR HIGHNESS! MUCH AS THE THOUGHT DELIGHTS ME -- I MUST RETURN TO MY RESPONSIBILITIES! OCHHH! WHAT A SHAME!
THE END

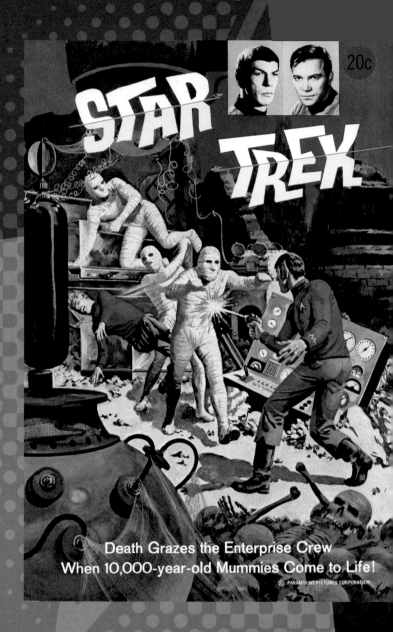

20c

Death Grazes the Enterprise Crew
When 10,000-year-old Mummies Come to Life!

© PARAMOUNT PICTURES CORPORATION

Chapter 5
The Mummies of Heitus VII

[Originally Published in November, 1973]

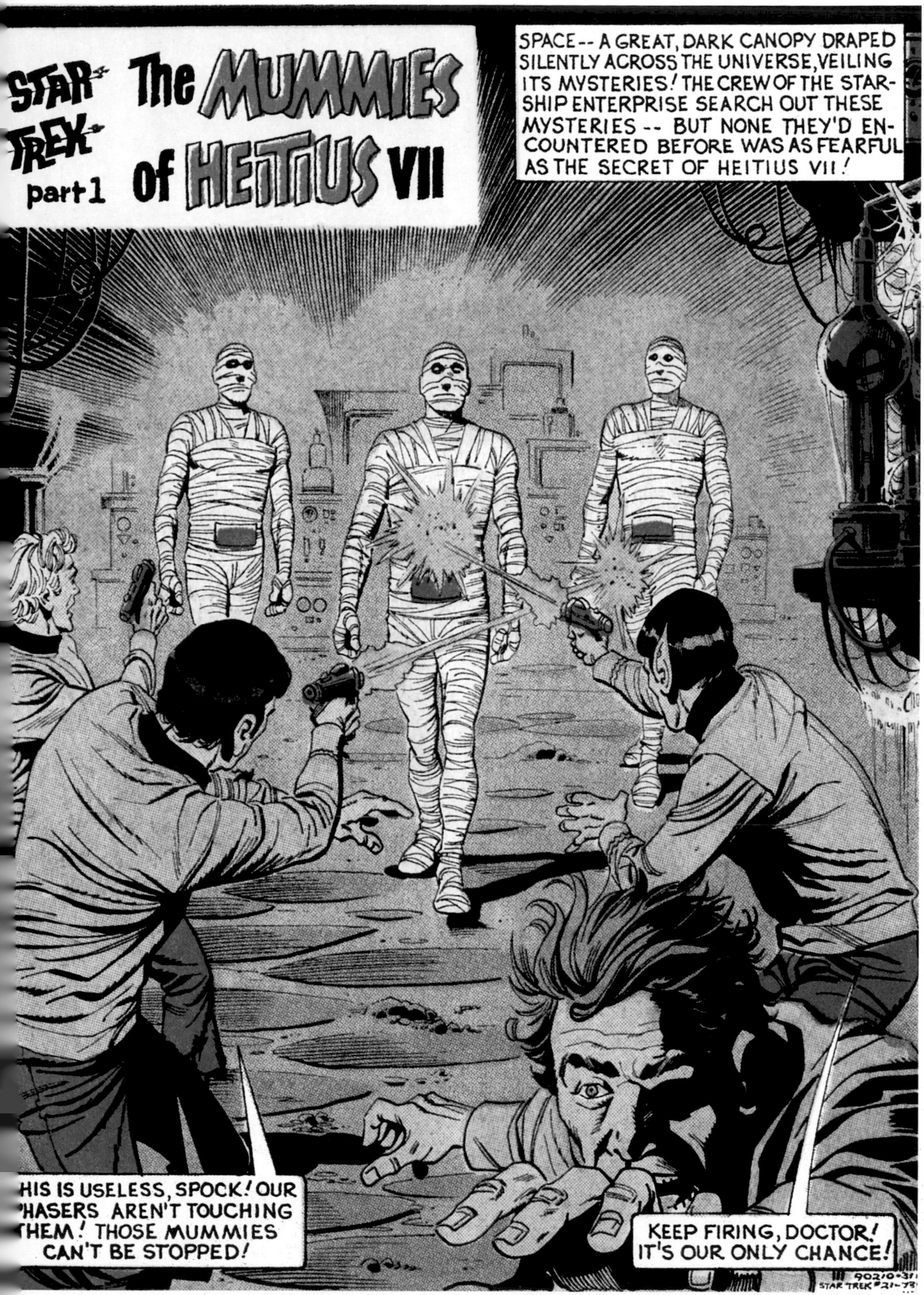
STAR TREK
part 1
The MUMMIES of HEITIUS VII
SPACE-- A GREAT, DARK CANOPY DRAPED SILENTLY ACROSS THE UNIVERSE, VEILING ITS MYSTERIES! THE CREW OF THE STAR-SHIP ENTERPRISE SEARCH OUT THESE MYSTERIES -- BUT NONE THEY'D EN-COUNTERED BEFORE WAS AS FEARFUL AS THE SECRET OF HEITIUS VII!
HIS IS USELESS, SPOCK! OUR HASERS AREN'T TOUCHING HEM! THOSE MUMMIES CAN'T BE STOPPED!
KEEP FIRING, DOCTOR! IT'S OUR ONLY CHANCE!

aptain's Log, Stardate 30:26.5 . . DATA REF . . 21.00-21.25

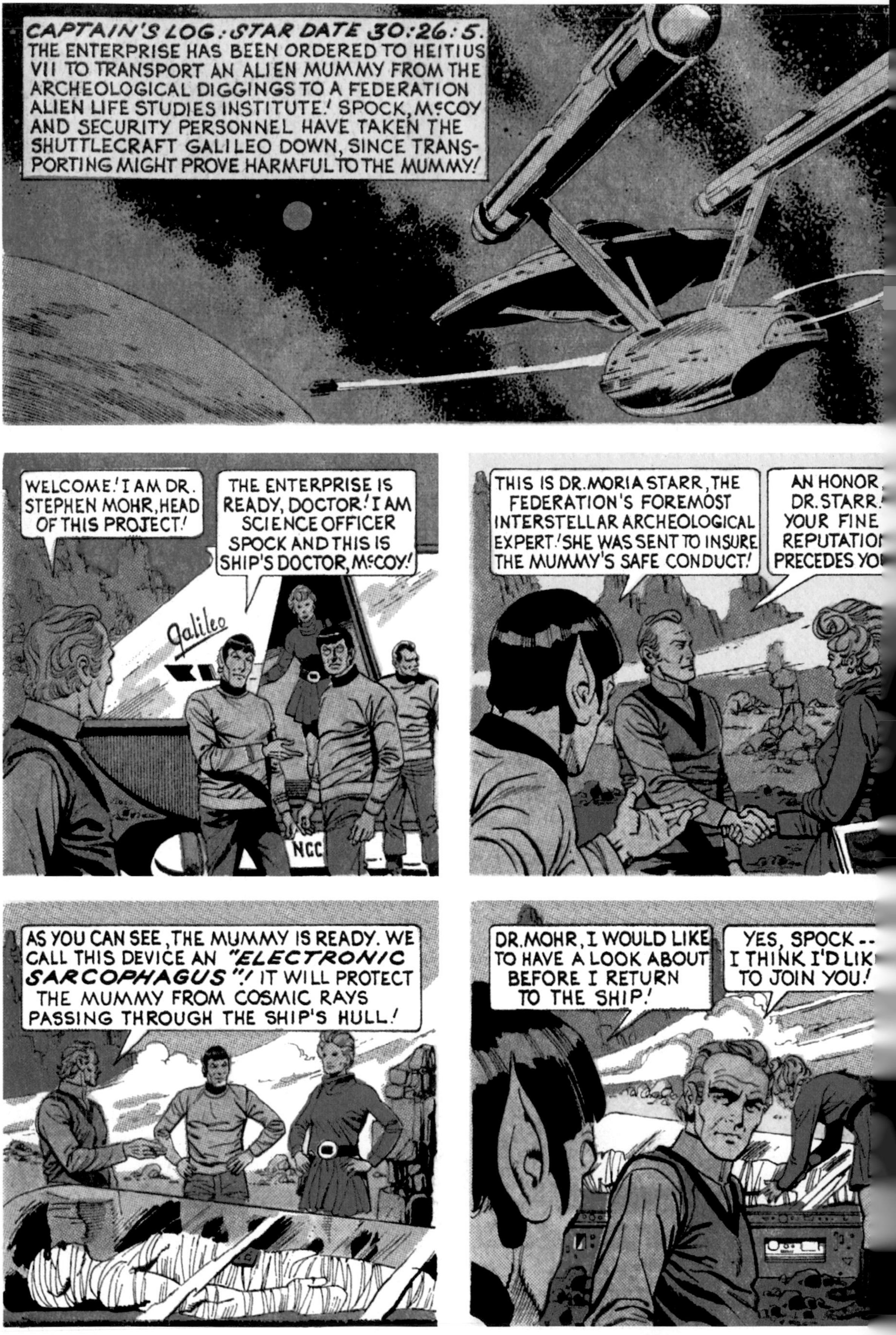
CAPTAIN'S LOG: STAR DATE 30:26:5. THE ENTERPRISE HAS BEEN ORDERED TO HEITIUS VII TO TRANSPORT AN ALIEN MUMMY FROM THE ARCHEOLOGICAL DIGGINGS TO A FEDERATION ALIEN LIFE STUDIES INSTITUTE! SPOCK, McCOY AND SECURITY PERSONNEL HAVE TAKEN THE SHUTTLECRAFT GALILEO DOWN, SINCE TRANSPORTING MIGHT PROVE HARMFUL TO THE MUMMY!
WELCOME! I AM DR. STEPHEN MOHR, HEAD OF THIS PROJECT!
THE ENTERPRISE IS READY, DOCTOR! I AM SCIENCE OFFICER SPOCK AND THIS IS SHIP'S DOCTOR, McCOY!
Galileo
NCC
THIS IS DR. MORIA STARR, THE FEDERATION'S FOREMOST INTERSTELLAR ARCHEOLOGICAL EXPERT! SHE WAS SENT TO INSURE THE MUMMY'S SAFE CONDUCT!
AN HONOR, DR. STARR! YOUR FINE REPUTATIO PRECEDES YO
AS YOU CAN SEE, THE MUMMY IS READY. WE CALL THIS DEVICE AN "ELECTRONIC SARCOPHAGUS"! IT WILL PROTECT THE MUMMY FROM COSMIC RAYS PASSING THROUGH THE SHIP'S HULL!
DR. MOHR, I WOULD LIKE TO HAVE A LOOK ABOUT BEFORE I RETURN TO THE SHIP!
YES, SPOCK -- I THINK I'D LIK TO JOIN YOU!

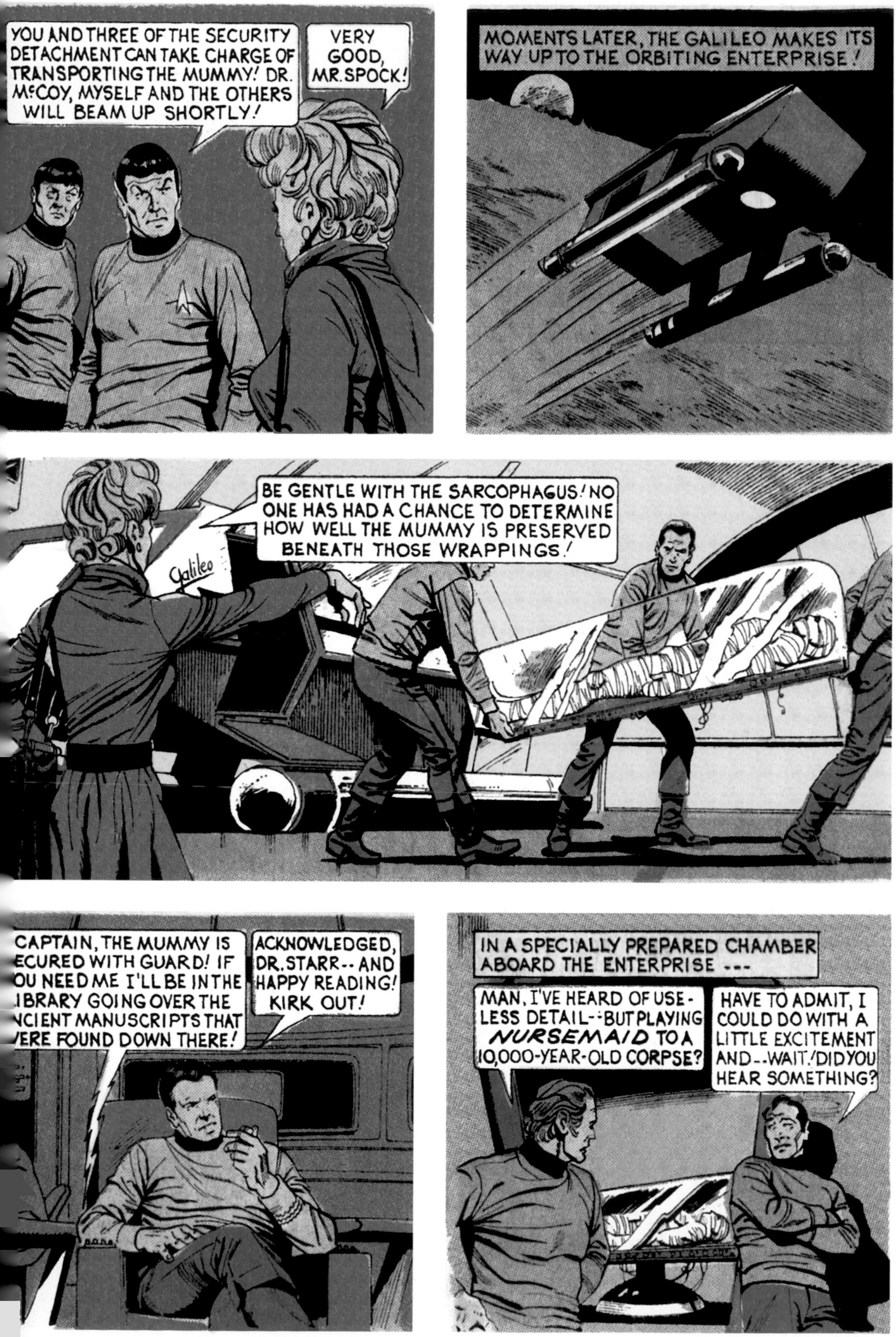
YOU AND THREE OF THE SECURITY DETACHMENT CAN TAKE CHARGE OF TRANSPORTING THE MUMMY! DR. McCOY, MYSELF AND THE OTHERS WILL BEAM UP SHORTLY!
VERY GOOD, MR. SPOCK!
MOMENTS LATER, THE GALILEO MAKES ITS WAY UP TO THE ORBITING ENTERPRISE!
BE GENTLE WITH THE SARCOPHAGUS! NO ONE HAS HAD A CHANCE TO DETERMINE HOW WELL THE MUMMY IS PRESERVED BENEATH THOSE WRAPPINGS!
Galileo
CAPTAIN, THE MUMMY IS ECURED WITH GUARD! IF OU NEED ME I'LL BE IN THE IBRARY GOING OVER THE NCIENT MANUSCRIPTS THAT VERE FOUND DOWN THERE!
ACKNOWLEDGED, DR. STARR-- AND HAPPY READING! KIRK OUT!
IN A SPECIALLY PREPARED CHAMBER ABOARD THE ENTERPRISE ---
MAN, I'VE HEARD OF USE-LESS DETAIL--BUT PLAYING NURSEMAID TO A 10,000-YEAR-OLD CORPSE?
HAVE TO ADMIT, I COULD DO WITH A LITTLE EXCITEMENT AND--WAIT! DID YOU HEAR SOMETHING?

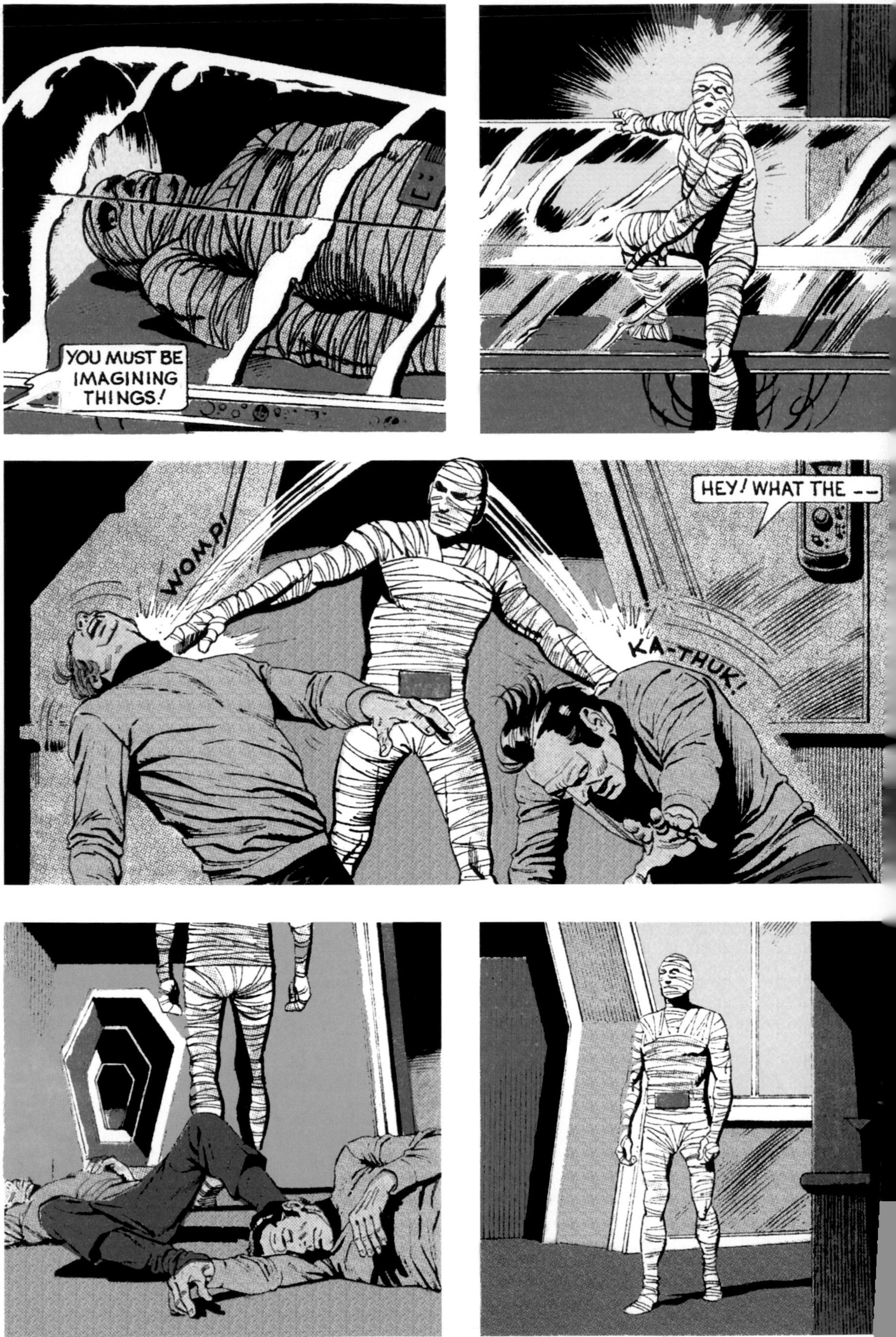
YOU MUST BE IMAGINING THINGS!
WOMP!
HEY! WHAT THE --
KA-THUK!

CAUTION-CENTRAL COMPUTER CORE
NO UNAUTHORIZED ADMITTANCE

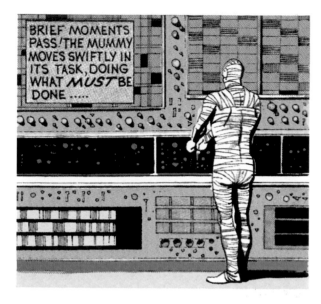

BRIEF MOMENTS PASS! THE MUMMY MOVES SWIFTLY IN ITS TASK, DOING WHAT *MUST* BE DONE ....

....AND RETURNING ONCE AGAIN TO ITS "SARCOPHAGUS"!

OMENTS LATER ....

OAH! WHAT HIT ME?

WHATEVER IT WAS, IT PACKED A MEAN WALLOP!

MANNING OF SECURITY, CAPTAIN! SOMEONE HIT US FROM BEHIND -- DIDN'T GET A LOOK AT WHO IT WAS!

THE MUMMY- IS IT ALL RIGHT?

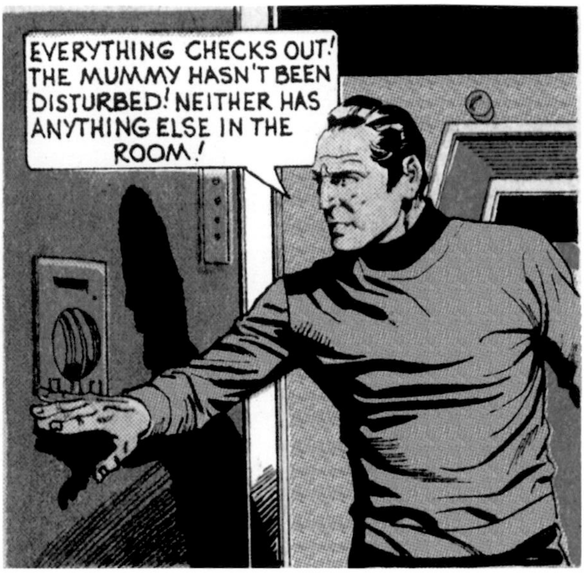
EVERYTHING CHECKS OUT! THE MUMMY HASN'T BEEN DISTURBED! NEITHER HAS ANYTHING ELSE IN THE ROOM!

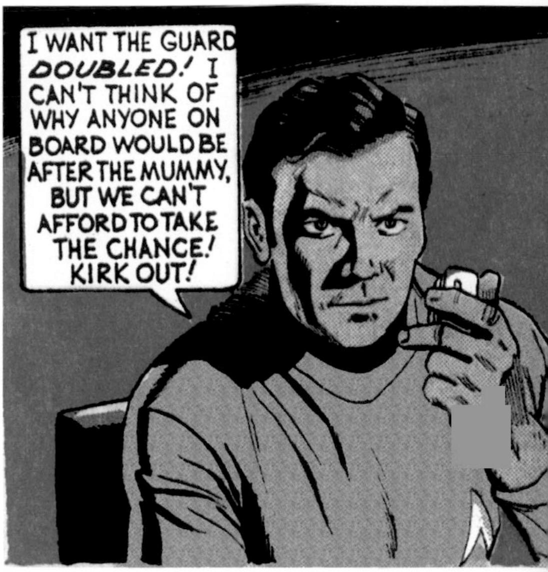
I WANT THE GUARD DOUBLED! I CAN'T THINK OF WHY ANYONE ON BOARD WOULD BE AFTER THE MUMMY, BUT WE CAN'T AFFORD TO TAKE THE CHANCE! KIRK OUT!

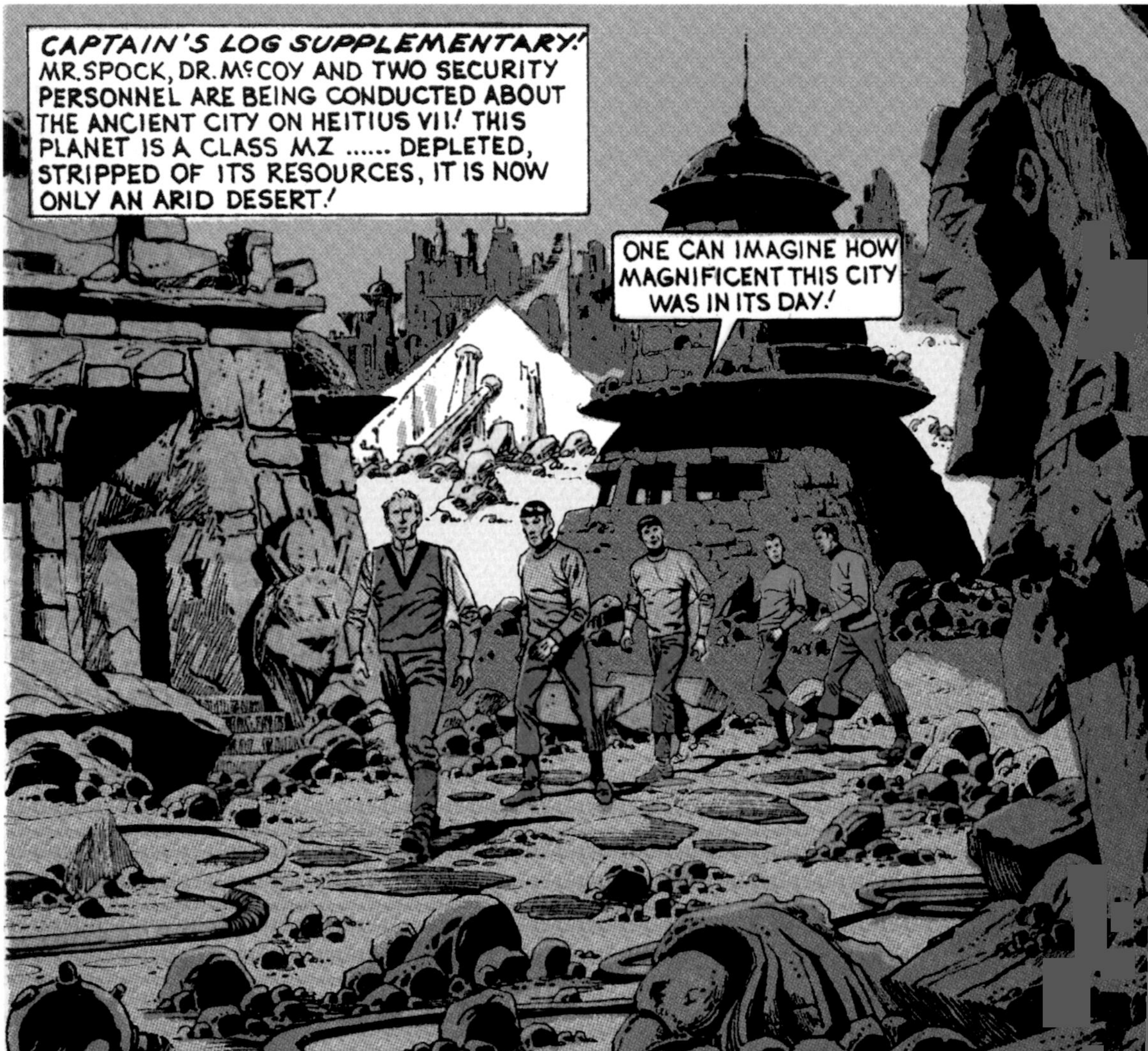
CAPTAIN'S LOG SUPPLEMENTARY! MR. SPOCK, DR. McCOY AND TWO SECURITY PERSONNEL ARE BEING CONDUCTED ABOUT THE ANCIENT CITY ON HEITIUS VII! THIS PLANET IS A CLASS MZ ...... DEPLETED, STRIPPED OF ITS RESOURCES, IT IS NOW ONLY AN ARID DESERT!
ONE CAN IMAGINE HOW MAGNIFICENT THIS CITY WAS IN ITS DAY!

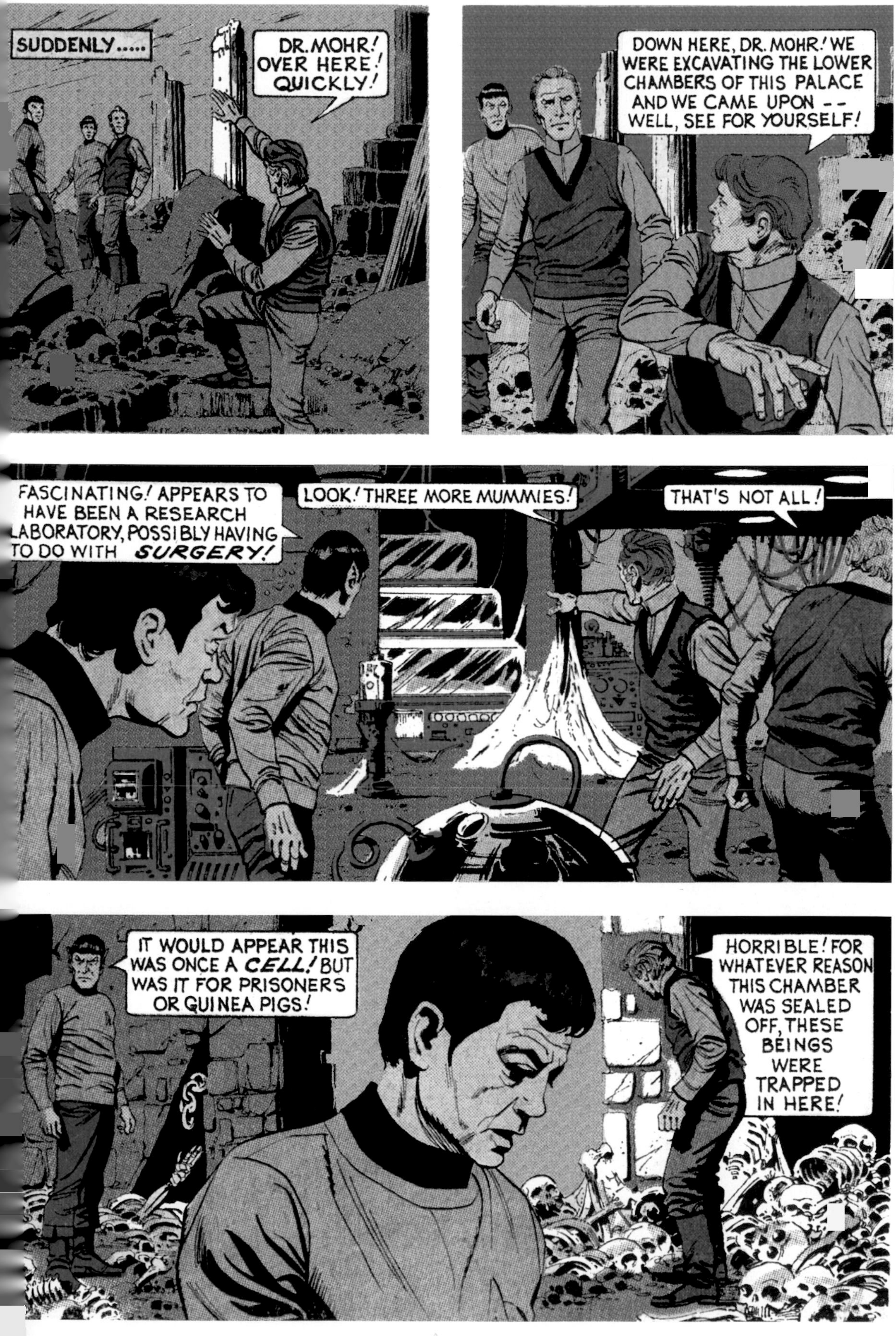
SUDDENLY.....
DR. MOHR! OVER HERE! QUICKLY!
DOWN HERE, DR. MOHR! WE WERE EXCAVATING THE LOWER CHAMBERS OF THIS PALACE AND WE CAME UPON -- WELL, SEE FOR YOURSELF!
FASCINATING! APPEARS TO HAVE BEEN A RESEARCH LABORATORY, POSSIBLY HAVING TO DO WITH SURGERY!
LOOK! THREE MORE MUMMIES!
THAT'S NOT ALL!
IT WOULD APPEAR THIS WAS ONCE A CELL! BUT WAS IT FOR PRISONERS OR GUINEA PIGS!
HORRIBLE! FOR WHATEVER REASON THIS CHAMBER WAS SEALED OFF, THESE BEINGS WERE TRAPPED IN HERE!

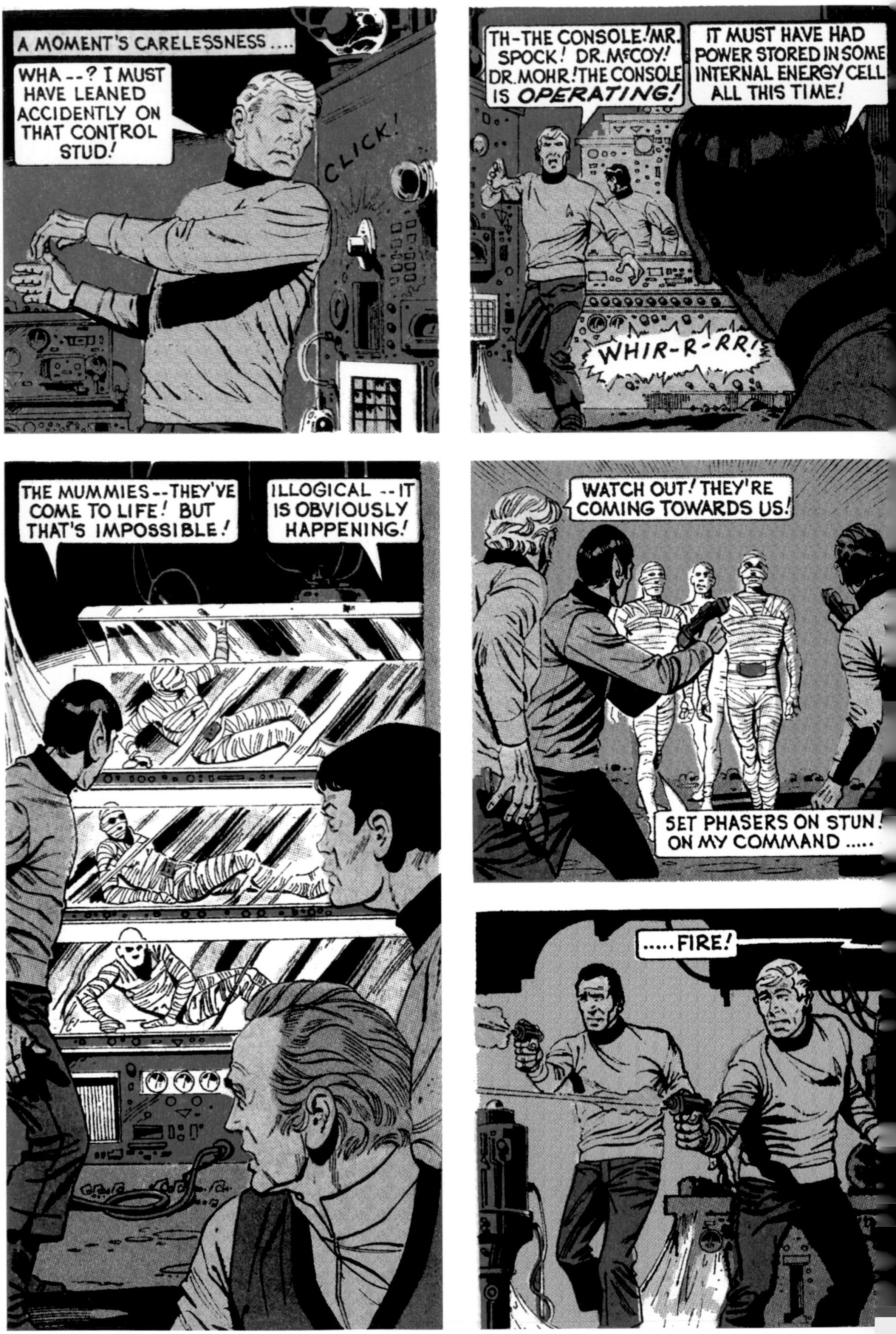
A MOMENT'S CARELESSNESS ....
WHA --? I MUST HAVE LEANED ACCIDENTLY ON THAT CONTROL STUD!
CLICK!
TH-THE CONSOLE! MR. SPOCK! DR. McCOY! DR. MOHR! THE CONSOLE IS OPERATING!
IT MUST HAVE HAD POWER STORED IN SOME INTERNAL ENERGY CELL ALL THIS TIME!
WHIR-R-RR!
THE MUMMIES--THEY'VE COME TO LIFE! BUT THAT'S IMPOSSIBLE!
ILLOGICAL --IT IS OBVIOUSLY HAPPENING!
WATCH OUT! THEY'RE COMING TOWARDS US!
SET PHASERS ON STUN! ON MY COMMAND .....
.....FIRE!

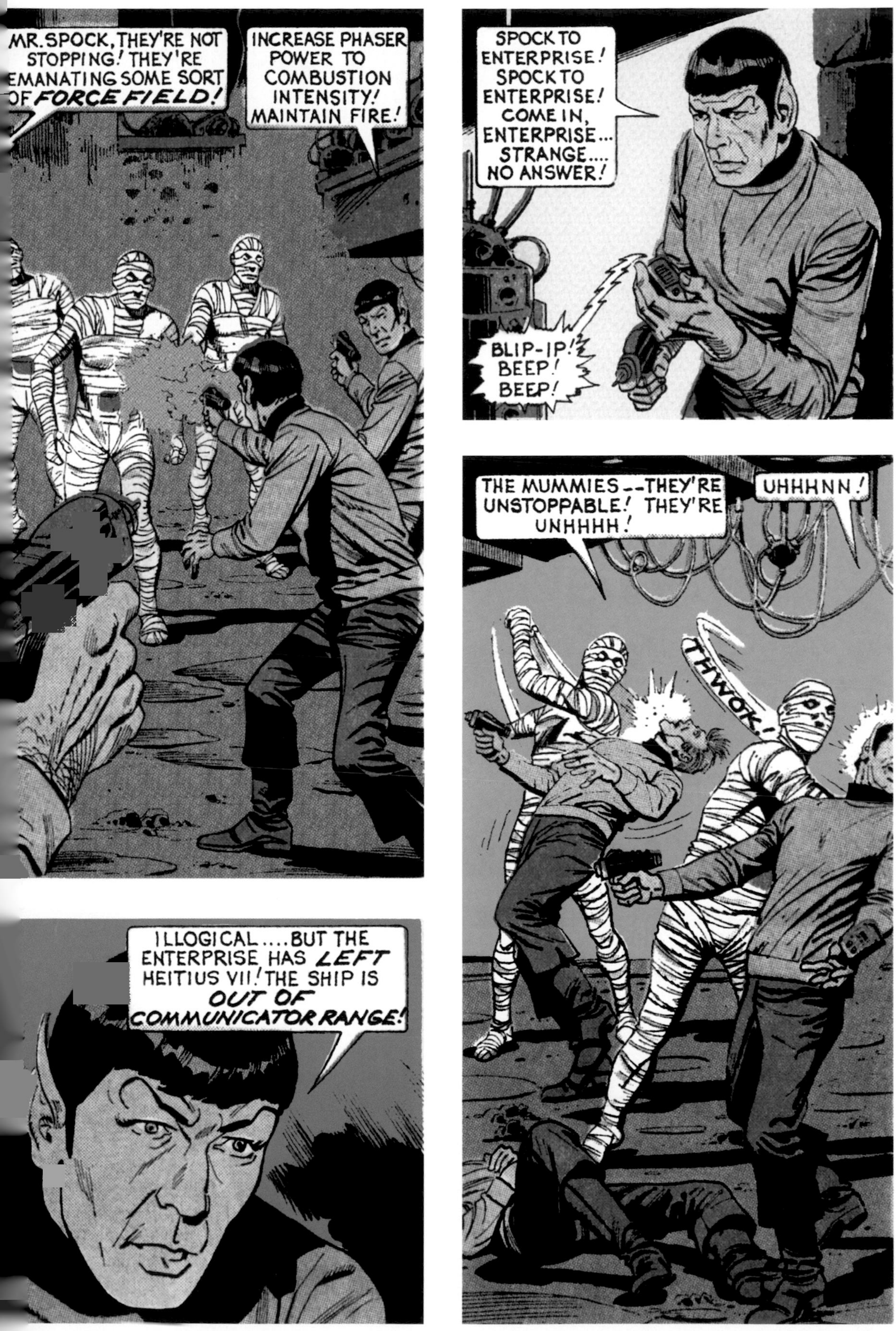

MR. SPOCK, THEY'RE NOT STOPPING! THEY'RE EMANATING SOME SORT OF FORCE FIELD!
INCREASE PHASER POWER TO COMBUSTION INTENSITY! MAINTAIN FIRE!
SPOCK TO ENTERPRISE! SPOCK TO ENTERPRISE! COME IN, ENTERPRISE... STRANGE.... NO ANSWER!
BLIP-IP! BEEP! BEEP!
ILLOGICAL.... BUT THE ENTERPRISE HAS LEFT HEITIUS VII! THE SHIP IS OUT OF COMMUNICATOR RANGE!
THE MUMMIES--THEY'RE UNSTOPPABLE! THEY'RE UNHHHH!
UHHHNN!
THWOK!

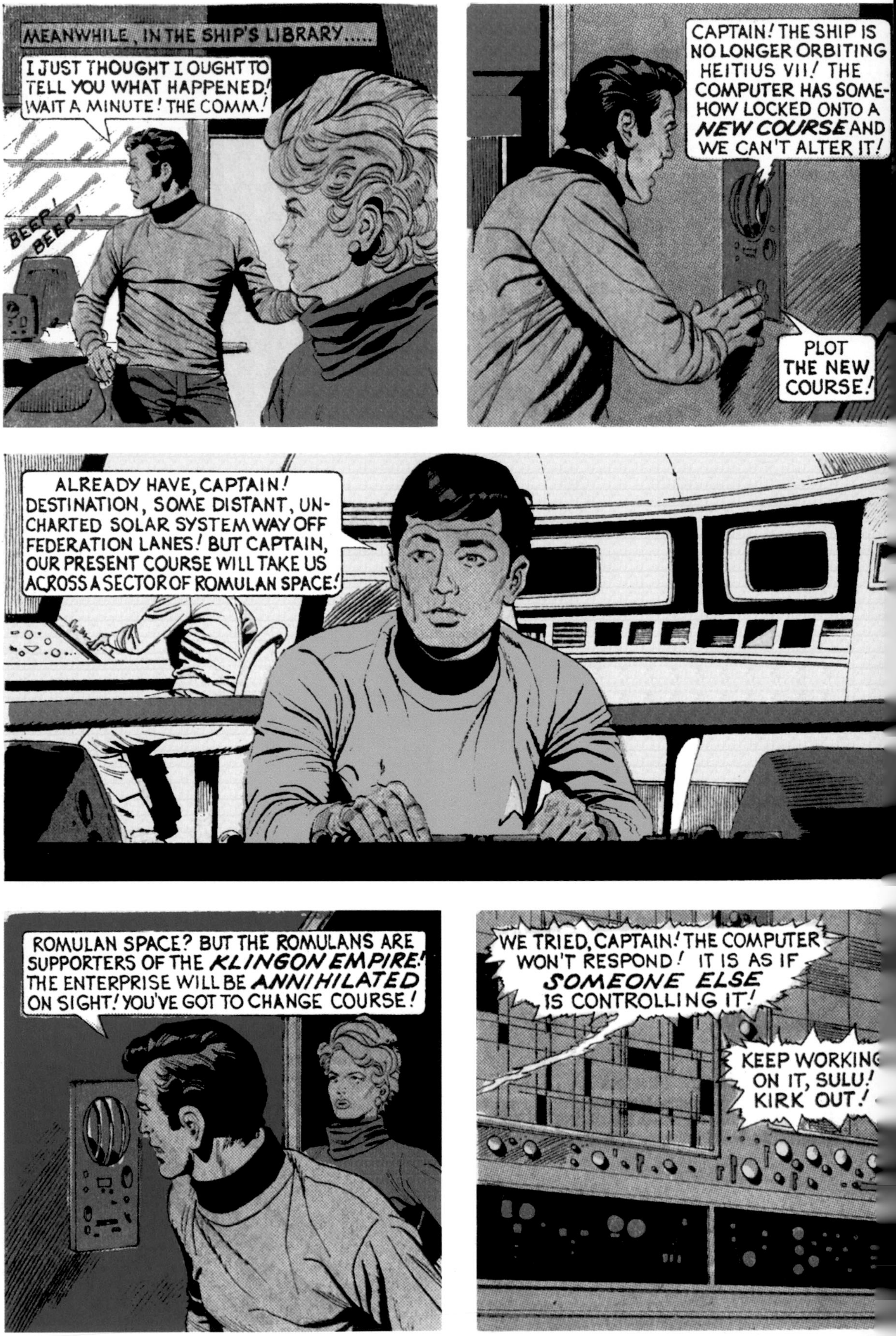
MEANWHILE, IN THE SHIP'S LIBRARY....
I JUST THOUGHT I OUGHT TO TELL YOU WHAT HAPPENED! WAIT A MINUTE! THE COMM!
BEEP! BEEP!
CAPTAIN! THE SHIP IS NO LONGER ORBITING HEITIUS VII! THE COMPUTER HAS SOMEHOW LOCKED ONTO A NEW COURSE AND WE CAN'T ALTER IT!
PLOT THE NEW COURSE!
ALREADY HAVE, CAPTAIN! DESTINATION, SOME DISTANT, UNCHARTED SOLAR SYSTEM WAY OFF FEDERATION LANES! BUT CAPTAIN, OUR PRESENT COURSE WILL TAKE US ACROSS A SECTOR OF ROMULAN SPACE!
ROMULAN SPACE? BUT THE ROMULANS ARE SUPPORTERS OF THE KLINGON EMPIRE! THE ENTERPRISE WILL BE ANNIHILATED ON SIGHT! YOU'VE GOT TO CHANGE COURSE!
WE TRIED, CAPTAIN! THE COMPUTER WON'T RESPOND! IT IS AS IF SOMEONE ELSE IS CONTROLLING IT!
KEEP WORKING ON IT, SULU! KIRK OUT!

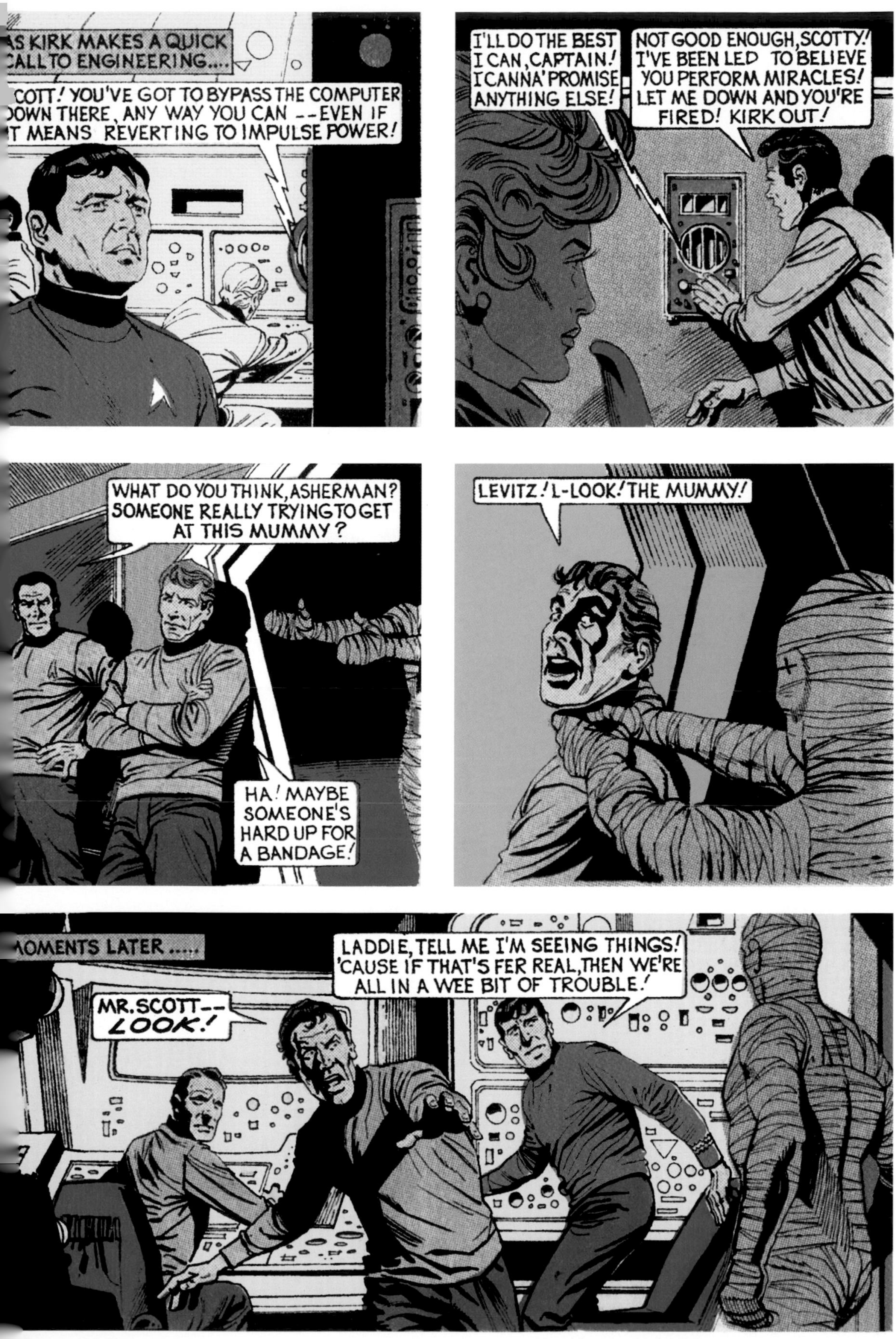
AS KIRK MAKES A QUICK CALL TO ENGINEERING....
COTT! YOU'VE GOT TO BYPASS THE COMPUTER DOWN THERE, ANY WAY YOU CAN --EVEN IF IT MEANS REVERTING TO IMPULSE POWER!
I'LL DO THE BEST I CAN, CAPTAIN! I CANNA' PROMISE ANYTHING ELSE!
NOT GOOD ENOUGH, SCOTTY! I'VE BEEN LED TO BELIEVE YOU PERFORM MIRACLES! LET ME DOWN AND YOU'RE FIRED! KIRK OUT!
WHAT DO YOU THINK, ASHERMAN? SOMEONE REALLY TRYING TO GET AT THIS MUMMY?
HA! MAYBE SOMEONE'S HARD UP FOR A BANDAGE!
LEVITZ! L-LOOK! THE MUMMY!
MOMENTS LATER .....
MR. SCOTT-- LOOK!
LADDIE, TELL ME I'M SEEING THINGS! 'CAUSE IF THAT'S FER REAL, THEN WE'RE ALL IN A WEE BIT OF TROUBLE!

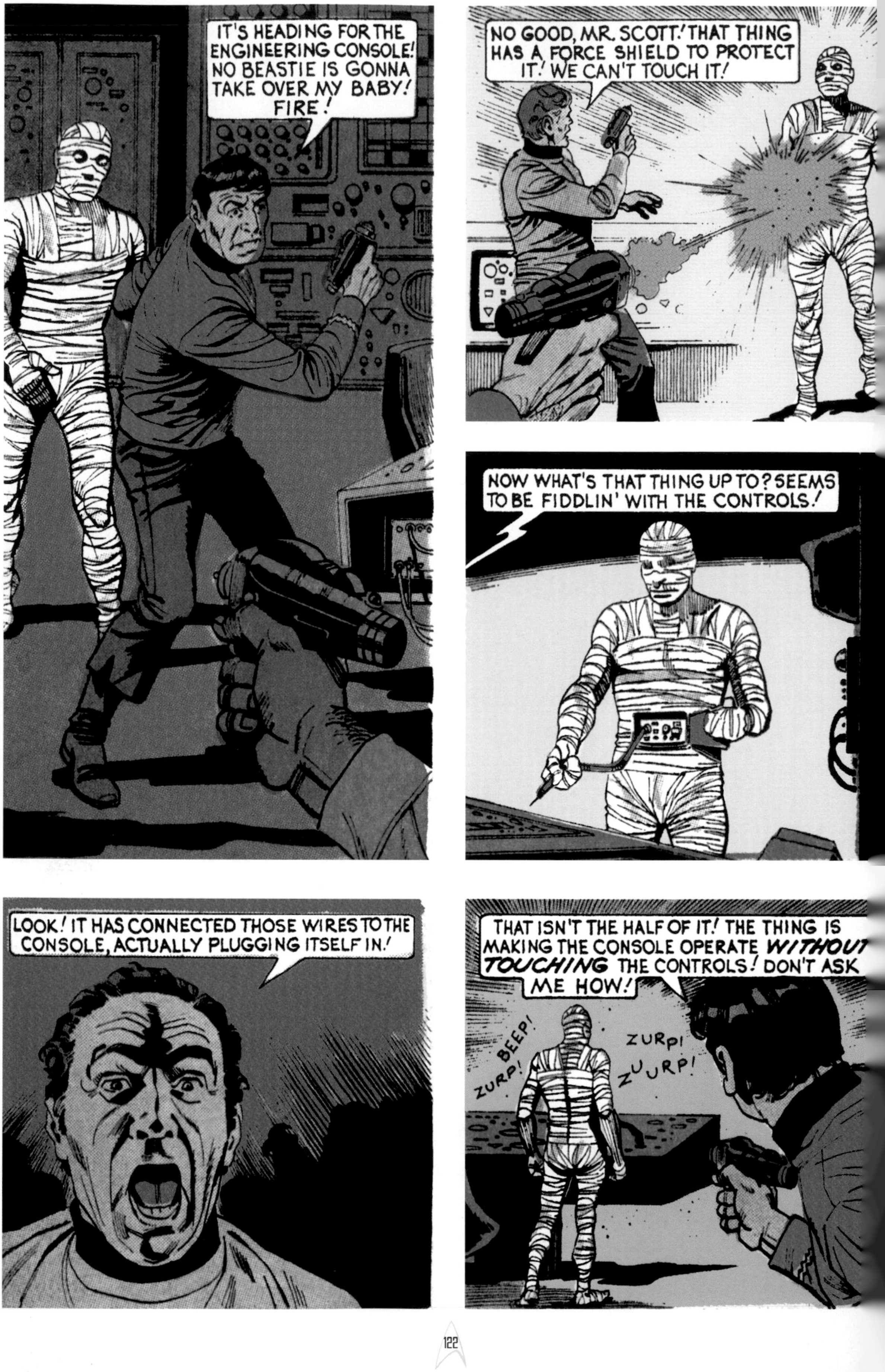
IT'S HEADING FOR THE ENGINEERING CONSOLE! NO BEASTIE IS GONNA TAKE OVER MY BABY! FIRE!
NO GOOD, MR. SCOTT! THAT THING HAS A FORCE SHIELD TO PROTECT IT! WE CAN'T TOUCH IT!
NOW WHAT'S THAT THING UP TO? SEEMS TO BE FIDDLIN' WITH THE CONTROLS!
LOOK! IT HAS CONNECTED THOSE WIRES TO THE CONSOLE, ACTUALLY PLUGGING ITSELF IN!
THAT ISN'T THE HALF OF IT! THE THING IS MAKING THE CONSOLE OPERATE WITHOUT TOUCHING THE CONTROLS! DON'T ASK ME HOW!
ZURP! BEEP!
ZURP! ZUURP!

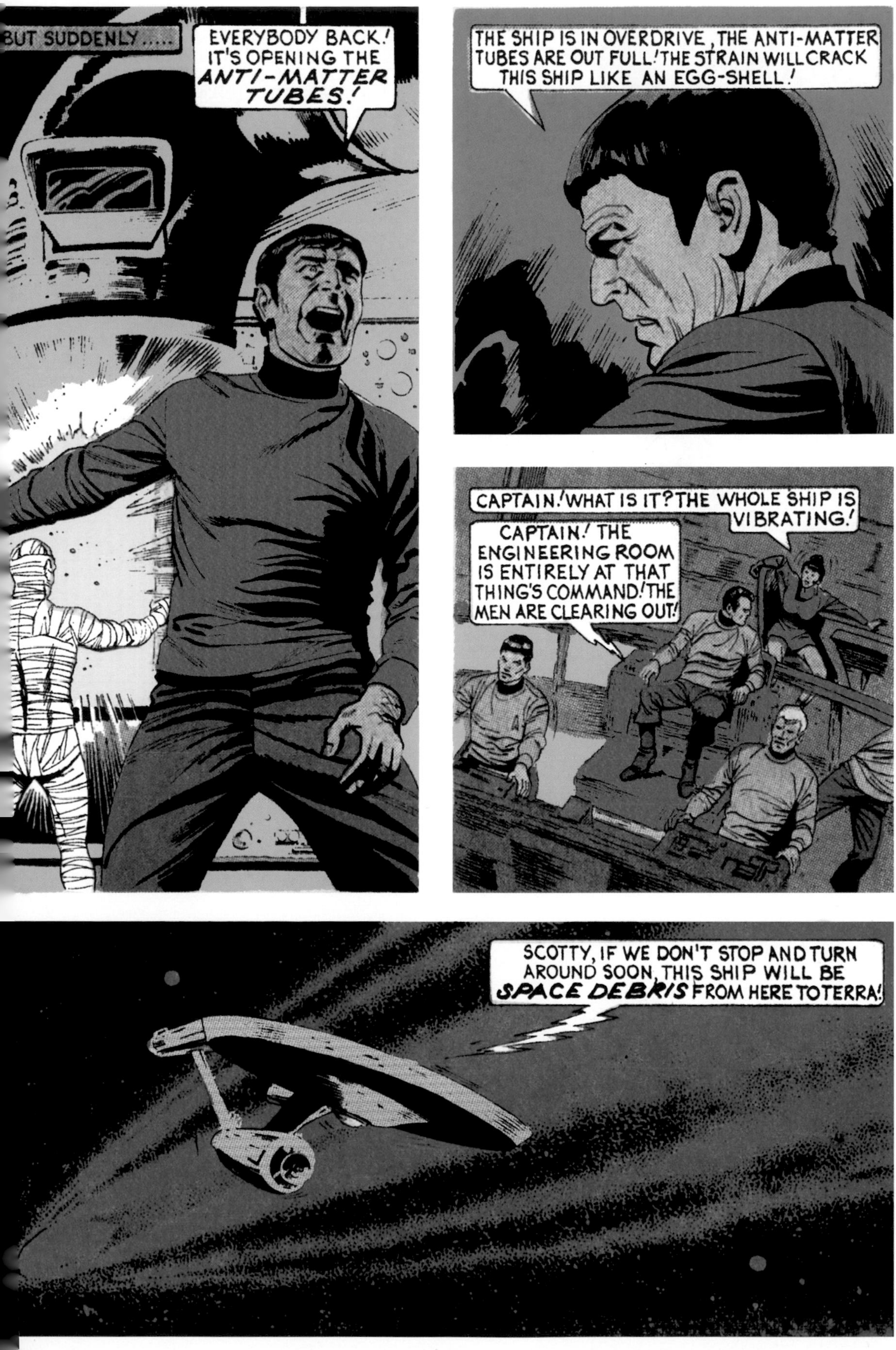
BUT SUDDENLY.....
EVERYBODY BACK! IT'S OPENING THE ANTI-MATTER TUBES!
THE SHIP IS IN OVERDRIVE, THE ANTI-MATTER TUBES ARE OUT FULL! THE STRAIN WILL CRACK THIS SHIP LIKE AN EGG-SHELL!
CAPTAIN! WHAT IS IT? THE WHOLE SHIP IS VIBRATING!
CAPTAIN! THE ENGINEERING ROOM IS ENTIRELY AT THAT THING'S COMMAND! THE MEN ARE CLEARING OUT!
SCOTTY, IF WE DON'T STOP AND TURN AROUND SOON, THIS SHIP WILL BE SPACE DEBRIS FROM HERE TO TERRA!

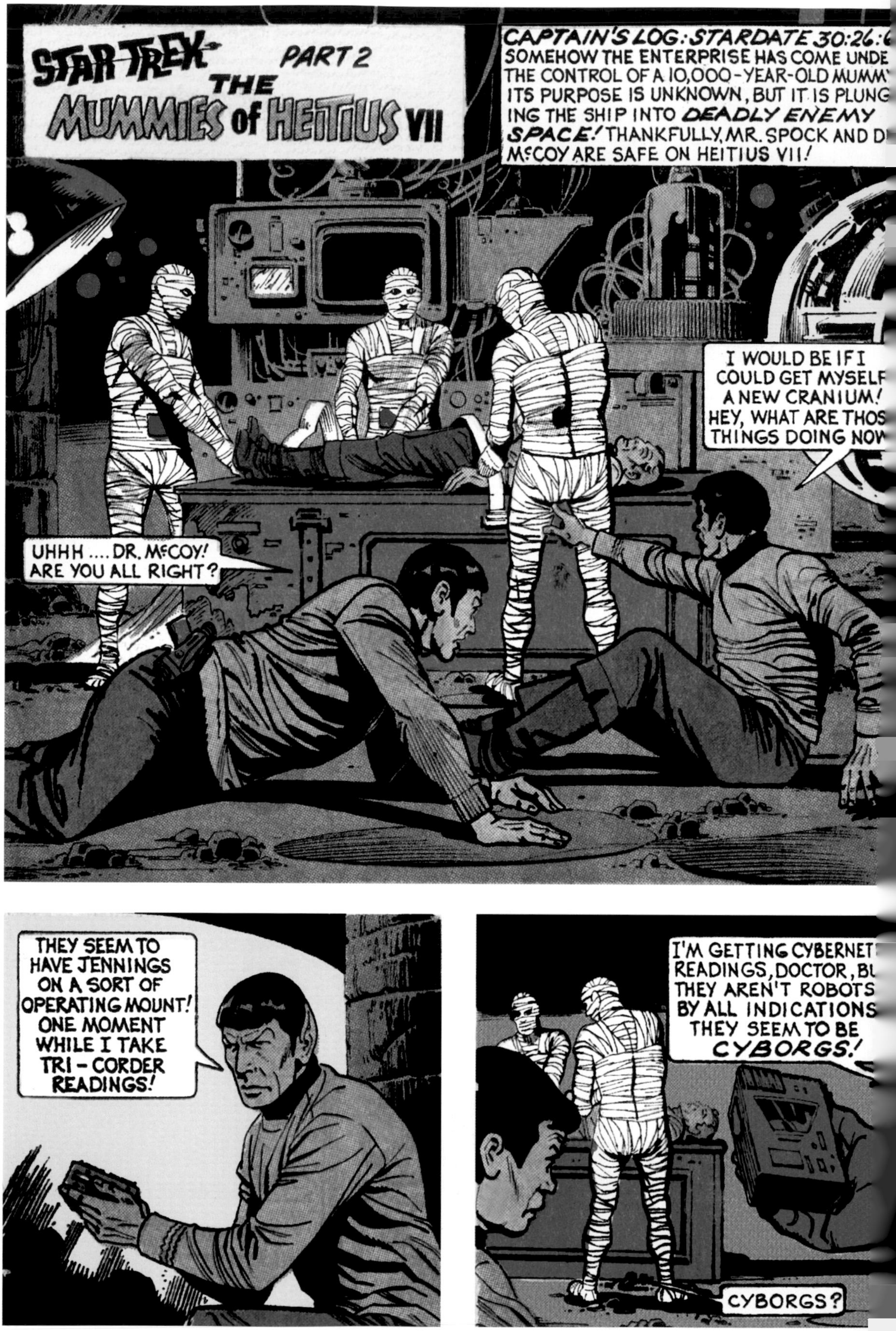

STAR TREK PART 2 THE MUMMIES of HEITIUS VII
CAPTAIN'S LOG: STARDATE 30:26:6 SOMEHOW THE ENTERPRISE HAS COME UNDE THE CONTROL OF A 10,000-YEAR-OLD MUMM ITS PURPOSE IS UNKNOWN, BUT IT IS PLUNG ING THE SHIP INTO DEADLY ENEMY SPACE! THANKFULLY, MR. SPOCK AND D McCOY ARE SAFE ON HEITIUS VII!
UHHH .... DR. McCOY! ARE YOU ALL RIGHT?
I WOULD BE IF I COULD GET MYSELF A NEW CRANIUM! HEY, WHAT ARE THOS THINGS DOING NOW
THEY SEEM TO HAVE JENNINGS ON A SORT OF OPERATING MOUNT! ONE MOMENT WHILE I TAKE TRI-CORDER READINGS!
I'M GETTING CYBERNET READINGS, DOCTOR, BU THEY AREN'T ROBOTS BY ALL INDICATIONS THEY SEEM TO BE CYBORGS!
CYBORGS?

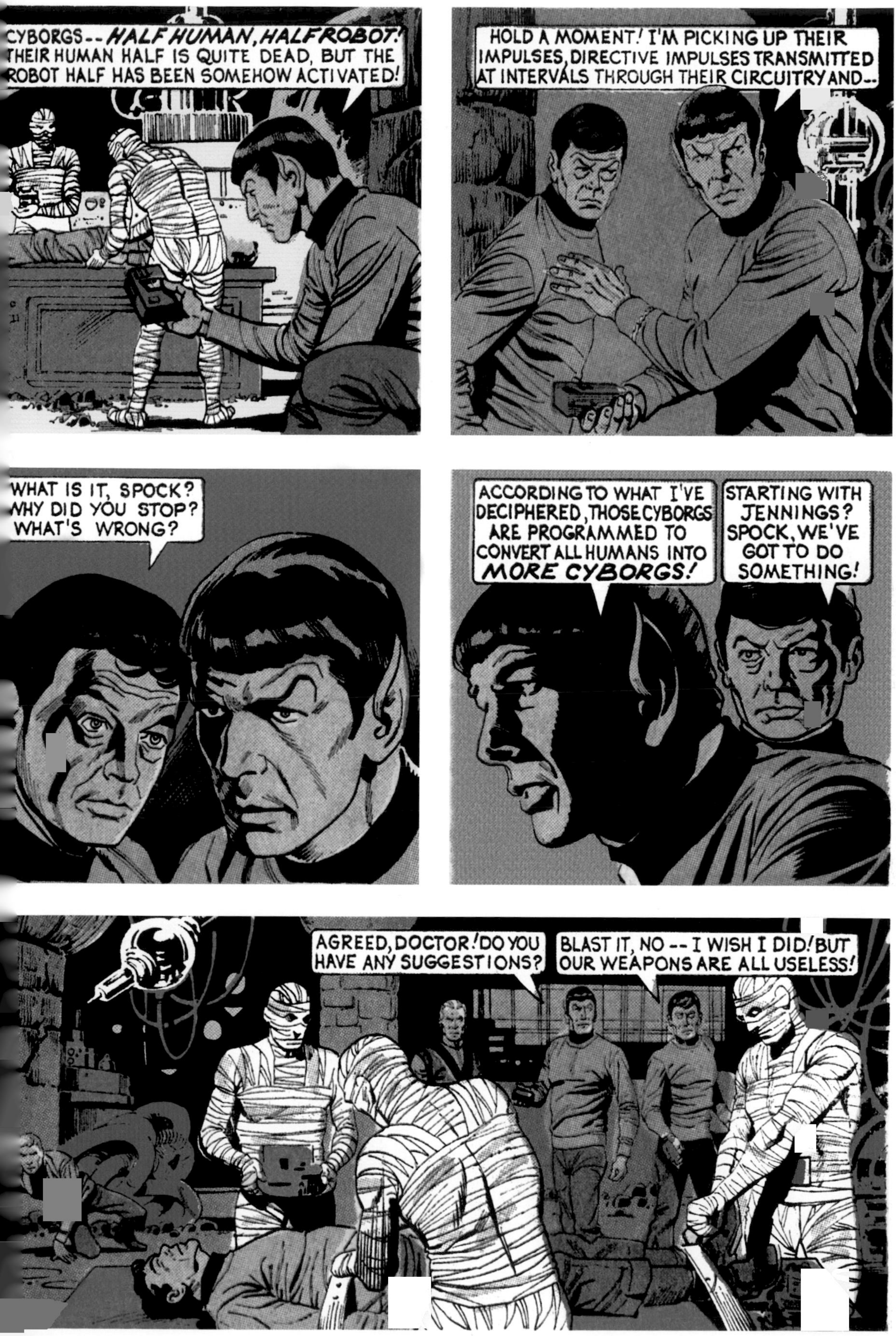
CYBORGS-- HALF HUMAN, HALF ROBOT! THEIR HUMAN HALF IS QUITE DEAD, BUT THE ROBOT HALF HAS BEEN SOMEHOW ACTIVATED!
HOLD A MOMENT! I'M PICKING UP THEIR IMPULSES, DIRECTIVE IMPULSES TRANSMITTED AT INTERVALS THROUGH THEIR CIRCUITRY AND--
WHAT IS IT, SPOCK? WHY DID YOU STOP? WHAT'S WRONG?
ACCORDING TO WHAT I'VE DECIPHERED, THOSE CYBORGS ARE PROGRAMMED TO CONVERT ALL HUMANS INTO MORE CYBORGS!
STARTING WITH JENNINGS? SPOCK, WE'VE GOT TO DO SOMETHING!
AGREED, DOCTOR! DO YOU HAVE ANY SUGGESTIONS?
BLAST IT, NO -- I WISH I DID! BUT OUR WEAPONS ARE ALL USELESS!

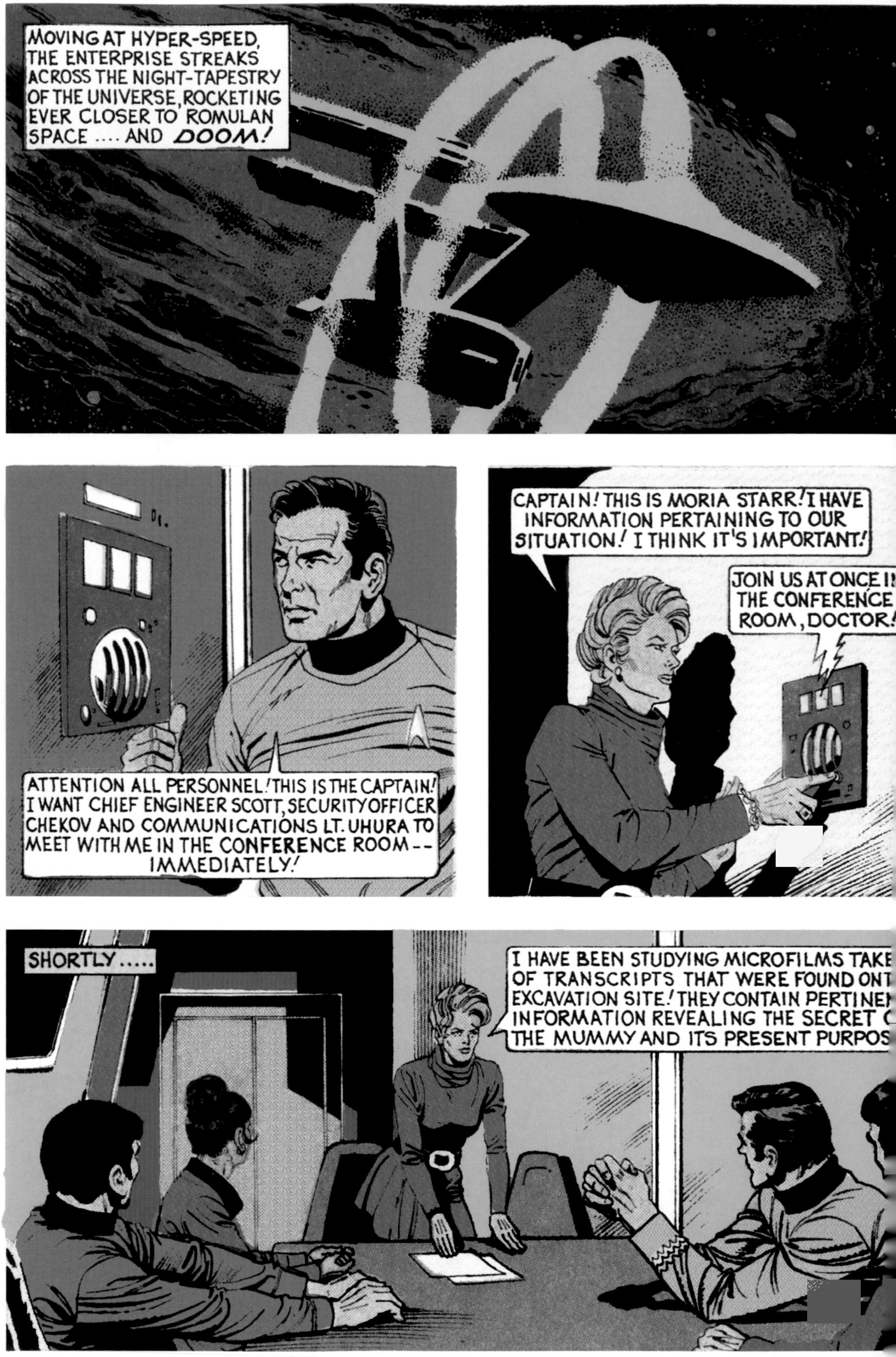

MOVING AT HYPER-SPEED, THE ENTERPRISE STREAKS ACROSS THE NIGHT-TAPESTRY OF THE UNIVERSE, ROCKETING EVER CLOSER TO ROMULAN SPACE .... AND DOOM!
ATTENTION ALL PERSONNEL! THIS IS THE CAPTAIN! I WANT CHIEF ENGINEER SCOTT, SECURITY OFFICER CHEKOV AND COMMUNICATIONS LT. UHURA TO MEET WITH ME IN THE CONFERENCE ROOM -- IMMEDIATELY!
CAPTAIN! THIS IS MORIA STARR! I HAVE INFORMATION PERTAINING TO OUR SITUATION! I THINK IT'S IMPORTANT!
JOIN US AT ONCE I
THE CONFERENCE
ROOM, DOCTOR!
SHORTLY .....
I HAVE BEEN STUDYING MICROFILMS TAKE
OF TRANSCRIPTS THAT WERE FOUND ONT
EXCAVATION SITE! THEY CONTAIN PERTINEN
INFORMATION REVEALING THE SECRET
THE MUMMY AND ITS PRESENT PURPOS

"AT THE TIME THESE MANUSCRIPTS WERE WRITTEN, HEITIUS VII WAS A DYING WORLD! THE PLANET'S RESOURCES HAD BEEN DRAINED BY OVERPOPULATION AND STRANGLED BY UN-CHECKED TECHNOLOGY! IT WAS ECOLOGICAL SUICIDE!"

"UPON THIS DESERT WORLD, ONE LAST STRONGHOLD OF LIFE STRUGGLED FOR EXISTENCE! BUT AL-THOUGH THE PLANET WAS DOOMED, THE PEOPLE HAD *OUTLAWED ALL TECHNOLOGY*, MAKING FLIGHT TO THE STARS HERESY!"

"THE SCIENCE MINISTRY HAD BECOME GRAVELY WORRIED, WHEN A NEW PROBLEM AROSE..."

THE KING IS DYING! WHAT WILL WE DO?

THE PEOPLE WILL GIVE WAY TO CHAOS! WE MUST ACT--TAKE THE INITIATIVE!

THE KING MUST LIVE --IF NOT IN REALITY, THEN IN MECHANICAL FANTASY! WE WILL CYBER-NETICALLY ALTER HIS BODY, CONVERTING HIM INTO A CYBORG!

BUT WILL HE APPROVE?

WE WILL DO IT -- WITH *OR* WITHOUT HIS APPROVAL!

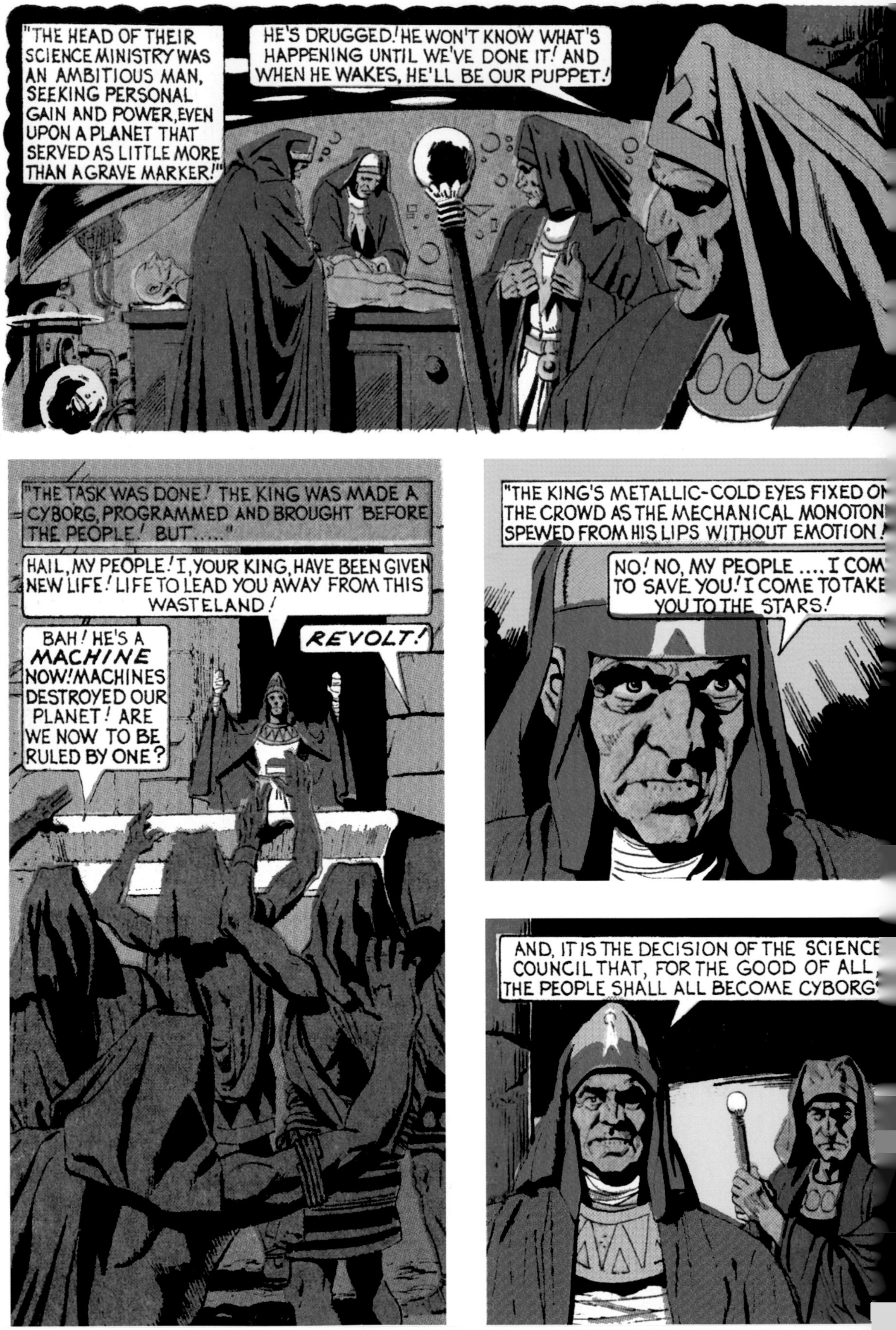
"THE HEAD OF THEIR SCIENCE MINISTRY WAS AN AMBITIOUS MAN, SEEKING PERSONAL GAIN AND POWER, EVEN UPON A PLANET THAT SERVED AS LITTLE MORE THAN A GRAVE MARKER!"
HE'S DRUGGED! HE WON'T KNOW WHAT'S HAPPENING UNTIL WE'VE DONE IT! AND WHEN HE WAKES, HE'LL BE OUR PUPPET!
"THE TASK WAS DONE! THE KING WAS MADE A CYBORG, PROGRAMMED AND BROUGHT BEFORE THE PEOPLE! BUT....."
HAIL, MY PEOPLE! I, YOUR KING, HAVE BEEN GIVEN NEW LIFE! LIFE TO LEAD YOU AWAY FROM THIS WASTELAND!
BAH! HE'S A MACHINE NOW! MACHINES DESTROYED OUR PLANET! ARE WE NOW TO BE RULED BY ONE?
REVOLT!
"THE KING'S METALLIC-COLD EYES FIXED ON THE CROWD AS THE MECHANICAL MONOTONE SPEWED FROM HIS LIPS WITHOUT EMOTION!
NO! NO, MY PEOPLE .... I COM TO SAVE YOU! I COME TO TAKE YOU TO THE STARS!
AND, IT IS THE DECISION OF THE SCIENCE COUNCIL THAT, FOR THE GOOD OF ALL, THE PEOPLE SHALL ALL BECOME CYBORG

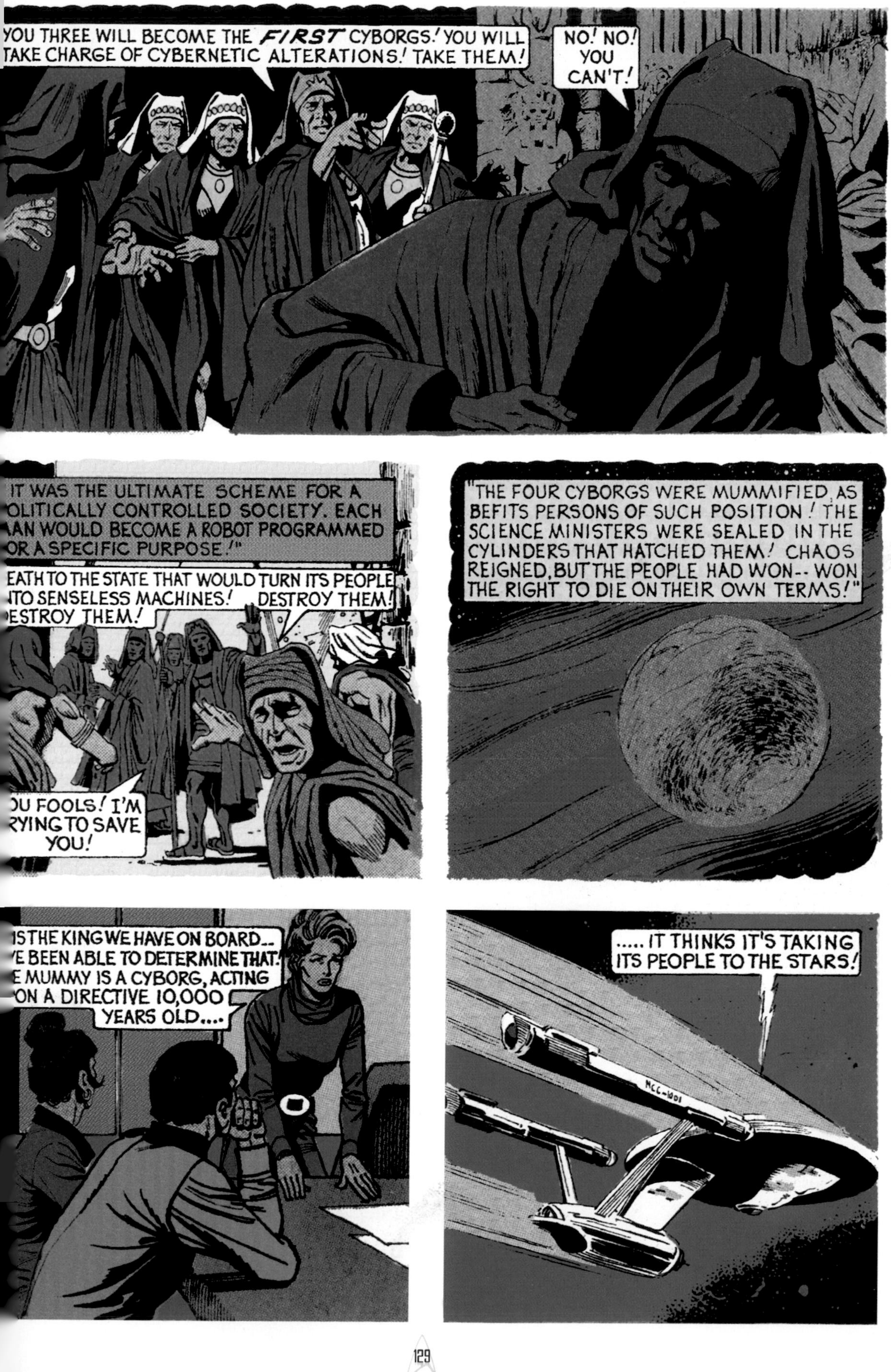
YOU THREE WILL BECOME THE FIRST CYBORGS! YOU WILL TAKE CHARGE OF CYBERNETIC ALTERATIONS! TAKE THEM!
NO! NO! YOU CAN'T!
IT WAS THE ULTIMATE SCHEME FOR A OLITICALLY CONTROLLED SOCIETY. EACH AN WOULD BECOME A ROBOT PROGRAMMED OR A SPECIFIC PURPOSE!"
EATH TO THE STATE THAT WOULD TURN ITS PEOPLE NTO SENSELESS MACHINES! ESTROY THEM!
DESTROY THEM!
OU FOOLS! I'M RYING TO SAVE YOU!
"THE FOUR CYBORGS WERE MUMMIFIED, AS BEFITS PERSONS OF SUCH POSITION! THE SCIENCE MINISTERS WERE SEALED IN THE CYLINDERS THAT HATCHED THEM! CHAOS REIGNED, BUT THE PEOPLE HAD WON-- WON THE RIGHT TO DIE ON THEIR OWN TERMS!"
IS THE KING WE HAVE ON BOARD.. E BEEN ABLE TO DETERMINE THAT! E MUMMY IS A CYBORG, ACTING ON A DIRECTIVE 10,000 YEARS OLD....
..... IT THINKS IT'S TAKING ITS PEOPLE TO THE STARS!
NCC-1701

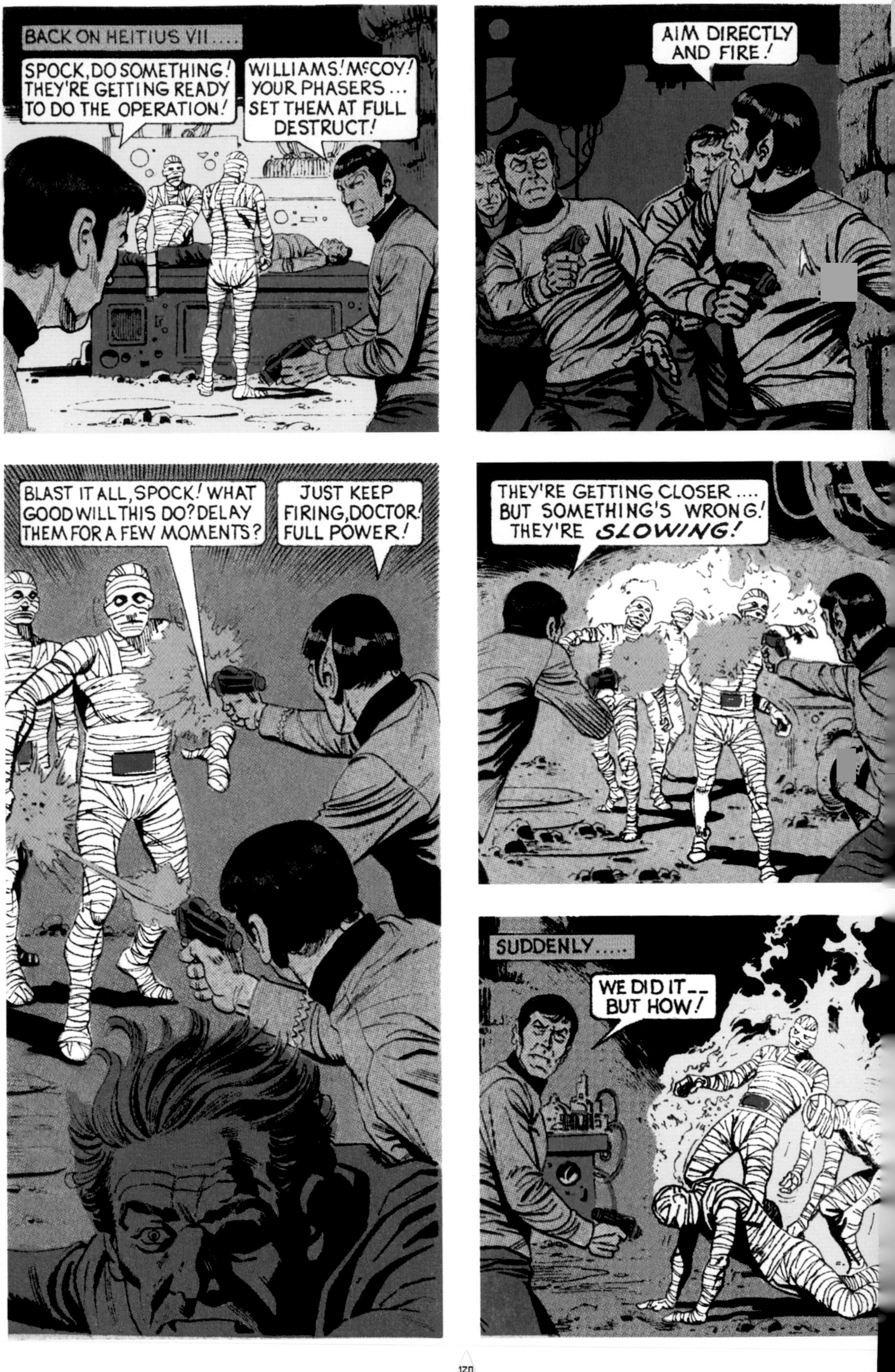
BACK ON HEITIUS VII....
SPOCK, DO SOMETHING! THEY'RE GETTING READY TO DO THE OPERATION!
WILLIAMS! McCOY! YOUR PHASERS... SET THEM AT FULL DESTRUCT!
AIM DIRECTLY AND FIRE!
BLAST IT ALL, SPOCK! WHAT GOOD WILL THIS DO? DELAY THEM FOR A FEW MOMENTS?
JUST KEEP FIRING, DOCTOR! FULL POWER!
THEY'RE GETTING CLOSER.... BUT SOMETHING'S WRONG! THEY'RE SLOWING!
SUDDENLY.....
WE DID IT-- BUT HOW!

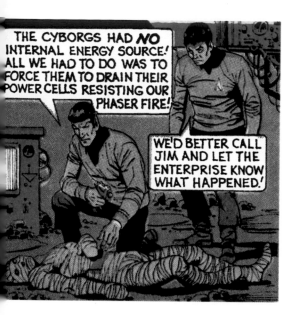

THE CYBORGS HAD *NO* INTERNAL ENERGY SOURCE! ALL WE HAD TO DO WAS TO FORCE THEM TO DRAIN THEIR POWER CELLS RESISTING OUR PHASER FIRE!

WE'D BETTER CALL JIM AND LET THE ENTERPRISE KNOW WHAT HAPPENED!

I WISH WE COULD, DOCTOR! THE ENTERPRISE HAS LEFT ORBIT! WE MUST THEREFORE ASSUME THAT THE *OTHER* MUMMY IS LOOSE -- WITH AN ALMOST *UNLIMITED* SUPPLY OF POWER!

AT THAT SAME MOMENT . . . . .

SCOTT, FOLLOW ME . . . . QUICKLY! I HAVE A PLAN TO STOP THE MUMMY, BUT I'LL NEED YOUR HELP!

YET, EVEN AS THE CAPTAIN SPEAKS, THE ENTERPRISE PLUMMETS TOWARDS DEADLY DANGER!

FEDERATION SHIP APPROACHING AT HYPERSPEED!

AND ON THE ROMULAN VESSEL . . . .

PREPARE AND ARM PHOTON TORPEDO DUCTS! SET FIRING INDICATOR AT THE EDGE OF OUR SECTOR ON THE INVADER'S COURSE!

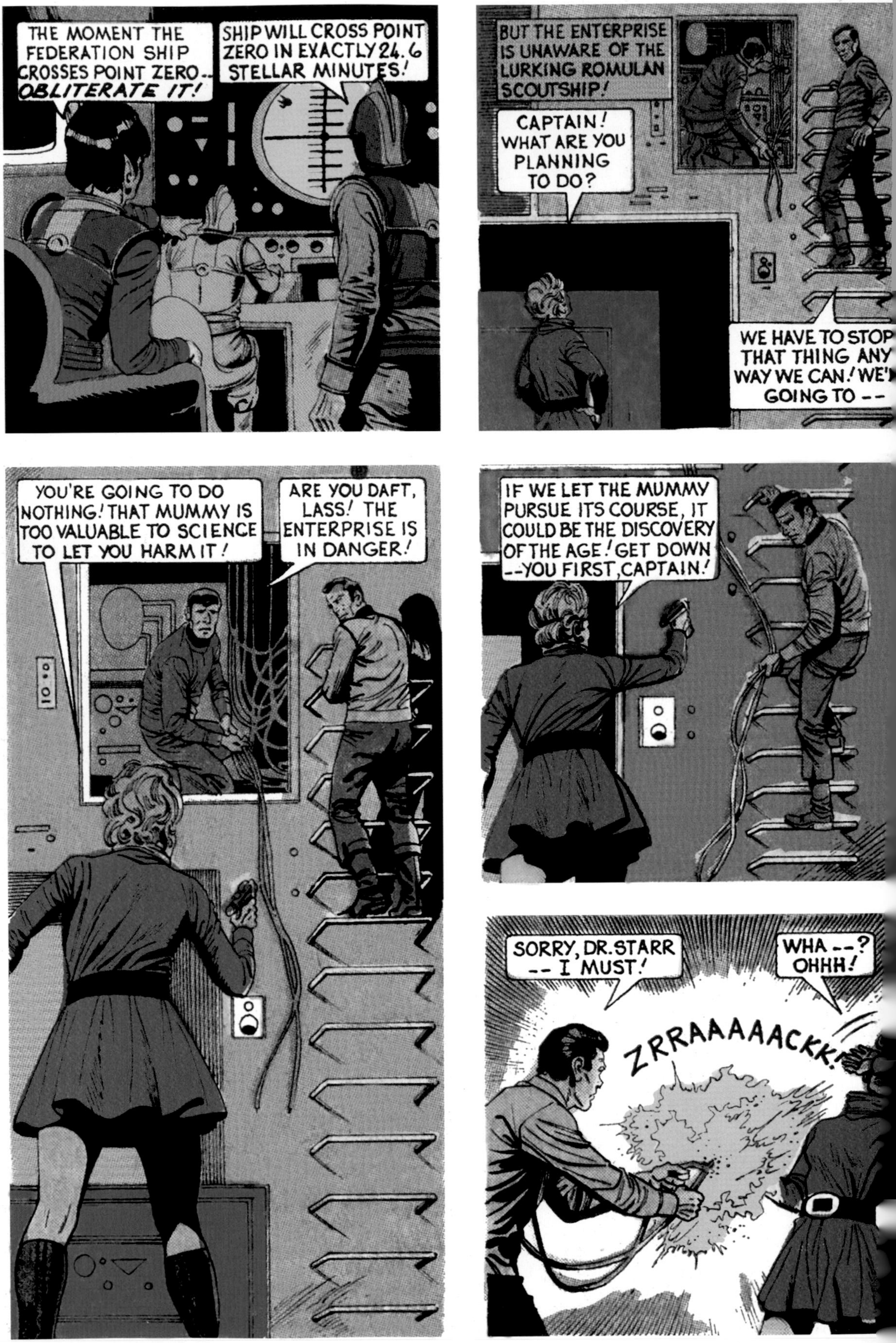
THE MOMENT THE FEDERATION SHIP CROSSES POINT ZERO -- *OBLITERATE IT!*
SHIP WILL CROSS POINT ZERO IN EXACTLY 24.6 STELLAR MINUTES!
BUT THE ENTERPRISE IS UNAWARE OF THE LURKING ROMULAN SCOUTSHIP!
CAPTAIN! WHAT ARE YOU PLANNING TO DO?
WE HAVE TO STOP THAT THING ANY WAY WE CAN! WE'
GOING TO --
YOU'RE GOING TO DO NOTHING! THAT MUMMY IS TOO VALUABLE TO SCIENCE TO LET YOU HARM IT!
ARE YOU DAFT, LASS! THE ENTERPRISE IS IN DANGER!
IF WE LET THE MUMMY PURSUE ITS COURSE, IT COULD BE THE DISCOVERY OF THE AGE! GET DOWN --YOU FIRST, CAPTAIN!
SORRY, DR. STARR -- I MUST!
WHA --? OHHH!
ZRRAAAAACKK!

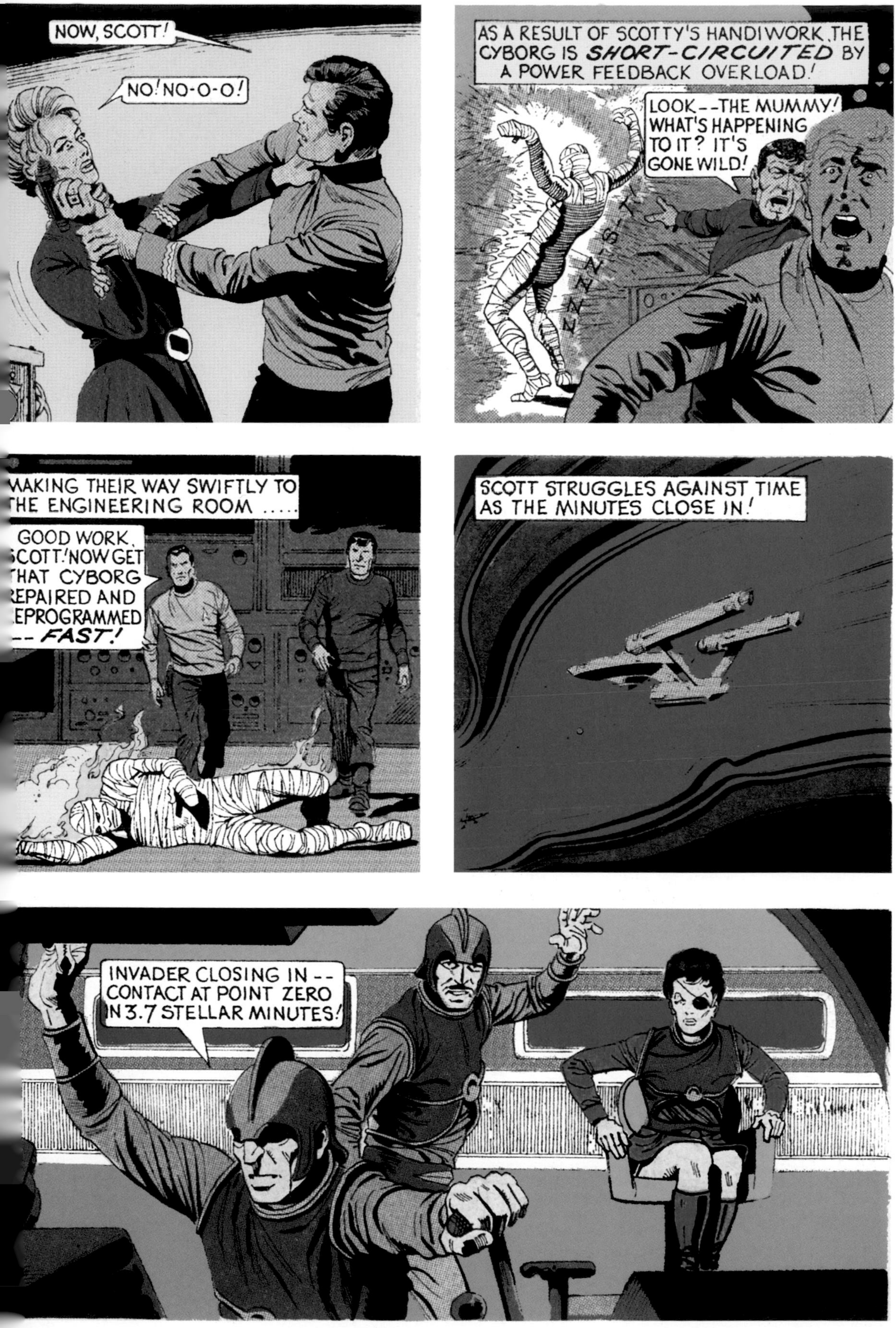
NOW, SCOTT!
NO! NO-O-O!
AS A RESULT OF SCOTTY'S HANDIWORK, THE CYBORG IS SHORT-CIRCUITED BY A POWER FEEDBACK OVERLOAD!
LOOK--THE MUMMY! WHAT'S HAPPENING TO IT? IT'S GONE WILD!
MAKING THEIR WAY SWIFTLY TO THE ENGINEERING ROOM .....
GOOD WORK, SCOTT! NOW GET THAT CYBORG REPAIRED AND REPROGRAMMED --FAST!
SCOTT STRUGGLES AGAINST TIME AS THE MINUTES CLOSE IN!
INVADER CLOSING IN-- CONTACT AT POINT ZERO IN 3.7 STELLAR MINUTES!

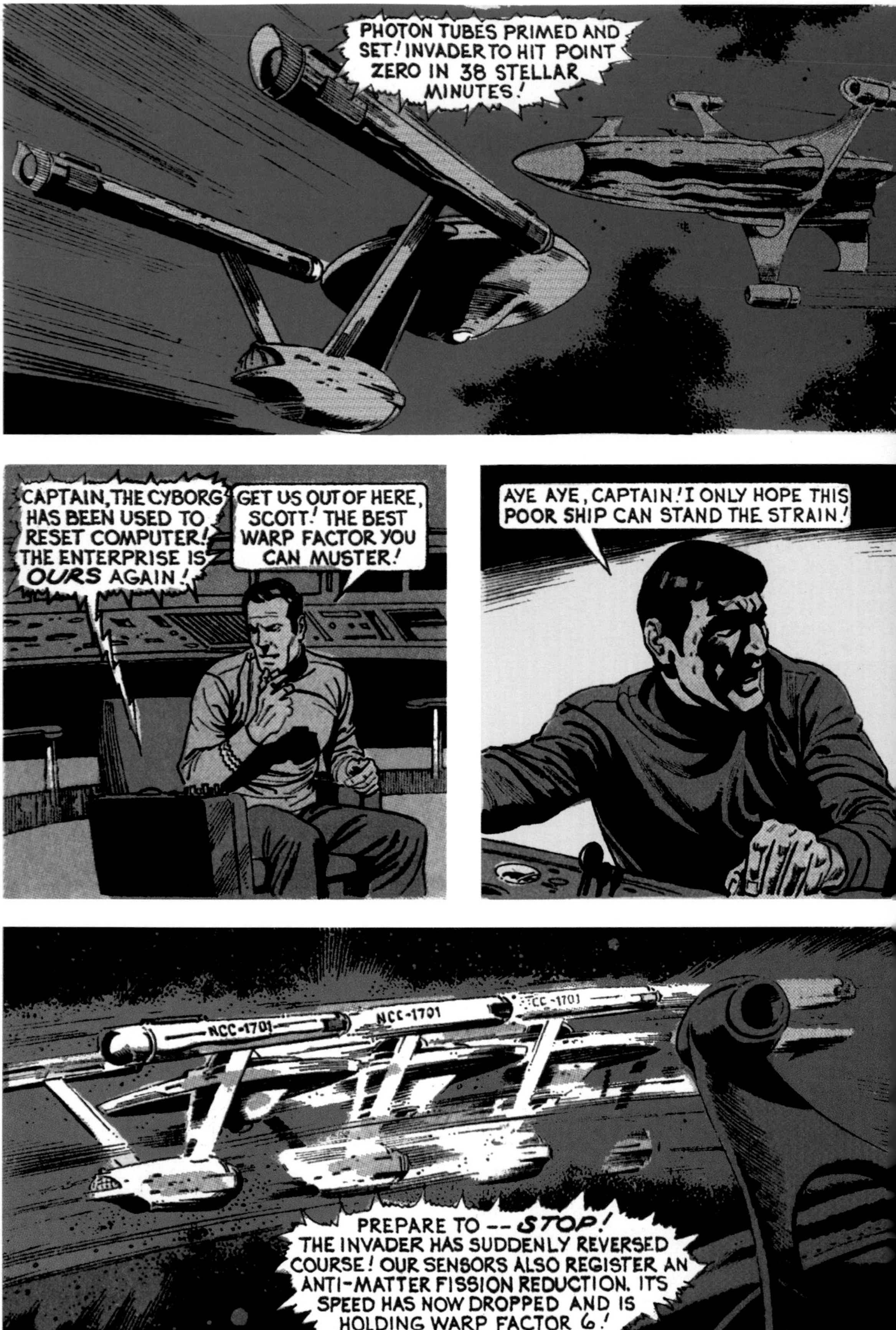
PHOTON TUBES PRIMED AND SET! INVADER TO HIT POINT ZERO IN 38 STELLAR MINUTES!
CAPTAIN, THE CYBORG HAS BEEN USED TO RESET COMPUTER! THE ENTERPRISE IS OURS AGAIN!
GET US OUT OF HERE, SCOTT! THE BEST WARP FACTOR YOU CAN MUSTER!
AYE AYE, CAPTAIN! I ONLY HOPE THIS POOR SHIP CAN STAND THE STRAIN!
NCC-1701
NCC-1701
CC-1701
PREPARE TO -- STOP! THE INVADER HAS SUDDENLY REVERSED COURSE! OUR SENSORS ALSO REGISTER AN ANTI-MATTER FISSION REDUCTION. ITS SPEED HAS NOW DROPPED AND IS HOLDING WARP FACTOR 6!

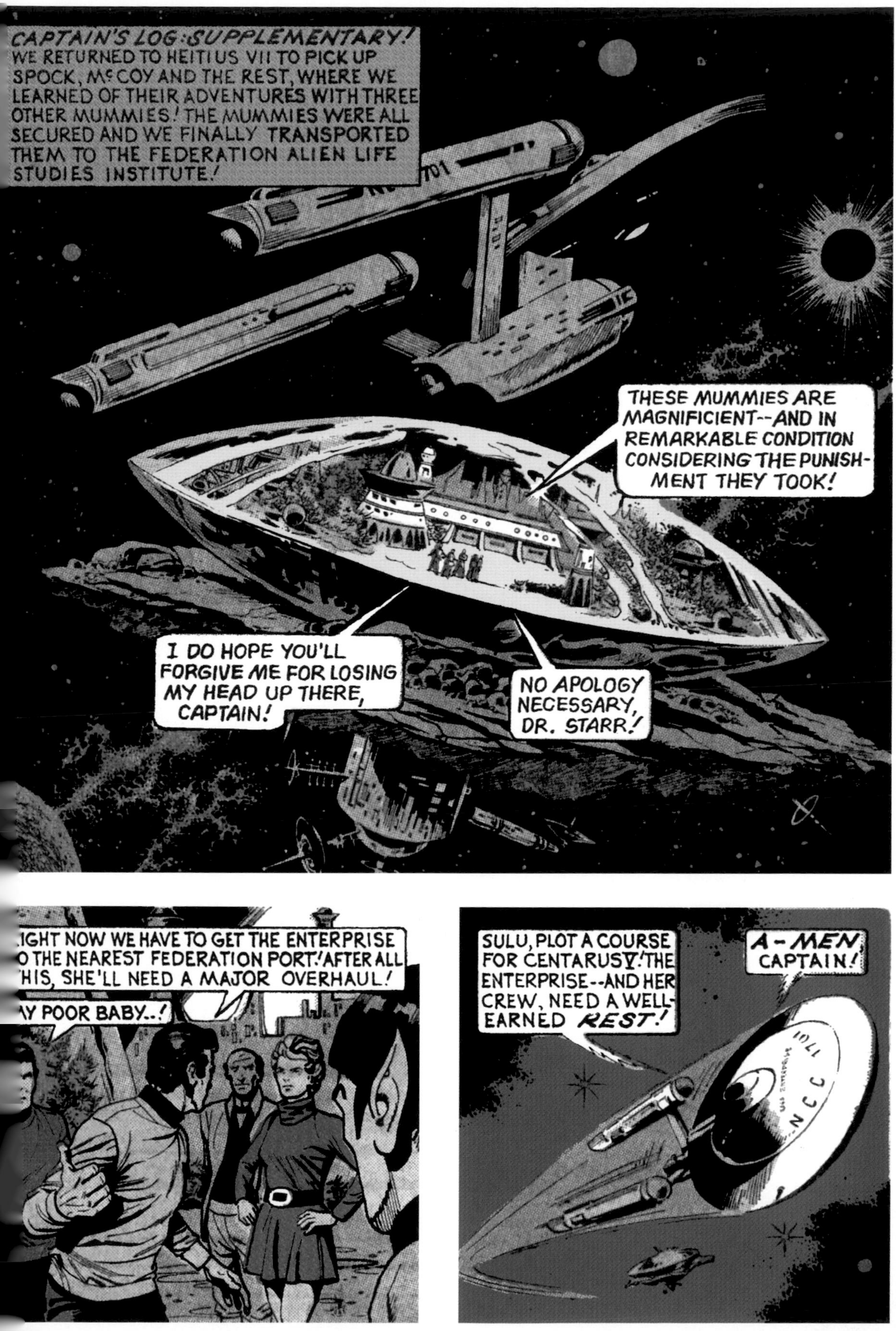
CAPTAIN'S LOG: SUPPLEMENTARY! WE RETURNED TO HEITIUS VII TO PICK UP SPOCK, McCOY AND THE REST, WHERE WE LEARNED OF THEIR ADVENTURES WITH THREE OTHER MUMMIES! THE MUMMIES WERE ALL SECURED AND WE FINALLY TRANSPORTED THEM TO THE FEDERATION ALIEN LIFE STUDIES INSTITUTE!
THESE MUMMIES ARE MAGNIFICIENT--AND IN REMARKABLE CONDITION CONSIDERING THE PUNISHMENT THEY TOOK!
I DO HOPE YOU'LL FORGIVE ME FOR LOSING MY HEAD UP THERE, CAPTAIN!
NO APOLOGY NECESSARY, DR. STARR!
IGHT NOW WE HAVE TO GET THE ENTERPRISE O THE NEAREST FEDERATION PORT! AFTER ALL HIS, SHE'LL NEED A MAJOR OVERHAUL!
Y POOR BABY..!
SULU, PLOT A COURSE FOR CENTARUS V! THE ENTERPRISE--AND HER CREW, NEED A WELL-EARNED REST!
A-MEN, CAPTAIN!

20c
STAR TREK
TRAPPED
IN SUPERSPACE,
THE ENTERPRISE
CREW IS RELENTLESSLY
HUNTED BY
A TERRIFYING WAR MACHINE!
© PARAMOUNT PICTURES CORPORATION

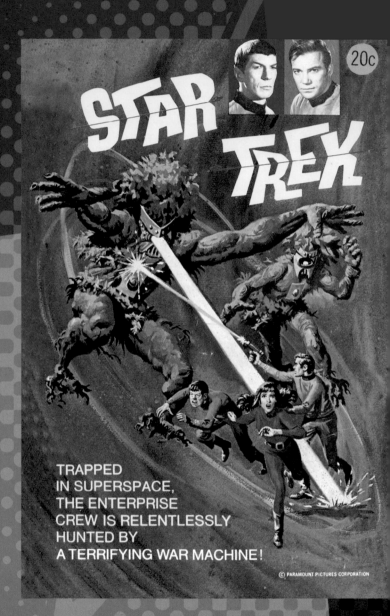

Chapter 6
Siege in Superspace

(Originally Published in January, 1974)

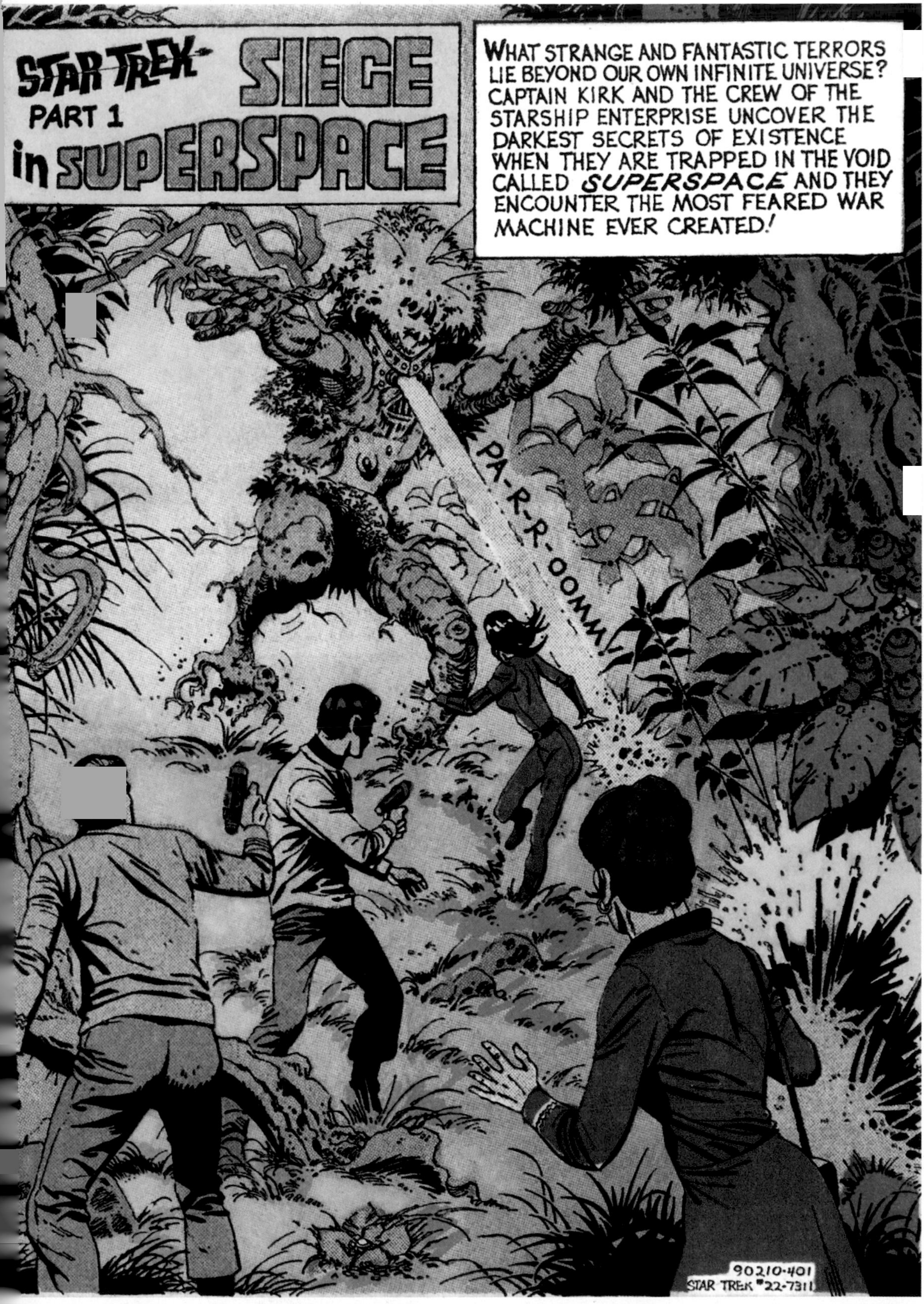
STAR TREK
PART 1
SIEGE in SUPERSPACE
WHAT STRANGE AND FANTASTIC TERRORS LIE BEYOND OUR OWN INFINITE UNIVERSE? CAPTAIN KIRK AND THE CREW OF THE STARSHIP ENTERPRISE UNCOVER THE DARKEST SECRETS OF EXISTENCE WHEN THEY ARE TRAPPED IN THE VOID CALLED SUPERSPACE AND THEY ENCOUNTER THE MOST FEARED WAR MACHINE EVER CREATED!
PA-R-R-OOMM!
90210-401
STAR TREK #22-7311

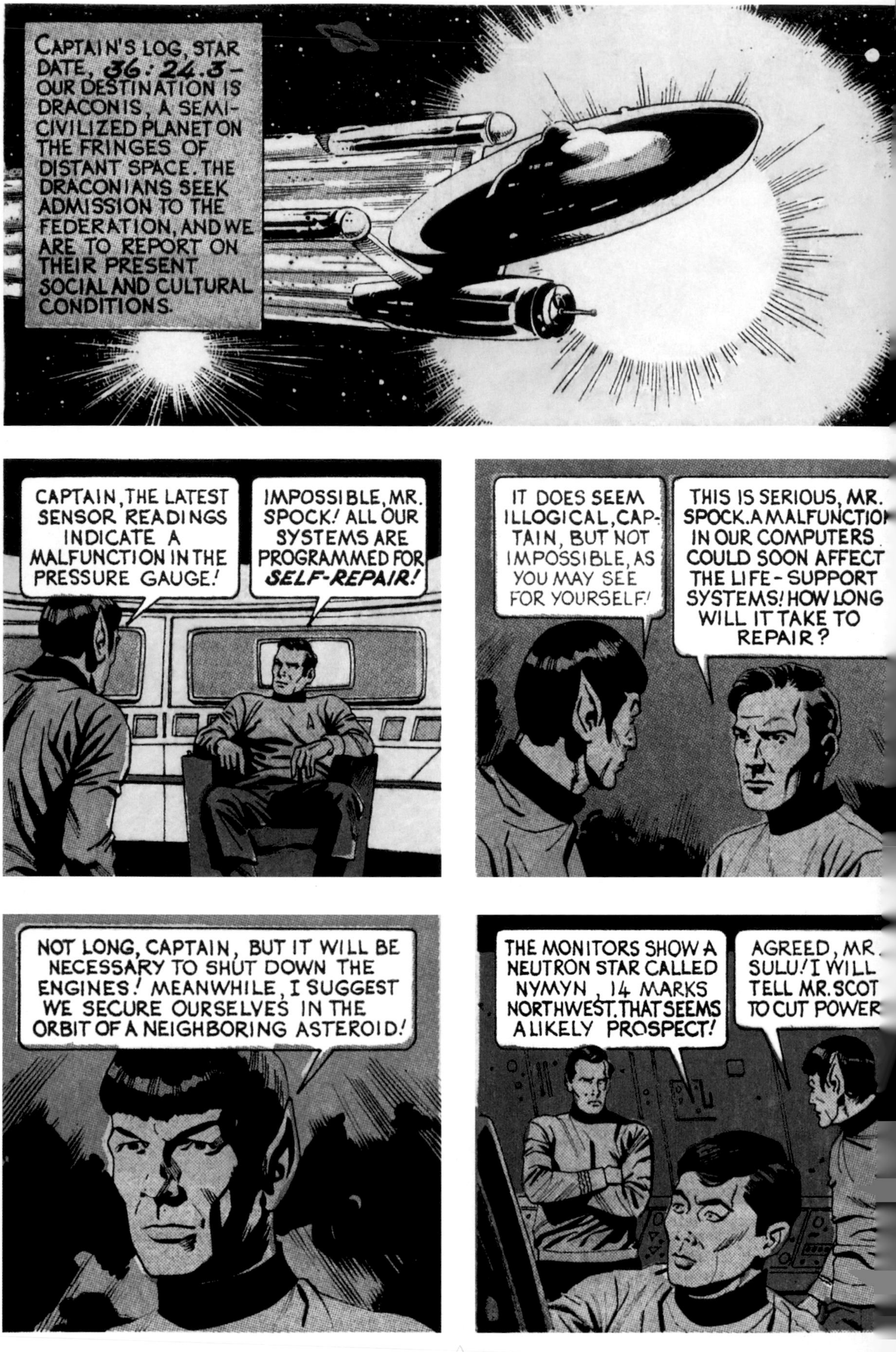
CAPTAIN'S LOG, STAR DATE, 36:24.3— OUR DESTINATION IS DRACONIS, A SEMI-CIVILIZED PLANET ON THE FRINGES OF DISTANT SPACE. THE DRACONIANS SEEK ADMISSION TO THE FEDERATION, AND WE ARE TO REPORT ON THEIR PRESENT SOCIAL AND CULTURAL CONDITIONS.
CAPTAIN, THE LATEST SENSOR READINGS INDICATE A MALFUNCTION IN THE PRESSURE GAUGE!
IMPOSSIBLE, MR. SPOCK! ALL OUR SYSTEMS ARE PROGRAMMED FOR SELF-REPAIR!
IT DOES SEEM ILLOGICAL, CAPTAIN, BUT NOT IMPOSSIBLE, AS YOU MAY SEE FOR YOURSELF!
THIS IS SERIOUS, MR. SPOCK. A MALFUNCTIO IN OUR COMPUTERS COULD SOON AFFECT THE LIFE-SUPPORT SYSTEMS! HOW LONG WILL IT TAKE TO REPAIR?
NOT LONG, CAPTAIN, BUT IT WILL BE NECESSARY TO SHUT DOWN THE ENGINES! MEANWHILE, I SUGGEST WE SECURE OURSELVES IN THE ORBIT OF A NEIGHBORING ASTEROID!
THE MONITORS SHOW A NEUTRON STAR CALLED NYMYN, 14 MARKS NORTHWEST. THAT SEEMS A LIKELY PROSPECT!
AGREED, MR. SULU! I WILL TELL MR. SCOT TO CUT POWER

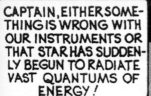

CAPTAIN, EITHER SOMETHING IS WRONG WITH OUR INSTRUMENTS OR THAT STAR HAS SUDDENLY BEGUN TO RADIATE VAST QUANTUMS OF ENERGY!

BOTH, MR. SCOTT! THE ENERGY IS OVERLOADING OUR COMPUTER SYSTEMS, CAUSING THEM TO MALFUNCTION!

WHERE IS THE ENERGY COMING FROM?

HAVE YOU EVER HEARD OF A *"BLACK HOLE"*, CAPTAIN?

I'M AFRAID NOT, MR. SPOCK! PLEASE EXPLAIN!

YOU SEE, CAPTAIN, GRAVITATIONAL PULL CONTINUES EVEN AFTER A STAR HAS BURNED ITSELF OUT. EVENTUALLY, THE DEAD STAR'S MASS SIMPLY COLLAPSES INTO OBLIVION. MY GUESS IS THAT NYMYN IS ABOUT TO UNDERGO GRAVITATIONAL COLLAPSE!

THEN WE'VE GOT TO GET THE ENTERPRISE OUT OF NYMYN'S RANGE BEFORE IT'S ---

TOO LATE, CAPTAIN! SHE'S OUT OF CONTROL!

THEN, AS THOUGH SQUEEZED THROUGH A KNOT-HOLE IN THE FABRIC OF SPACE, THE STAR AND ALL IN ITS WAKE.... DISAPPEAR!

SCIENTISTS SAY IN A "BLACK HOLE", TIME AND SPACE ARE INTERCHANGABLE: WAS IT A MOMENT OR AN ETERNITY THAT THE ENTERPRISE HOVERED IN THAT NAMELESS VOID BEFORE IT SLOWLY SOLIDIFIED ONCE MORE?

CAPTAIN, WE APPEAR TO BE ORBITING A PLANET OF CONSIDERABLE SIZE!

OUR NAVIGATIONAL MONITORS ARE USELESS, MR. SPOCK. ANY GUESSES AS TO WHERE WE ARE?

YES, CAPTAIN. I BELIEVE IT IS CALLED SUPERSPACE, THE ALL ENCOMPASSING ENTITY WHICH EXISTS BEYOND OUR OWN INFINITE UNIVERSE!

IN OTHER WORDS, MR. SPOCK, WE COULD BE *ANYWHERE*!

THAT SUMS IT UP QUITE EFFECTIVELY, CAPTAIN!

EVERYTHING INDICATES THAT THE ATMOSPHERE BELOW IS CONDUCIVE TO LIFE! I SUGGEST WE SEND DOWN A RECONNAISANCE PARTY!

EXCELLENT IDEA! YOU AND LT. UHURA COME WITH ME WHILE SCOTTY AND SPOCK MAKE ANY NECESSARY REPAIRS!

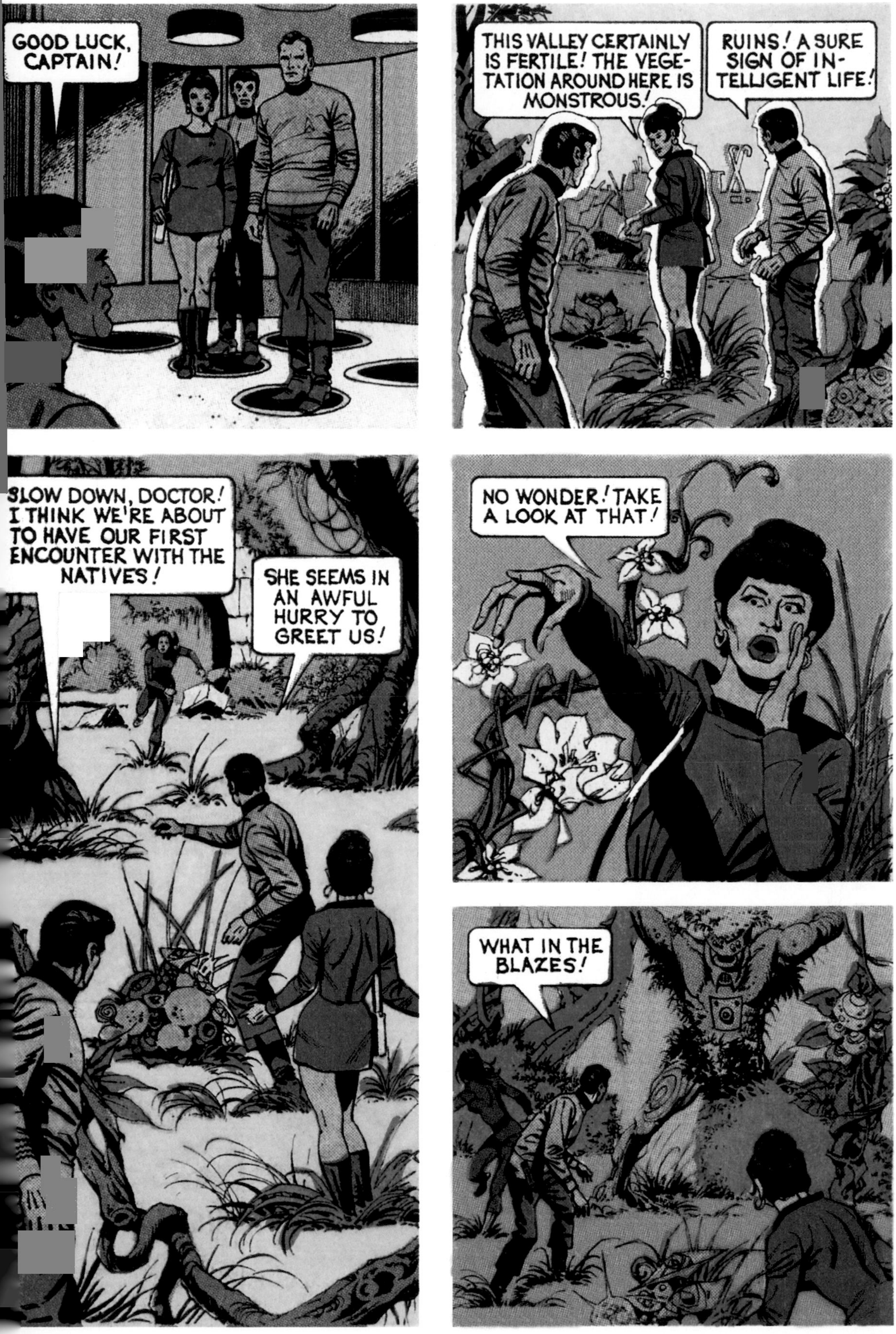
GOOD LUCK, CAPTAIN!
THIS VALLEY CERTAINLY IS FERTILE! THE VEGETATION AROUND HERE IS MONSTROUS!
RUINS! A SURE SIGN OF INTELLIGENT LIFE!
SLOW DOWN, DOCTOR! I THINK WE'RE ABOUT TO HAVE OUR FIRST ENCOUNTER WITH THE NATIVES!
SHE SEEMS IN AN AWFUL HURRY TO GREET US!
NO WONDER! TAKE A LOOK AT THAT!
WHAT IN THE BLAZES!

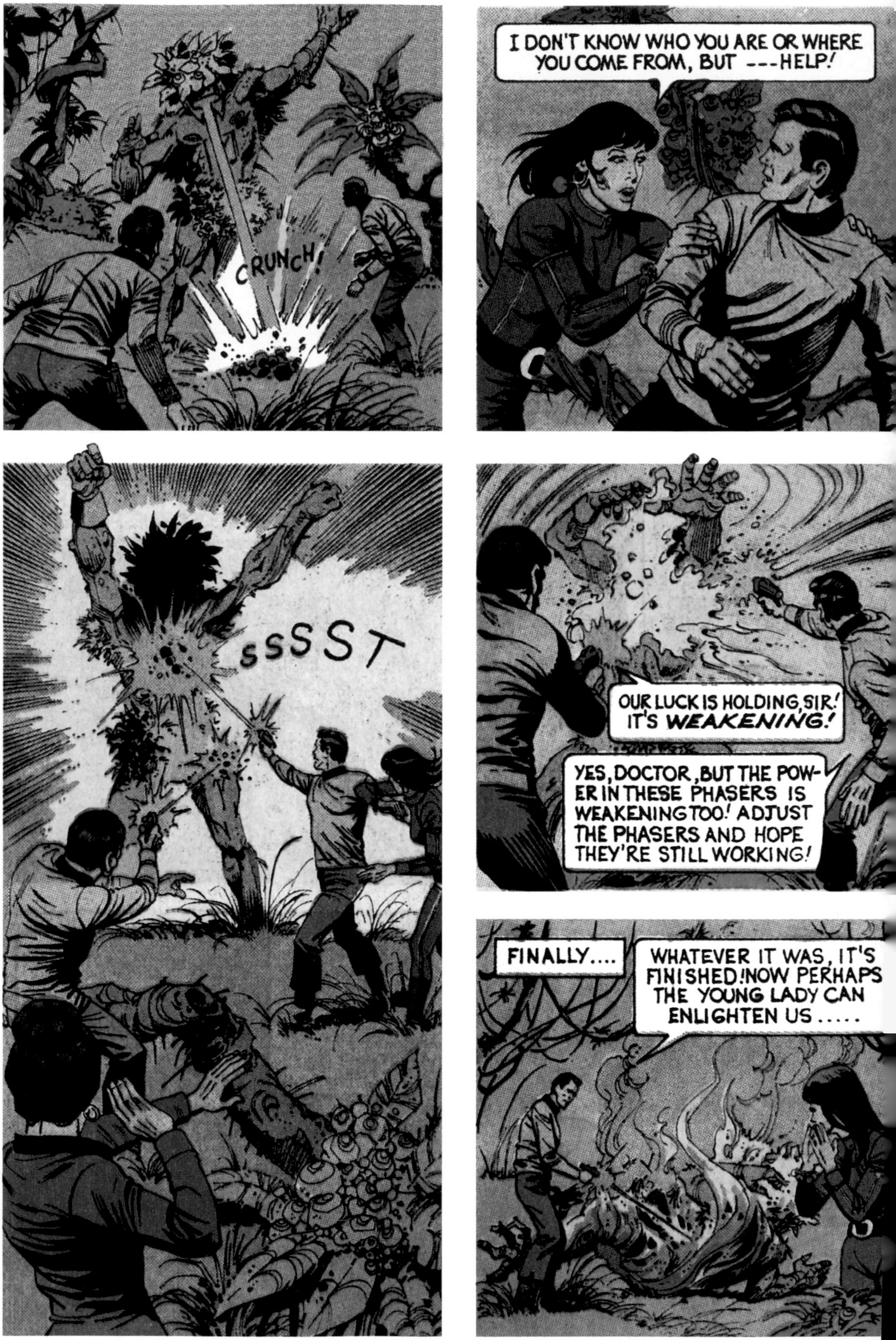
CRUNCH!
I DON'T KNOW WHO YOU ARE OR WHERE YOU COME FROM, BUT ---HELP!
SSSST
OUR LUCK IS HOLDING, SIR! IT'S WEAKENING!
YES, DOCTOR, BUT THE POWER IN THESE PHASERS IS WEAKENING TOO! ADJUST THE PHASERS AND HOPE THEY'RE STILL WORKING!
FINALLY....
WHATEVER IT WAS, IT'S FINISHED! NOW PERHAPS THE YOUNG LADY CAN ENLIGHTEN US .....

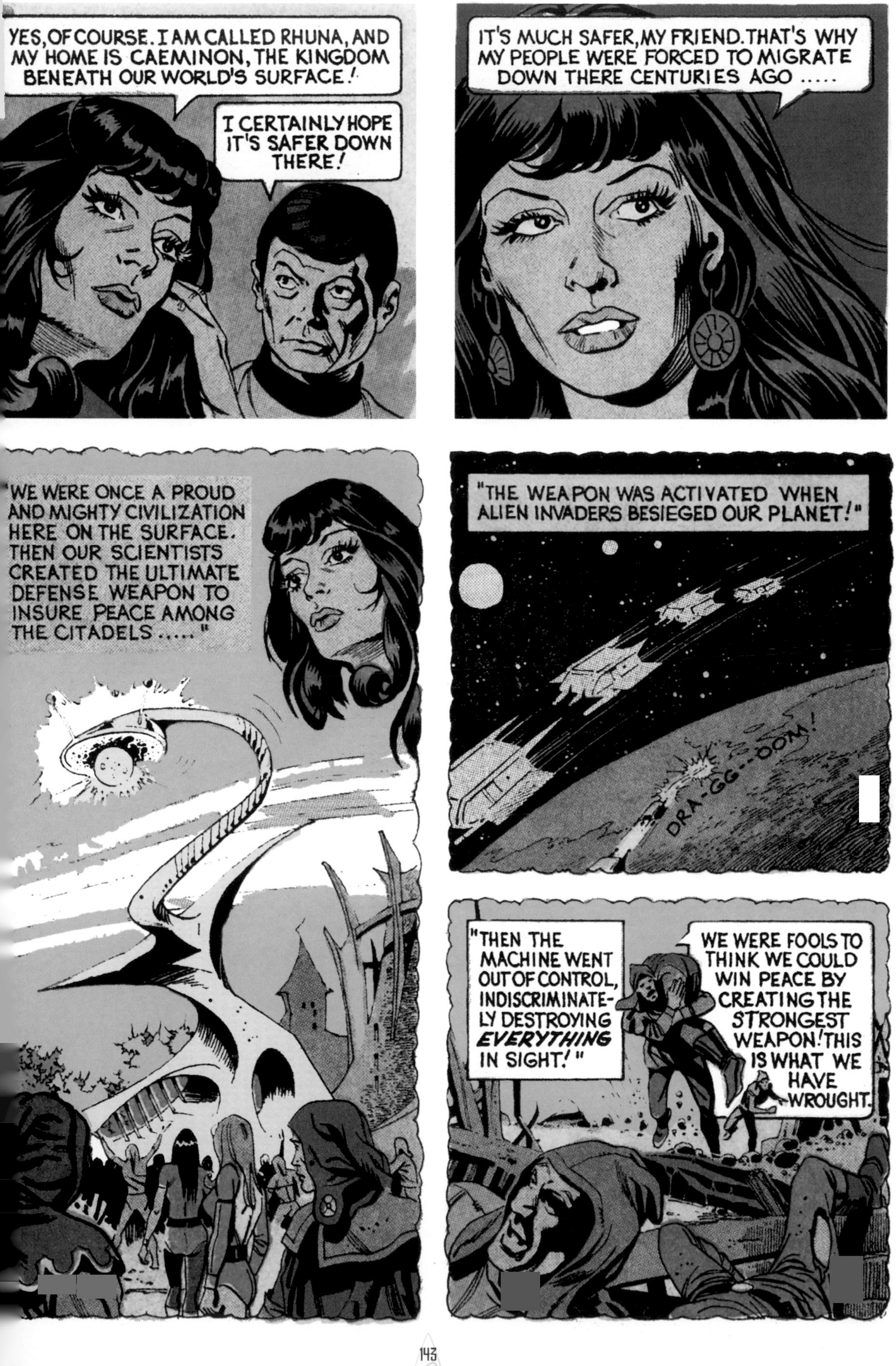
YES, OF COURSE. I AM CALLED RHUNA, AND MY HOME IS CAEMINON, THE KINGDOM BENEATH OUR WORLD'S SURFACE!
I CERTAINLY HOPE IT'S SAFER DOWN THERE!
IT'S MUCH SAFER, MY FRIEND. THAT'S WHY MY PEOPLE WERE FORCED TO MIGRATE DOWN THERE CENTURIES AGO .....
"WE WERE ONCE A PROUD AND MIGHTY CIVILIZATION HERE ON THE SURFACE. THEN OUR SCIENTISTS CREATED THE ULTIMATE DEFENSE WEAPON TO INSURE PEACE AMONG THE CITADELS ....."
"THE WEAPON WAS ACTIVATED WHEN ALIEN INVADERS BESIEGED OUR PLANET!"
DRA-GG-OOM!
"THEN THE MACHINE WENT OUT OF CONTROL, INDISCRIMINATELY DESTROYING *EVERYTHING* IN SIGHT!"
WE WERE FOOLS TO THINK WE COULD WIN PEACE BY CREATING THE STRONGEST WEAPON! THIS IS WHAT WE HAVE WROUGHT.

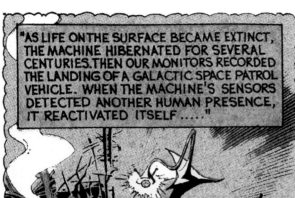

"AS LIFE ON THE SURFACE BECAME EXTINCT, THE MACHINE HIBERNATED FOR SEVERAL CENTURIES. THEN OUR MONITORS RECORDED THE LANDING OF A GALACTIC SPACE PATROL VEHICLE. WHEN THE MACHINE'S SENSORS DETECTED ANOTHER HUMAN PRESENCE, IT REACTIVATED ITSELF....."

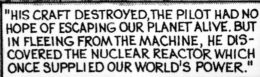

"HIS CRAFT DESTROYED, THE PILOT HAD NO HOPE OF ESCAPING OUR PLANET ALIVE. BUT IN FLEEING FROM THE MACHINE, HE DIS-COVERED THE NUCLEAR REACTOR WHICH ONCE SUPPLIED OUR WORLD'S POWER."

PAR-OOOM!

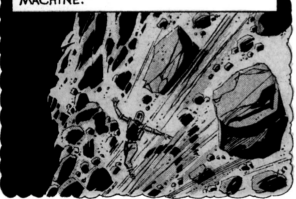

"REALIZING HE WAS DOOMED ANYWAY, HE SET THE ENERGY CONTROLS FAR BEYOND THE DANGER LEVEL AND SET OFF A NUCLEAR HOLOCAUST, KILLING BOTH HIM AND THE MACHINE."

"WE CAN ONLY GUESS WHAT HAPPENED NEXT, BUT WE SUSPECT THAT THE *MIND MODULE* WHICH CONTROLLED THE MACHINE SOMEHOW SURVIVED ....."

"SINCE THE MIND-MODULE HAD BEEN PROGRAMMED FOR SELF-SURVIVAL, IT PROTECTED ITSELF BY GENETICALLY ALTERING THE VEGETATION TO CREATE AN ARMY OF VEGETABLE CREATURES LIKE THE ONE WE ENCOUNTERED EARLIER."

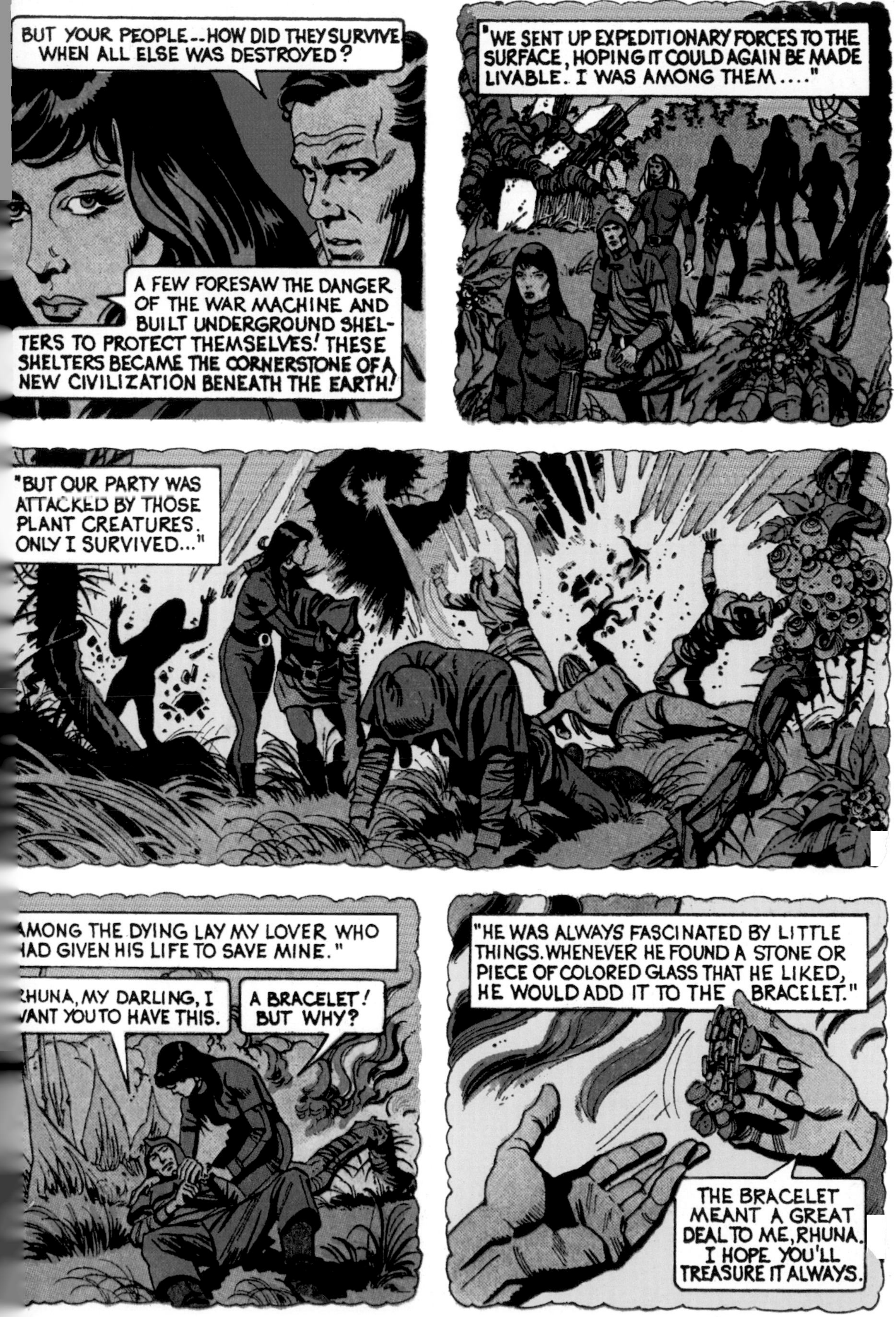
BUT YOUR PEOPLE--HOW DID THEY SURVIVE WHEN ALL ELSE WAS DESTROYED?
A FEW FORESAW THE DANGER OF THE WAR MACHINE AND BUILT UNDERGROUND SHELTERS TO PROTECT THEMSELVES! THESE SHELTERS BECAME THE CORNERSTONE OF A NEW CIVILIZATION BENEATH THE EARTH!
"WE SENT UP EXPEDITIONARY FORCES TO THE SURFACE, HOPING IT COULD AGAIN BE MADE LIVABLE. I WAS AMONG THEM...."
"BUT OUR PARTY WAS ATTACKED BY THOSE PLANT CREATURES. ONLY I SURVIVED..."
AMONG THE DYING LAY MY LOVER WHO HAD GIVEN HIS LIFE TO SAVE MINE."
RHUNA, MY DARLING, I WANT YOU TO HAVE THIS.
A BRACELET! BUT WHY?
"HE WAS ALWAYS FASCINATED BY LITTLE THINGS. WHENEVER HE FOUND A STONE OR PIECE OF COLORED GLASS THAT HE LIKED, HE WOULD ADD IT TO THE BRACELET."
THE BRACELET MEANT A GREAT DEAL TO ME, RHUNA. I HOPE YOU'LL TREASURE IT ALWAYS.

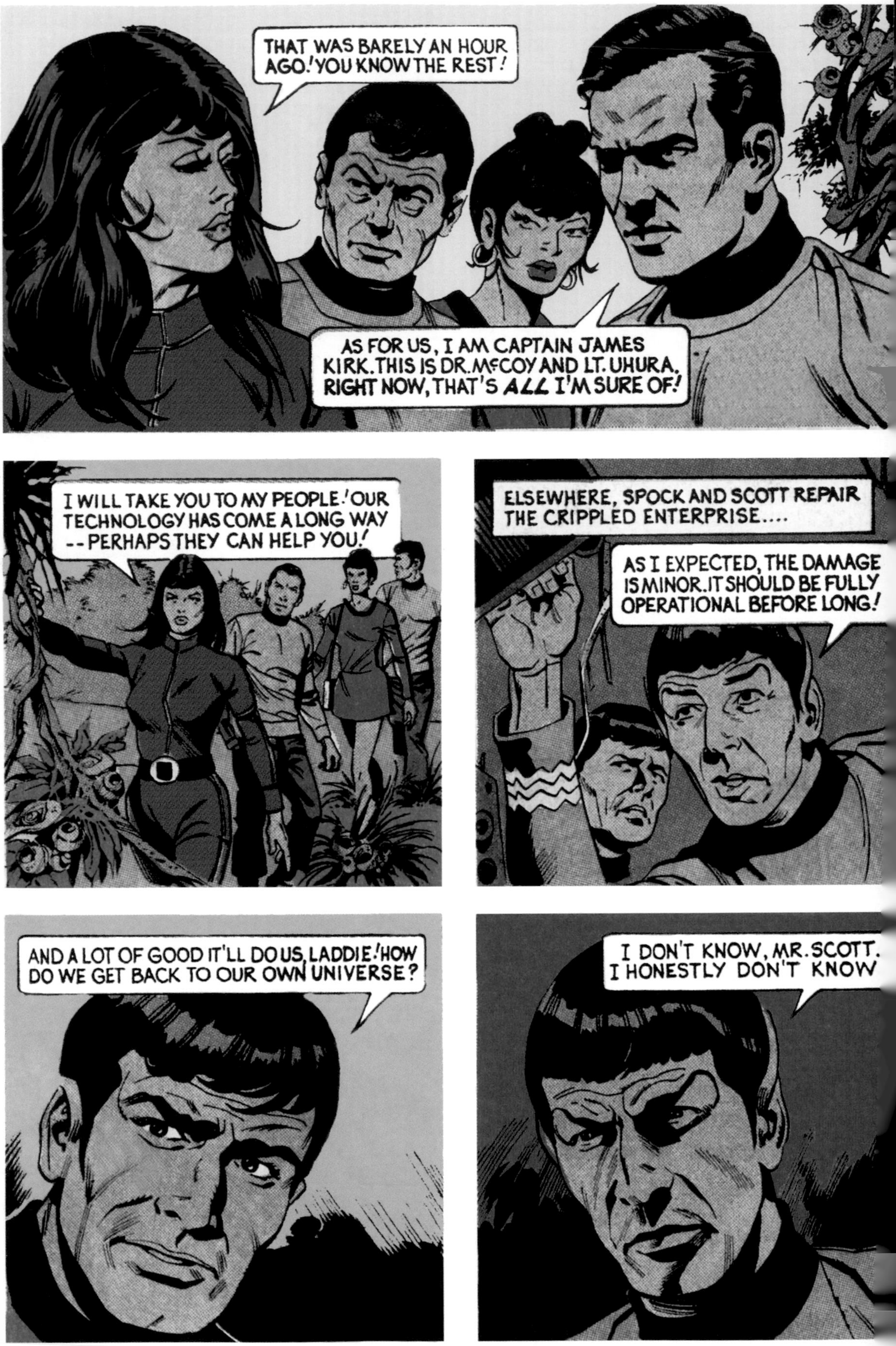
THAT WAS BARELY AN HOUR AGO! YOU KNOW THE REST!
AS FOR US, I AM CAPTAIN JAMES KIRK. THIS IS DR. McCOY AND LT. UHURA. RIGHT NOW, THAT'S ALL I'M SURE OF!
I WILL TAKE YOU TO MY PEOPLE! OUR TECHNOLOGY HAS COME A LONG WAY -- PERHAPS THEY CAN HELP YOU!
ELSEWHERE, SPOCK AND SCOTT REPAIR THE CRIPPLED ENTERPRISE....
AS I EXPECTED, THE DAMAGE IS MINOR. IT SHOULD BE FULLY OPERATIONAL BEFORE LONG!
AND A LOT OF GOOD IT'LL DO US, LADDIE! HOW DO WE GET BACK TO OUR OWN UNIVERSE?
I DON'T KNOW, MR. SCOTT. I HONESTLY DON'T KNOW

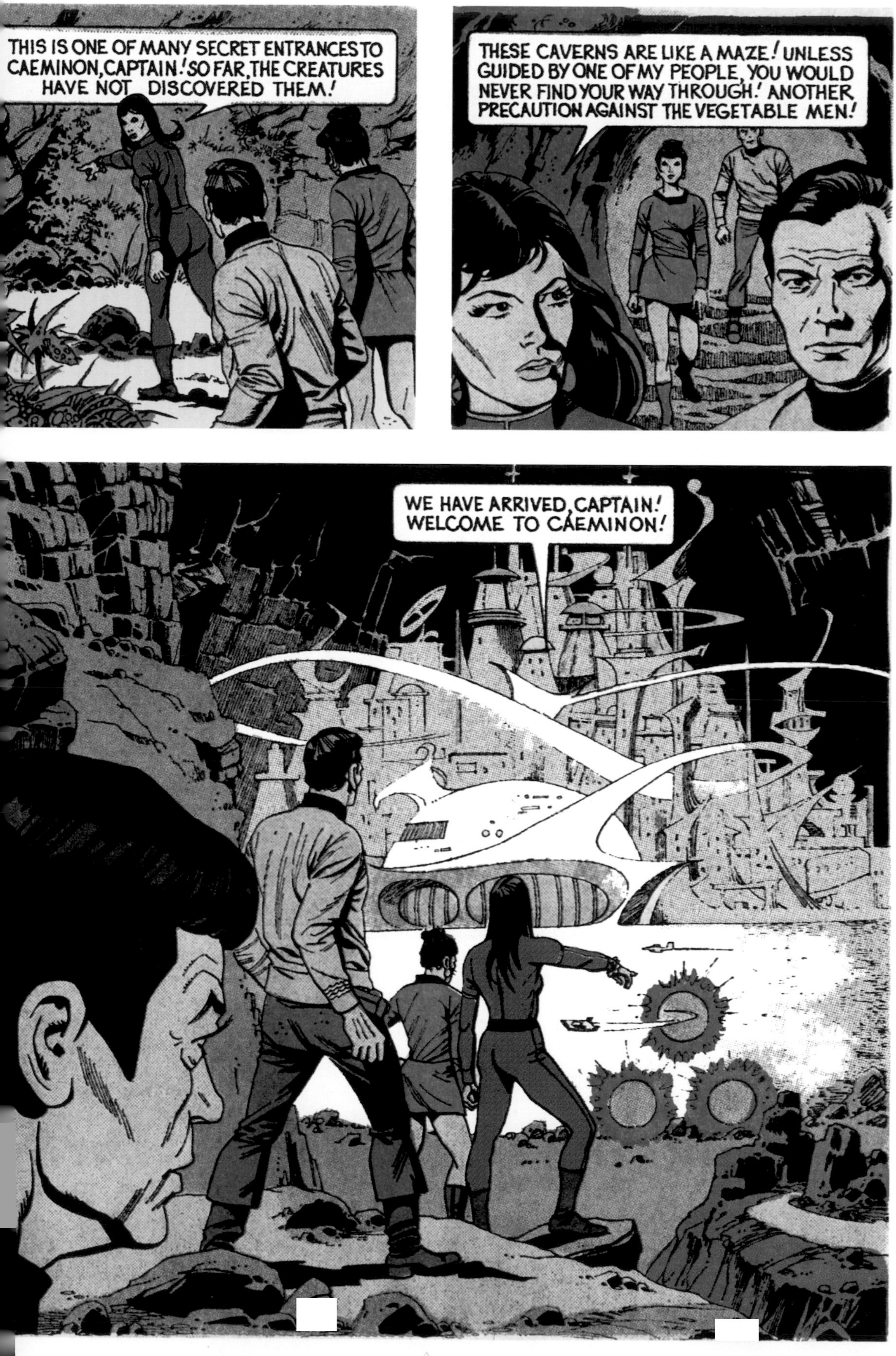
THIS IS ONE OF MANY SECRET ENTRANCES TO CAEMINON, CAPTAIN! SO FAR, THE CREATURES HAVE NOT DISCOVERED THEM!
THESE CAVERNS ARE LIKE A MAZE! UNLESS GUIDED BY ONE OF MY PEOPLE, YOU WOULD NEVER FIND YOUR WAY THROUGH! ANOTHER PRECAUTION AGAINST THE VEGETABLE MEN!
WE HAVE ARRIVED, CAPTAIN! WELCOME TO CAEMINON!

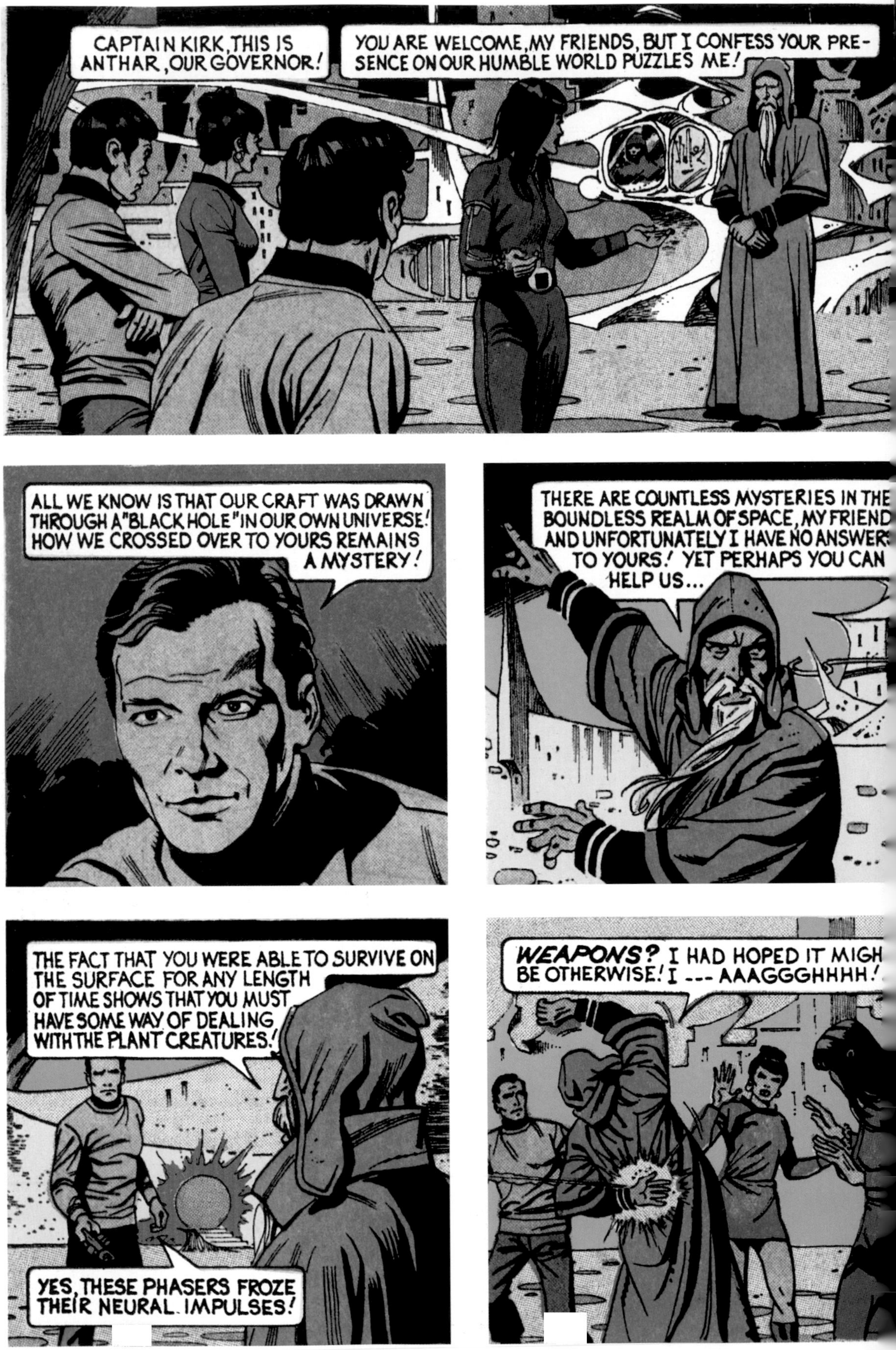
CAPTAIN KIRK, THIS IS ANTHAR, OUR GOVERNOR!
YOU ARE WELCOME, MY FRIENDS, BUT I CONFESS YOUR PRESENCE ON OUR HUMBLE WORLD PUZZLES ME!
ALL WE KNOW IS THAT OUR CRAFT WAS DRAWN THROUGH A "BLACK HOLE" IN OUR OWN UNIVERSE! HOW WE CROSSED OVER TO YOURS REMAINS A MYSTERY!
THERE ARE COUNTLESS MYSTERIES IN THE BOUNDLESS REALM OF SPACE, MY FRIEND AND UNFORTUNATELY I HAVE NO ANSWERS TO YOURS! YET PERHAPS YOU CAN HELP US...
THE FACT THAT YOU WERE ABLE TO SURVIVE ON THE SURFACE FOR ANY LENGTH OF TIME SHOWS THAT YOU MUST HAVE SOME WAY OF DEALING WITH THE PLANT CREATURES!
YES, THESE PHASERS FROZE THEIR NEURAL IMPULSES!
WEAPONS? I HAD HOPED IT MIGH BE OTHERWISE! I --- AAAGGGHHHH!

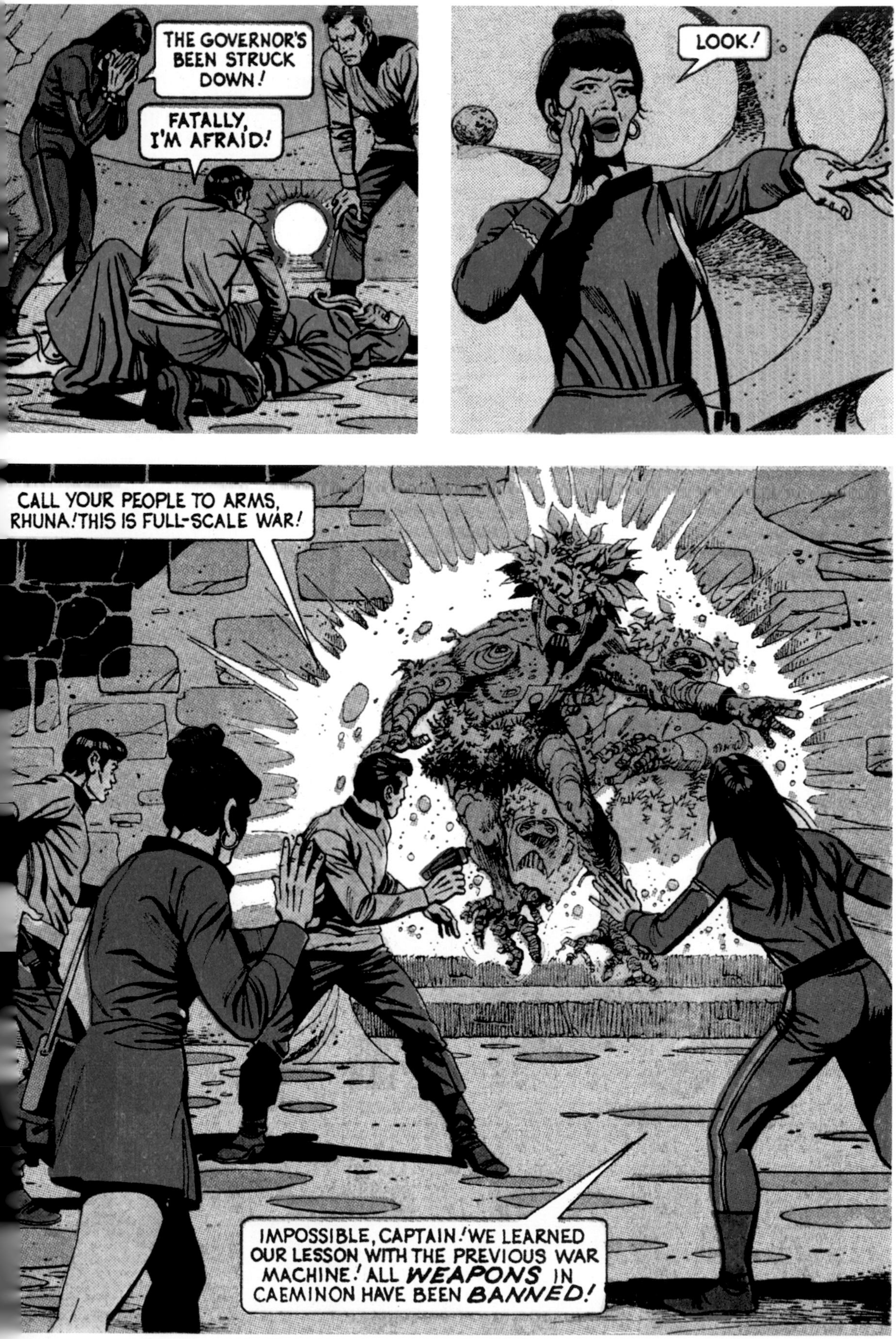
THE GOVERNOR'S BEEN STRUCK DOWN!
FATALLY, I'M AFRAID!
LOOK!
CALL YOUR PEOPLE TO ARMS, RHUNA! THIS IS FULL-SCALE WAR!
IMPOSSIBLE, CAPTAIN! WE LEARNED OUR LESSON WITH THE PREVIOUS WAR MACHINE! ALL *WEAPONS* IN CAEMINON HAVE BEEN *BANNED*!

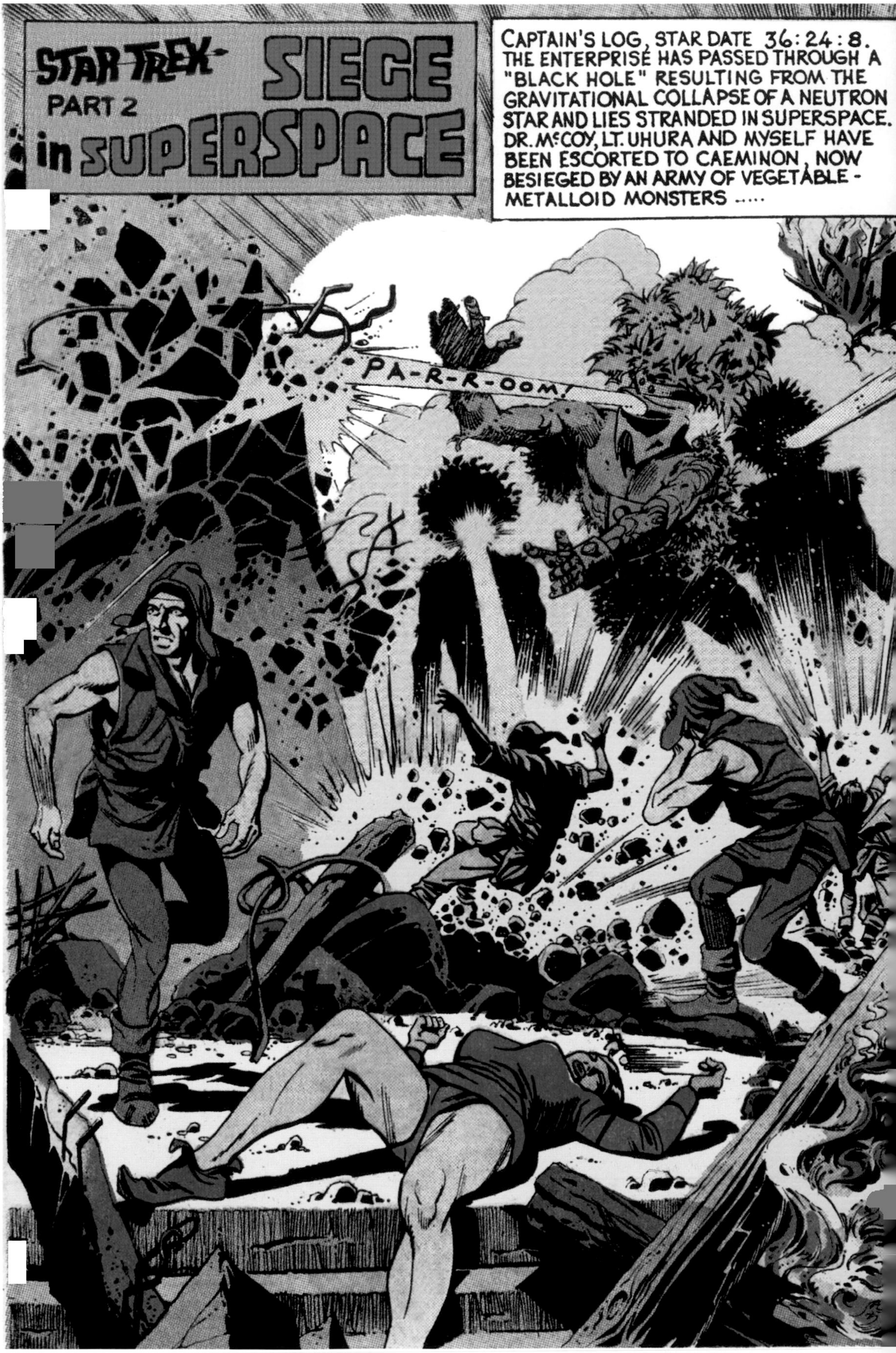
STAR TREK
PART 2
SIEGE in SUPERSPACE
CAPTAIN'S LOG, STAR DATE 36:24:8. THE ENTERPRISE HAS PASSED THROUGH A "BLACK HOLE" RESULTING FROM THE GRAVITATIONAL COLLAPSE OF A NEUTRON STAR AND LIES STRANDED IN SUPERSPACE. DR. McCOY, LT. UHURA AND MYSELF HAVE BEEN ESCORTED TO CAEMINON, NOW BESIEGED BY AN ARMY OF VEGETABLE-METALLOID MONSTERS .....
PA-R-R-OOM!

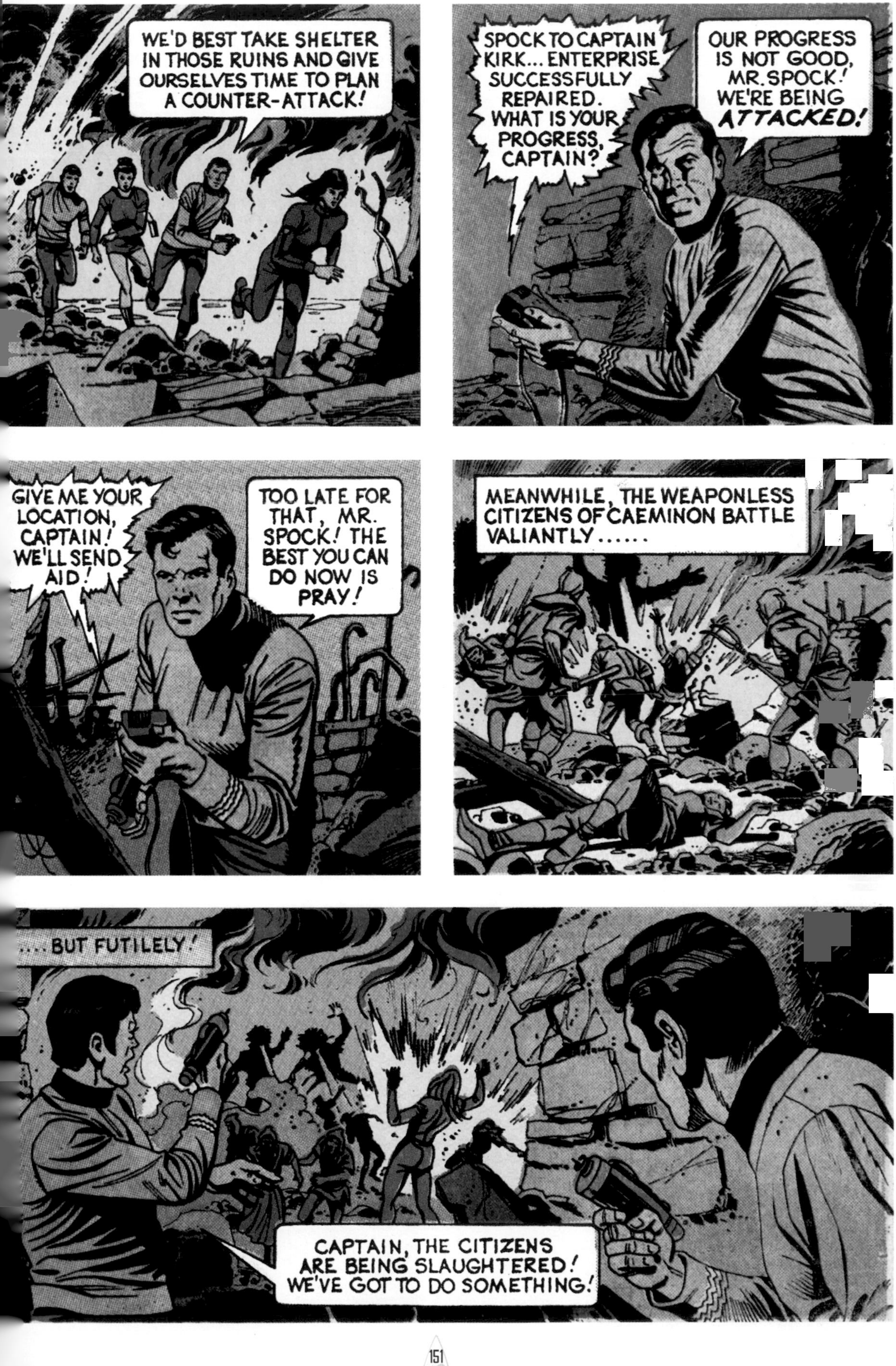
WE'D BEST TAKE SHELTER IN THOSE RUINS AND GIVE OURSELVES TIME TO PLAN A COUNTER-ATTACK!
SPOCK TO CAPTAIN KIRK... ENTERPRISE SUCCESSFULLY REPAIRED. WHAT IS YOUR PROGRESS, CAPTAIN?
OUR PROGRESS IS NOT GOOD, MR. SPOCK! WE'RE BEING ATTACKED!
GIVE ME YOUR LOCATION, CAPTAIN! WE'LL SEND AID!
TOO LATE FOR THAT, MR. SPOCK! THE BEST YOU CAN DO NOW IS PRAY!
MEANWHILE, THE WEAPONLESS CITIZENS OF CAEMINON BATTLE VALIANTLY......
....BUT FUTILELY!
CAPTAIN, THE CITIZENS ARE BEING SLAUGHTERED! WE'VE GOT TO DO SOMETHING!

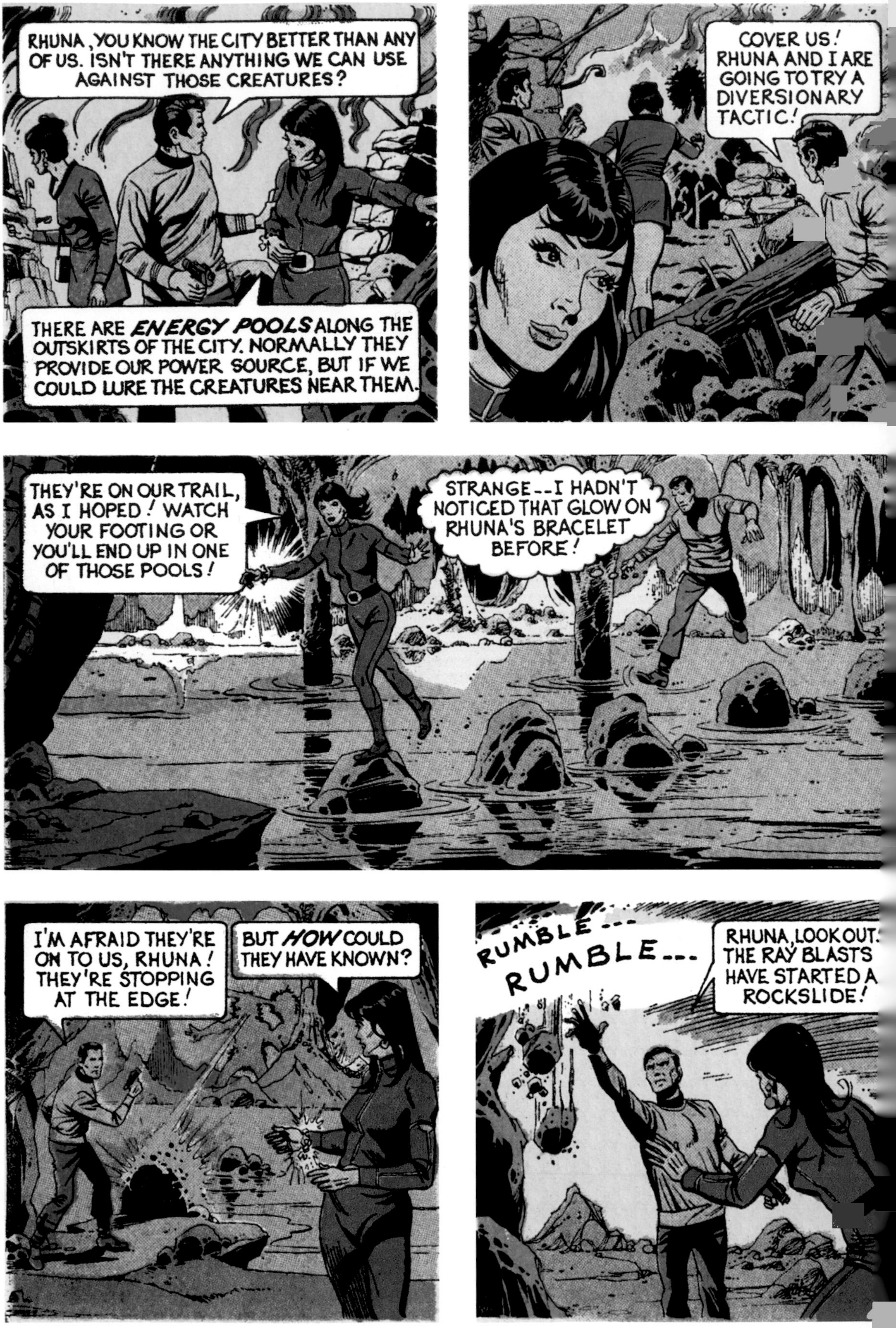

RHUNA, YOU KNOW THE CITY BETTER THAN ANY OF US. ISN'T THERE ANYTHING WE CAN USE AGAINST THOSE CREATURES?
THERE ARE ENERGY POOLS ALONG THE OUTSKIRTS OF THE CITY. NORMALLY THEY PROVIDE OUR POWER SOURCE, BUT IF WE COULD LURE THE CREATURES NEAR THEM.
COVER US! RHUNA AND I ARE GOING TO TRY A DIVERSIONARY TACTIC!
THEY'RE ON OUR TRAIL, AS I HOPED! WATCH YOUR FOOTING OR YOU'LL END UP IN ONE OF THOSE POOLS!
STRANGE--I HADN'T NOTICED THAT GLOW ON RHUNA'S BRACELET BEFORE!
I'M AFRAID THEY'RE ON TO US, RHUNA! THEY'RE STOPPING AT THE EDGE!
BUT HOW COULD THEY HAVE KNOWN?
RUMBLE--- RUMBLE---
RHUNA, LOOK OUT! THE RAY BLASTS HAVE STARTED A ROCKSLIDE!

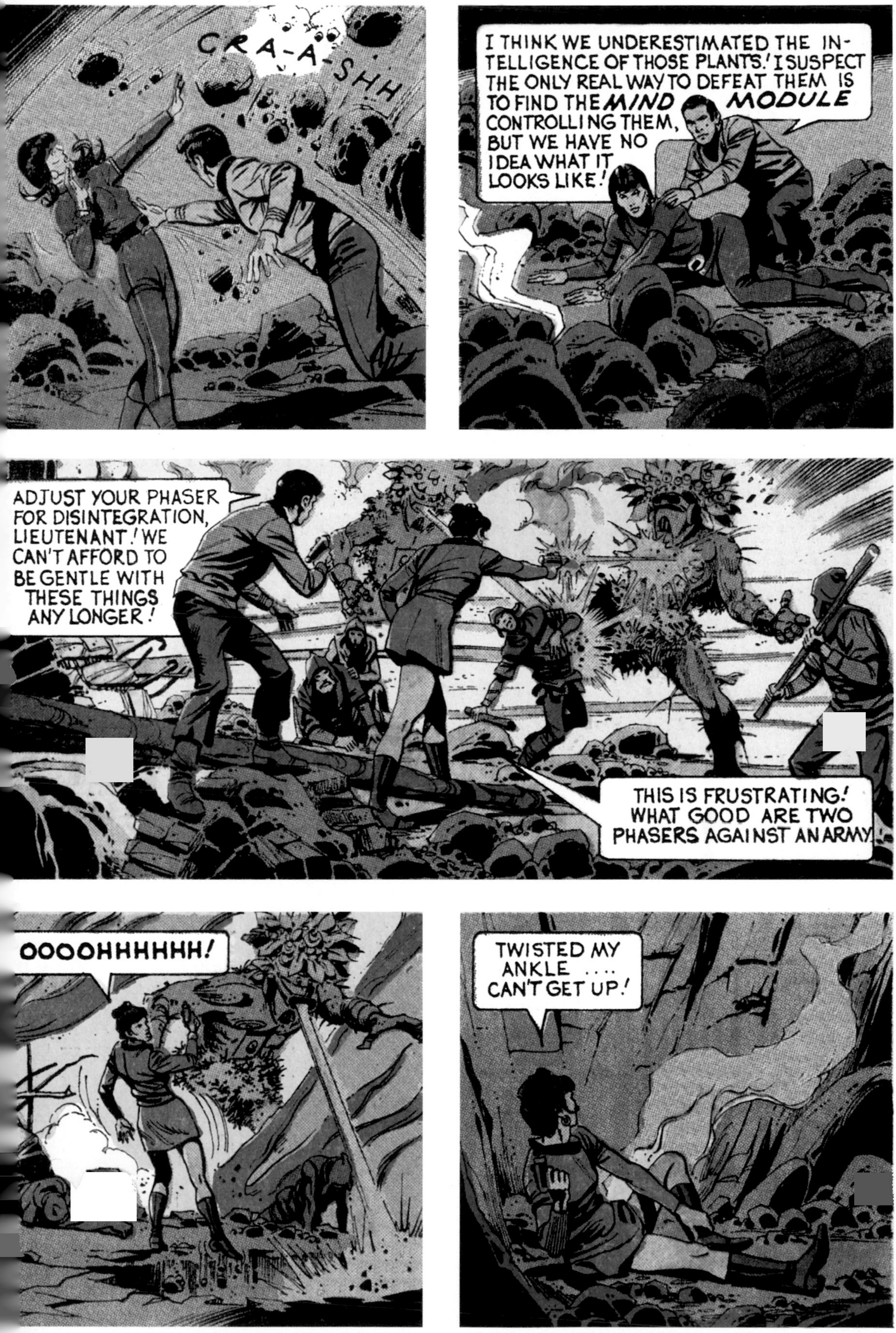
CRA-A-SHH
I THINK WE UNDERESTIMATED THE INTELLIGENCE OF THOSE PLANTS! I SUSPECT THE ONLY REAL WAY TO DEFEAT THEM IS TO FIND THE MIND MODULE CONTROLLING THEM, BUT WE HAVE NO IDEA WHAT IT LOOKS LIKE!
ADJUST YOUR PHASER FOR DISINTEGRATION, LIEUTENANT! WE CAN'T AFFORD TO BE GENTLE WITH THESE THINGS ANY LONGER!
THIS IS FRUSTRATING! WHAT GOOD ARE TWO PHASERS AGAINST AN ARMY!
OOOOHHHHHH!
TWISTED MY ANKLE .... CAN'T GET UP!

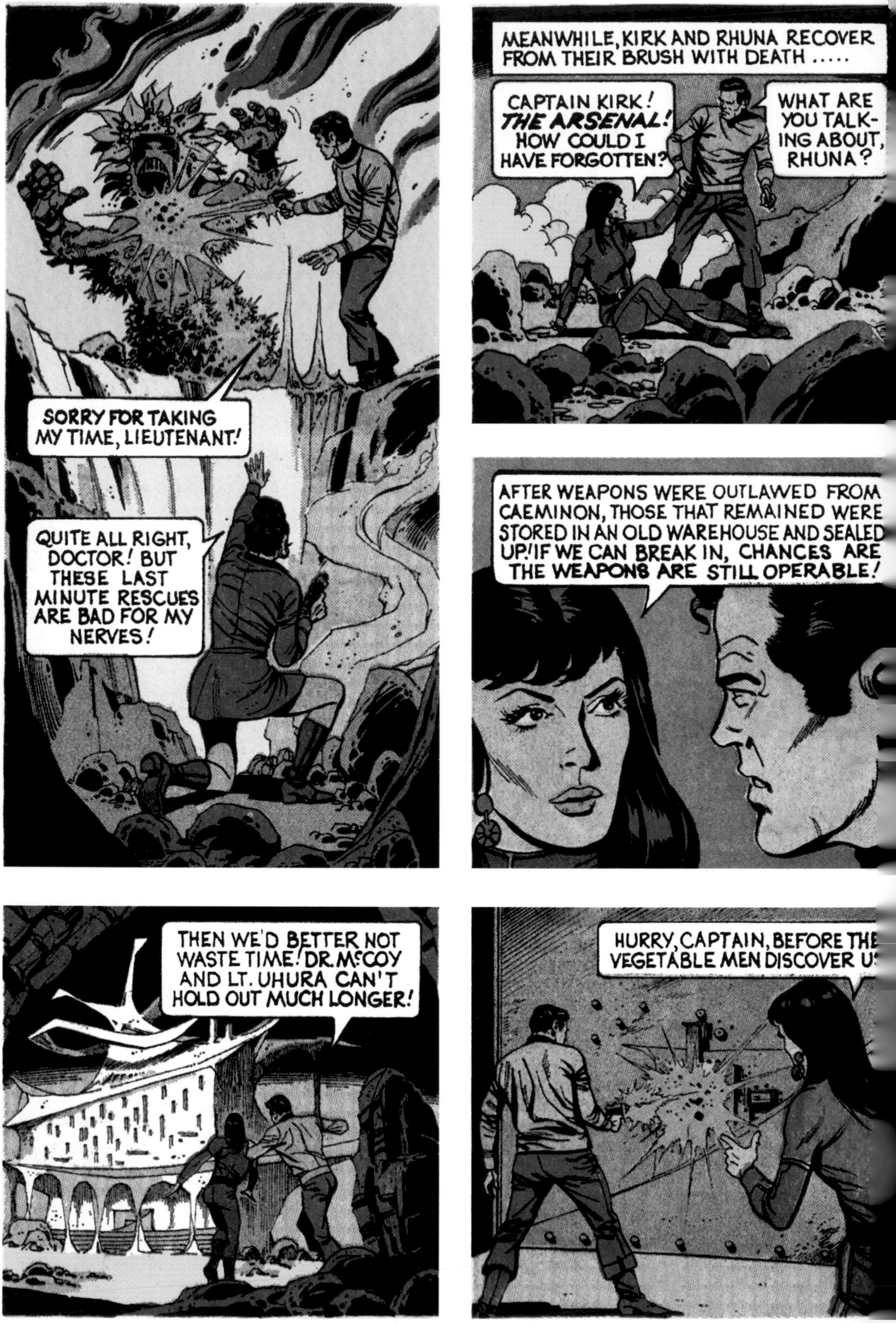
SORRY FOR TAKING MY TIME, LIEUTENANT!
QUITE ALL RIGHT, DOCTOR! BUT THESE LAST MINUTE RESCUES ARE BAD FOR MY NERVES!
MEANWHILE, KIRK AND RHUNA RECOVER FROM THEIR BRUSH WITH DEATH .....
CAPTAIN KIRK! THE ARSENAL! HOW COULD I HAVE FORGOTTEN?
WHAT ARE YOU TALKING ABOUT, RHUNA?
AFTER WEAPONS WERE OUTLAWED FROM CAEMINON, THOSE THAT REMAINED WERE STORED IN AN OLD WAREHOUSE AND SEALED UP! IF WE CAN BREAK IN, CHANCES ARE THE WEAPONS ARE STILL OPERABLE!
THEN WE'D BETTER NOT WASTE TIME! DR. McCOY AND LT. UHURA CAN'T HOLD OUT MUCH LONGER!
HURRY, CAPTAIN, BEFORE THE VEGETABLE MEN DISCOVER US

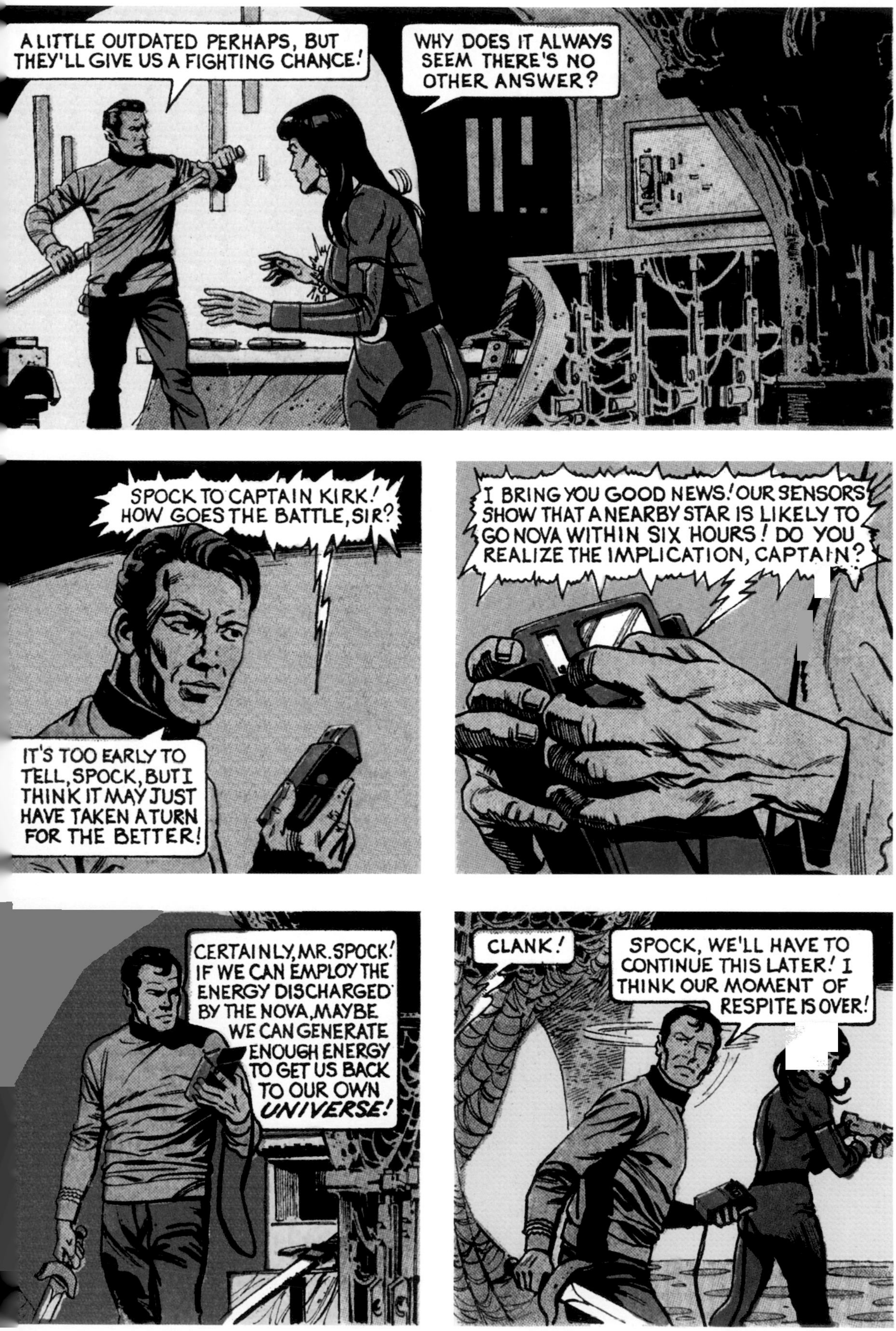
A LITTLE OUTDATED PERHAPS, BUT THEY'LL GIVE US A FIGHTING CHANCE!
WHY DOES IT ALWAYS SEEM THERE'S NO OTHER ANSWER?
SPOCK TO CAPTAIN KIRK! HOW GOES THE BATTLE, SIR?
IT'S TOO EARLY TO TELL, SPOCK, BUT I THINK IT MAY JUST HAVE TAKEN A TURN FOR THE BETTER!
I BRING YOU GOOD NEWS! OUR SENSORS SHOW THAT A NEARBY STAR IS LIKELY TO GO NOVA WITHIN SIX HOURS! DO YOU REALIZE THE IMPLICATION, CAPTAIN?
CERTAINLY, MR. SPOCK! IF WE CAN EMPLOY THE ENERGY DISCHARGED BY THE NOVA, MAYBE WE CAN GENERATE ENOUGH ENERGY TO GET US BACK TO OUR OWN UNIVERSE!
CLANK!
SPOCK, WE'LL HAVE TO CONTINUE THIS LATER! I THINK OUR MOMENT OF RESPITE IS OVER!

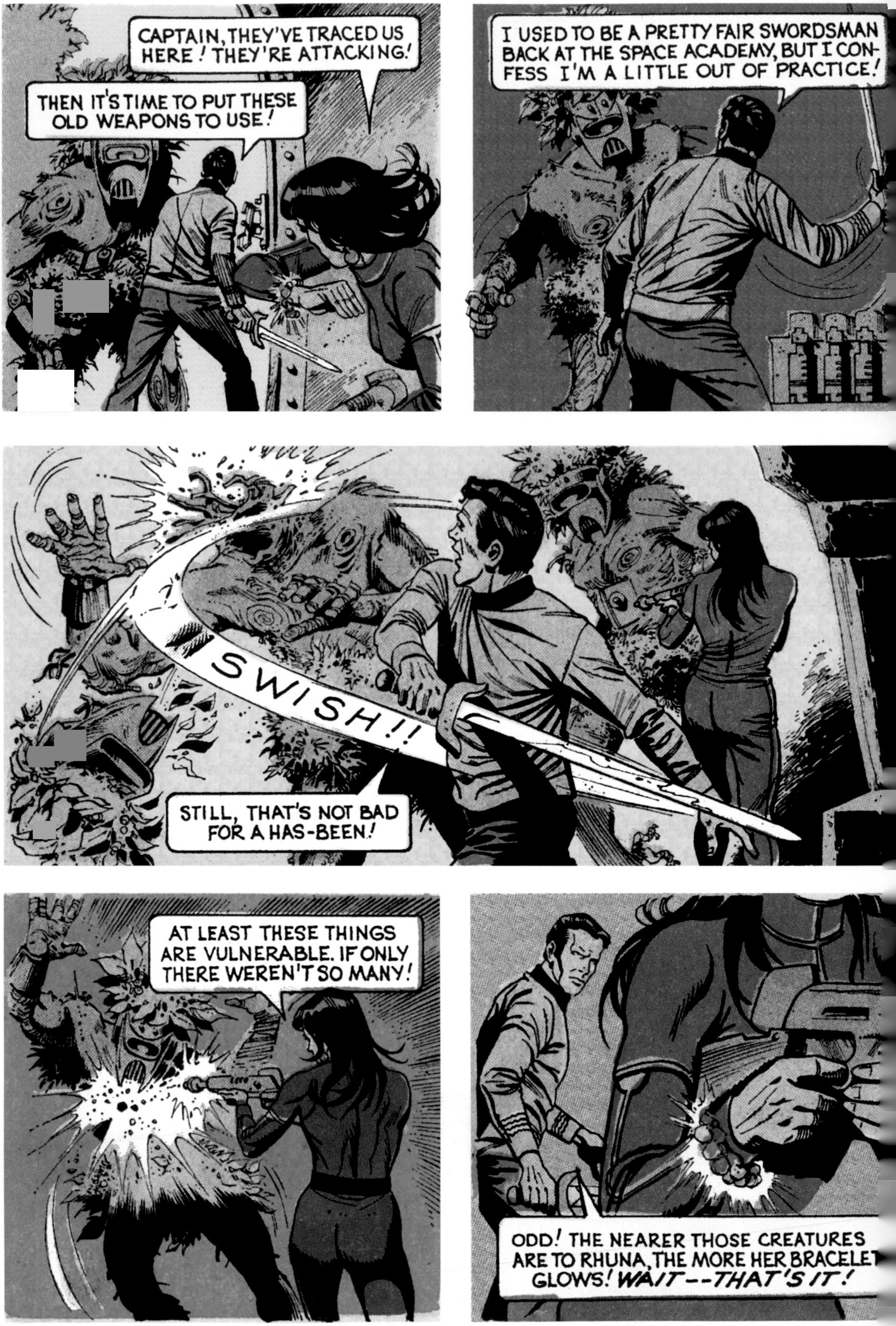
CAPTAIN, THEY'VE TRACED US HERE! THEY'RE ATTACKING!
THEN IT'S TIME TO PUT THESE OLD WEAPONS TO USE!
I USED TO BE A PRETTY FAIR SWORDSMAN BACK AT THE SPACE ACADEMY, BUT I CONFESS I'M A LITTLE OUT OF PRACTICE!
SWISH!!
STILL, THAT'S NOT BAD FOR A HAS-BEEN!
AT LEAST THESE THINGS ARE VULNERABLE. IF ONLY THERE WEREN'T SO MANY!
ODD! THE NEARER THOSE CREATURES ARE TO RHUNA, THE MORE HER BRACELET GLOWS! *WAIT--THAT'S IT!*

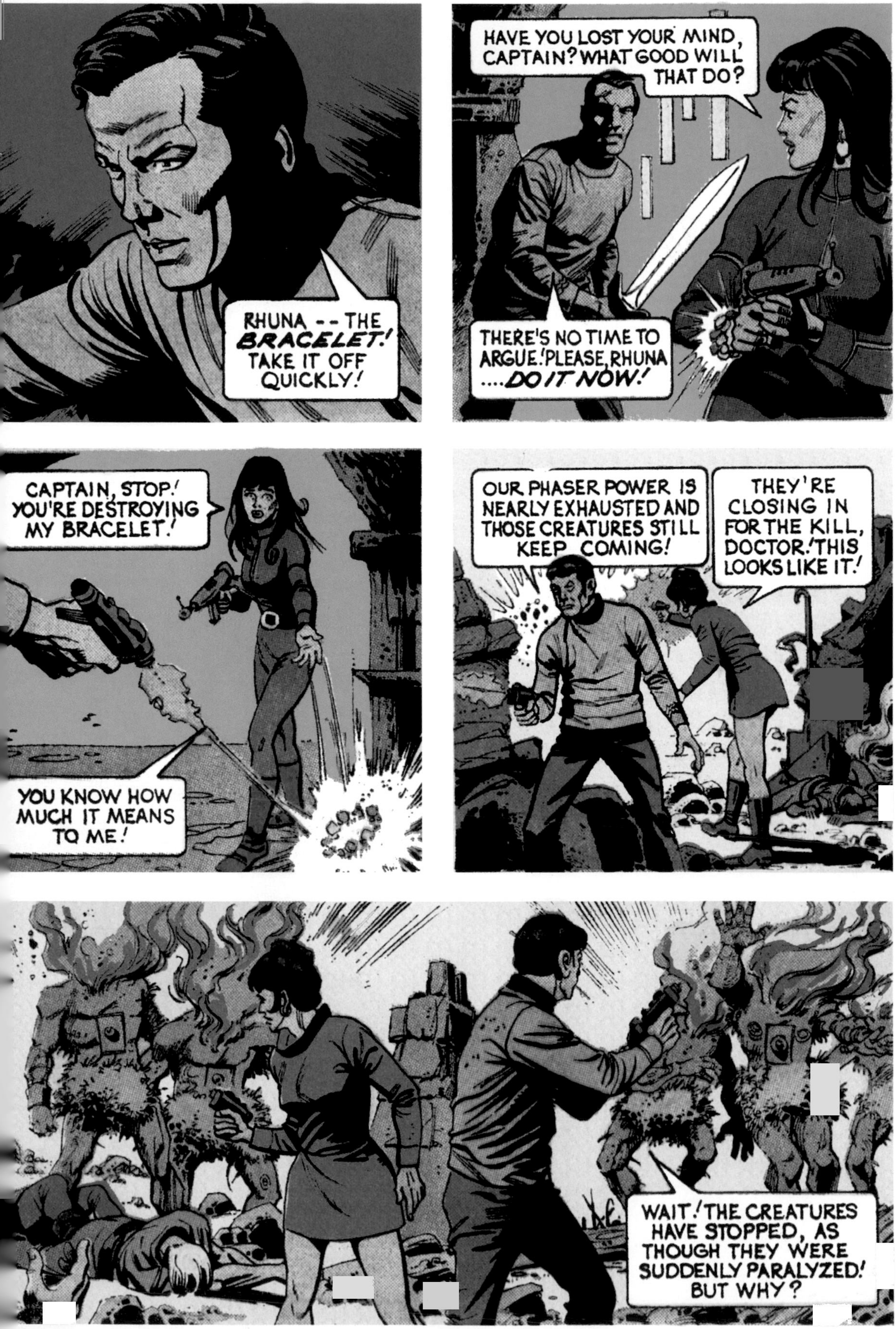
RHUNA -- THE BRACELET! TAKE IT OFF QUICKLY!
HAVE YOU LOST YOUR MIND, CAPTAIN? WHAT GOOD WILL THAT DO?
THERE'S NO TIME TO ARGUE! PLEASE, RHUNA ....DO IT NOW!
CAPTAIN, STOP! YOU'RE DESTROYING MY BRACELET!
YOU KNOW HOW MUCH IT MEANS TO ME!
OUR PHASER POWER IS NEARLY EXHAUSTED AND THOSE CREATURES STILL KEEP COMING!
THEY'RE CLOSING IN FOR THE KILL, DOCTOR! THIS LOOKS LIKE IT!
WAIT! THE CREATURES HAVE STOPPED, AS THOUGH THEY WERE SUDDENLY PARALYZED! BUT WHY?

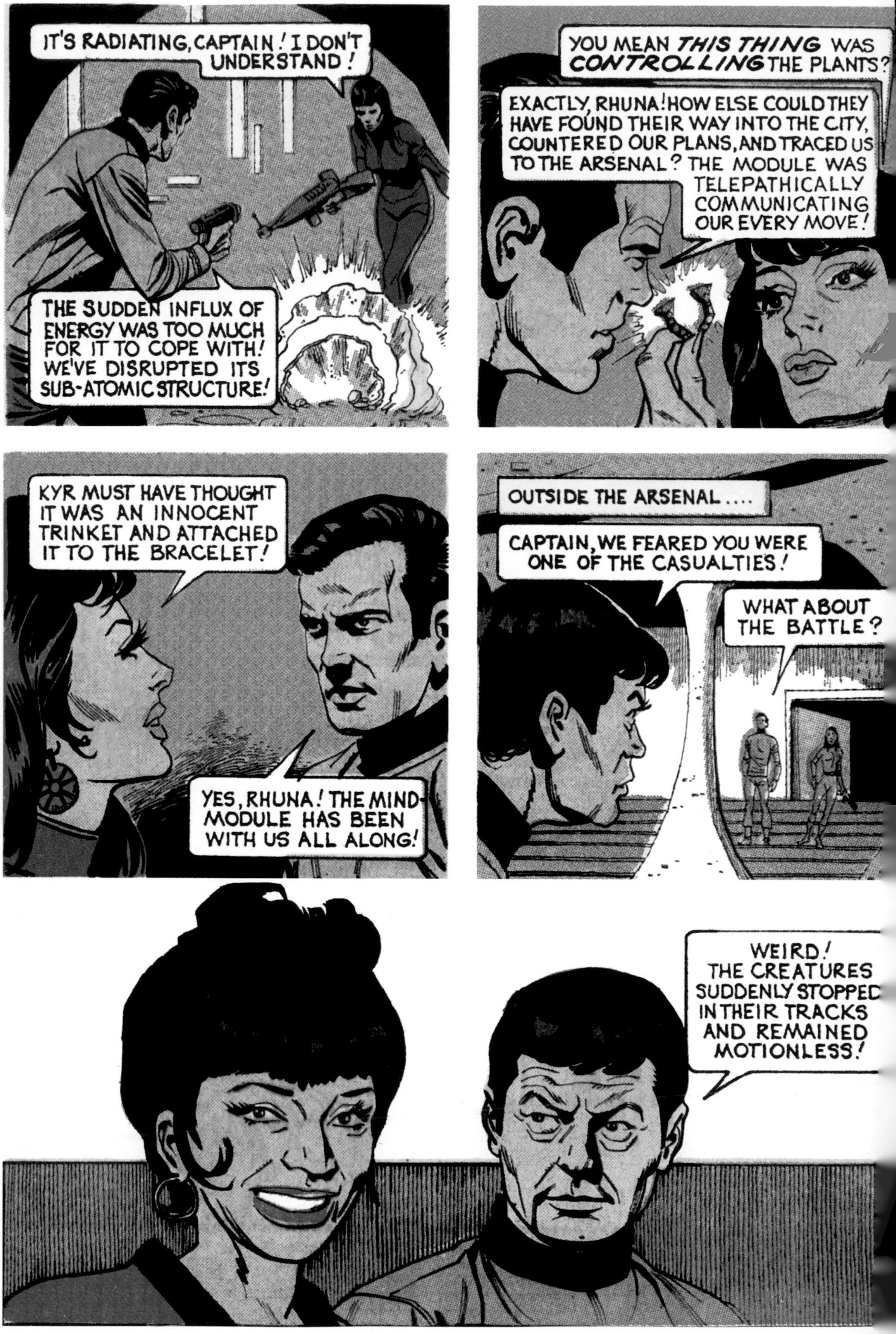

IT'S RADIATING, CAPTAIN! I DON'T UNDERSTAND!
THE SUDDEN INFLUX OF ENERGY WAS TOO MUCH FOR IT TO COPE WITH! WE'VE DISRUPTED ITS SUB-ATOMIC STRUCTURE!
YOU MEAN THIS THING WAS CONTROLLING THE PLANTS?
EXACTLY, RHUNA! HOW ELSE COULD THEY HAVE FOUND THEIR WAY INTO THE CITY, COUNTERED OUR PLANS, AND TRACED US TO THE ARSENAL? THE MODULE WAS TELEPATHICALLY COMMUNICATING OUR EVERY MOVE!
KYR MUST HAVE THOUGHT IT WAS AN INNOCENT TRINKET AND ATTACHED IT TO THE BRACELET!
YES, RHUNA! THE MIND-MODULE HAS BEEN WITH US ALL ALONG!
OUTSIDE THE ARSENAL....
CAPTAIN, WE FEARED YOU WERE ONE OF THE CASUALTIES!
WHAT ABOUT THE BATTLE?
WEIRD! THE CREATURES SUDDENLY STOPPED IN THEIR TRACKS AND REMAINED MOTIONLESS!

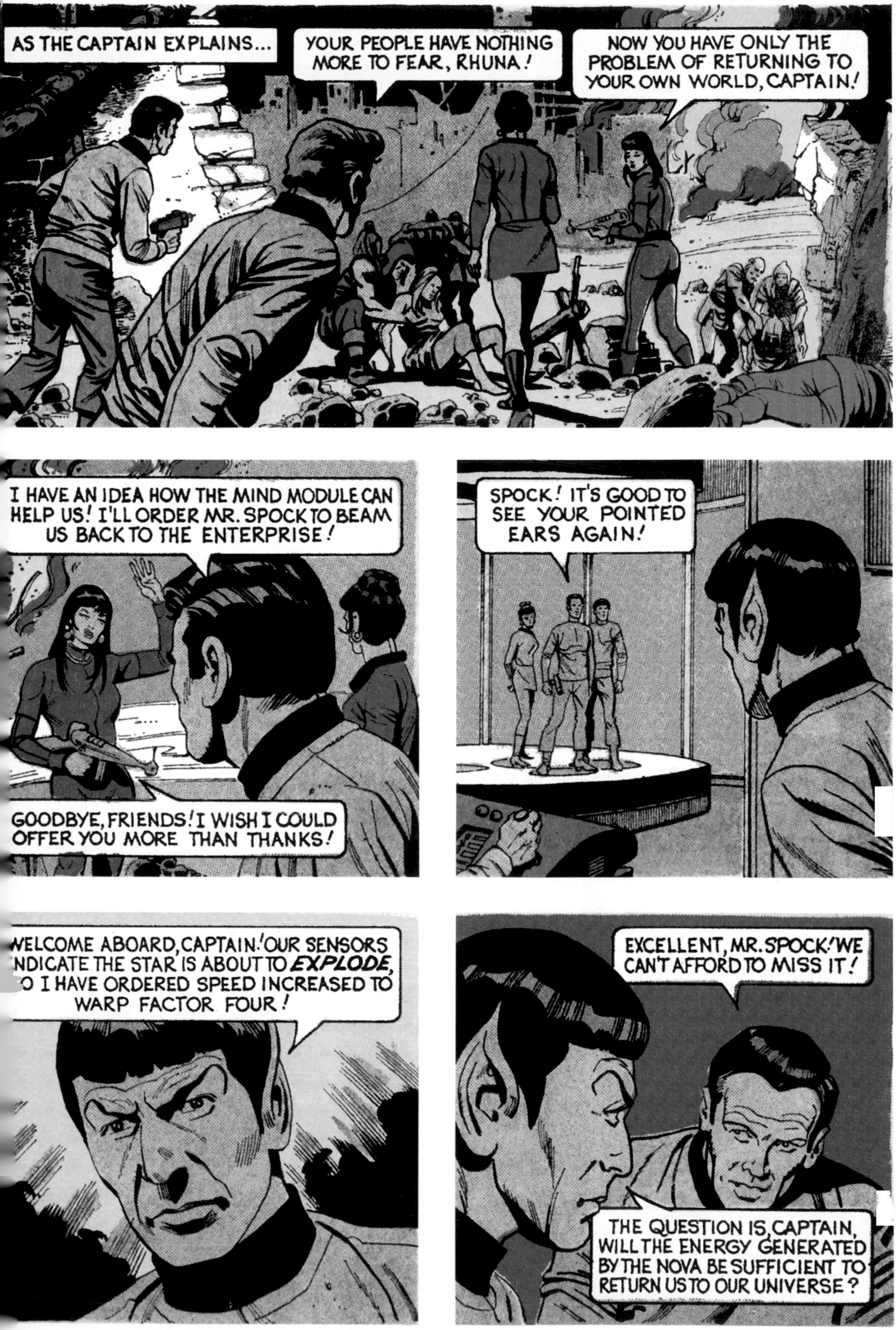
AS THE CAPTAIN EXPLAINS...
YOUR PEOPLE HAVE NOTHING MORE TO FEAR, RHUNA!
NOW YOU HAVE ONLY THE PROBLEM OF RETURNING TO YOUR OWN WORLD, CAPTAIN!
I HAVE AN IDEA HOW THE MIND MODULE CAN HELP US! I'LL ORDER MR. SPOCK TO BEAM US BACK TO THE ENTERPRISE!
GOODBYE, FRIENDS! I WISH I COULD OFFER YOU MORE THAN THANKS!
SPOCK! IT'S GOOD TO SEE YOUR POINTED EARS AGAIN!
WELCOME ABOARD, CAPTAIN! OUR SENSORS INDICATE THE STAR IS ABOUT TO EXPLODE, SO I HAVE ORDERED SPEED INCREASED TO WARP FACTOR FOUR!
EXCELLENT, MR. SPOCK! WE CAN'T AFFORD TO MISS IT!
THE QUESTION IS, CAPTAIN, WILL THE ENERGY GENERATED BY THE NOVA BE SUFFICIENT TO RETURN US TO OUR UNIVERSE?

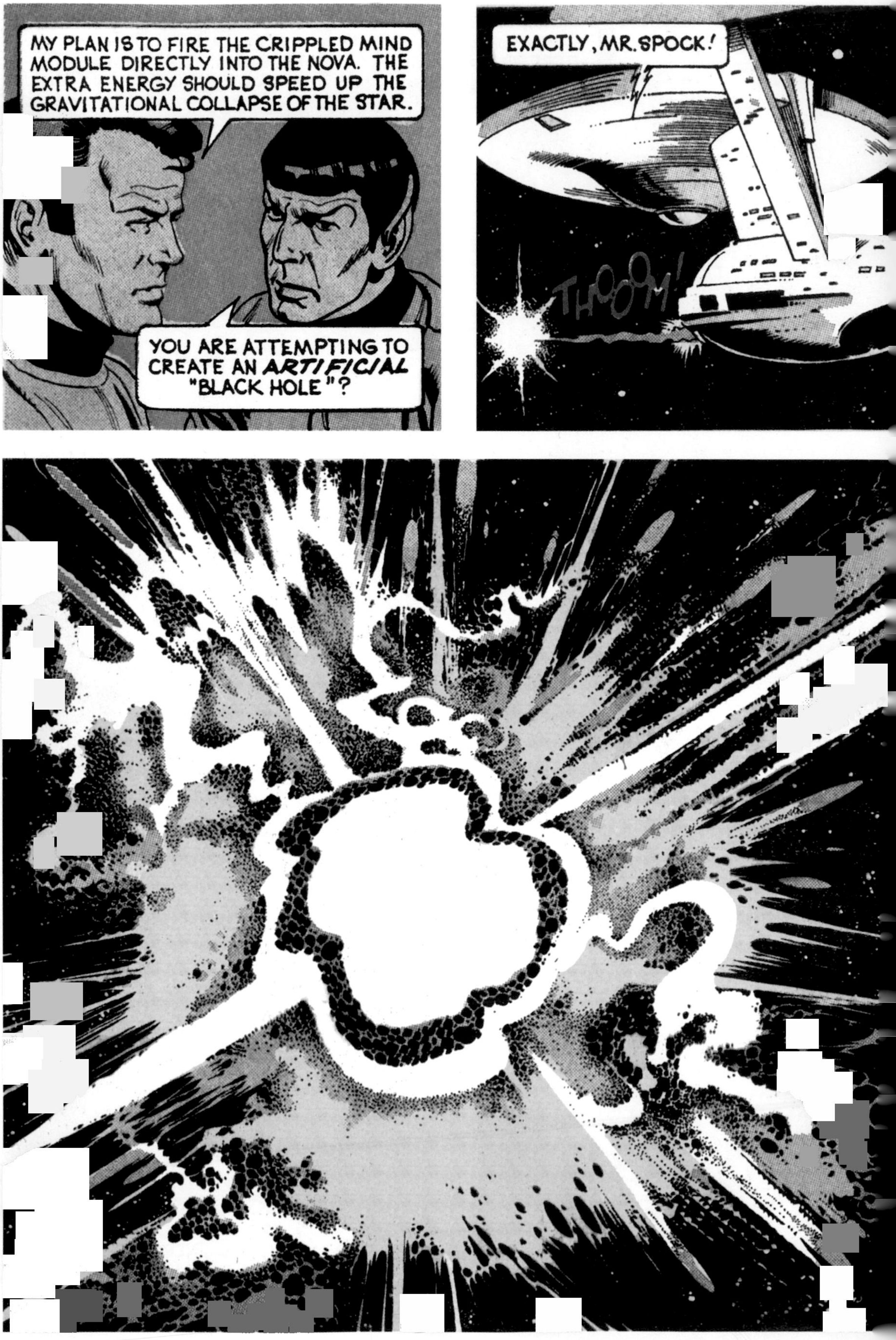
MY PLAN IS TO FIRE THE CRIPPLED MIND MODULE DIRECTLY INTO THE NOVA. THE EXTRA ENERGY SHOULD SPEED UP THE GRAVITATIONAL COLLAPSE OF THE STAR.
YOU ARE ATTEMPTING TO CREATE AN ARTIFICIAL "BLACK HOLE"?
EXACTLY, MR. SPOCK!
THOOOM!

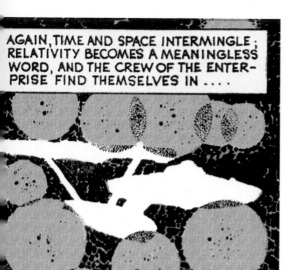

AGAIN, TIME AND SPACE INTERMINGLE; RELATIVITY BECOMES A MEANINGLESS WORD, AND THE CREW OF THE ENTERPRISE FIND THEMSELVES IN ....

....THEIR OWN UNIVERSE!

WE SUCCEEDED, CAPTAIN! WE HAVE ONCE MORE CROSSED THE BARRIERS OF SUPERSPACE!

AND THE MIND MODULE WAS DESTROYED IN THE NOVA! THE CAEMINONS HAVE NOTHING MORE TO FEAR!

RHUNA WAS QUITE AN AMAZING WOMAN. IF ONLY INFINITY DIDN'T BLOCK OUR PATHS....

CAPTAIN'S LOG ... STAR DATE 36:25.2. SAFELY IN OUR OWN ERA, WE CONTINUE OUR TREK TO DRACONIS. IN SPITE OF EVERYTHING, I DON'T THINK I WILL EVER BE ABLE TO FORGET BEING TRAPPED IN THAT VOID CALLED *SUPERSPACE!*

THE END

20c

STAR TREK

A planetful of doomed children—playing their deadliest game!

© PARAMOUNT PICTURES CORPORATION

Chapter 7
Child's Play

(Originally Published in 1974)

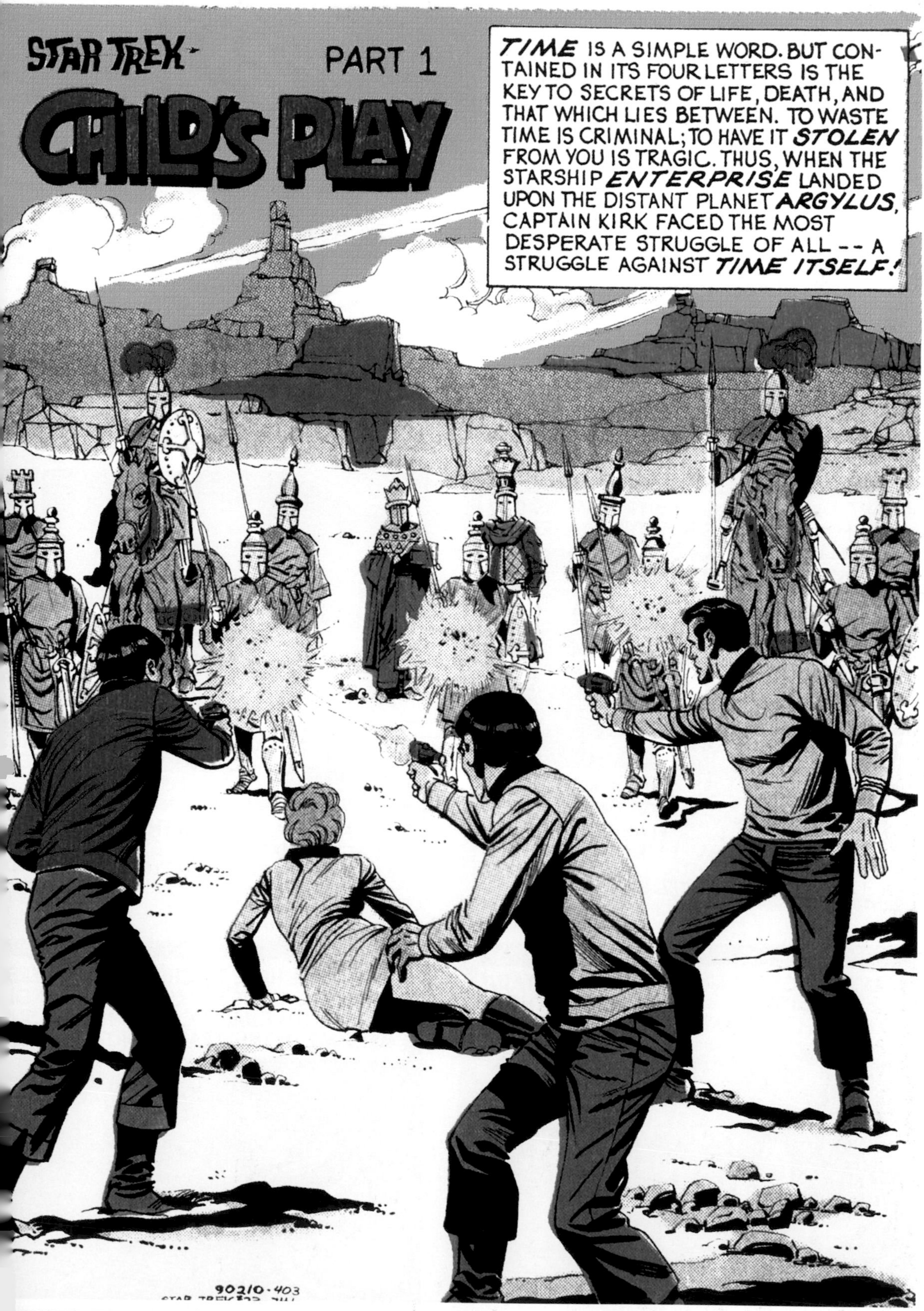
STAR TREK
PART 1
CHILD'S PLAY
TIME IS A SIMPLE WORD. BUT CONTAINED IN ITS FOUR LETTERS IS THE KEY TO SECRETS OF LIFE, DEATH, AND THAT WHICH LIES BETWEEN. TO WASTE TIME IS CRIMINAL; TO HAVE IT STOLEN FROM YOU IS TRAGIC. THUS, WHEN THE STARSHIP ENTERPRISE LANDED UPON THE DISTANT PLANET ARGYLUS, CAPTAIN KIRK FACED THE MOST DESPERATE STRUGGLE OF ALL -- A STRUGGLE AGAINST TIME ITSELF!
90210-403

CAPTAIN'S LOG, STAR DATE 17:23.4. HAVING SUCCESSFULLY COMPLETED OUR MISSION ON THE PLANET KYNARDI, WE NOW CRUISE TOWARD THE SOLAR SYSTEM, ZETA CENTAURI, SEEKING FURTHER CLASS M PLANETS FOR STUDY......

CAPTAIN, AN EMERGENCY TRANSMISSION! ITS POINT OF ORIGIN IS THE PLANET ARGYLUS, 13 MARK 4 BELOW US!

I WANT A SCHEMATIC OF THE PLANET FLASHED ON THE VIEWING SCREEN IMMEDIATELY!

ARGYLUS IS A CLASS M PLANET: ITS ATMOSPHERIC CONDITIONS ARE ROUGHLY COMPARABLE TO THOSE OF EARTH!

IT IS ALSO RATED 17 ON THE INDUSTRIAL SCALE! THAT INDICATES A HIGHLY ADVANCED CIVILIZATION, CAPTAIN.

ANY SUCCESS IN ESTABLISHING CONTACT, LT. UHURA?

NONE YET, CAPTAIN! APPARENTLY THEIR RECEIVING EQUIPMENT HAS BEEN DAMAGED!

THEN WE'LL HAVE TO CHECK IT OUT PERSONALLY! MR. SPOCK, ORGANIZE A LANDING PARTY! HAVE MR. SCOTT AND MR. SULU MEET ME IN THE TRANSPORTER ROOM!

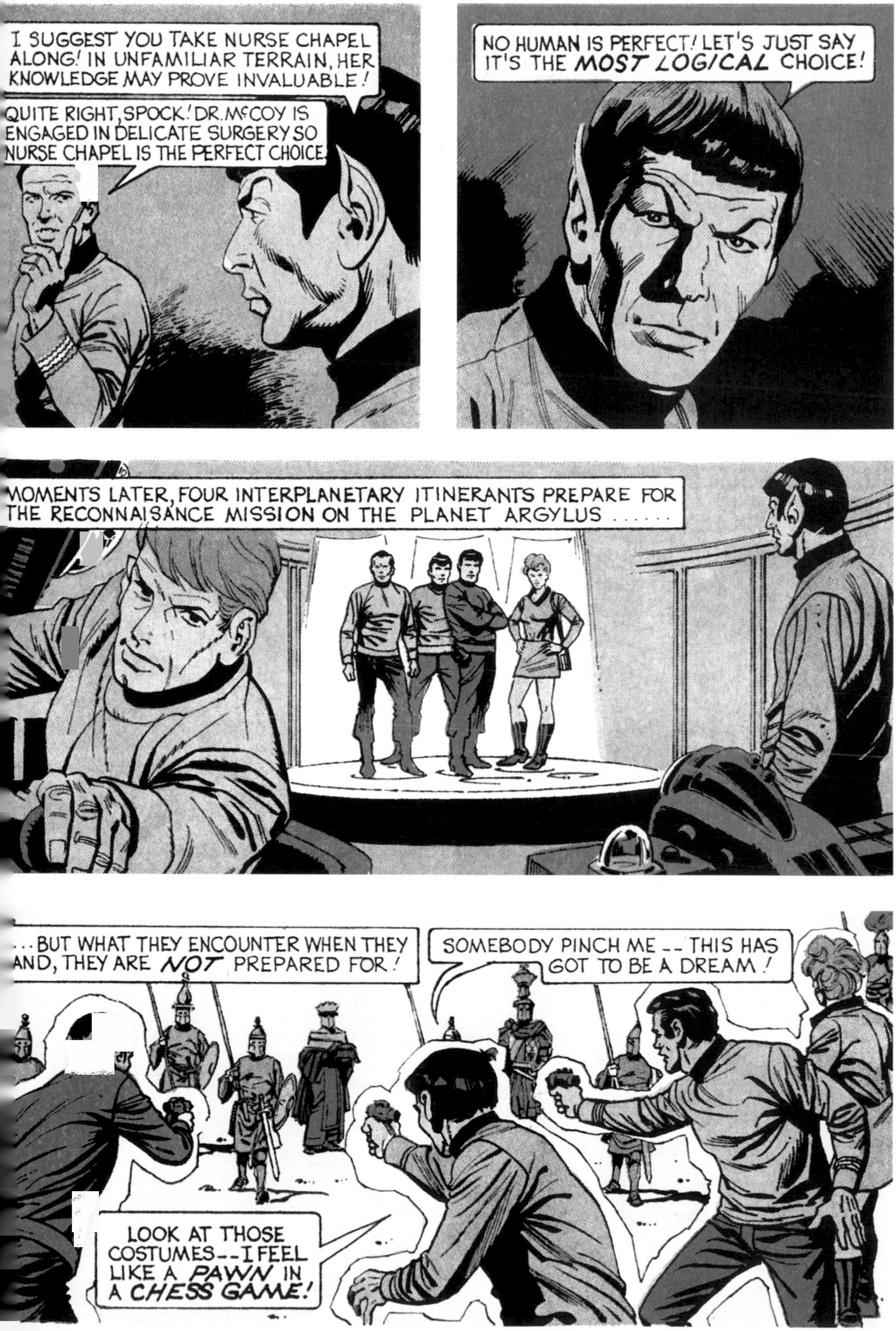

I SUGGEST YOU TAKE NURSE CHAPEL ALONG! IN UNFAMILIAR TERRAIN, HER KNOWLEDGE MAY PROVE INVALUABLE!
QUITE RIGHT, SPOCK! DR. McCOY IS ENGAGED IN DELICATE SURGERY SO NURSE CHAPEL IS THE PERFECT CHOICE.
NO HUMAN IS PERFECT! LET'S JUST SAY IT'S THE MOST LOGICAL CHOICE!
MOMENTS LATER, FOUR INTERPLANETARY ITINERANTS PREPARE FOR THE RECONNAISANCE MISSION ON THE PLANET ARGYLUS ......
...BUT WHAT THEY ENCOUNTER WHEN THEY AND, THEY ARE NOT PREPARED FOR!
SOMEBODY PINCH ME -- THIS HAS GOT TO BE A DREAM!
LOOK AT THOSE COSTUMES--I FEEL LIKE A PAWN IN A CHESS GAME!

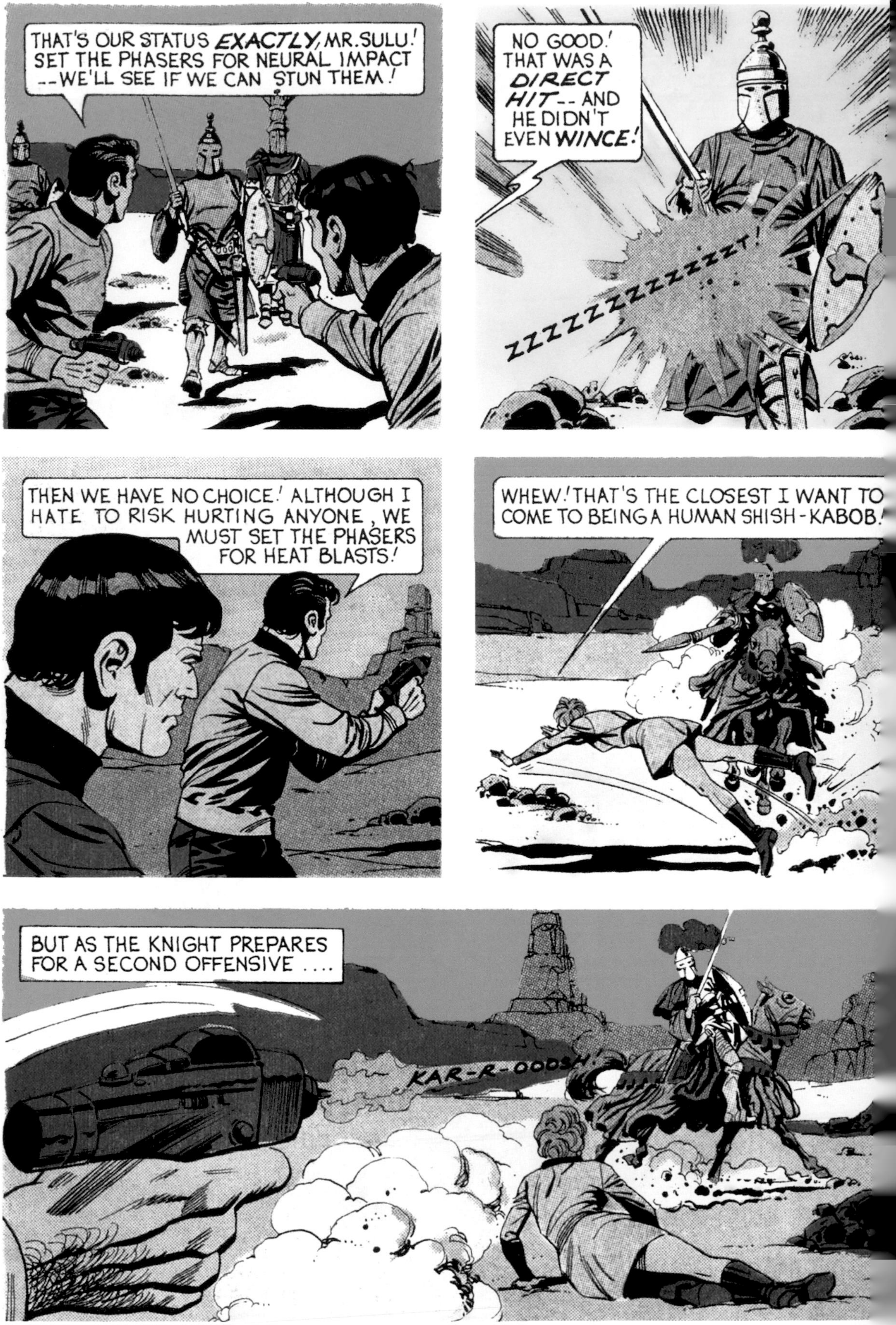
THAT'S OUR STATUS EXACTLY, MR. SULU! SET THE PHASERS FOR NEURAL IMPACT --WE'LL SEE IF WE CAN STUN THEM!
NO GOOD! THAT WAS A DIRECT HIT-- AND HE DIDN'T EVEN WINCE!
ZZZZZZZZZZZZZZZT!
THEN WE HAVE NO CHOICE! ALTHOUGH I HATE TO RISK HURTING ANYONE, WE MUST SET THE PHASERS FOR HEAT BLASTS!
WHEW! THAT'S THE CLOSEST I WANT TO COME TO BEING A HUMAN SHISH-KABOB!
BUT AS THE KNIGHT PREPARES FOR A SECOND OFFENSIVE ....
KAR-R-OOOSH!

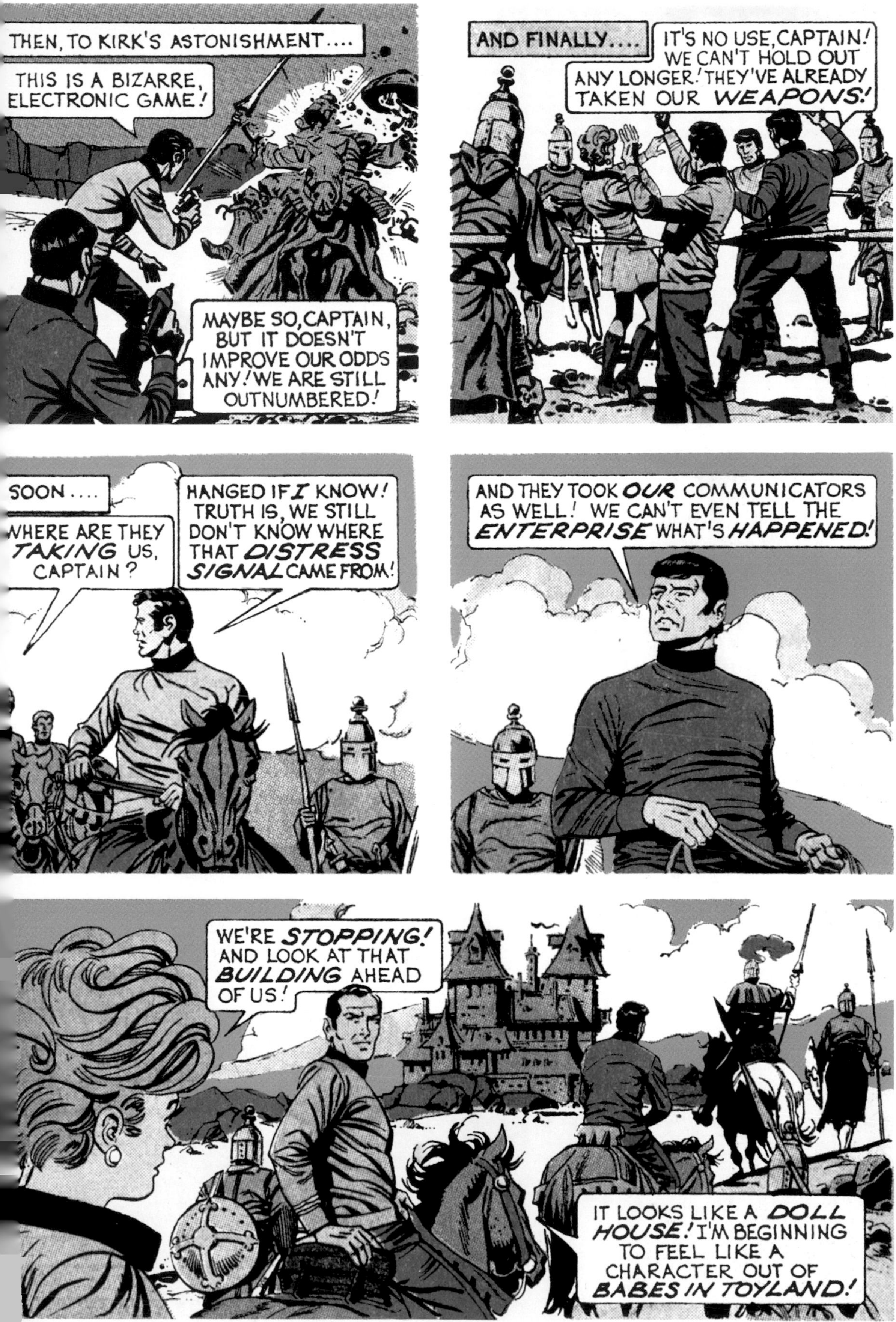
THEN, TO KIRK'S ASTONISHMENT....
THIS IS A BIZARRE, ELECTRONIC GAME!
MAYBE SO, CAPTAIN, BUT IT DOESN'T IMPROVE OUR ODDS ANY! WE ARE STILL OUTNUMBERED!
AND FINALLY....
IT'S NO USE, CAPTAIN! WE CAN'T HOLD OUT ANY LONGER! THEY'VE ALREADY TAKEN OUR WEAPONS!
SOON....
WHERE ARE THEY TAKING US, CAPTAIN?
HANGED IF I KNOW! TRUTH IS, WE STILL DON'T KNOW WHERE THAT DISTRESS SIGNAL CAME FROM!
AND THEY TOOK OUR COMMUNICATORS AS WELL! WE CAN'T EVEN TELL THE ENTERPRISE WHAT'S HAPPENED!
WE'RE STOPPING! AND LOOK AT THAT BUILDING AHEAD OF US!
IT LOOKS LIKE A DOLL HOUSE! I'M BEGINNING TO FEEL LIKE A CHARACTER OUT OF BABES IN TOYLAND!

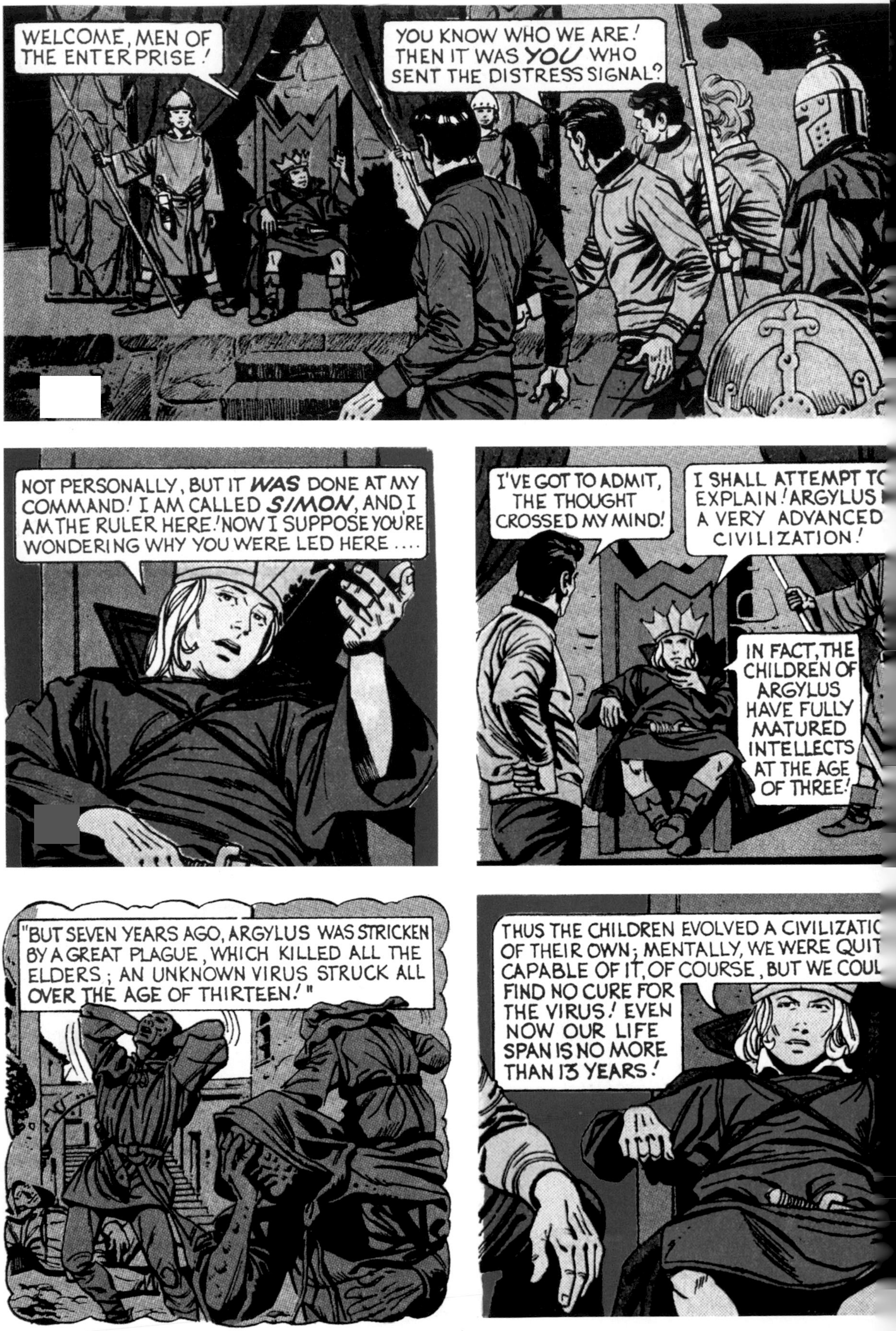
WELCOME, MEN OF THE ENTERPRISE!
YOU KNOW WHO WE ARE! THEN IT WAS YOU WHO SENT THE DISTRESS SIGNAL?
NOT PERSONALLY, BUT IT WAS DONE AT MY COMMAND! I AM CALLED SIMON, AND I AM THE RULER HERE! NOW I SUPPOSE YOU'RE WONDERING WHY YOU WERE LED HERE....
I'VE GOT TO ADMIT, THE THOUGHT CROSSED MY MIND!
I SHALL ATTEMPT TO EXPLAIN! ARGYLUS A VERY ADVANCED CIVILIZATION!
IN FACT, THE CHILDREN OF ARGYLUS HAVE FULLY MATURED INTELLECTS AT THE AGE OF THREE!
"BUT SEVEN YEARS AGO, ARGYLUS WAS STRICKEN BY A GREAT PLAGUE, WHICH KILLED ALL THE ELDERS; AN UNKNOWN VIRUS STRUCK ALL OVER THE AGE OF THIRTEEN!"
THUS THE CHILDREN EVOLVED A CIVILIZATI OF THEIR OWN; MENTALLY, WE WERE QUIT CAPABLE OF IT, OF COURSE, BUT WE COUL FIND NO CURE FOR THE VIRUS! EVEN NOW OUR LIFE SPAN IS NO MORE THAN 13 YEARS!

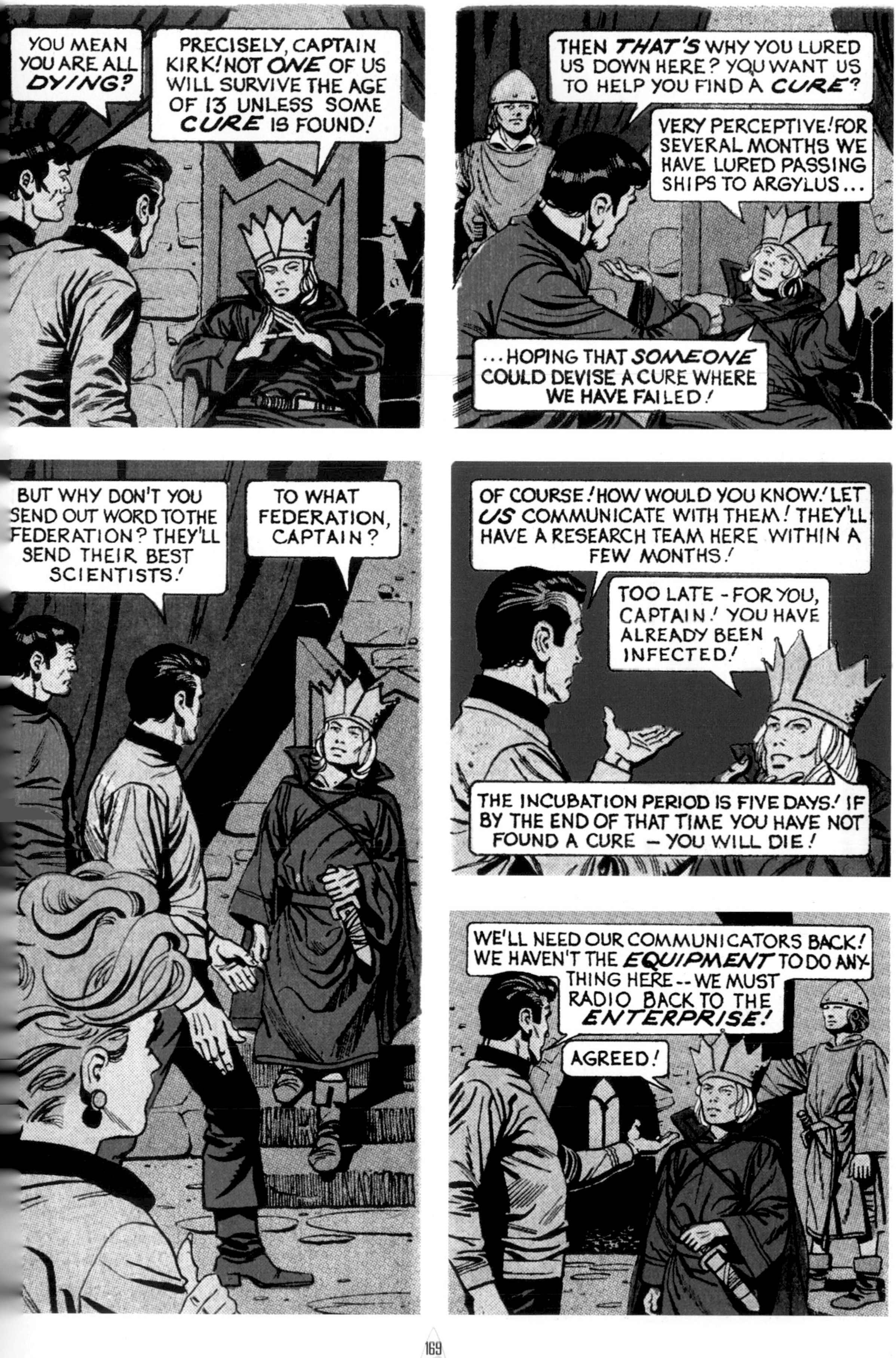
YOU MEAN YOU ARE ALL DYING?
PRECISELY, CAPTAIN KIRK! NOT ONE OF US WILL SURVIVE THE AGE OF 13 UNLESS SOME CURE IS FOUND!
THEN THAT'S WHY YOU LURED US DOWN HERE? YOU WANT US TO HELP YOU FIND A CURE?
VERY PERCEPTIVE! FOR SEVERAL MONTHS WE HAVE LURED PASSING SHIPS TO ARGYLUS...
...HOPING THAT SOMEONE COULD DEVISE A CURE WHERE WE HAVE FAILED!
BUT WHY DON'T YOU SEND OUT WORD TO THE FEDERATION? THEY'LL SEND THEIR BEST SCIENTISTS!
TO WHAT FEDERATION, CAPTAIN?
OF COURSE! HOW WOULD YOU KNOW! LET US COMMUNICATE WITH THEM! THEY'LL HAVE A RESEARCH TEAM HERE WITHIN A FEW MONTHS!
TOO LATE - FOR YOU, CAPTAIN! YOU HAVE ALREADY BEEN INFECTED!
THE INCUBATION PERIOD IS FIVE DAYS! IF BY THE END OF THAT TIME YOU HAVE NOT FOUND A CURE - YOU WILL DIE!
WE'LL NEED OUR COMMUNICATORS BACK! WE HAVEN'T THE EQUIPMENT TO DO ANYTHING HERE -- WE MUST RADIO BACK TO THE ENTERPRISE!
AGREED!

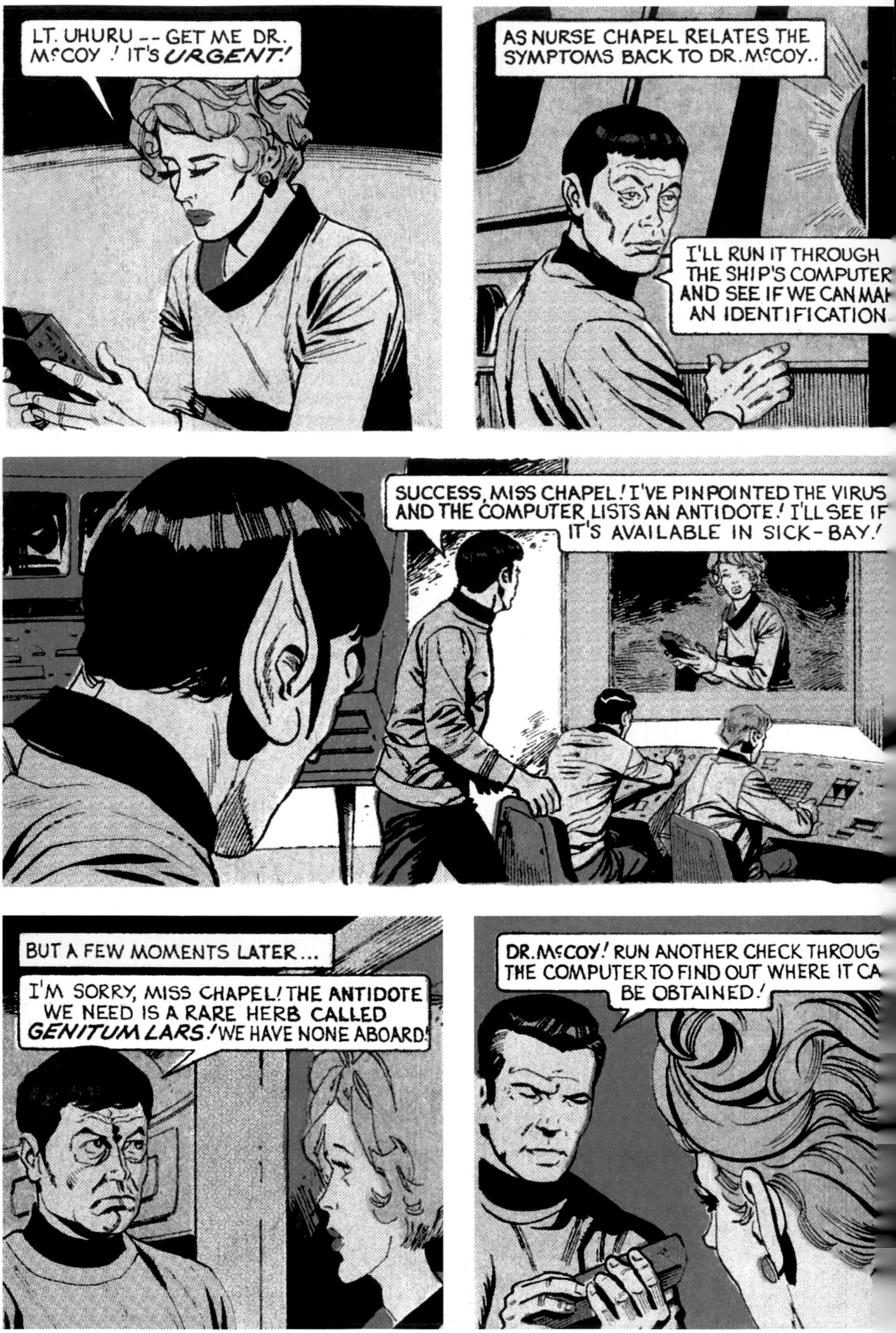
LT. UHURU -- GET ME DR. McCOY! IT'S URGENT!
AS NURSE CHAPEL RELATES THE SYMPTOMS BACK TO DR. McCOY..
I'LL RUN IT THROUGH THE SHIP'S COMPUTER AND SEE IF WE CAN MA AN IDENTIFICATION.
SUCCESS, MISS CHAPEL! I'VE PINPOINTED THE VIRUS AND THE COMPUTER LISTS AN ANTIDOTE! I'LL SEE IF IT'S AVAILABLE IN SICK-BAY!
BUT A FEW MOMENTS LATER...
I'M SORRY, MISS CHAPEL! THE ANTIDOTE WE NEED IS A RARE HERB CALLED GENITUM LARS! WE HAVE NONE ABOARD!
DR. McCOY! RUN ANOTHER CHECK THROUG THE COMPUTER TO FIND OUT WHERE IT CA BE OBTAINED!

OMINNUS
176 MARK 899

THE NEAREST PLANET ON WHICH GENITUM LARS CAN BE FOUND IS OMINNUS! BUT OMINNUS IS ON THE *OTHER EDGE OF THE GALAXY!* HOW LONG DO WE HAVE?

FIVE DAYS AT THE MOST! THINK YOU CAN MAKE IT?

I WOULDN'T LAY ANY ODDS ON IT! IT'S A TWO-DAY JOURNEY EACH WAY! IF ANYTHING SHOULD DELAY US....

IF ANYTHING SHOULD DELAY YOU, DOCTOR, YOU'RE GOING TO LOSE A CAPTAIN, A CHIEF ENGINEER, A NAVIGATOR, AND A GOOD NURSE!

ENOUGH TIME WASTED! I WILL ESCORT YOU ALL TO A MEDICAL RESEARCH CENTER. PERHAPS THERE, YOU WILL FIND SOME OTHER HOPE..

WITH FIRST OFFICER SPOCK IN COMMAND, THE ENTERPRISE ACCELERATES TOWARD THE PLANET OMINNUS ....

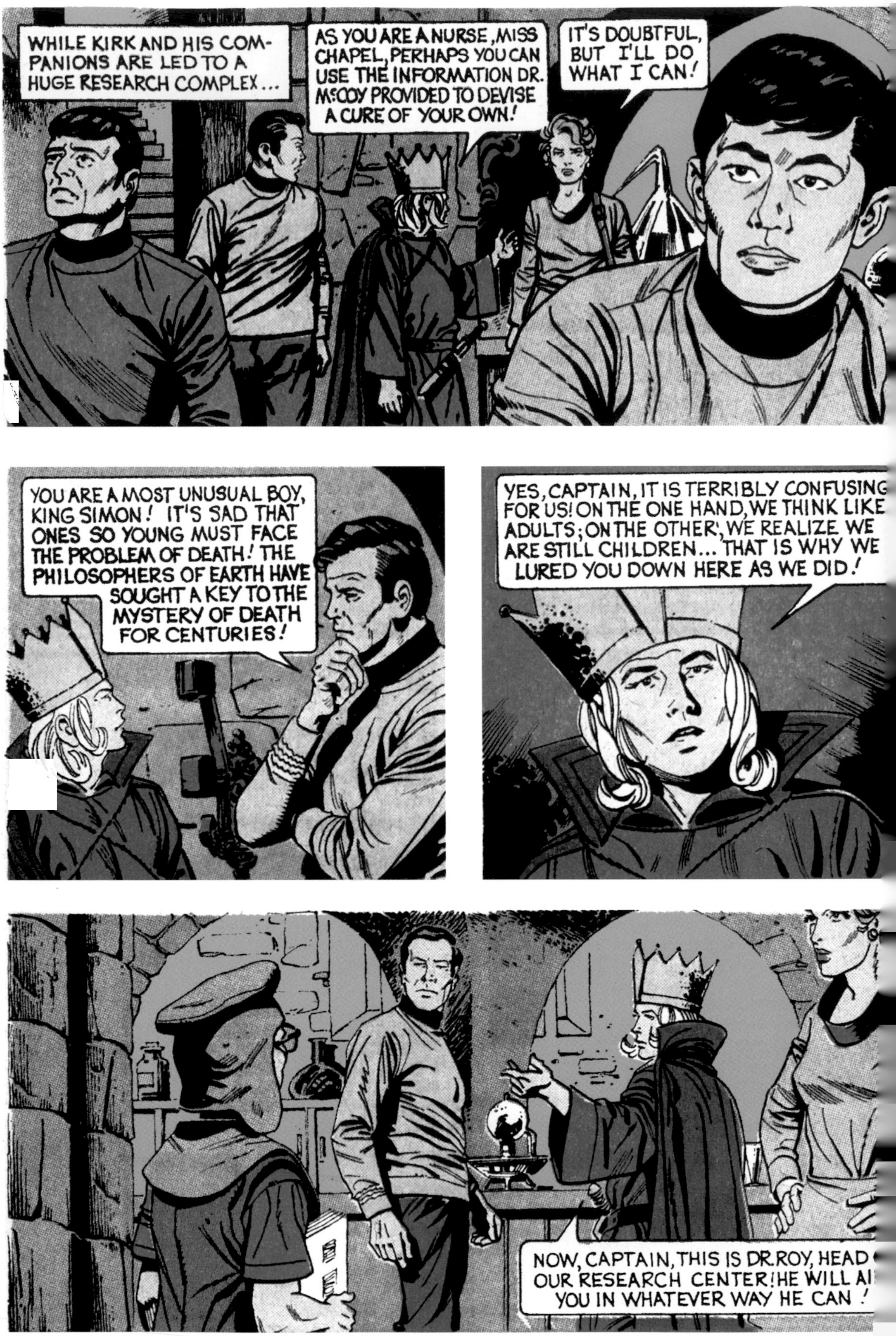
WHILE KIRK AND HIS COMPANIONS ARE LED TO A HUGE RESEARCH COMPLEX...
AS YOU ARE A NURSE, MISS CHAPEL, PERHAPS YOU CAN USE THE INFORMATION DR. McCOY PROVIDED TO DEVISE A CURE OF YOUR OWN!
IT'S DOUBTFUL, BUT I'LL DO WHAT I CAN!
YOU ARE A MOST UNUSUAL BOY, KING SIMON! IT'S SAD THAT ONES SO YOUNG MUST FACE THE PROBLEM OF DEATH! THE PHILOSOPHERS OF EARTH HAVE SOUGHT A KEY TO THE MYSTERY OF DEATH FOR CENTURIES!
YES, CAPTAIN, IT IS TERRIBLY CONFUSING FOR US! ON THE ONE HAND, WE THINK LIKE ADULTS; ON THE OTHER, WE REALIZE WE ARE STILL CHILDREN... THAT IS WHY WE LURED YOU DOWN HERE AS WE DID!
NOW, CAPTAIN, THIS IS DR. ROY, HEAD
OUR RESEARCH CENTER! HE WILL AI
YOU IN WHATEVER WAY HE CAN!

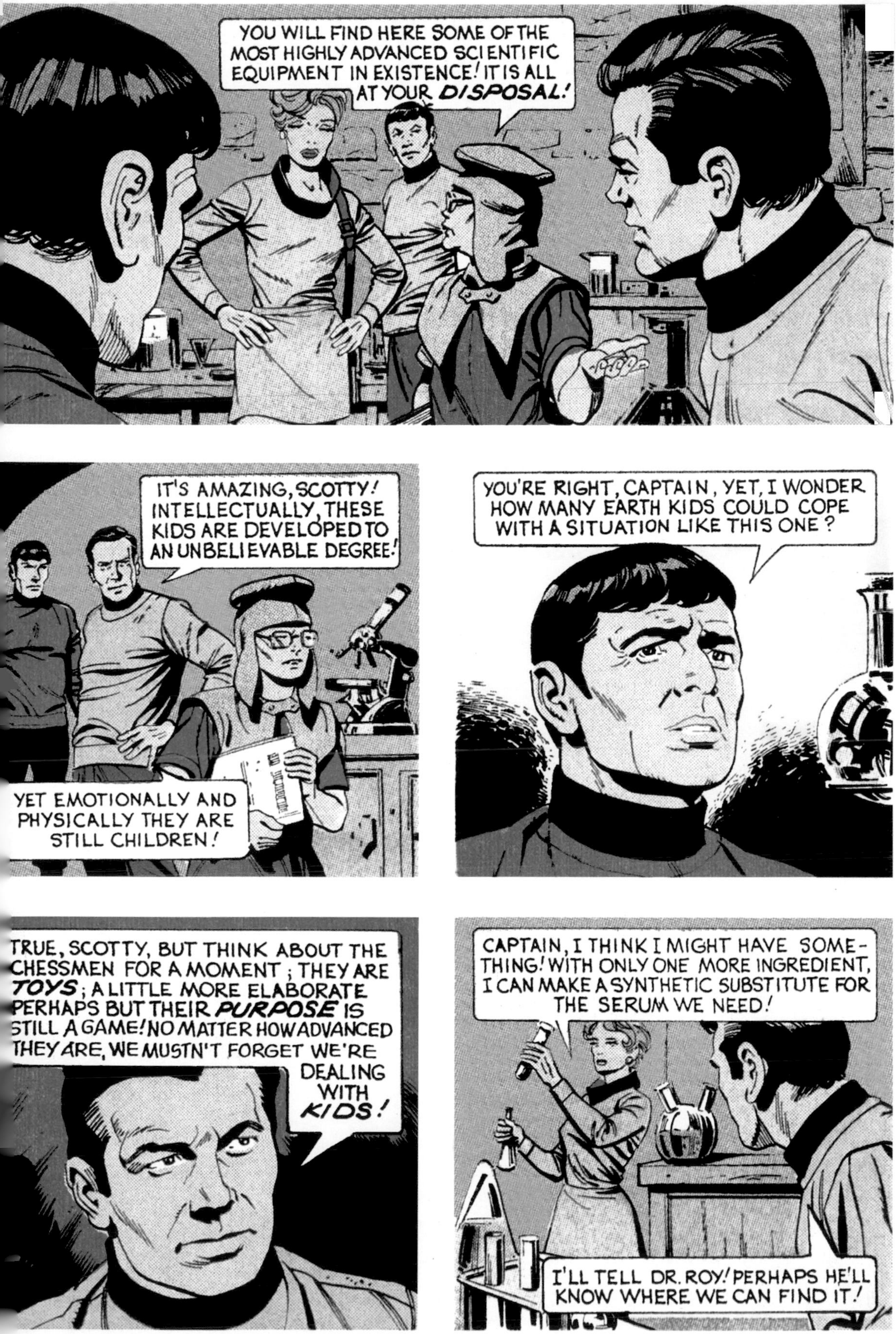
YOU WILL FIND HERE SOME OF THE MOST HIGHLY ADVANCED SCIENTIFIC EQUIPMENT IN EXISTENCE! IT IS ALL AT YOUR DISPOSAL!
IT'S AMAZING, SCOTTY! INTELLECTUALLY, THESE KIDS ARE DEVELOPED TO AN UNBELIEVABLE DEGREE!
YET EMOTIONALLY AND PHYSICALLY THEY ARE STILL CHILDREN!
YOU'RE RIGHT, CAPTAIN, YET, I WONDER HOW MANY EARTH KIDS COULD COPE WITH A SITUATION LIKE THIS ONE?
TRUE, SCOTTY, BUT THINK ABOUT THE CHESSMEN FOR A MOMENT; THEY ARE TOYS; A LITTLE MORE ELABORATE PERHAPS BUT THEIR PURPOSE IS STILL A GAME! NO MATTER HOW ADVANCED THEY ARE, WE MUSTN'T FORGET WE'RE DEALING WITH KIDS!
CAPTAIN, I THINK I MIGHT HAVE SOMETHING! WITH ONLY ONE MORE INGREDIENT, I CAN MAKE A SYNTHETIC SUBSTITUTE FOR THE SERUM WE NEED!
I'LL TELL DR. ROY! PERHAPS HE'LL KNOW WHERE WE CAN FIND IT!

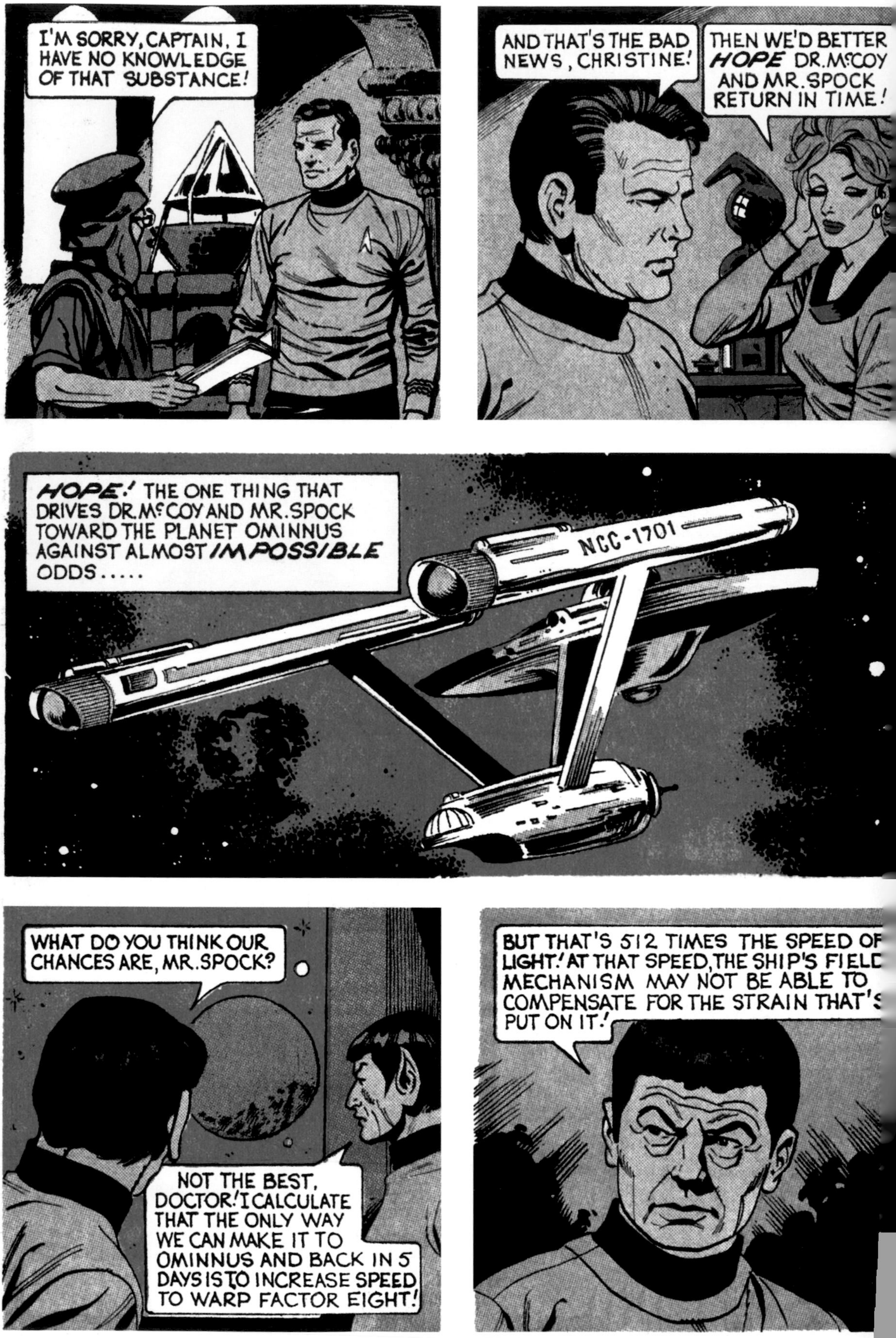
I'M SORRY, CAPTAIN, I HAVE NO KNOWLEDGE OF THAT SUBSTANCE!
AND THAT'S THE BAD NEWS, CHRISTINE!
THEN WE'D BETTER HOPE DR. McCOY AND MR. SPOCK RETURN IN TIME!
HOPE! THE ONE THING THAT DRIVES DR. McCOY AND MR. SPOCK TOWARD THE PLANET OMINNUS AGAINST ALMOST IMPOSSIBLE ODDS.....
NCC-1701
WHAT DO YOU THINK OUR CHANCES ARE, MR. SPOCK?
NOT THE BEST, DOCTOR! I CALCULATE THAT THE ONLY WAY WE CAN MAKE IT TO OMINNUS AND BACK IN 5 DAYS IS TO INCREASE SPEED TO WARP FACTOR EIGHT!
BUT THAT'S 512 TIMES THE SPEED OF LIGHT! AT THAT SPEED, THE SHIP'S FIELD MECHANISM MAY NOT BE ABLE TO COMPENSATE FOR THE STRAIN THAT'S PUT ON IT!

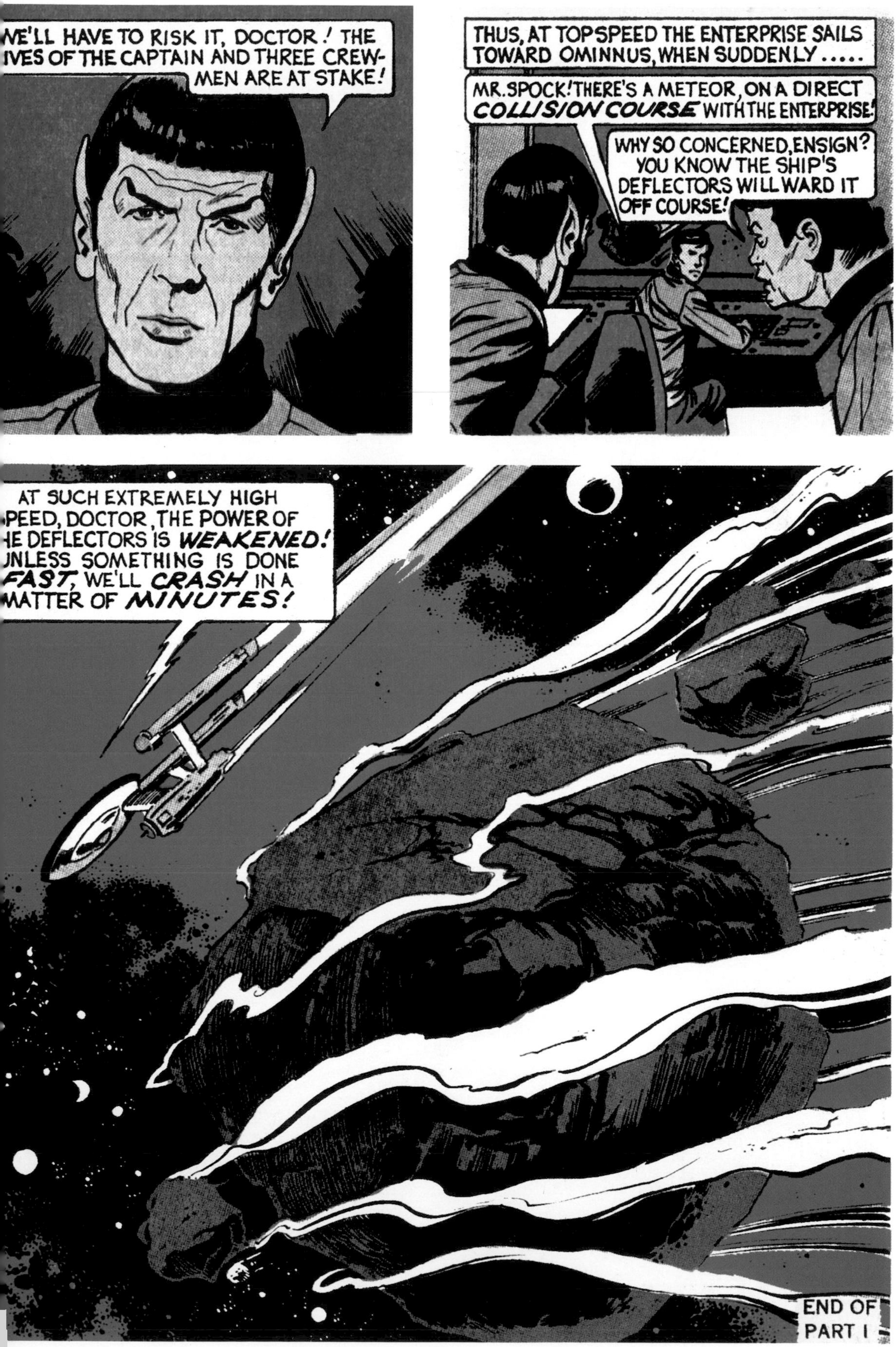

VE'LL HAVE TO RISK IT, DOCTOR! THE IVES OF THE CAPTAIN AND THREE CREW-MEN ARE AT STAKE!
THUS, AT TOPSPEED THE ENTERPRISE SAILS TOWARD OMINNUS, WHEN SUDDENLY.....
MR. SPOCK! THERE'S A METEOR, ON A DIRECT COLLISION COURSE WITH THE ENTERPRISE!
WHY SO CONCERNED, ENSIGN? YOU KNOW THE SHIP'S DEFLECTORS WILL WARD IT OFF COURSE!
AT SUCH EXTREMELY HIGH PEED, DOCTOR, THE POWER OF HE DEFLECTORS IS WEAKENED! JNLESS SOMETHING IS DONE FAST, WE'LL CRASH IN A MATTER OF MINUTES!
END OF PART I

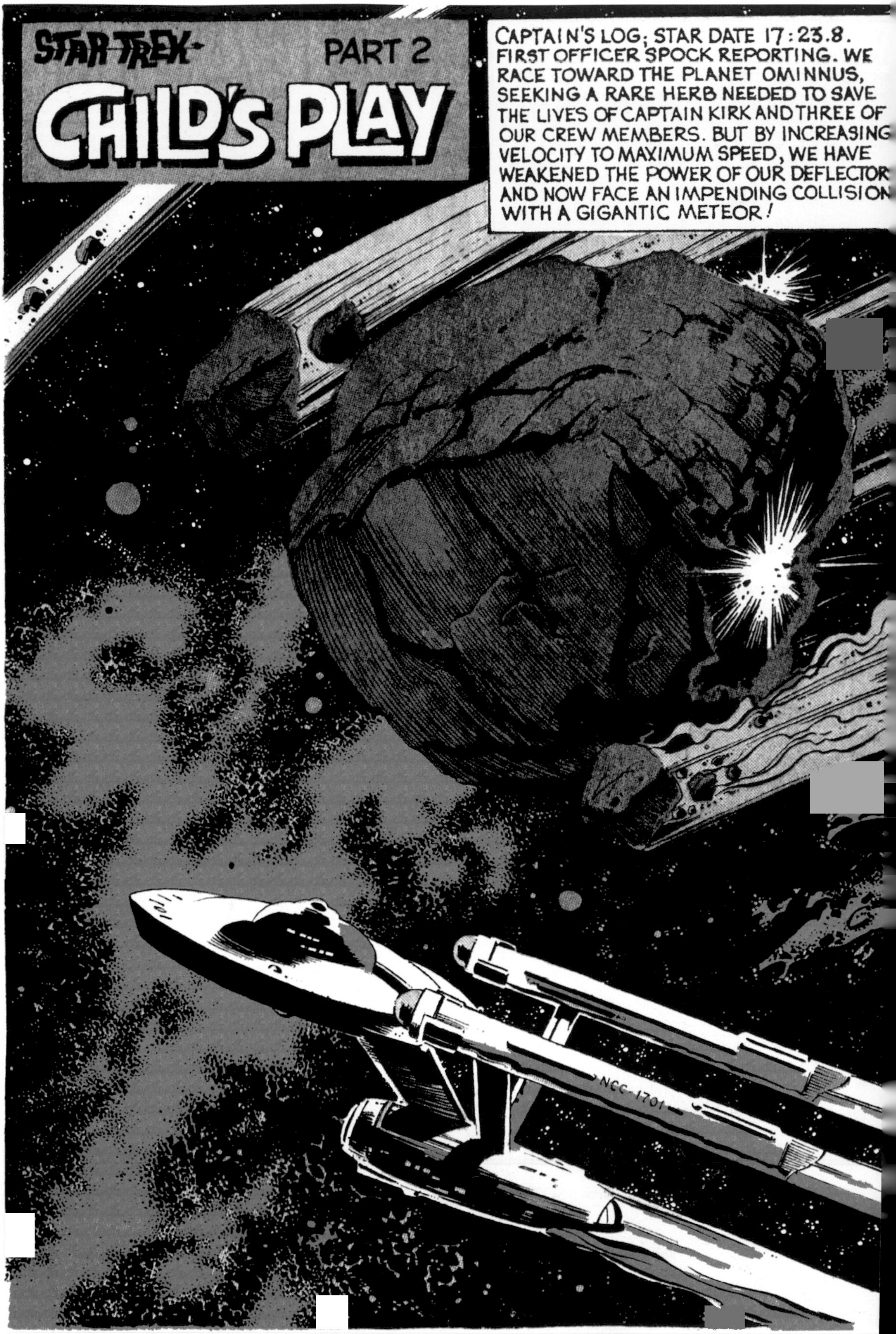
STAR TREK
PART 2
CHILD'S PLAY
CAPTAIN'S LOG; STAR DATE 17:23.8. FIRST OFFICER SPOCK REPORTING. WE RACE TOWARD THE PLANET OMINNUS, SEEKING A RARE HERB NEEDED TO SAVE THE LIVES OF CAPTAIN KIRK AND THREE OF OUR CREW MEMBERS. BUT BY INCREASING VELOCITY TO MAXIMUM SPEED, WE HAVE WEAKENED THE POWER OF OUR DEFLECTOR AND NOW FACE AN IMPENDING COLLISION WITH A GIGANTIC METEOR!
NCC-1701

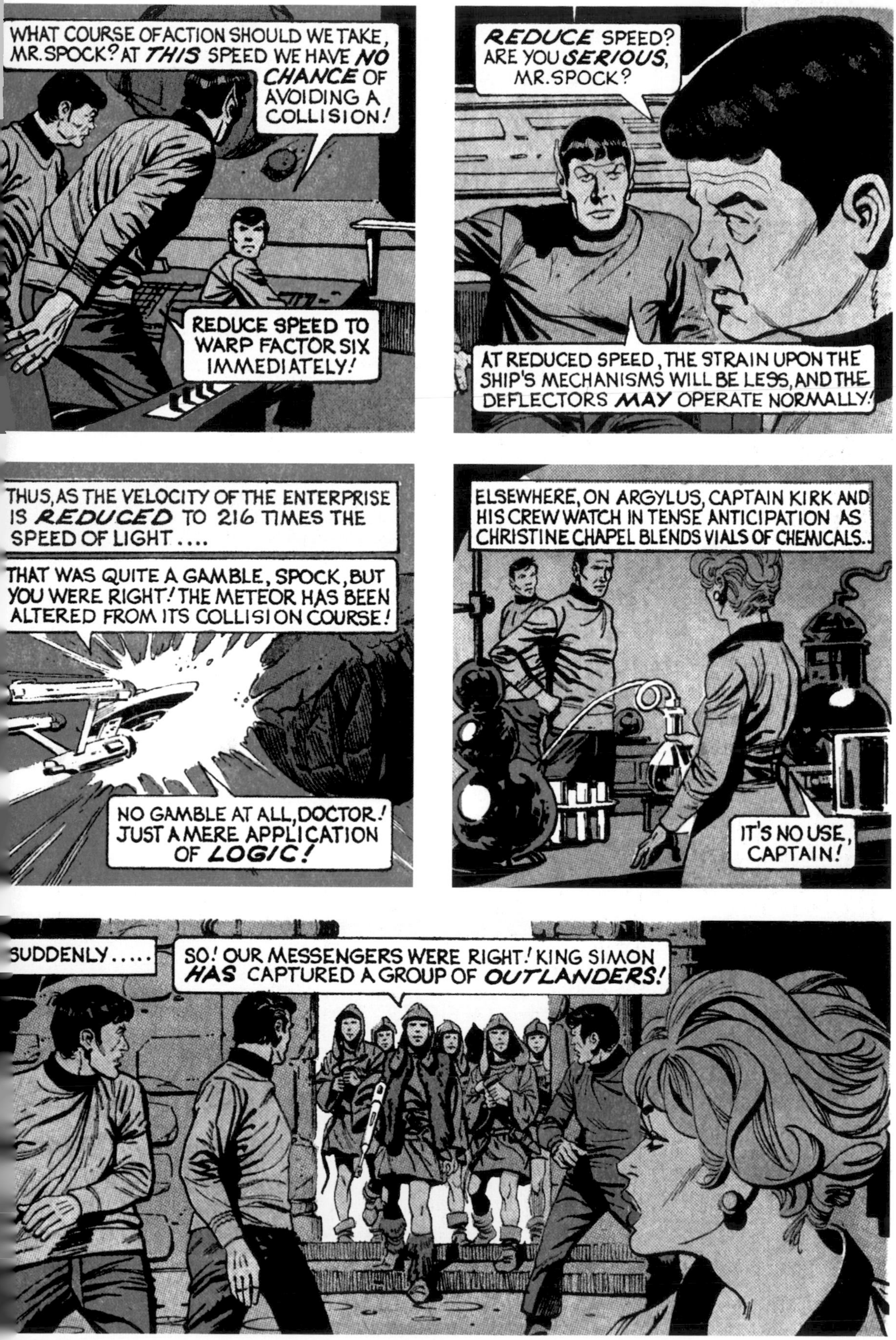
WHAT COURSE OF ACTION SHOULD WE TAKE, MR. SPOCK? AT THIS SPEED WE HAVE NO CHANCE OF AVOIDING A COLLISION!
REDUCE SPEED TO WARP FACTOR SIX IMMEDIATELY!
REDUCE SPEED? ARE YOU SERIOUS, MR. SPOCK?
AT REDUCED SPEED, THE STRAIN UPON THE SHIP'S MECHANISMS WILL BE LESS, AND THE DEFLECTORS MAY OPERATE NORMALLY!
THUS, AS THE VELOCITY OF THE ENTERPRISE IS REDUCED TO 216 TIMES THE SPEED OF LIGHT....
THAT WAS QUITE A GAMBLE, SPOCK, BUT YOU WERE RIGHT! THE METEOR HAS BEEN ALTERED FROM ITS COLLISION COURSE!
NO GAMBLE AT ALL, DOCTOR! JUST A MERE APPLICATION OF LOGIC!
ELSEWHERE, ON ARGYLUS, CAPTAIN KIRK AND HIS CREW WATCH IN TENSE ANTICIPATION AS CHRISTINE CHAPEL BLENDS VIALS OF CHEMICALS..
IT'S NO USE, CAPTAIN!
SUDDENLY.....
SO! OUR MESSENGERS WERE RIGHT! KING SIMON HAS CAPTURED A GROUP OF OUTLANDERS!

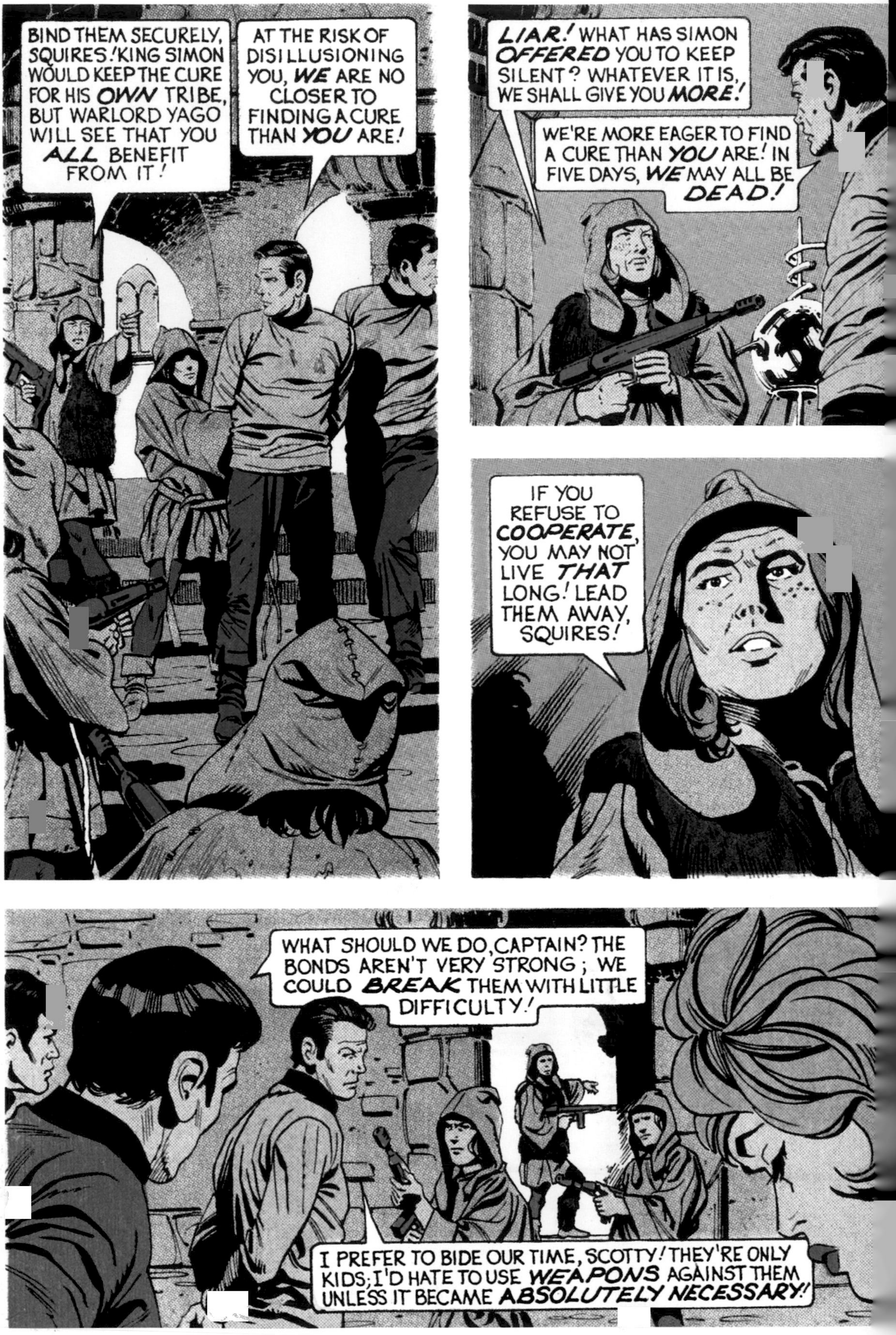
BIND THEM SECURELY, SQUIRES! KING SIMON WOULD KEEP THE CURE FOR HIS OWN TRIBE, BUT WARLORD YAGO WILL SEE THAT YOU ALL BENEFIT FROM IT!
AT THE RISK OF DISILLUSIONING YOU, WE ARE NO CLOSER TO FINDING A CURE THAN YOU ARE!
LIAR! WHAT HAS SIMON OFFERED YOU TO KEEP SILENT? WHATEVER IT IS, WE SHALL GIVE YOU MORE!
WE'RE MORE EAGER TO FIND A CURE THAN YOU ARE! IN FIVE DAYS, WE MAY ALL BE DEAD!
IF YOU REFUSE TO COOPERATE, YOU MAY NOT LIVE THAT LONG! LEAD THEM AWAY, SQUIRES!
WHAT SHOULD WE DO, CAPTAIN? THE BONDS AREN'T VERY STRONG; WE COULD BREAK THEM WITH LITTLE DIFFICULTY!
I PREFER TO BIDE OUR TIME, SCOTTY! THEY'RE ONLY KIDS; I'D HATE TO USE WEAPONS AGAINST THEM UNLESS IT BECAME ABSOLUTELY NECESSARY!

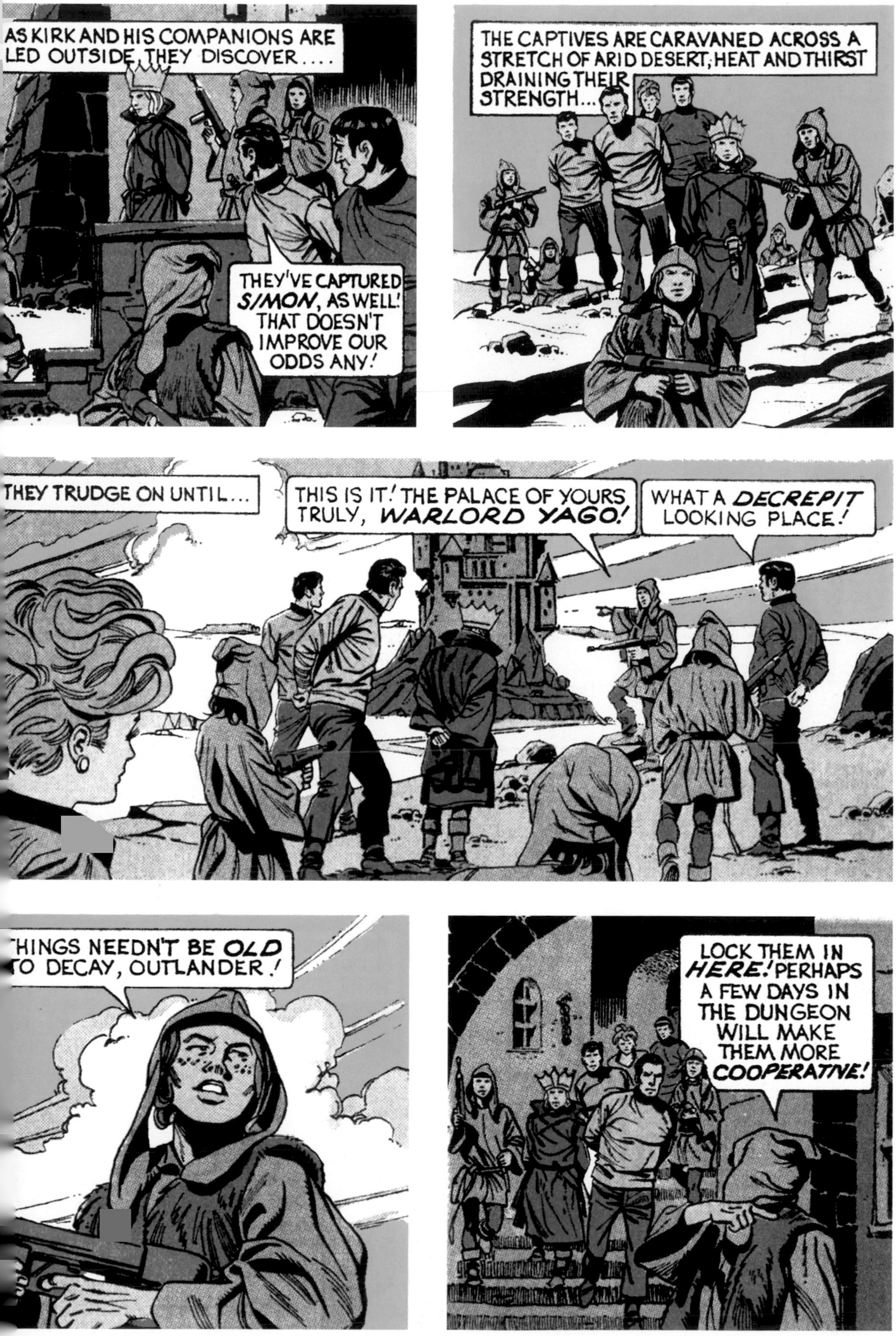
AS KIRK AND HIS COMPANIONS ARE LED OUTSIDE, THEY DISCOVER....
THEY'VE CAPTURED SIMON, AS WELL! THAT DOESN'T IMPROVE OUR ODDS ANY!
THE CAPTIVES ARE CARAVANED ACROSS A STRETCH OF ARID DESERT; HEAT AND THIRST DRAINING THEIR STRENGTH...
THEY TRUDGE ON UNTIL...
THIS IS IT! THE PALACE OF YOURS TRULY, WARLORD YAGO!
WHAT A DECREPIT LOOKING PLACE!
THINGS NEEDN'T BE OLD TO DECAY, OUTLANDER!
LOCK THEM IN HERE! PERHAPS A FEW DAYS IN THE DUNGEON WILL MAKE THEM MORE COOPERATIVE!

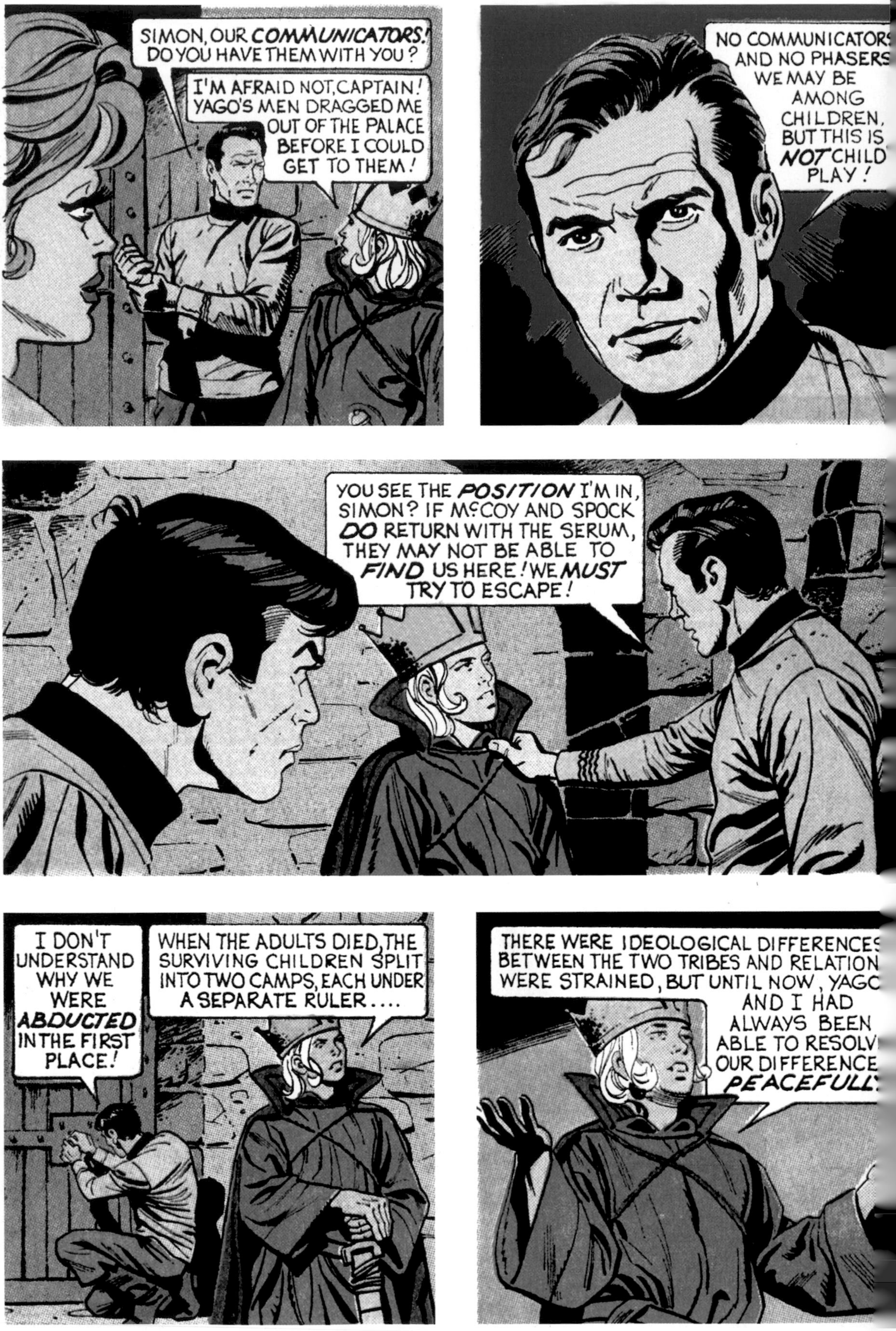
SIMON, OUR COMMUNICATORS! DO YOU HAVE THEM WITH YOU?
I'M AFRAID NOT, CAPTAIN! YAGO'S MEN DRAGGED ME OUT OF THE PALACE BEFORE I COULD GET TO THEM!
NO COMMUNICATORS AND NO PHASERS WE MAY BE AMONG CHILDREN, BUT THIS IS NOT CHILD PLAY!
YOU SEE THE POSITION I'M IN, SIMON? IF McCOY AND SPOCK DO RETURN WITH THE SERUM, THEY MAY NOT BE ABLE TO FIND US HERE! WE MUST TRY TO ESCAPE!
I DON'T UNDERSTAND WHY WE WERE ABDUCTED IN THE FIRST PLACE!
WHEN THE ADULTS DIED, THE SURVIVING CHILDREN SPLIT INTO TWO CAMPS, EACH UNDER A SEPARATE RULER....
THERE WERE IDEOLOGICAL DIFFERENCES BETWEEN THE TWO TRIBES AND RELATION WERE STRAINED, BUT UNTIL NOW, YAGO AND I HAD ALWAYS BEEN ABLE TO RESOLV OUR DIFFERENCE PEACEFULL

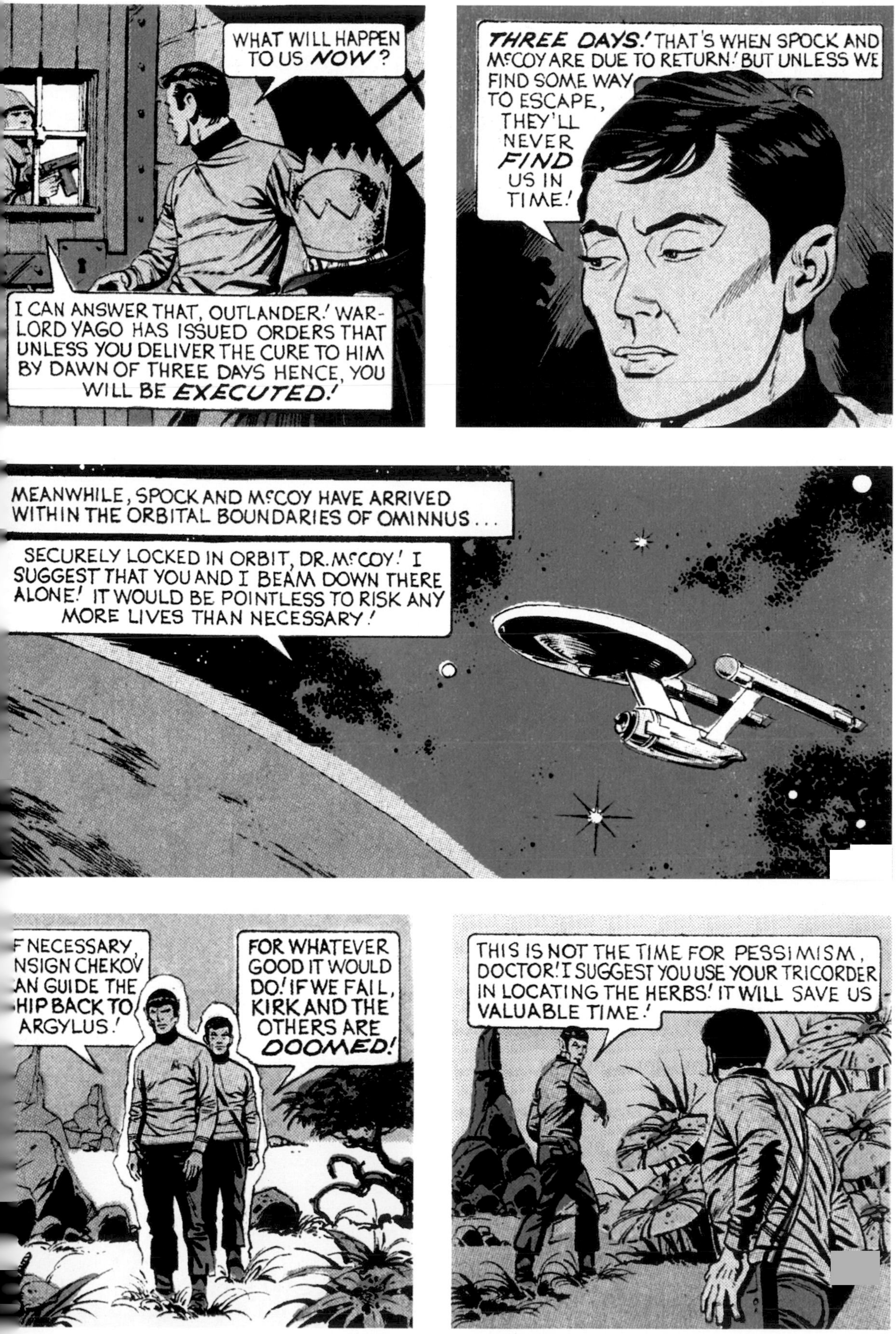
WHAT WILL HAPPEN TO US NOW?
I CAN ANSWER THAT, OUTLANDER! WAR-LORD YAGO HAS ISSUED ORDERS THAT UNLESS YOU DELIVER THE CURE TO HIM BY DAWN OF THREE DAYS HENCE, YOU WILL BE EXECUTED!
THREE DAYS! THAT'S WHEN SPOCK AND McCOY ARE DUE TO RETURN! BUT UNLESS WE FIND SOME WAY TO ESCAPE, THEY'LL NEVER FIND US IN TIME!
MEANWHILE, SPOCK AND McCOY HAVE ARRIVED WITHIN THE ORBITAL BOUNDARIES OF OMINNUS...
SECURELY LOCKED IN ORBIT, DR. McCOY! I SUGGEST THAT YOU AND I BEAM DOWN THERE ALONE! IT WOULD BE POINTLESS TO RISK ANY MORE LIVES THAN NECESSARY!
F NECESSARY, NSIGN CHEKOV AN GUIDE THE HIP BACK TO ARGYLUS!
FOR WHATEVER GOOD IT WOULD DO! IF WE FAIL, KIRK AND THE OTHERS ARE DOOMED!
THIS IS NOT THE TIME FOR PESSIMISM, DOCTOR! I SUGGEST YOU USE YOUR TRICORDER IN LOCATING THE HERBS! IT WILL SAVE US VALUABLE TIME!

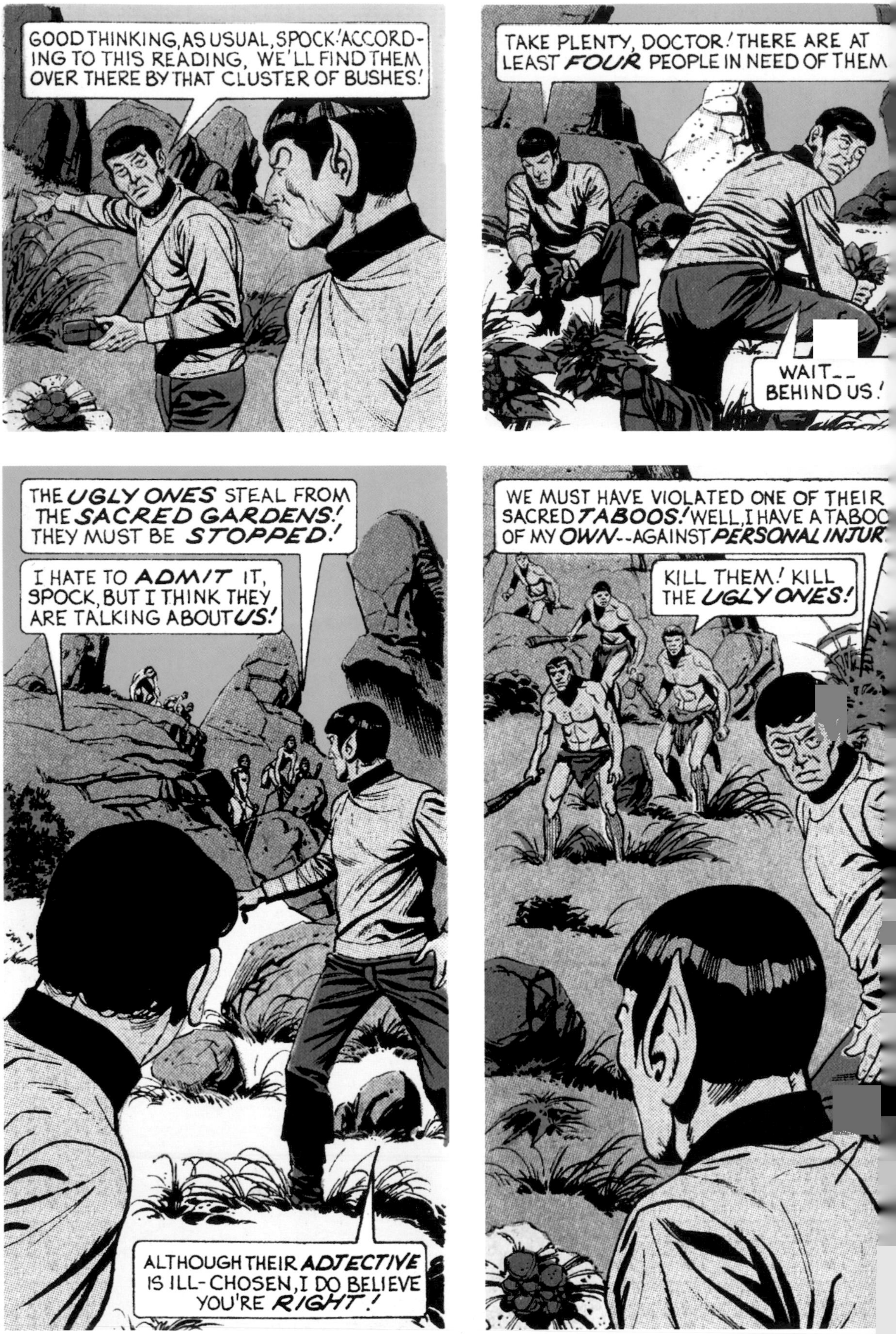
GOOD THINKING, AS USUAL, SPOCK! ACCORDING TO THIS READING, WE'LL FIND THEM OVER THERE BY THAT CLUSTER OF BUSHES!
TAKE PLENTY, DOCTOR! THERE ARE AT LEAST FOUR PEOPLE IN NEED OF THEM
WAIT-- BEHIND US!
THE UGLY ONES STEAL FROM THE SACRED GARDENS! THEY MUST BE STOPPED!
I HATE TO ADMIT IT, SPOCK, BUT I THINK THEY ARE TALKING ABOUT US!
ALTHOUGH THEIR ADJECTIVE IS ILL-CHOSEN, I DO BELIEVE YOU'RE RIGHT!
WE MUST HAVE VIOLATED ONE OF THEIR SACRED TABOOS! WELL, I HAVE A TABOC OF MY OWN--AGAINST PERSONAL INJUR
KILL THEM! KILL THE UGLY ONES!

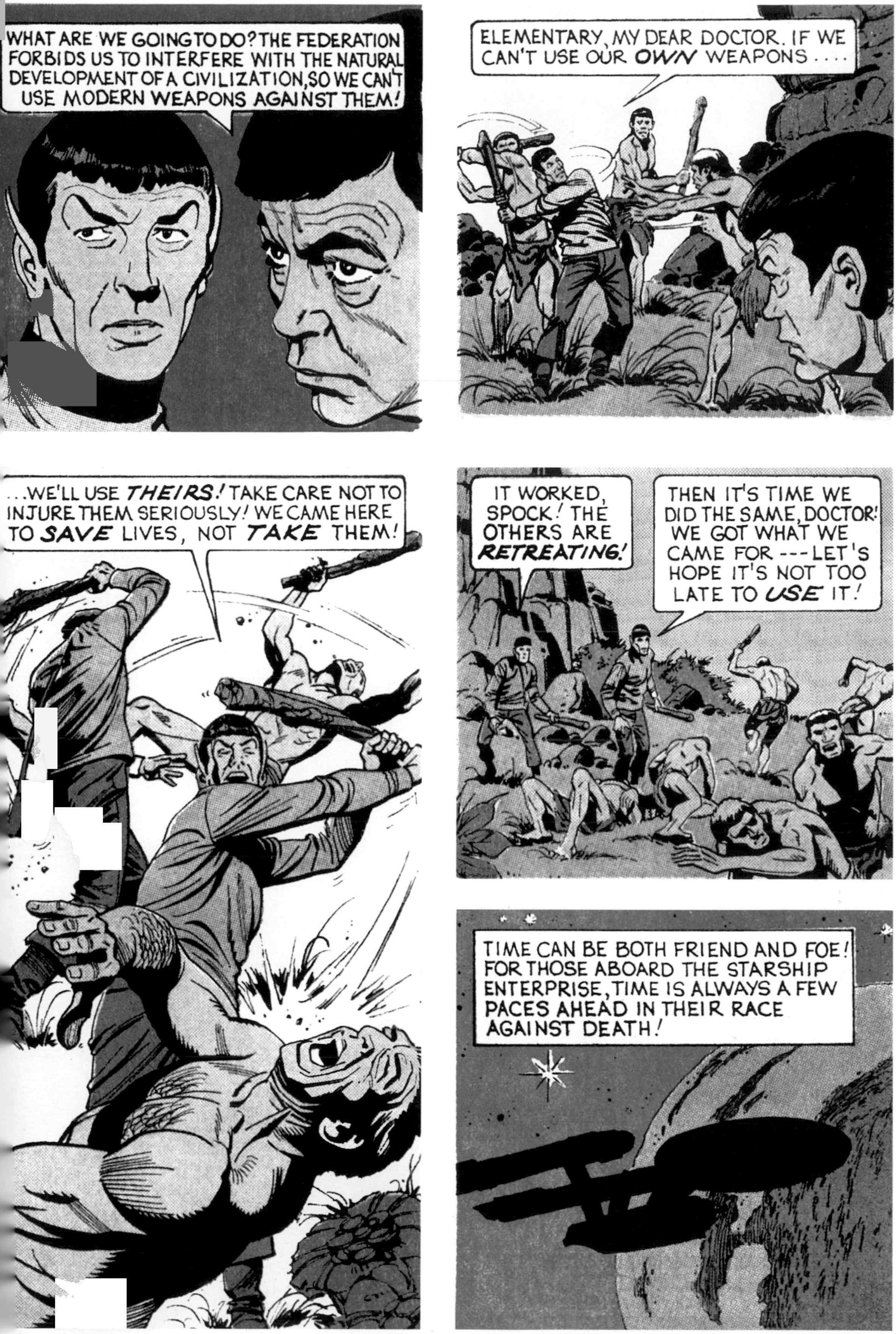

WHAT ARE WE GOING TO DO? THE FEDERATION FORBIDS US TO INTERFERE WITH THE NATURAL DEVELOPMENT OF A CIVILIZATION, SO WE CAN'T USE MODERN WEAPONS AGAINST THEM!
ELEMENTARY, MY DEAR DOCTOR. IF WE CAN'T USE OUR OWN WEAPONS....
...WE'LL USE THEIRS! TAKE CARE NOT TO INJURE THEM SERIOUSLY! WE CAME HERE TO SAVE LIVES, NOT TAKE THEM!
IT WORKED, SPOCK! THE OTHERS ARE RETREATING!
THEN IT'S TIME WE DID THE SAME, DOCTOR! WE GOT WHAT WE CAME FOR---LET'S HOPE IT'S NOT TOO LATE TO USE IT!
TIME CAN BE BOTH FRIEND AND FOE! FOR THOSE ABOARD THE STARSHIP ENTERPRISE, TIME IS ALWAYS A FEW PACES AHEAD IN THEIR RACE AGAINST DEATH!

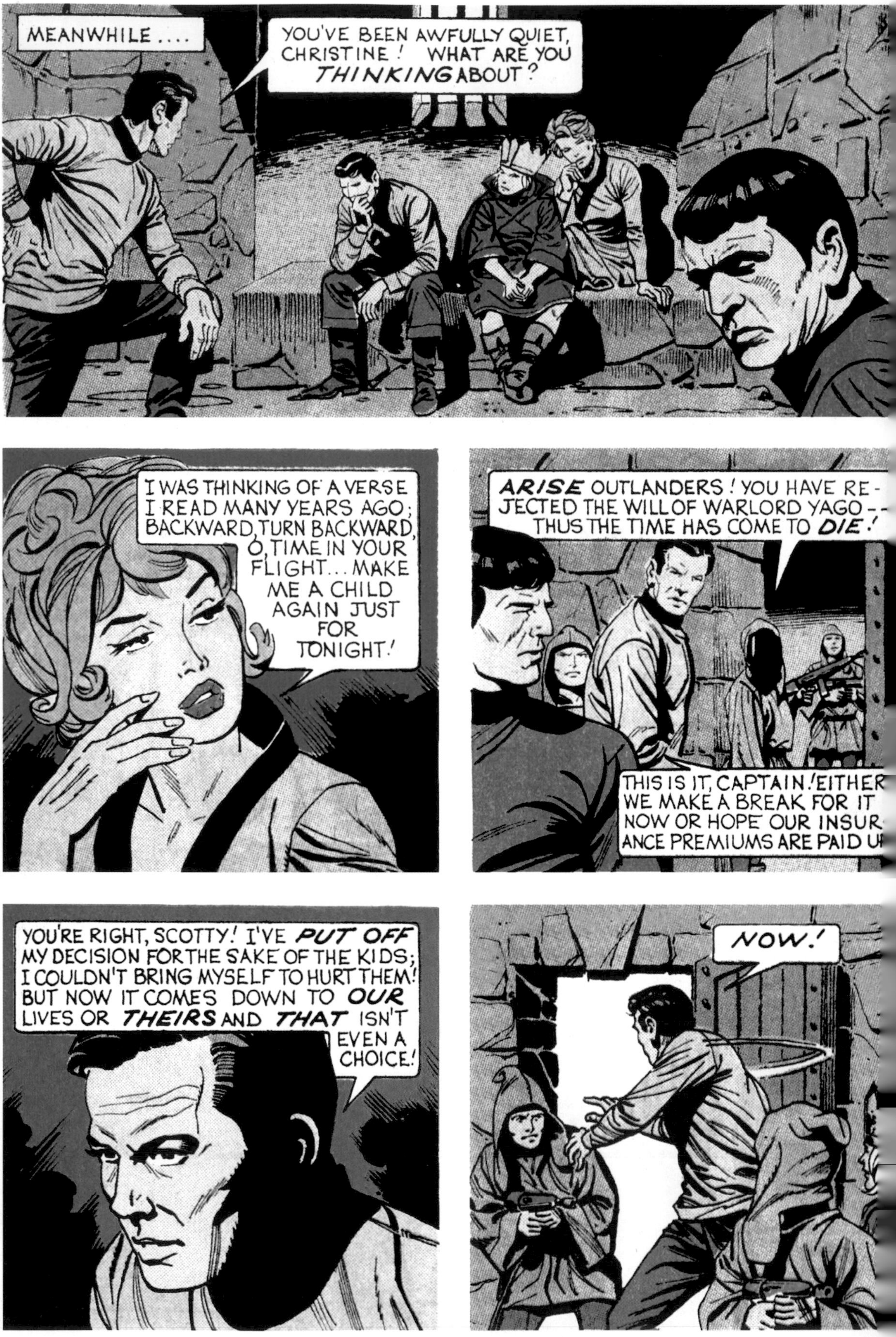

MEANWHILE....
YOU'VE BEEN AWFULLY QUIET, CHRISTINE! WHAT ARE YOU THINKING ABOUT?
I WAS THINKING OF A VERSE I READ MANY YEARS AGO; BACKWARD, TURN BACKWARD, O, TIME IN YOUR FLIGHT... MAKE ME A CHILD AGAIN JUST FOR TONIGHT!
ARISE OUTLANDERS! YOU HAVE REJECTED THE WILL OF WARLORD YAGO -- THUS THE TIME HAS COME TO DIE!
THIS IS IT, CAPTAIN! EITHER WE MAKE A BREAK FOR IT NOW OR HOPE OUR INSURANCE PREMIUMS ARE PAID U
YOU'RE RIGHT, SCOTTY! I'VE PUT OFF MY DECISION FOR THE SAKE OF THE KIDS; I COULDN'T BRING MYSELF TO HURT THEM! BUT NOW IT COMES DOWN TO OUR LIVES OR THEIRS AND THAT ISN'T EVEN A CHOICE!
NOW!

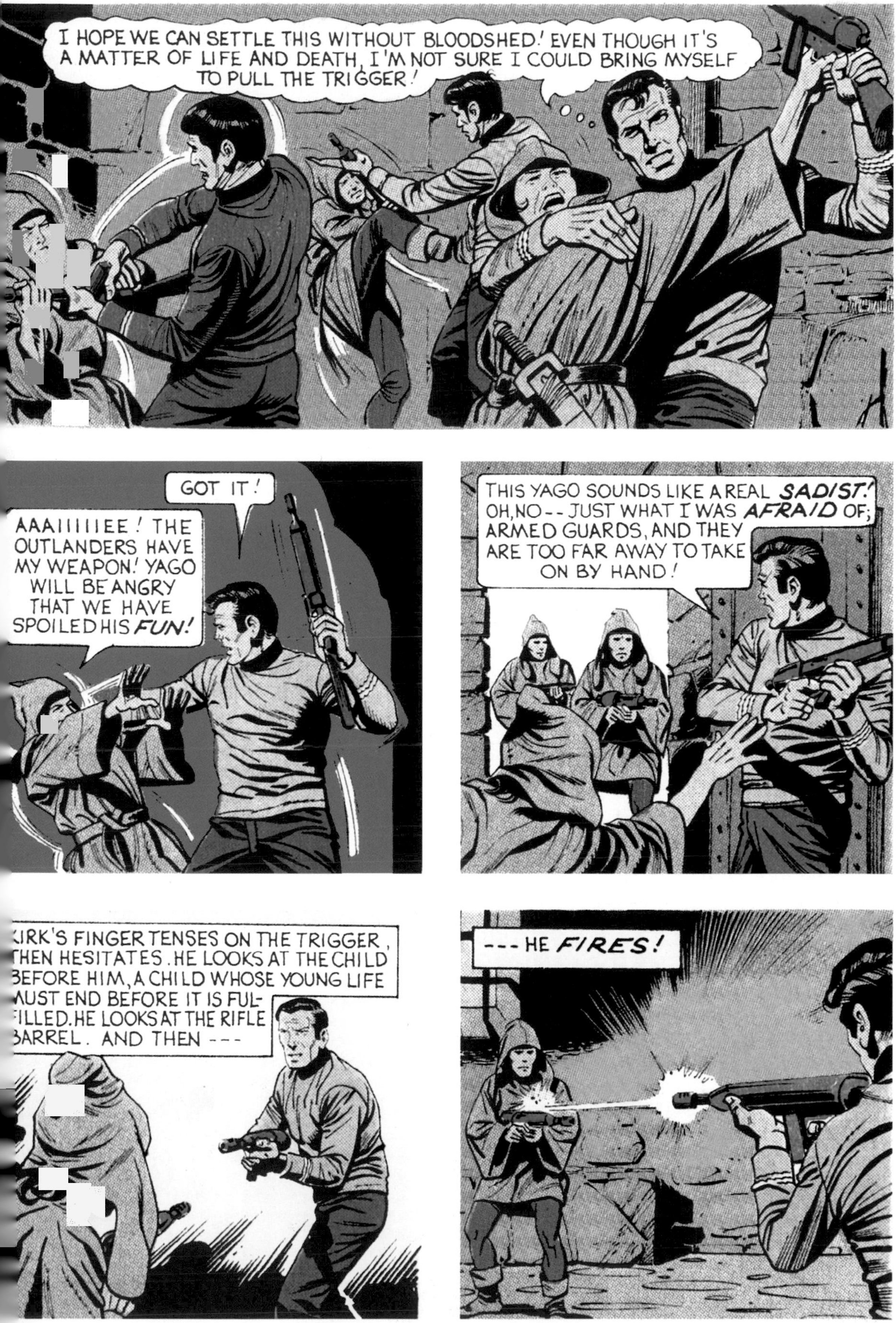
I HOPE WE CAN SETTLE THIS WITHOUT BLOODSHED! EVEN THOUGH IT'S A MATTER OF LIFE AND DEATH, I'M NOT SURE I COULD BRING MYSELF TO PULL THE TRIGGER!
GOT IT!
AAAIIIIIEE! THE OUTLANDERS HAVE MY WEAPON! YAGO WILL BE ANGRY THAT WE HAVE SPOILED HIS *FUN!*
THIS YAGO SOUNDS LIKE A REAL *SADIST!* OH, NO -- JUST WHAT I WAS *AFRAID* OF; ARMED GUARDS, AND THEY ARE TOO FAR AWAY TO TAKE ON BY HAND!
KIRK'S FINGER TENSES ON THE TRIGGER, THEN HESITATES. HE LOOKS AT THE CHILD BEFORE HIM, A CHILD WHOSE YOUNG LIFE MUST END BEFORE IT IS FULFILLED. HE LOOKS AT THE RIFLE BARREL. AND THEN ---
--- HE *FIRES!*

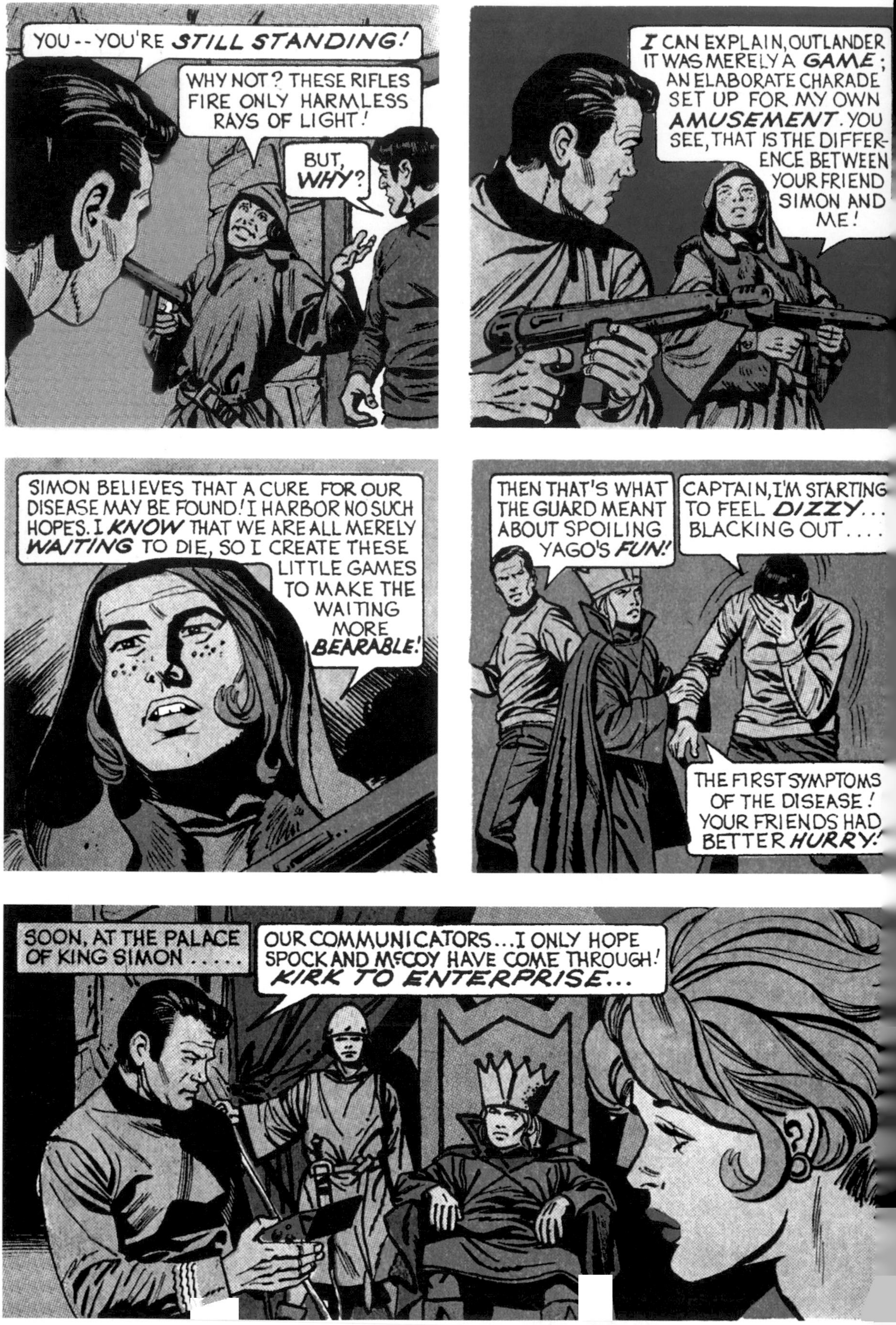
YOU -- YOU'RE STILL STANDING!
WHY NOT? THESE RIFLES FIRE ONLY HARMLESS RAYS OF LIGHT!
BUT, WHY?
I CAN EXPLAIN, OUTLANDER IT WAS MERELY A GAME; AN ELABORATE CHARADE SET UP FOR MY OWN AMUSEMENT. YOU SEE, THAT IS THE DIFFERENCE BETWEEN YOUR FRIEND SIMON AND ME!
SIMON BELIEVES THAT A CURE FOR OUR DISEASE MAY BE FOUND! I HARBOR NO SUCH HOPES. I KNOW THAT WE ARE ALL MERELY WAITING TO DIE, SO I CREATE THESE LITTLE GAMES TO MAKE THE WAITING MORE BEARABLE!
THEN THAT'S WHAT THE GUARD MEANT ABOUT SPOILING YAGO'S FUN!
CAPTAIN, I'M STARTING TO FEEL DIZZY... BLACKING OUT....
THE FIRST SYMPTOMS OF THE DISEASE! YOUR FRIENDS HAD BETTER HURRY!
SOON, AT THE PALACE OF KING SIMON.....
OUR COMMUNICATORS...I ONLY HOPE SPOCK AND McCOY HAVE COME THROUGH! KIRK TO ENTERPRISE...

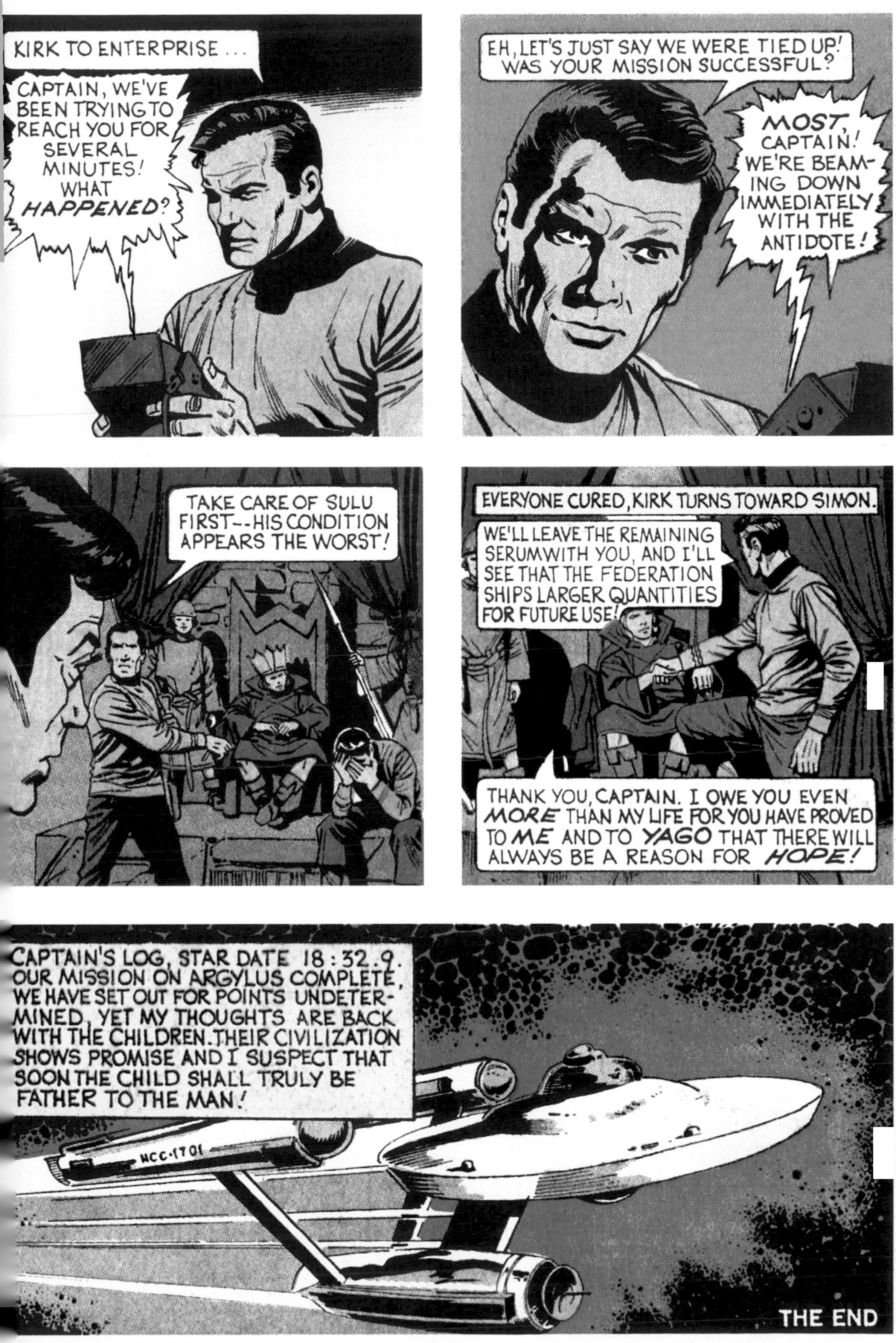
KIRK TO ENTERPRISE . . .
CAPTAIN, WE'VE BEEN TRYING TO REACH YOU FOR SEVERAL MINUTES! WHAT HAPPENED?
EH, LET'S JUST SAY WE WERE TIED UP! WAS YOUR MISSION SUCCESSFUL?
MOST, CAPTAIN! WE'RE BEAMING DOWN IMMEDIATELY WITH THE ANTIDOTE!
TAKE CARE OF SULU FIRST--HIS CONDITION APPEARS THE WORST!
EVERYONE CURED, KIRK TURNS TOWARD SIMON.
WE'LL LEAVE THE REMAINING SERUM WITH YOU, AND I'LL SEE THAT THE FEDERATION SHIPS LARGER QUANTITIES FOR FUTURE USE!
THANK YOU, CAPTAIN. I OWE YOU EVEN MORE THAN MY LIFE FOR YOU HAVE PROVED TO ME AND TO YAGO THAT THERE WILL ALWAYS BE A REASON FOR HOPE!
CAPTAIN'S LOG, STAR DATE 18:32.9. OUR MISSION ON ARGYLUS COMPLETE, WE HAVE SET OUT FOR POINTS UNDETERMINED, YET MY THOUGHTS ARE BACK WITH THE CHILDREN. THEIR CIVILIZATION SHOWS PROMISE AND I SUSPECT THAT SOON THE CHILD SHALL TRULY BE FATHER TO THE MAN!
NCC-1701
THE END

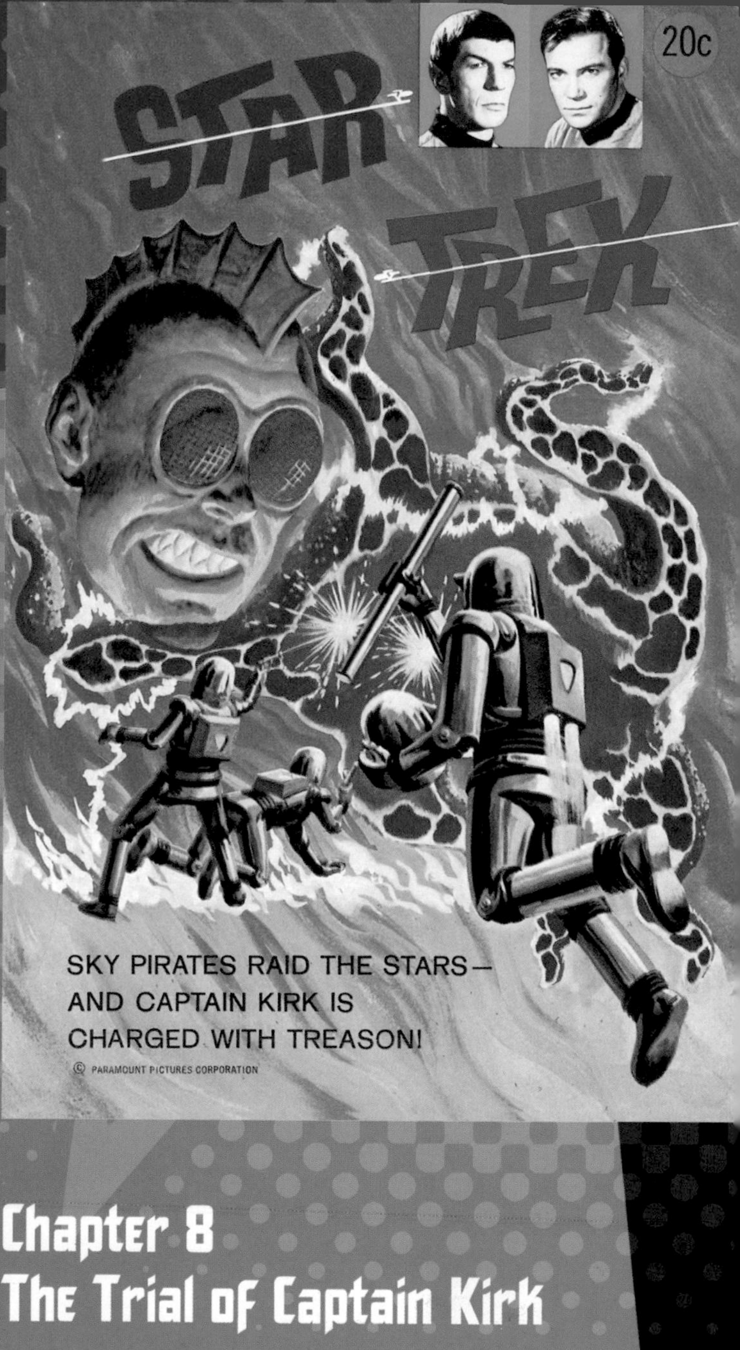
20c
STAR TREK
SKY PIRATES RAID THE STARS—
AND CAPTAIN KIRK IS
CHARGED WITH TREASON!
© PARAMOUNT PICTURES CORPORATION

Chapter 8
The Trial of Captain Kirk

(Originally Published in May, 1974)

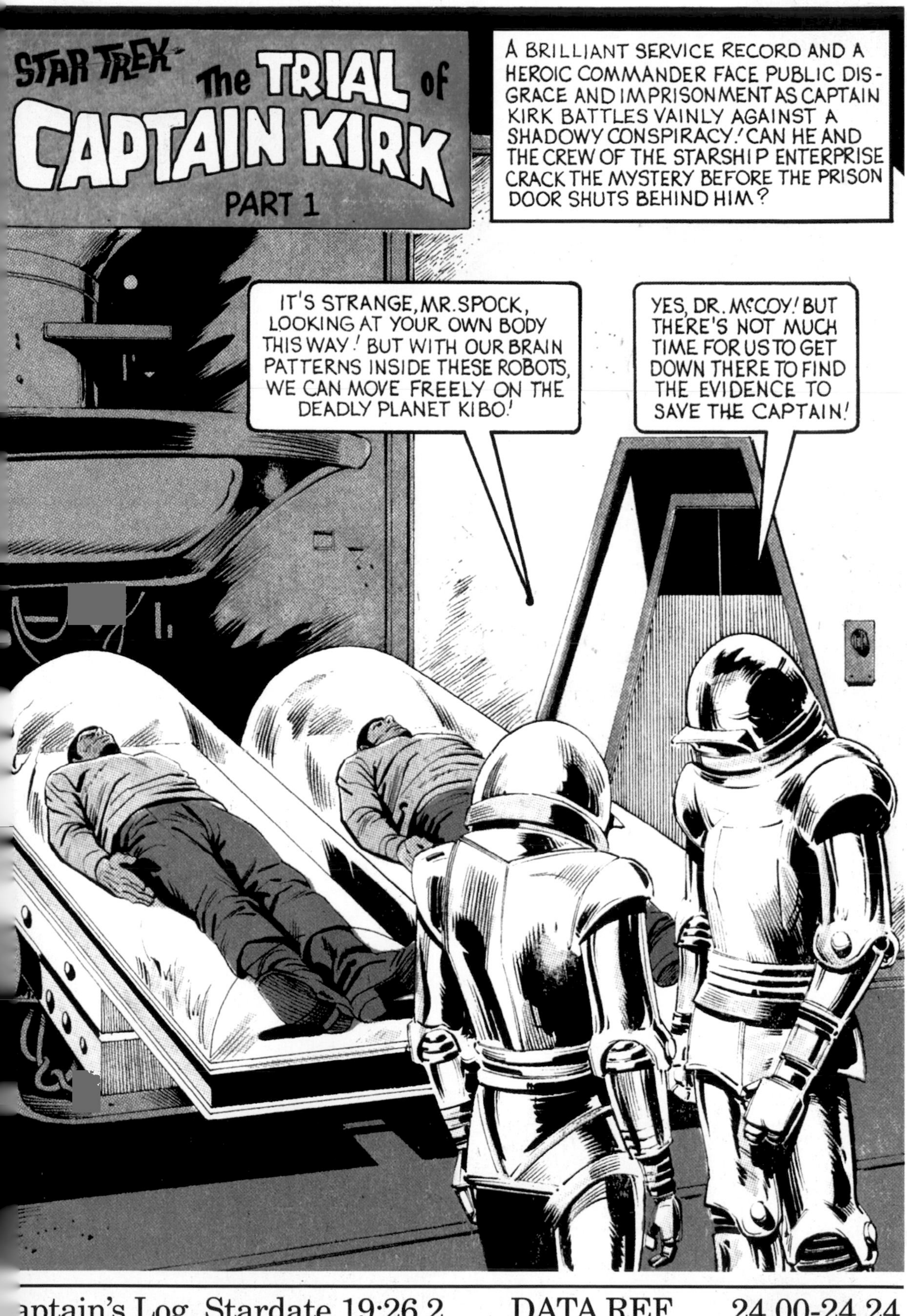
STAR TREK
The TRIAL of CAPTAIN KIRK
PART 1
A BRILLIANT SERVICE RECORD AND A HEROIC COMMANDER FACE PUBLIC DISGRACE AND IMPRISONMENT AS CAPTAIN KIRK BATTLES VAINLY AGAINST A SHADOWY CONSPIRACY! CAN HE AND THE CREW OF THE STARSHIP ENTERPRISE CRACK THE MYSTERY BEFORE THE PRISON DOOR SHUTS BEHIND HIM?
IT'S STRANGE, MR. SPOCK, LOOKING AT YOUR OWN BODY THIS WAY! BUT WITH OUR BRAIN PATTERNS INSIDE THESE ROBOTS, WE CAN MOVE FREELY ON THE DEADLY PLANET KIBO!
YES, DR. McCOY! BUT THERE'S NOT MUCH TIME FOR US TO GET DOWN THERE TO FIND THE EVIDENCE TO SAVE THE CAPTAIN!

aptain's Log, Stardate 19:26.2 . . DATA REF . . 24.00-24.24

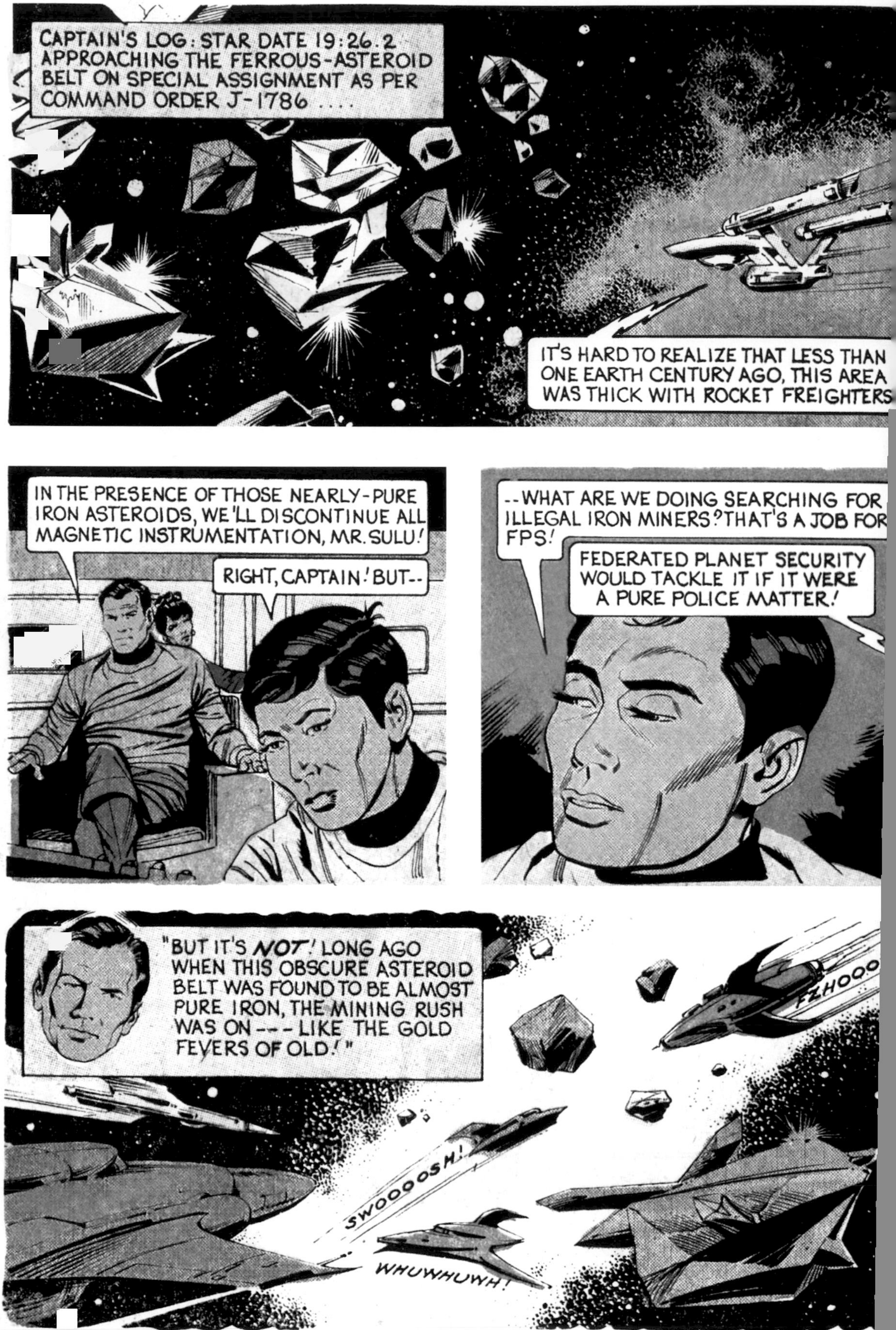
CAPTAIN'S LOG: STAR DATE 19:26.2 APPROACHING THE FERROUS-ASTEROID BELT ON SPECIAL ASSIGNMENT AS PER COMMAND ORDER J-1786 ....
IT'S HARD TO REALIZE THAT LESS THAN ONE EARTH CENTURY AGO, THIS AREA WAS THICK WITH ROCKET FREIGHTERS
IN THE PRESENCE OF THOSE NEARLY-PURE IRON ASTEROIDS, WE'LL DISCONTINUE ALL MAGNETIC INSTRUMENTATION, MR. SULU!
RIGHT, CAPTAIN! BUT--
--WHAT ARE WE DOING SEARCHING FOR ILLEGAL IRON MINERS? THAT'S A JOB FOR FPS!
FEDERATED PLANET SECURITY WOULD TACKLE IT IF IT WERE A PURE POLICE MATTER!
"BUT IT'S NOT! LONG AGO WHEN THIS OBSCURE ASTEROID BELT WAS FOUND TO BE ALMOST PURE IRON, THE MINING RUSH WAS ON --- LIKE THE GOLD FEVERS OF OLD!"
FZHOOO
SWOOOOOSH!
WHUWHUWH!

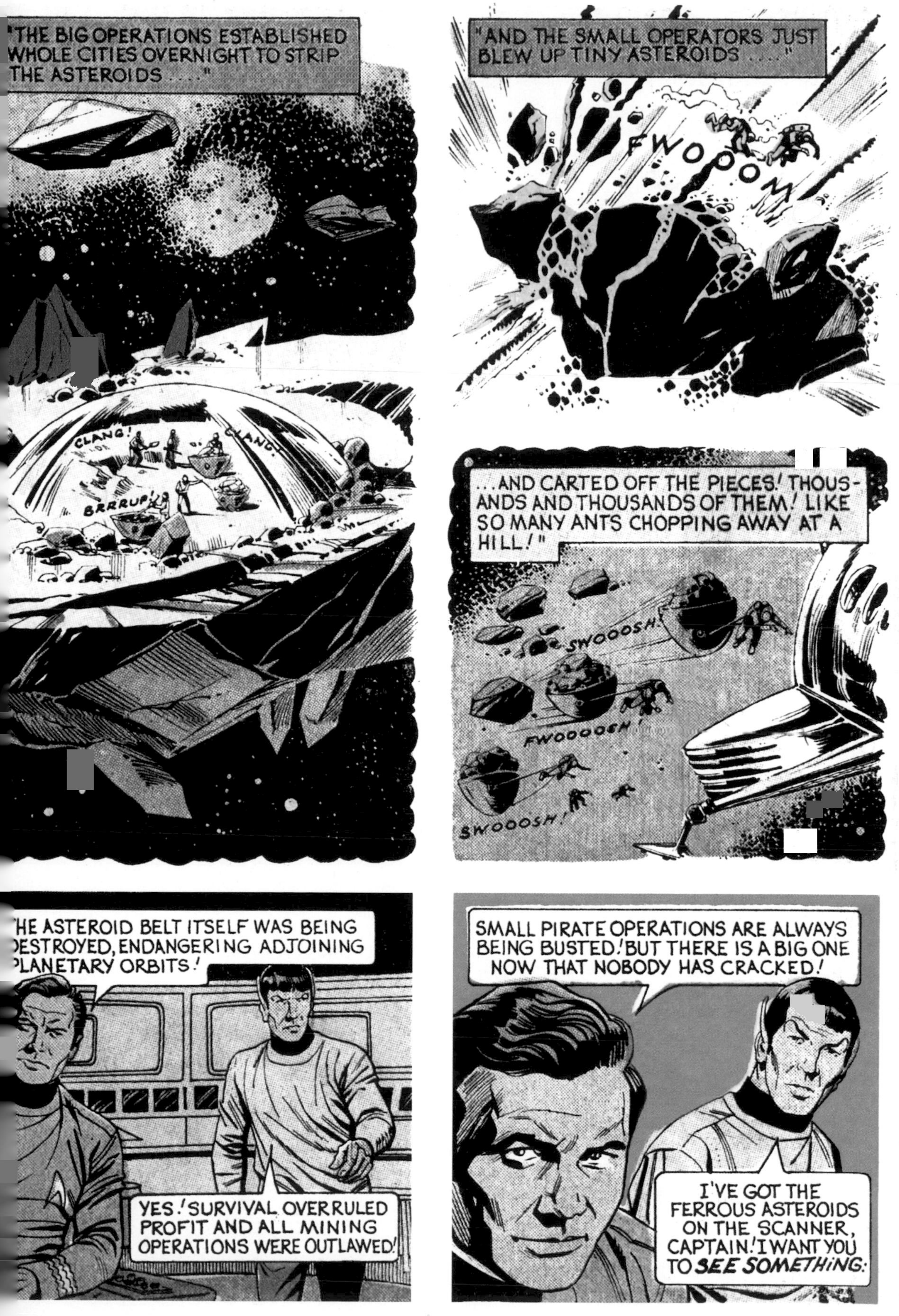
"THE BIG OPERATIONS ESTABLISHED WHOLE CITIES OVERNIGHT TO STRIP THE ASTEROIDS . . . ."
CLANG!
CLANG!
BRRRUP!
"AND THE SMALL OPERATORS JUST BLEW UP TINY ASTEROIDS . . . ."
FWOOOM
...AND CARTED OFF THE PIECES! THOUSANDS AND THOUSANDS OF THEM! LIKE SO MANY ANTS CHOPPING AWAY AT A HILL!"
SWOOOSH
FWOOOOSH!
SWOOOSH!
HE ASTEROID BELT ITSELF WAS BEING ESTROYED, ENDANGERING ADJOINING LANETARY ORBITS!
YES! SURVIVAL OVERRULED PROFIT AND ALL MINING OPERATIONS WERE OUTLAWED!
SMALL PIRATE OPERATIONS ARE ALWAYS BEING BUSTED! BUT THERE IS A BIG ONE NOW THAT NOBODY HAS CRACKED!
I'VE GOT THE FERROUS ASTEROIDS ON THE SCANNER, CAPTAIN! I WANT YOU TO SEE SOMETHING:

YES -- THERE'S THE *CAMEL*, ONE OF THE BEST KNOWN OF THOSE ODDLY SHAPED BODIES!

PRECISELY. NOW LET ME SHOW YOU THE SUB-SECTOR CHART!

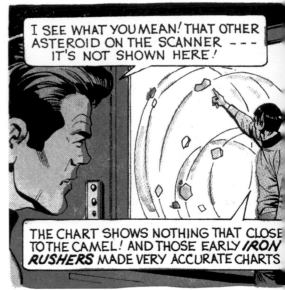

I SEE WHAT YOU MEAN! THAT OTHER ASTEROID ON THE SCANNER --- IT'S NOT SHOWN HERE!

THE CHART SHOWS NOTHING THAT CLOSE TO THE CAMEL! AND THOSE EARLY *IRON RUSHERS* MADE VERY ACCURATE CHARTS

I'M GOING OUT THERE TO HAVE A LOOK! THIS MAY BE THE FIRST BREAK IN THIS CASE IN YEARS!

MR. SCOTT! REPORT TO SPACE HATCH READY FOR EXTRA-VEHICULAR-ACTION!

AND SHORTLY....

IT DOESN'T LOOK LIKE THERE'S MUCH DOIN' THERE, CAP'N!

RIGHT! WE CAN SEARCH EVERY CRANNY OF THAT ROCK IN TEN MINUTES! LET'S GET AT IT!

TEN MINUTES LATER, ALMOST TO THE SECOND...

I SPOTTED NARY A THING, CAP'N! SHE'S A BARE HUNK OF IRON LIKE THE REST!

STRANGE! IT'S HARD TO BELIEVE THOSE OLD IRON RUSHERS' CHARTS WERE WRONG!

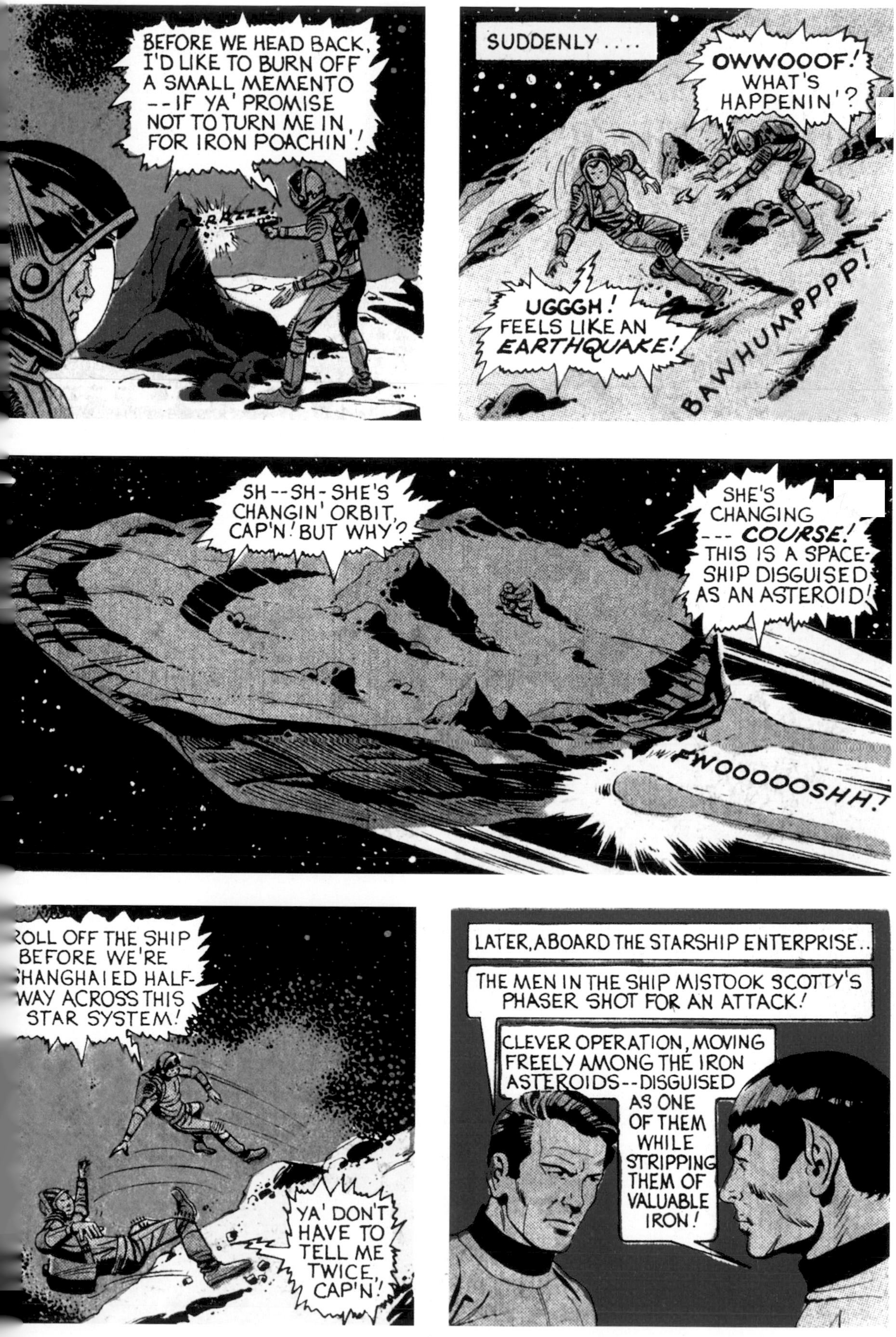
BEFORE WE HEAD BACK, I'D LIKE TO BURN OFF A SMALL MEMENTO --IF YA' PROMISE NOT TO TURN ME IN FOR IRON POACHIN'!
SUDDENLY....
OWWOOOF! WHAT'S HAPPENIN'?
UGGGH! FEELS LIKE AN EARTHQUAKE!
BAWHUMPPPP!
SH--SH-SHE'S CHANGIN' ORBIT, CAP'N! BUT WHY?
SHE'S CHANGING --- COURSE! THIS IS A SPACE-SHIP DISGUISED AS AN ASTEROID!
FWOOOOOOSHH!
ROLL OFF THE SHIP BEFORE WE'RE SHANGHAIED HALF-WAY ACROSS THIS STAR SYSTEM!
YA' DON'T HAVE TO TELL ME TWICE, CAP'N!
LATER, ABOARD THE STARSHIP ENTERPRISE..
THE MEN IN THE SHIP MISTOOK SCOTTY'S PHASER SHOT FOR AN ATTACK!
CLEVER OPERATION, MOVING FREELY AMONG THE IRON ASTEROIDS--DISGUISED AS ONE OF THEM WHILE STRIPPING THEM OF VALUABLE IRON!

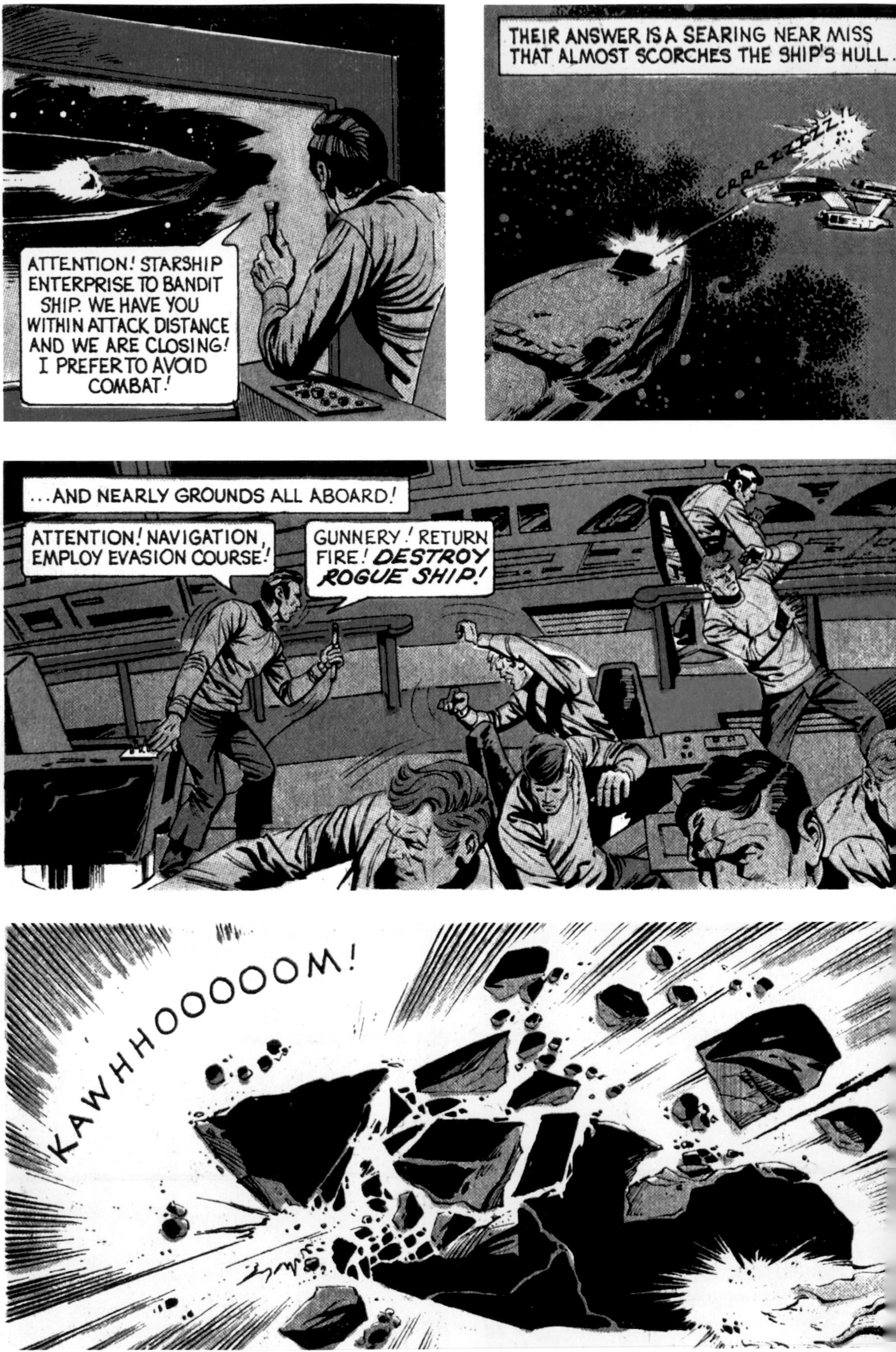
ATTENTION! STARSHIP ENTERPRISE TO BANDIT SHIP. WE HAVE YOU WITHIN ATTACK DISTANCE AND WE ARE CLOSING! I PREFER TO AVOID COMBAT!
THEIR ANSWER IS A SEARING NEAR MISS THAT ALMOST SCORCHES THE SHIP'S HULL...
CRRRZZZZZ
...AND NEARLY GROUNDS ALL ABOARD!
ATTENTION! NAVIGATION, EMPLOY EVASION COURSE!
GUNNERY! RETURN FIRE! DESTROY ROGUE SHIP!
KAWHHOOOOOM!

SHORTLY....

UNFORTUNATELY, NO DEFENSE SHORT OF TOTAL DESTRUCTION WAS POSSIBLE, COMMANDER DAR.

TOO BAD! WE WOULD HAVE LIKED PRISONERS TO QUESTION! RESUME COURSE 127-K UNTIL YOUR NEW ORDERS HAVE BEEN CUT!

FOR A NON-HOSTILE OPERATION, YOU COMMITTED YOURSELVES LIKE A TRUE FIGHTING SHIP! RELAX! ENJOY YOURSELVES!

ENJOY, HE SAYS! HALFWAY TO NOWHERE! SHALL WE STEP OUTSIDE THE SHIP AND GO TO THE BEACH, KRAD?

LOVELY! THEN PERHAPS A GOOD SHOW AND A NIGHTCLUB OR TWO, XANA!

ATTENTION STARSHIP ENTERPRISE! YOUR NEW ORDERS DIRECT FROM THE FEDERATED PLANETS SUPREME HEADQUARTERS! RETURN TO STARSHIP CENTRAL AT ONCE!

GO BACK? BUT WHY? WE JUST STARTED OUR TOUR!

WHAT D'YE MAKE OF IT, CAP'N?

"OURS NOT TO REASON WHY---". THAT'S A NINETEENTH CENTURY EARTH POET NAMED TENNYSON!

A PERCEPTIVE GENTLEMAN!

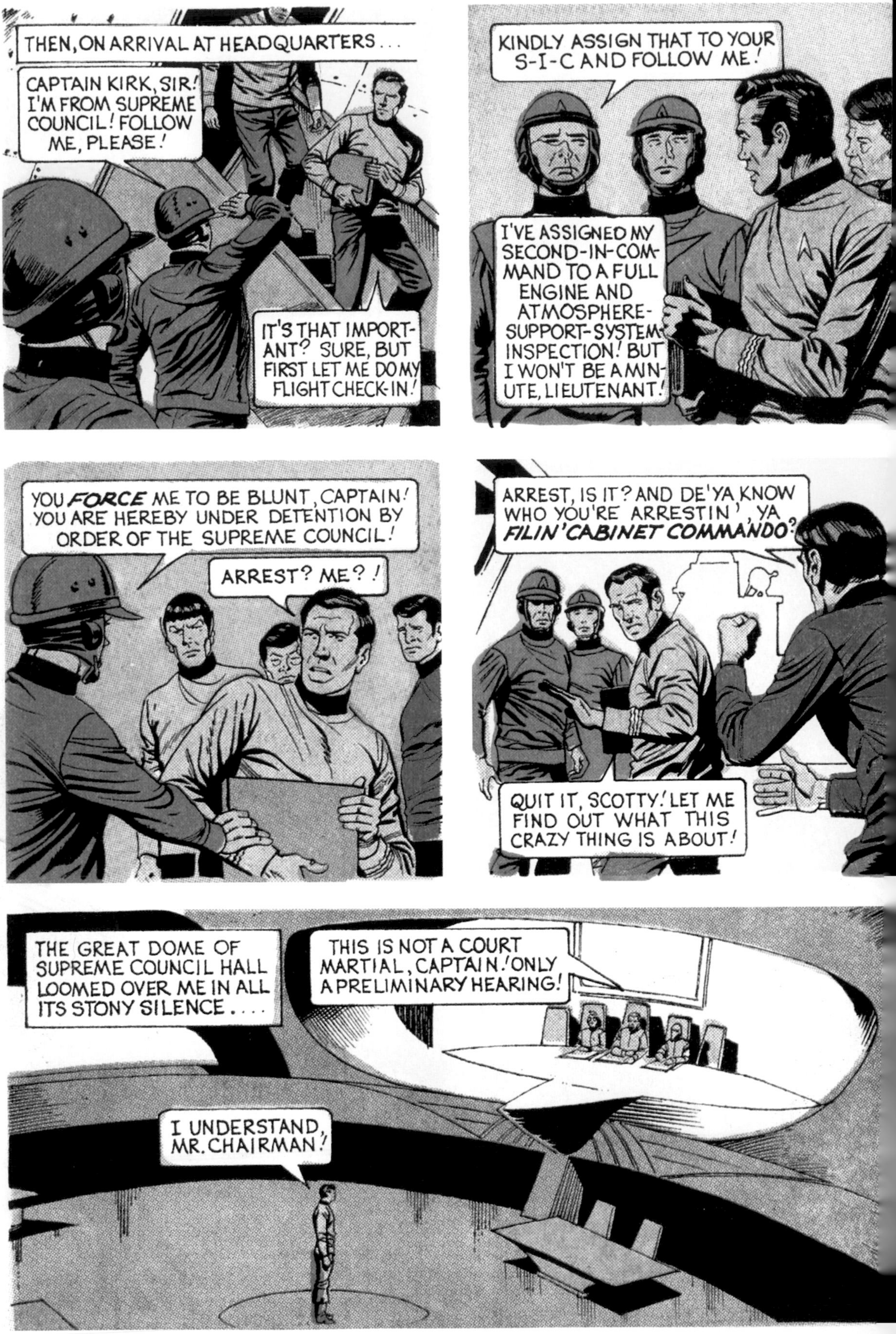
THEN, ON ARRIVAL AT HEADQUARTERS . . .
CAPTAIN KIRK, SIR! I'M FROM SUPREME COUNCIL! FOLLOW ME, PLEASE!
IT'S THAT IMPORTANT? SURE, BUT FIRST LET ME DO MY FLIGHT CHECK-IN!
KINDLY ASSIGN THAT TO YOUR S-I-C AND FOLLOW ME!
I'VE ASSIGNED MY SECOND-IN-COMMAND TO A FULL ENGINE AND ATMOSPHERE-SUPPORT-SYSTEM INSPECTION! BUT I WON'T BE A MINUTE, LIEUTENANT!
YOU FORCE ME TO BE BLUNT, CAPTAIN! YOU ARE HEREBY UNDER DETENTION BY ORDER OF THE SUPREME COUNCIL!
ARREST? ME?!
ARREST, IS IT? AND DE'YA KNOW WHO YOU'RE ARRESTIN', YA FILIN' CABINET COMMANDO?
QUIT IT, SCOTTY! LET ME FIND OUT WHAT THIS CRAZY THING IS ABOUT!
THE GREAT DOME OF SUPREME COUNCIL HALL LOOMED OVER ME IN ALL ITS STONY SILENCE . . . .
THIS IS NOT A COURT MARTIAL, CAPTAIN! ONLY A PRELIMINARY HEARING!
I UNDERSTAND, MR. CHAIRMAN!

BE ASSURED, THAT ONLY THE GREATEST RESPECT FOR YOUR PAST RECORD DICTATED THIS PRIVATE PRELIMINARY HEARING RATHER THAN NORMAL PUBLIC TRIAL!

SUPPOSE YOU TELL ME WHAT I'M BEING INVESTIGATED FOR!

YOU HAVE PROBABLY SEEN VICE CHAIRMEN, FADO AND HAJARA BEFORE...FADO, OUTLINE THE INQUIRY TARGET!

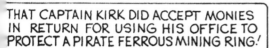

THAT CAPTAIN KIRK DID ACCEPT MONIES IN RETURN FOR USING HIS OFFICE TO PROTECT A PIRATE FERROUS MINING RING!

THAT'S A PACK OF LIES!

EVIDENTIAL ENTRY NUMBER ONE--YOUR BANK ACCOUNT--SHOWING A RECENT DEPOSIT OF SEVEN MILLION CREDITS!

THAT'S INSANE! I COULDN'T EARN THAT IN A LIFETIME!

PRECISELY, CAPTAIN! EVIDENTIAL ENTRY NUMBER TWO--A VIDEO TAPE OF CAPTAIN KIRK MEETING WITH THE SELF-CONFESSED PIRATE LEADER!

WHA-A-A-T?!

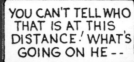

THIS CLANDESTINE MEETING ON THE FAMED CHROME ARCH OF PLANET ZEAYANA IS BETWEEN THE SUSPECT AND ONE LIJI BRAGG, HEAD OF THE MINING OPERATION!

YOU CAN'T TELL WHO THAT IS AT THIS DISTANCE! WHAT'S GOING ON HE--

TO BE SURE, CAPTAIN! I'LL HAVE THEM EXPAND THE IMAGE!

THERE, CAPTAIN! THAT PICTURE SHOULD BE CLEAR ENOUGH, EVEN TO A MAN WHOSE VISION IS CLOUDED WITH GUILT!

THAT'S UNCALLED FOR, VICE CHAIRMAN FADO! PRESUMPTION OF INNOCENCE MUST BE MAINTAINED! ESPECIALLY WITH --

--THE MOST HONORED STARSHIP COMMANDER IN THE FLEET! CERTAINLY, VICE-CHAIRMAN HAJARA!

A MOMENT'S CONSULTATION AND THEN ...

IT IS OUR FINDING THAT YOU BE BOUND OVER FOR COURT MARTIAL! YOU ARE UNDER CITY DETENTION UNTIL THEN!

MR. CHAIRMAN! IT'S A CONSPIRACY! A FRAMEUP! DON'T YOU SEE!

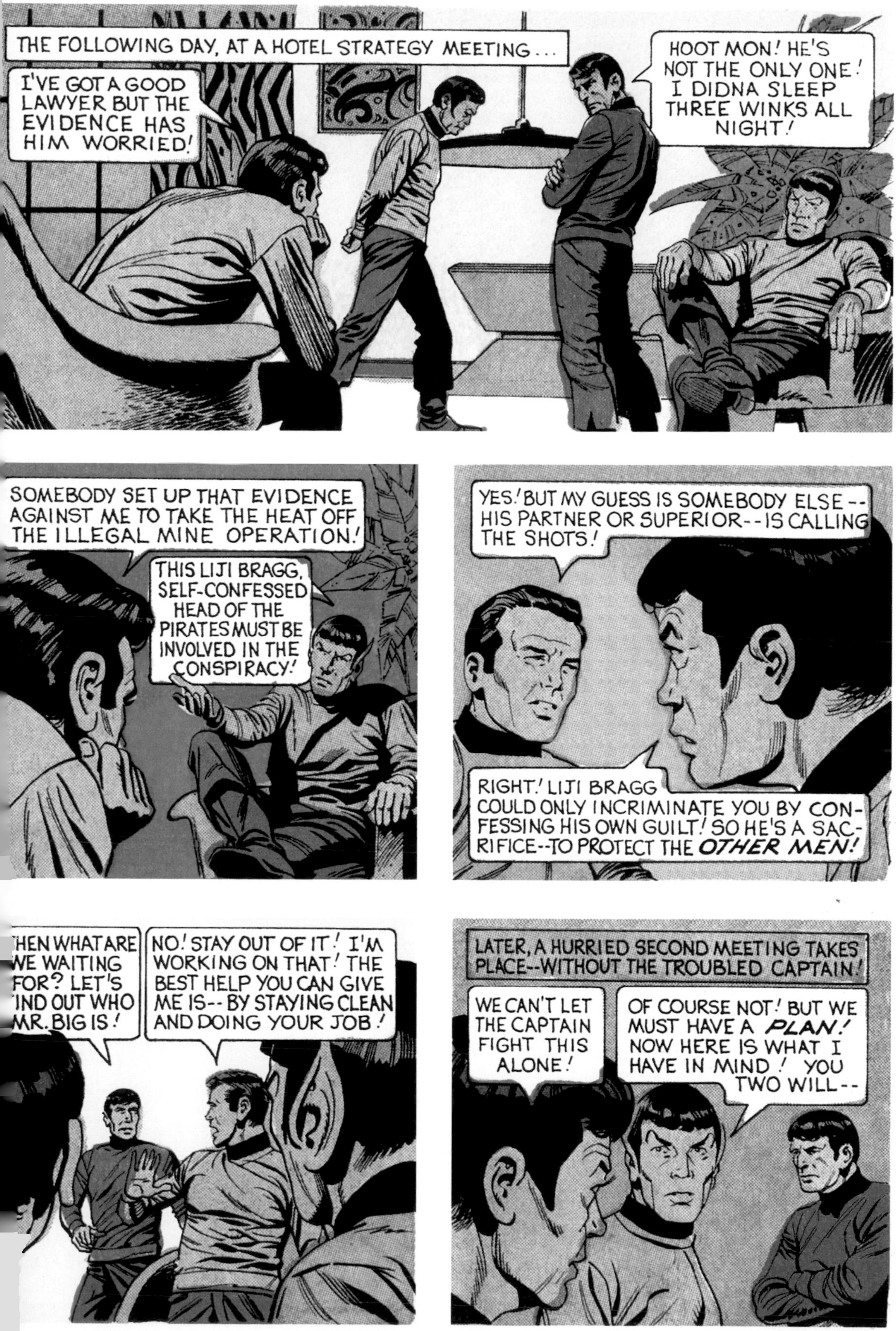
THE FOLLOWING DAY, AT A HOTEL STRATEGY MEETING...
I'VE GOT A GOOD LAWYER BUT THE EVIDENCE HAS HIM WORRIED!
HOOT MON! HE'S NOT THE ONLY ONE! I DIDNA SLEEP THREE WINKS ALL NIGHT!
SOMEBODY SET UP THAT EVIDENCE AGAINST ME TO TAKE THE HEAT OFF THE ILLEGAL MINE OPERATION!
THIS LIJI BRAGG, SELF-CONFESSED HEAD OF THE PIRATES MUST BE INVOLVED IN THE CONSPIRACY!
YES! BUT MY GUESS IS SOMEBODY ELSE--HIS PARTNER OR SUPERIOR--IS CALLING THE SHOTS!
RIGHT! LIJI BRAGG COULD ONLY INCRIMINATE YOU BY CONFESSING HIS OWN GUILT! SO HE'S A SACRIFICE--TO PROTECT THE *OTHER MEN!*
HEN WHATARE WE WAITING FOR? LET'S IND OUT WHO MR.BIG IS!
NO! STAY OUT OF IT! I'M WORKING ON THAT! THE BEST HELP YOU CAN GIVE ME IS--BY STAYING CLEAN AND DOING YOUR JOB!
LATER, A HURRIED SECOND MEETING TAKES PLACE--WITHOUT THE TROUBLED CAPTAIN!
WE CAN'T LET THE CAPTAIN FIGHT THIS ALONE!
OF COURSE NOT! BUT WE MUST HAVE A *PLAN!* NOW HERE IS WHAT I HAVE IN MIND! YOU TWO WILL--

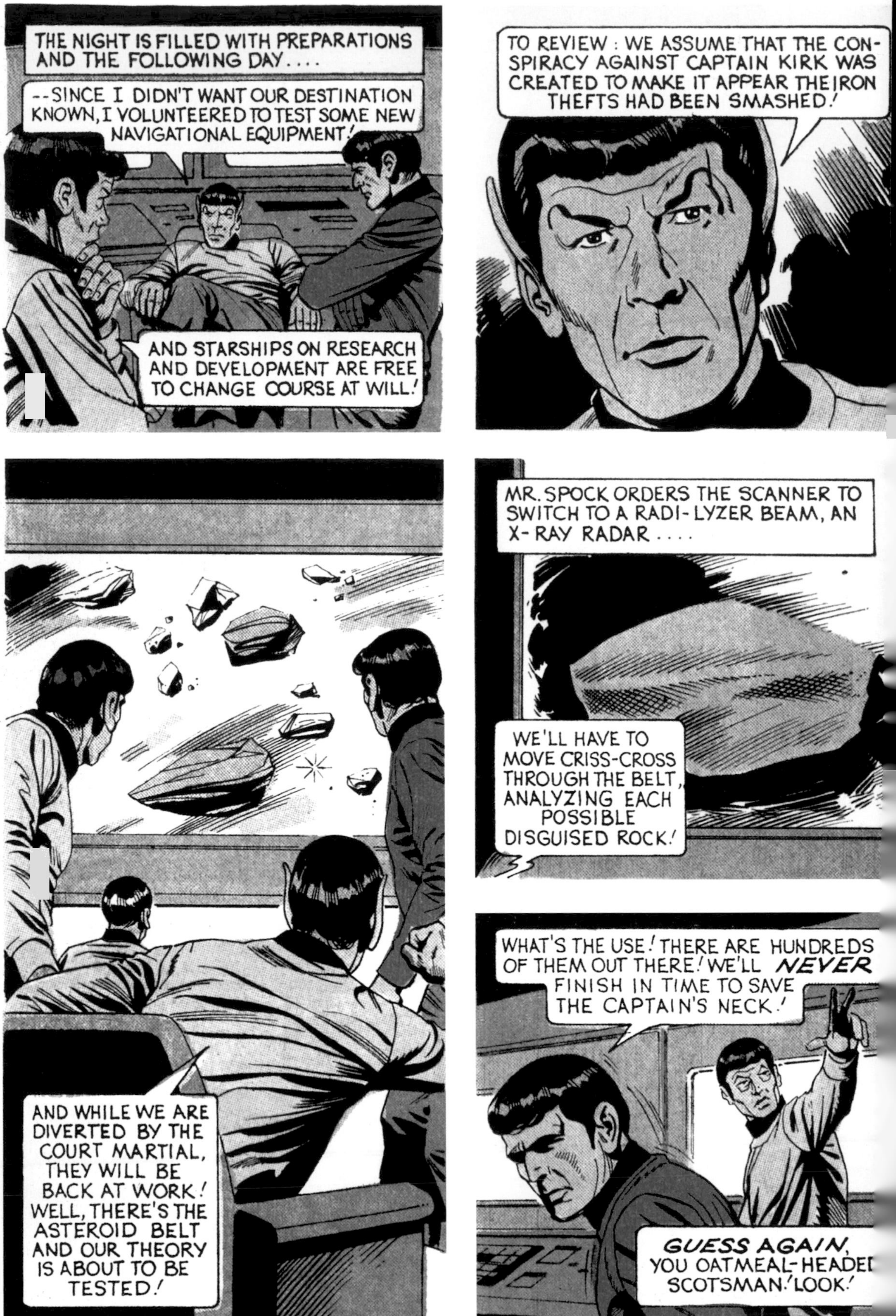
THE NIGHT IS FILLED WITH PREPARATIONS AND THE FOLLOWING DAY....
--SINCE I DIDN'T WANT OUR DESTINATION KNOWN, I VOLUNTEERED TO TEST SOME NEW NAVIGATIONAL EQUIPMENT!
AND STARSHIPS ON RESEARCH AND DEVELOPMENT ARE FREE TO CHANGE COURSE AT WILL!
TO REVIEW: WE ASSUME THAT THE CONSPIRACY AGAINST CAPTAIN KIRK WAS CREATED TO MAKE IT APPEAR THE IRON THEFTS HAD BEEN SMASHED!
AND WHILE WE ARE DIVERTED BY THE COURT MARTIAL, THEY WILL BE BACK AT WORK! WELL, THERE'S THE ASTEROID BELT AND OUR THEORY IS ABOUT TO BE TESTED!
MR. SPOCK ORDERS THE SCANNER TO SWITCH TO A RADI-LYZER BEAM, AN X-RAY RADAR....
WE'LL HAVE TO MOVE CRISS-CROSS THROUGH THE BELT, ANALYZING EACH POSSIBLE DISGUISED ROCK!
WHAT'S THE USE! THERE ARE HUNDREDS OF THEM OUT THERE! WE'LL NEVER FINISH IN TIME TO SAVE THE CAPTAIN'S NECK!
GUESS AGAIN, YOU OATMEAL-HEADED SCOTSMAN! LOOK!

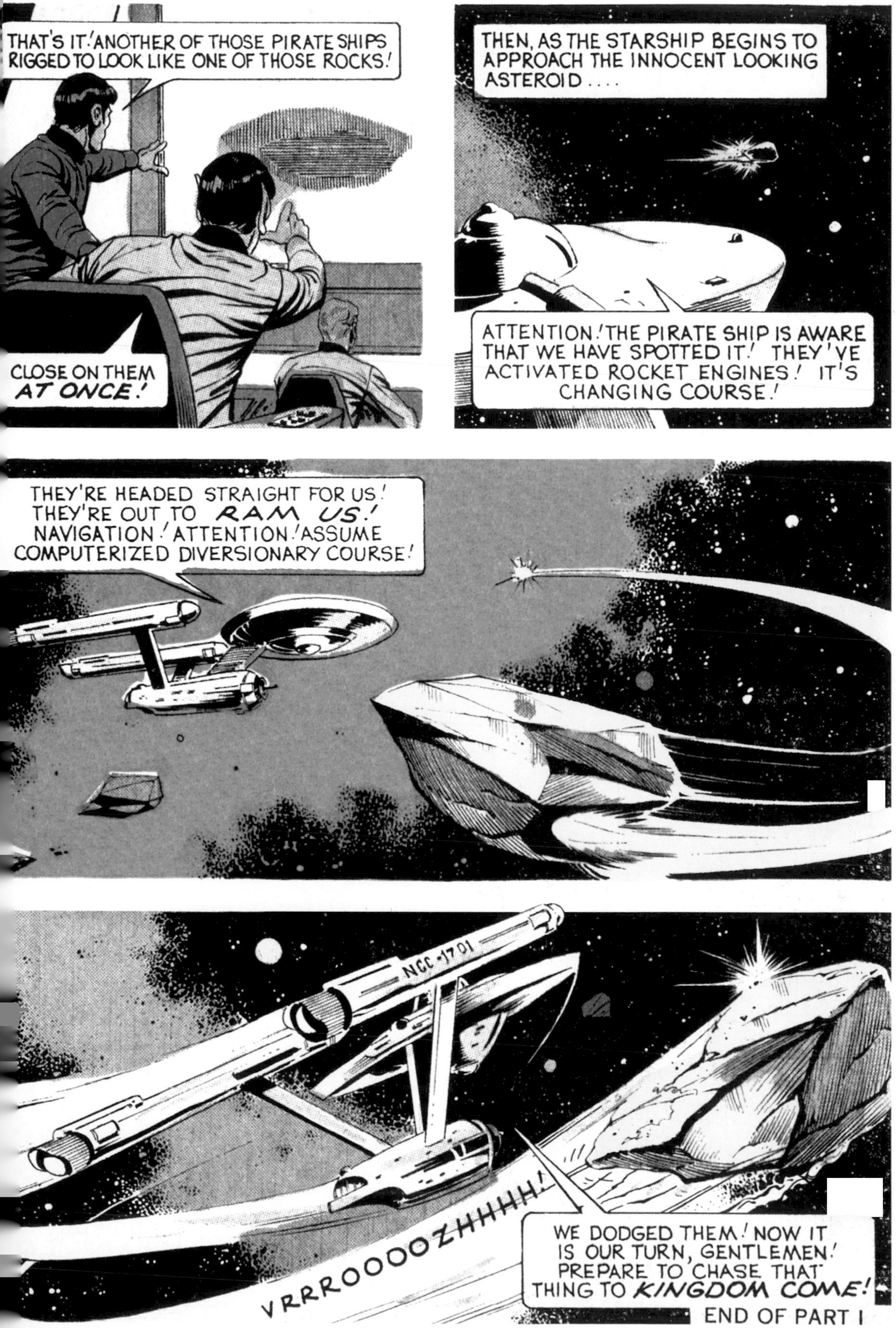
THAT'S IT! ANOTHER OF THOSE PIRATE SHIPS RIGGED TO LOOK LIKE ONE OF THOSE ROCKS!
CLOSE ON THEM AT ONCE!
THEN, AS THE STARSHIP BEGINS TO APPROACH THE INNOCENT LOOKING ASTEROID....
ATTENTION! THE PIRATE SHIP IS AWARE THAT WE HAVE SPOTTED IT! THEY'VE ACTIVATED ROCKET ENGINES! IT'S CHANGING COURSE!
THEY'RE HEADED STRAIGHT FOR US! THEY'RE OUT TO RAM US! NAVIGATION! ATTENTION! ASSUME COMPUTERIZED DIVERSIONARY COURSE!
NCC-1701
VRRROOOOZHHHH!
WE DODGED THEM! NOW IT IS OUR TURN, GENTLEMEN! PREPARE TO CHASE THAT THING TO KINGDOM COME!
END OF PART I

STAR TREK
The TRIAL of CAPTAIN KIRK
PART 2

CAPTAIN'S LOG: STAR DATE 19:26.3 I HAVE THE FREEDOM OF THE CITY AND A LIMITED TIME IN WHICH TO FIGHT BACK AGAINST THE CHARGES AIMED AT ME. WHAT I NEED DESPERATELY IS INFORMATION--AND THE ANONYMITY WITH WHICH TO GAIN IT!

DR. STILLER WILL SEE YOU NOW, CAPTAIN!

THANK YOU, NURSE.

QUICKLY, KIRK OUTLINES HIS PROBLEM TO HIS OLD FRIEND, A LEADING COSMETIC SURGEON....

YOU UNDERSTAND, DWAYNE, THAT IF I'M CAUGHT, YOU COULD BE IMPLICATED!

AT MY AGE, FEAR DOESN'T MOVE ME--BUT ADVENTURE STILL DOES! I'M TOTALLY BORED WITH REMOVING WRINKLES! LET'S GO, JIM!

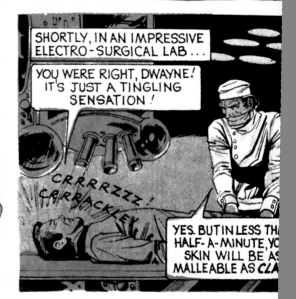

SHORTLY, IN AN IMPRESSIVE ELECTRO-SURGICAL LAB...

YOU WERE RIGHT, DWAYNE! IT'S JUST A TINGLING SENSATION!

CRRRRZZZ! CRRRACKLE!

YES. BUT IN LESS THA HALF-A-MINUTE, YO SKIN WILL BE AS MALLEABLE AS CLA

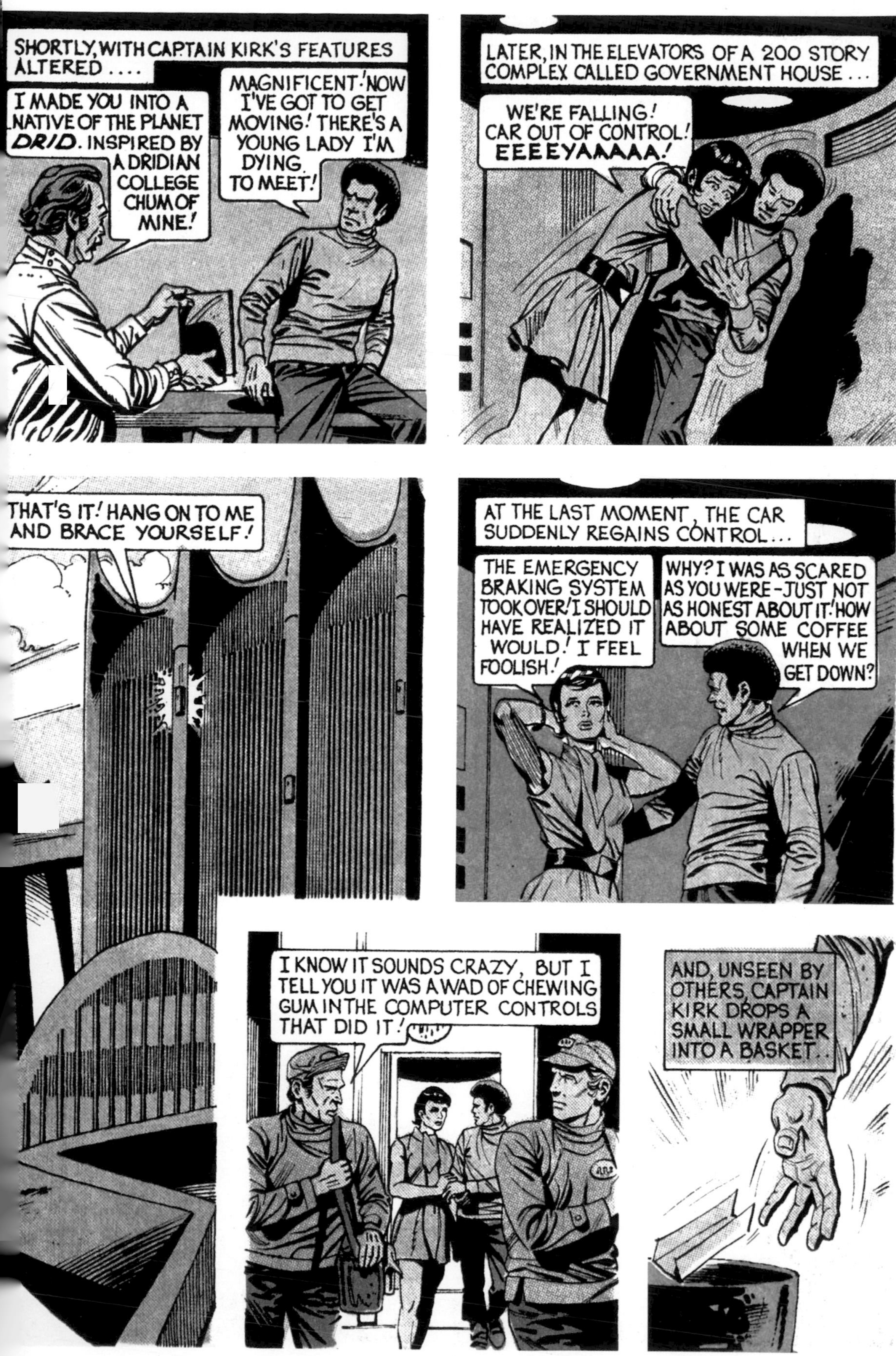
SHORTLY, WITH CAPTAIN KIRK'S FEATURES ALTERED ....
I MADE YOU INTO A NATIVE OF THE PLANET DRID. INSPIRED BY A DRIDIAN COLLEGE CHUM OF MINE!
MAGNIFICENT! NOW I'VE GOT TO GET MOVING! THERE'S A YOUNG LADY I'M DYING TO MEET!
LATER, IN THE ELEVATORS OF A 200 STORY COMPLEX CALLED GOVERNMENT HOUSE ...
WE'RE FALLING! CAR OUT OF CONTROL! EEEEYAAAAA!
THAT'S IT! HANG ON TO ME AND BRACE YOURSELF!
AT THE LAST MOMENT, THE CAR SUDDENLY REGAINS CONTROL ...
THE EMERGENCY BRAKING SYSTEM TOOK OVER! I SHOULD HAVE REALIZED IT WOULD! I FEEL FOOLISH!
WHY? I WAS AS SCARED AS YOU WERE - JUST NOT AS HONEST ABOUT IT! HOW ABOUT SOME COFFEE WHEN WE GET DOWN?
I KNOW IT SOUNDS CRAZY, BUT I TELL YOU IT WAS A WAD OF CHEWING GUM IN THE COMPUTER CONTROLS THAT DID IT!
AND, UNSEEN BY OTHERS, CAPTAIN KIRK DROPS A SMALL WRAPPER INTO A BASKET.

MEANWHILE, ABOARD THE ENTERPRISE....

WE'RE OVERTAKING THEM! WE SHOULD CLOSE ON THEM WITHIN--

HOLD IT! THEY FIRED SOME KIND OF MISSILE! AIMED STRAIGHT AT THAT PLANET WAY OFF THERE!

THE QUESTION IS, WHY? TO DIVERT US --CAUSE US TO CHASE THAT THING?

OR ARE THEY GETTING RID OF SOME EVIDENC LET'S FIND OUT WHAT PLANET THAT IS!

NAVI-COMP REPORTS THE PLANET IN QUESTION IS KIBO, 5TH. PLANET OF SYSTEM C-71.

YES, YES! I KNOW KIBO! COMPLETELY BATHED IN DEADLY HIGH ENERGY! NO LIVING BEING HAS EVER WALKED ON IT!

THERE IS A WAY WE CAN WALK THERE THOUGH!

EH? OH, OF COURS THE VERY THING DR. McCOY! WE'LL EMPLOY CEREBOTS.

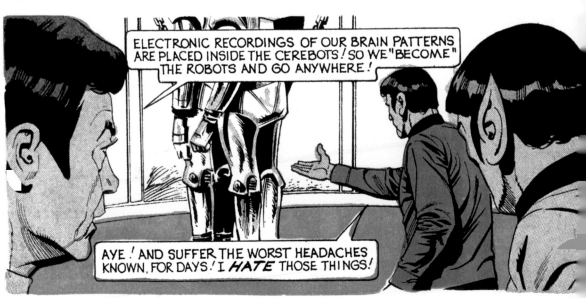

ELECTRONIC RECORDINGS OF OUR BRAIN PATTERNS ARE PLACED INSIDE THE CEREBOTS! SO WE "BECOME" THE ROBOTS AND GO ANYWHERE!

AYE! AND SUFFER THE WORST HEADACHES KNOWN, FOR DAYS! I HATE THOSE THINGS!

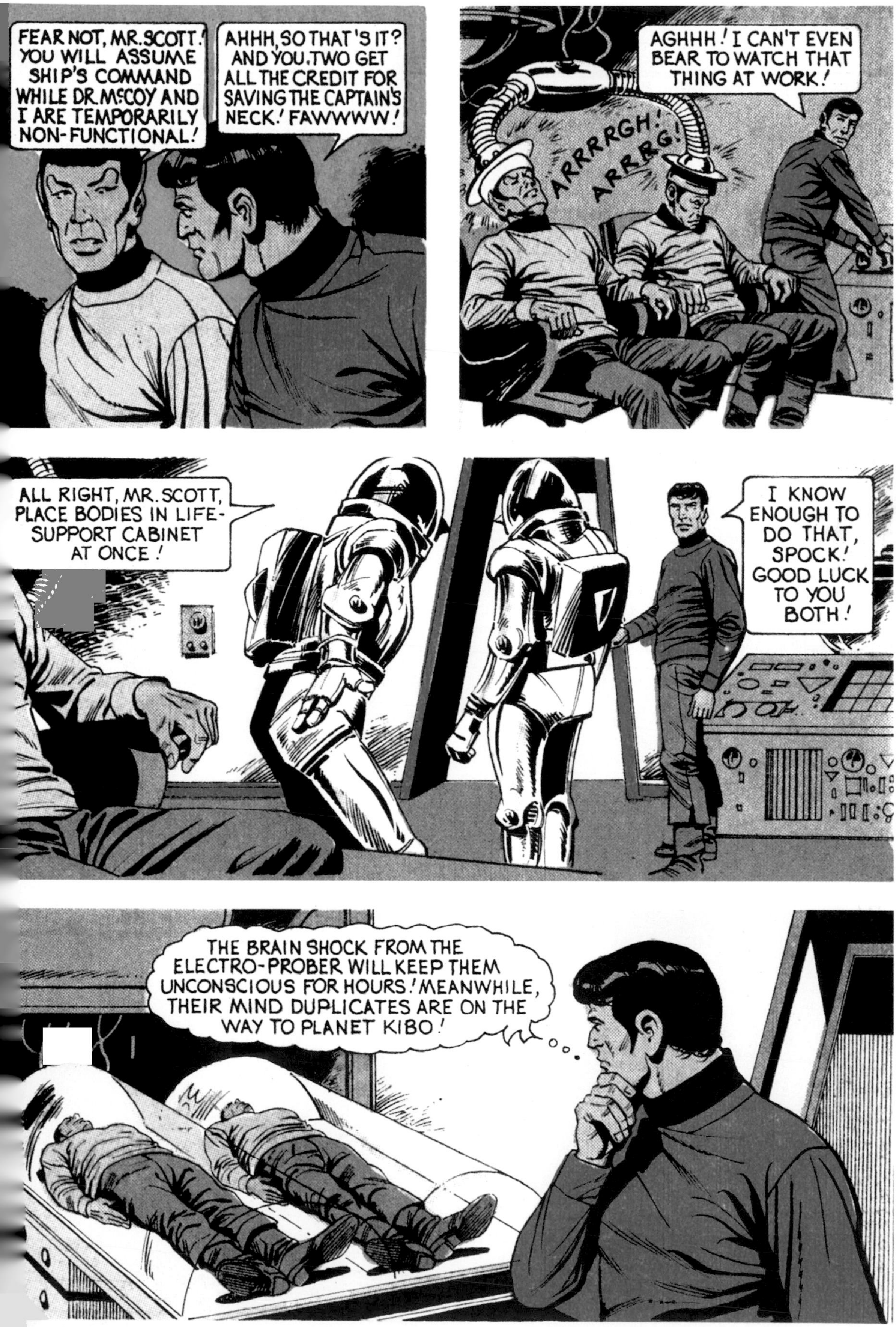

FEAR NOT, MR. SCOTT. YOU WILL ASSUME SHIP'S COMMAND WHILE DR. McCOY AND I ARE TEMPORARILY NON-FUNCTIONAL!
AHHH, SO THAT'S IT? AND YOU TWO GET ALL THE CREDIT FOR SAVING THE CAPTAIN'S NECK! FAWWWW!
AGHHH! I CAN'T EVEN BEAR TO WATCH THAT THING AT WORK!
ARRRRGH!
ARRRG!
ALL RIGHT, MR. SCOTT, PLACE BODIES IN LIFE-SUPPORT CABINET AT ONCE!
I KNOW ENOUGH TO DO THAT, SPOCK! GOOD LUCK TO YOU BOTH!
THE BRAIN SHOCK FROM THE ELECTRO-PROBER WILL KEEP THEM UNCONSCIOUS FOR HOURS! MEANWHILE, THEIR MIND DUPLICATES ARE ON THE WAY TO PLANET KIBO!

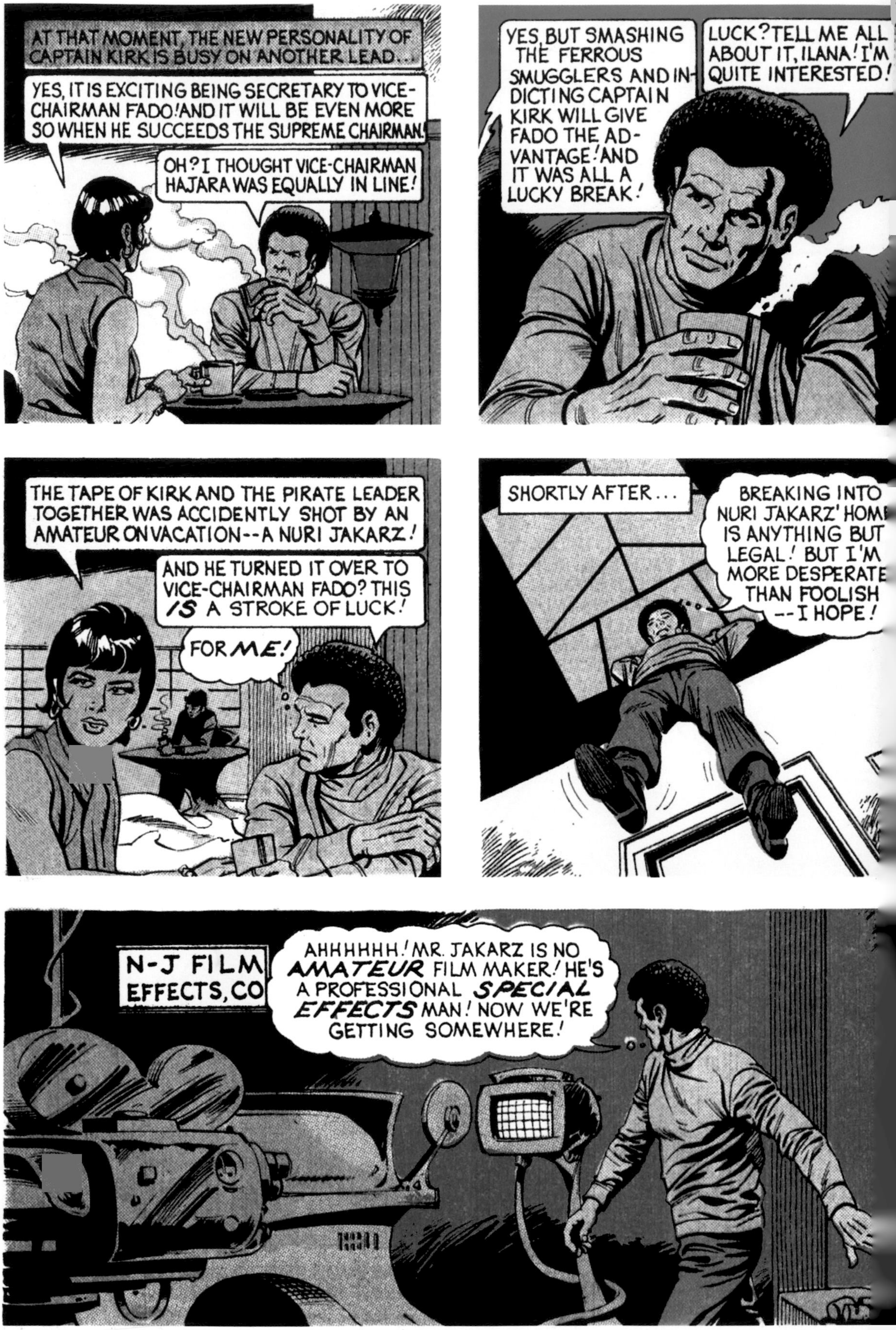
AT THAT MOMENT, THE NEW PERSONALITY OF CAPTAIN KIRK IS BUSY ON ANOTHER LEAD...
YES, IT IS EXCITING BEING SECRETARY TO VICE-CHAIRMAN FADO! AND IT WILL BE EVEN MORE SO WHEN HE SUCCEEDS THE SUPREME CHAIRMAN!
OH? I THOUGHT VICE-CHAIRMAN HAJARA WAS EQUALLY IN LINE!
YES, BUT SMASHING THE FERROUS SMUGGLERS AND INDICTING CAPTAIN KIRK WILL GIVE FADO THE ADVANTAGE! AND IT WAS ALL A LUCKY BREAK!
LUCK? TELL ME ALL ABOUT IT, ILANA! I'M QUITE INTERESTED!
THE TAPE OF KIRK AND THE PIRATE LEADER TOGETHER WAS ACCIDENTLY SHOT BY AN AMATEUR ON VACATION--A NURI JAKARZ!
AND HE TURNED IT OVER TO VICE-CHAIRMAN FADO? THIS *IS* A STROKE OF LUCK!
FOR *ME*!
SHORTLY AFTER...
BREAKING INTO NURI JAKARZ' HOME IS ANYTHING BUT LEGAL! BUT I'M MORE DESPERATE THAN FOOLISH --I HOPE!
N-J FILM EFFECTS, CO
AHHHHHH! MR. JAKARZ IS NO *AMATEUR* FILM MAKER! HE'S A PROFESSIONAL *SPECIAL EFFECTS* MAN! NOW WE'RE GETTING SOMEWHERE!

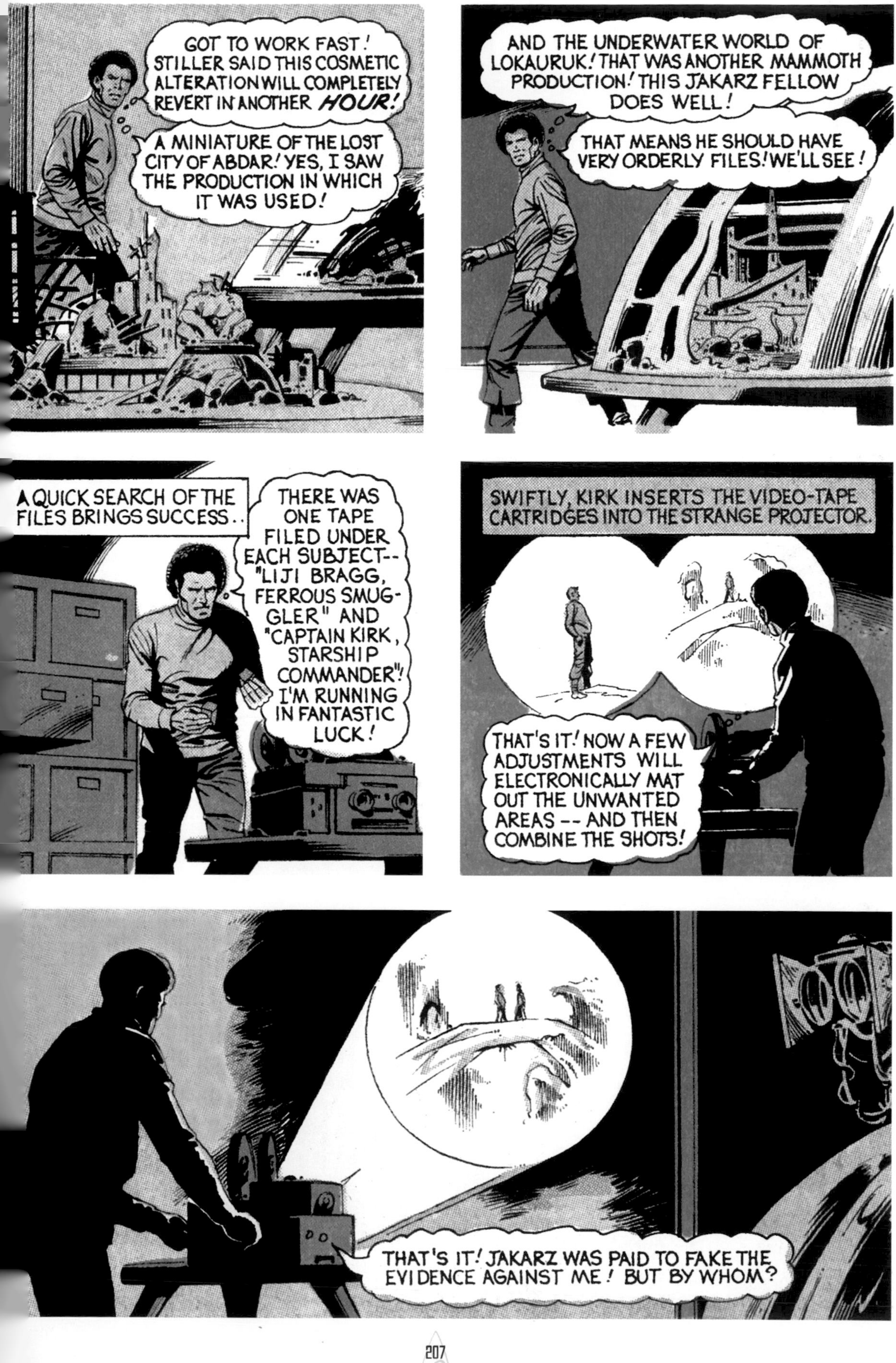
GOT TO WORK FAST! STILLER SAID THIS COSMETIC ALTERATION WILL COMPLETELY REVERT IN ANOTHER HOUR!
A MINIATURE OF THE LOST CITY OF ABDAR! YES, I SAW THE PRODUCTION IN WHICH IT WAS USED!
AND THE UNDERWATER WORLD OF LOKAURUK! THAT WAS ANOTHER MAMMOTH PRODUCTION! THIS JAKARZ FELLOW DOES WELL!
THAT MEANS HE SHOULD HAVE VERY ORDERLY FILES! WE'LL SEE!
A QUICK SEARCH OF THE FILES BRINGS SUCCESS..
THERE WAS ONE TAPE FILED UNDER EACH SUBJECT-- "LIJI BRAGG, FERROUS SMUGGLER" AND "CAPTAIN KIRK, STARSHIP COMMANDER"! I'M RUNNING IN FANTASTIC LUCK!
SWIFTLY, KIRK INSERTS THE VIDEO-TAPE CARTRIDGES INTO THE STRANGE PROJECTOR.
THAT'S IT! NOW A FEW ADJUSTMENTS WILL ELECTRONICALLY MAT OUT THE UNWANTED AREAS -- AND THEN COMBINE THE SHOTS!
THAT'S IT! JAKARZ WAS PAID TO FAKE THE EVIDENCE AGAINST ME! BUT BY WHOM?

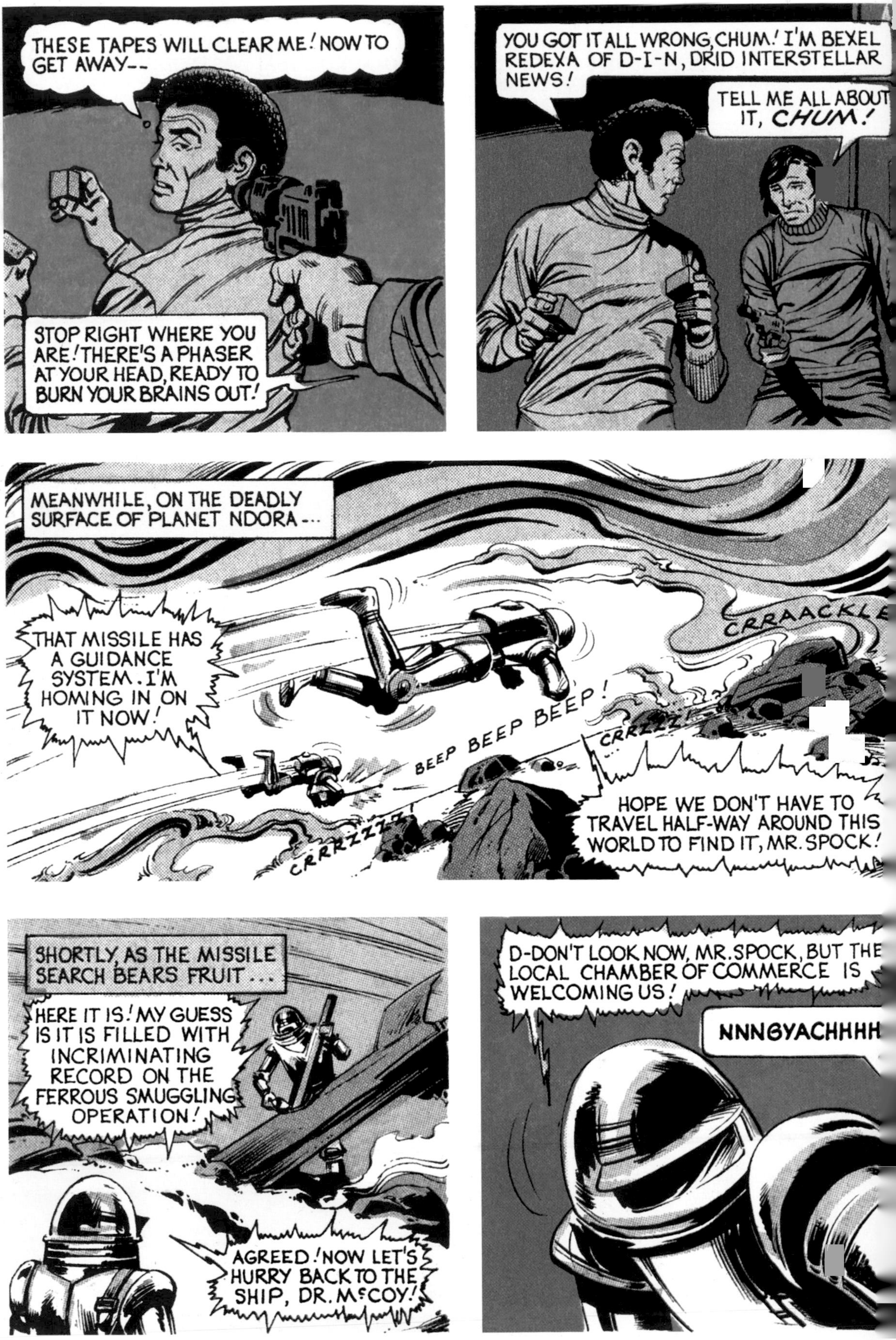
THESE TAPES WILL CLEAR ME! NOW TO GET AWAY--
STOP RIGHT WHERE YOU ARE! THERE'S A PHASER AT YOUR HEAD, READY TO BURN YOUR BRAINS OUT!
YOU GOT IT ALL WRONG, CHUM! I'M BEXEL REDEXA OF D-I-N, DRID INTERSTELLAR NEWS!
TELL ME ALL ABOUT IT, CHUM!
MEANWHILE, ON THE DEADLY SURFACE OF PLANET NDORA...
CRRAACKLE
THAT MISSILE HAS A GUIDANCE SYSTEM. I'M HOMING IN ON IT NOW!
BEEP BEEP BEEP BEEP!
CRRZZZ
HOPE WE DON'T HAVE TO TRAVEL HALF-WAY AROUND THIS WORLD TO FIND IT, MR. SPOCK!
CRRRZZZZ
SHORTLY, AS THE MISSILE SEARCH BEARS FRUIT...
HERE IT IS! MY GUESS IS IT IS FILLED WITH INCRIMINATING RECORD ON THE FERROUS SMUGGLING OPERATION!
AGREED! NOW LET'S HURRY BACK TO THE SHIP, DR. McCOY!
D-DON'T LOOK NOW, MR. SPOCK, BUT THE LOCAL CHAMBER OF COMMERCE IS WELCOMING US!
NNNGYACHHHH

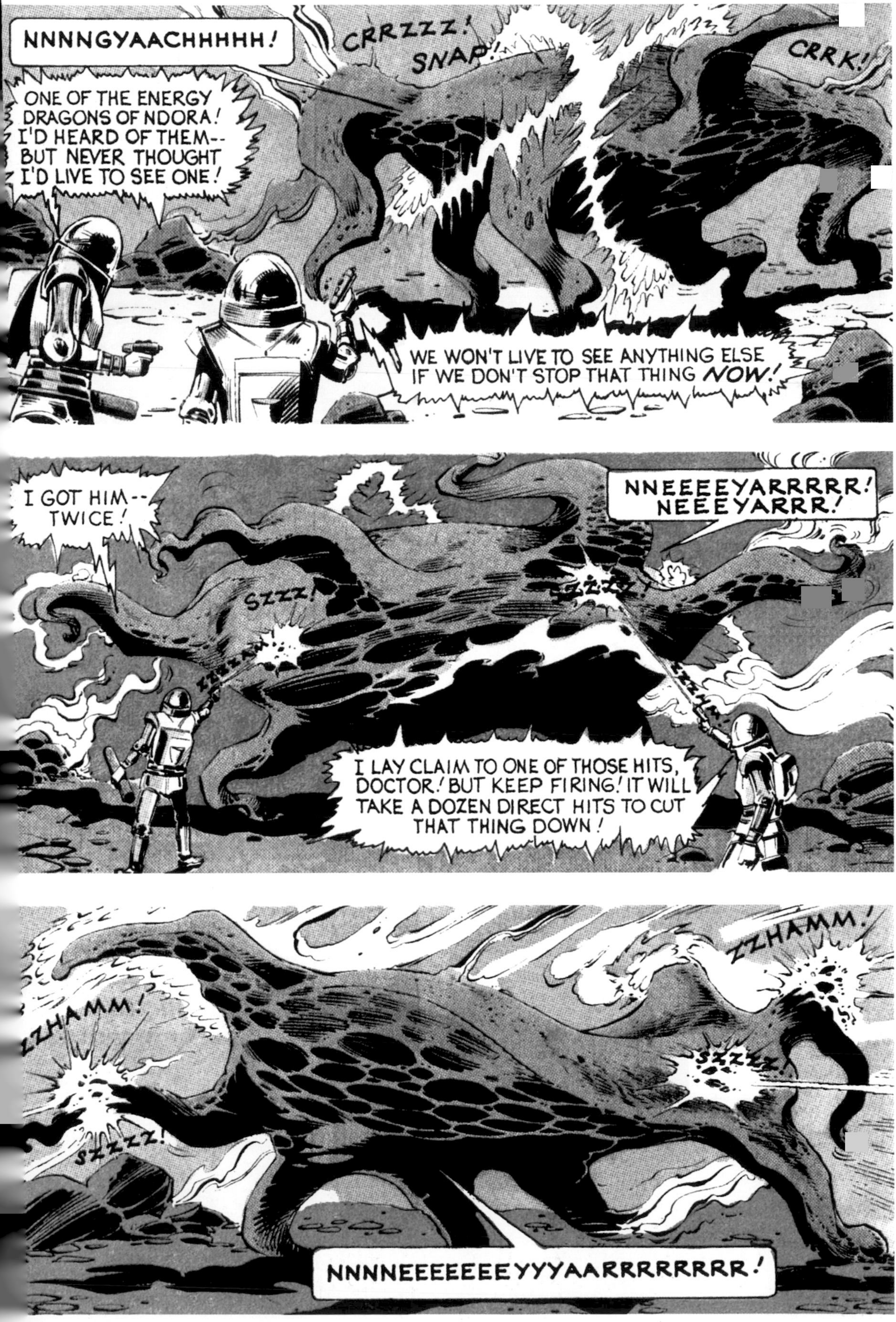
NNNNGYAACHHHHH!
CRRZZZ!
SNAP!
CRRK!
ONE OF THE ENERGY DRAGONS OF NDORA! I'D HEARD OF THEM-- BUT NEVER THOUGHT I'D LIVE TO SEE ONE!
WE WON'T LIVE TO SEE ANYTHING ELSE IF WE DON'T STOP THAT THING NOW!
I GOT HIM-- TWICE!
NNEEEEYARRRRR! NEEEYARRR!
SZZZ!
I LAY CLAIM TO ONE OF THOSE HITS, DOCTOR! BUT KEEP FIRING! IT WILL TAKE A DOZEN DIRECT HITS TO CUT THAT THING DOWN!
ZZHAMM!
ZZHAMM!
SZZZZ!
SZZZZ!
NNNNEEEEEEEYYYAARRRRRRR!

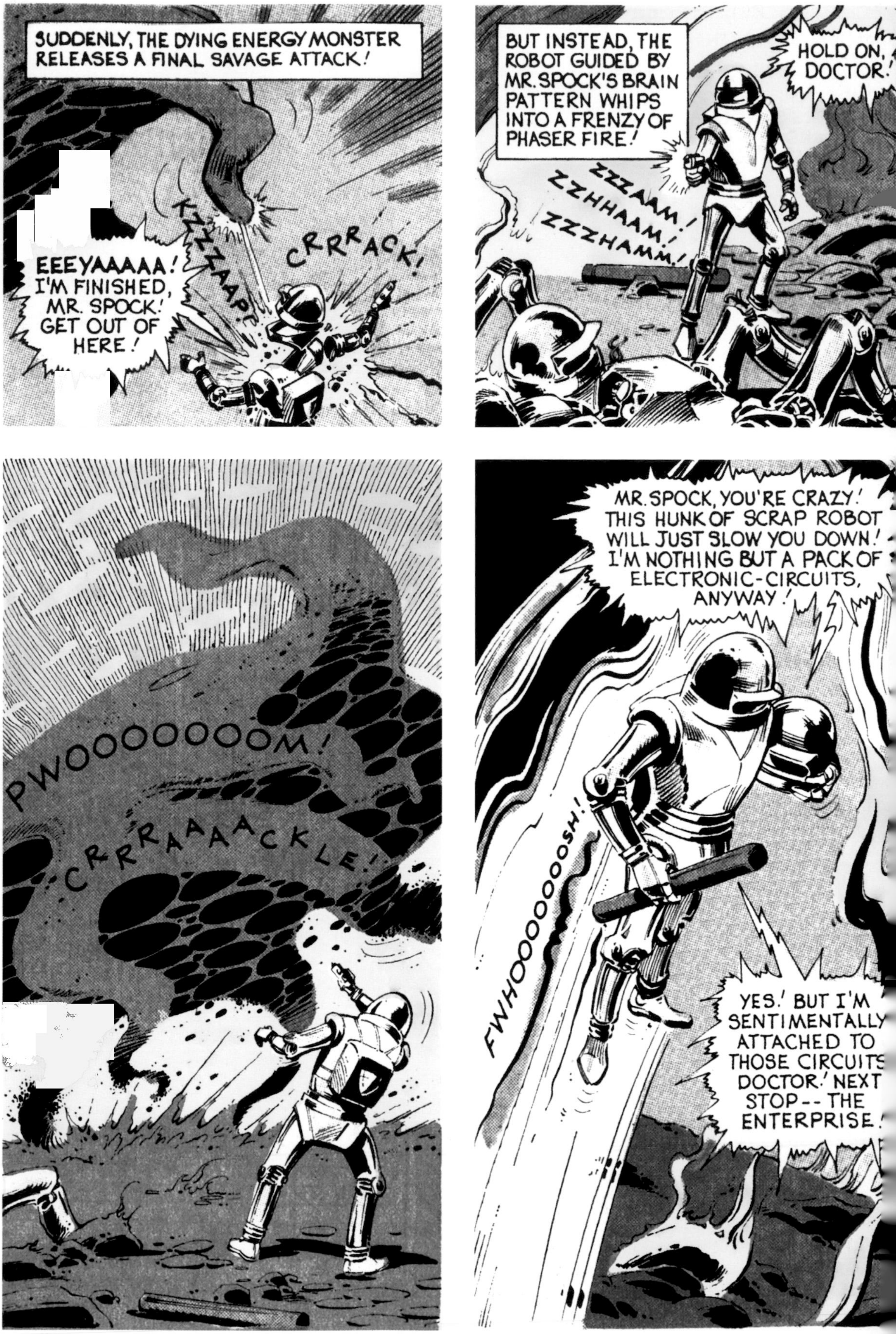
SUDDENLY, THE DYING ENERGY MONSTER RELEASES A FINAL SAVAGE ATTACK!
KZZZAAAP!
CRRRACK!
EEEYAAAAA! I'M FINISHED, MR. SPOCK! GET OUT OF HERE!
BUT INSTEAD, THE ROBOT GUIDED BY MR. SPOCK'S BRAIN PATTERN WHIPS INTO A FRENZY OF PHASER FIRE!
HOLD ON, DOCTOR!
ZZZZAAM!
ZZHHAAM!
ZZZHAMM!
PWOOOOOOOM!
CRRRAAAACKLE!
MR. SPOCK, YOU'RE CRAZY! THIS HUNK OF SCRAP ROBOT WILL JUST SLOW YOU DOWN! I'M NOTHING BUT A PACK OF ELECTRONIC-CIRCUITS, ANYWAY!
FWHOOOOOOSH!
YES! BUT I'M SENTIMENTALLY ATTACHED TO THOSE CIRCUITS DOCTOR! NEXT STOP -- THE ENTERPRISE!

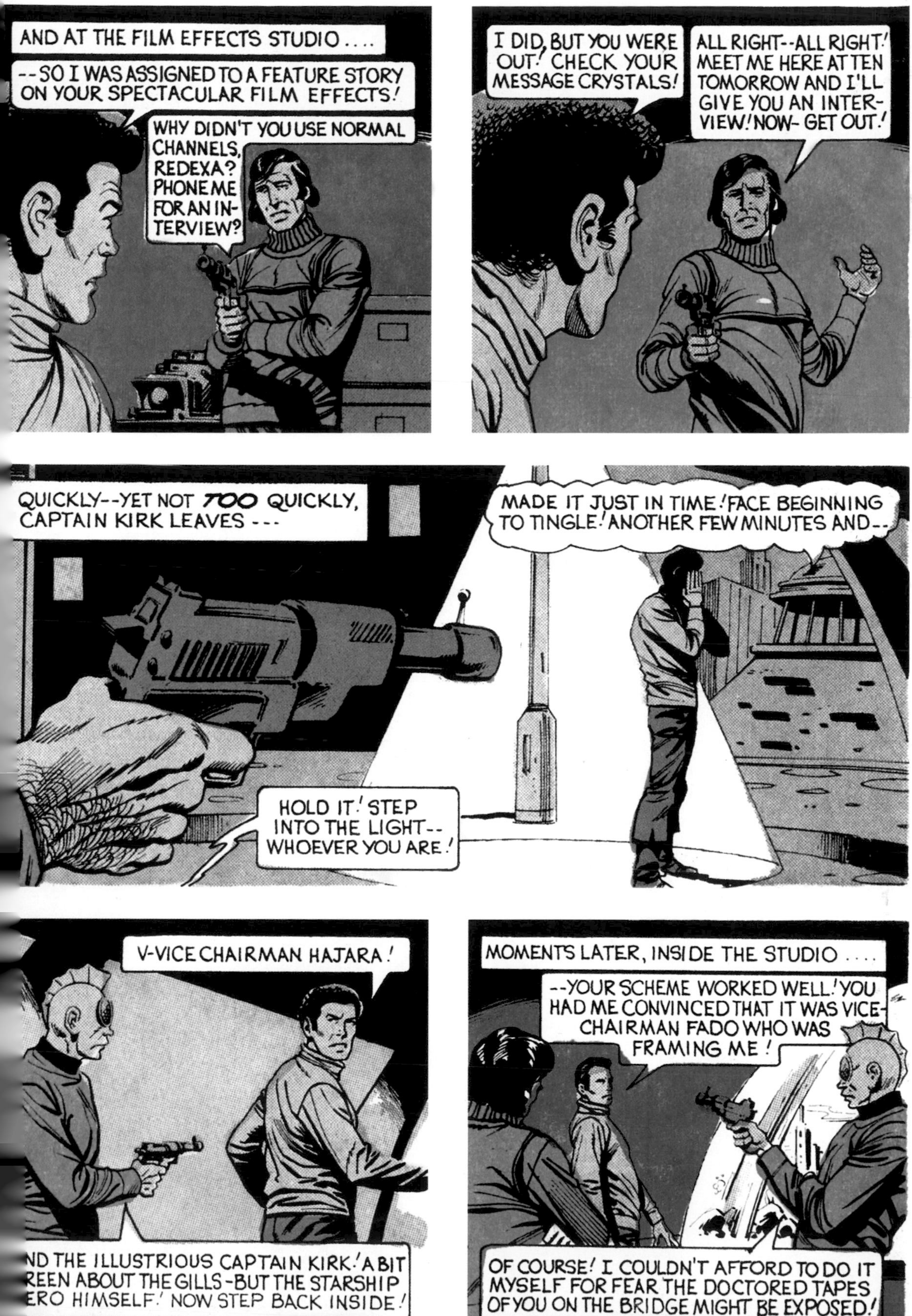
AND AT THE FILM EFFECTS STUDIO....
--SO I WAS ASSIGNED TO A FEATURE STORY ON YOUR SPECTACULAR FILM EFFECTS!
WHY DIDN'T YOU USE NORMAL CHANNELS, REDEXA? PHONE ME FOR AN INTERVIEW?
I DID, BUT YOU WERE OUT! CHECK YOUR MESSAGE CRYSTALS!
ALL RIGHT--ALL RIGHT! MEET ME HERE AT TEN TOMORROW AND I'LL GIVE YOU AN INTERVIEW! NOW- GET OUT!
QUICKLY--YET NOT TOO QUICKLY, CAPTAIN KIRK LEAVES---
MADE IT JUST IN TIME! FACE BEGINNING TO TINGLE! ANOTHER FEW MINUTES AND--
HOLD IT! STEP INTO THE LIGHT--WHOEVER YOU ARE!
V-VICE CHAIRMAN HAJARA!
ND THE ILLUSTRIOUS CAPTAIN KIRK! A BIT REEN ABOUT THE GILLS-BUT THE STARSHIP ERO HIMSELF! NOW STEP BACK INSIDE!
MOMENTS LATER, INSIDE THE STUDIO....
--YOUR SCHEME WORKED WELL! YOU HAD ME CONVINCED THAT IT WAS VICE-CHAIRMAN FADO WHO WAS FRAMING ME!
OF COURSE! I COULDN'T AFFORD TO DO IT MYSELF FOR FEAR THE DOCTORED TAPES OF YOU ON THE BRIDGE MIGHT BE EXPOSED!

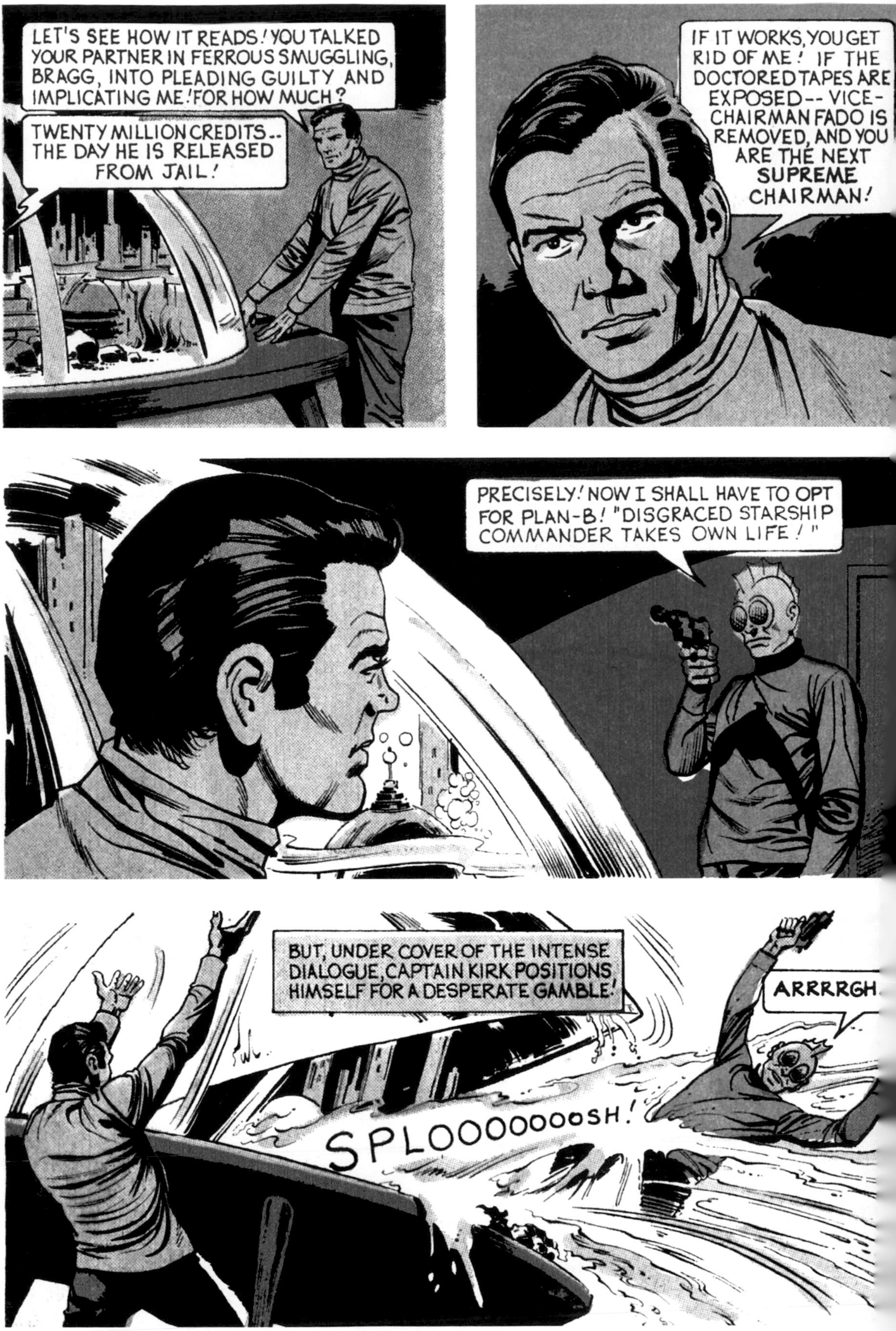
LET'S SEE HOW IT READS! YOU TALKED YOUR PARTNER IN FERROUS SMUGGLING, BRAGG, INTO PLEADING GUILTY AND IMPLICATING ME! FOR HOW MUCH?
TWENTY MILLION CREDITS.. THE DAY HE IS RELEASED FROM JAIL!
IF IT WORKS, YOU GET RID OF ME! IF THE DOCTORED TAPES ARE EXPOSED-- VICE-CHAIRMAN FADO IS REMOVED, AND YOU ARE THE NEXT SUPREME CHAIRMAN!
PRECISELY! NOW I SHALL HAVE TO OPT FOR PLAN-B! "DISGRACED STARSHIP COMMANDER TAKES OWN LIFE!"
BUT, UNDER COVER OF THE INTENSE DIALOGUE, CAPTAIN KIRK POSITIONS HIMSELF FOR A DESPERATE GAMBLE!
ARRRRGH
SPLOOOOOOOOSH!

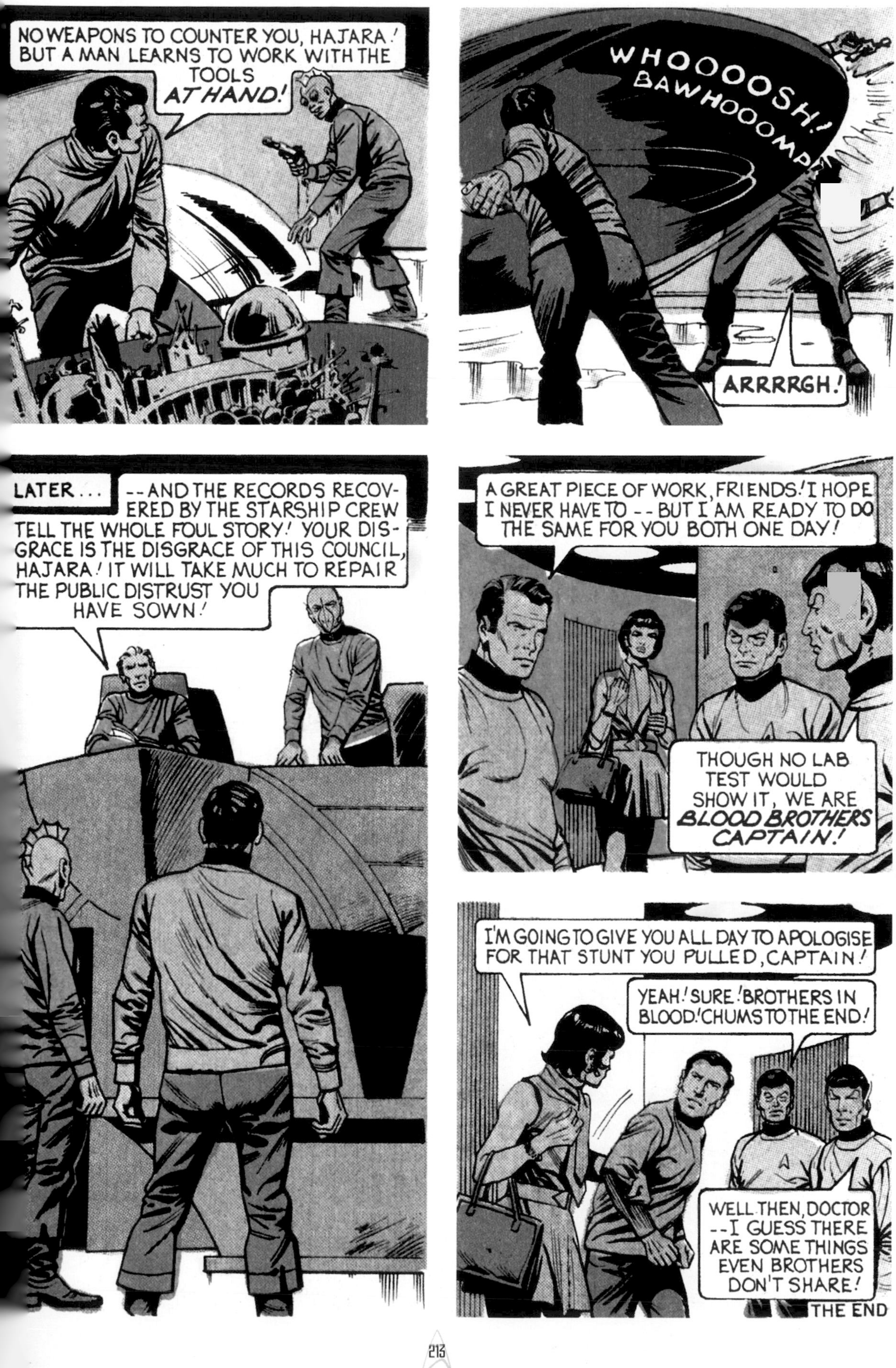
NO WEAPONS TO COUNTER YOU, HAJARA! BUT A MAN LEARNS TO WORK WITH THE TOOLS AT HAND!
WHOOOOSH! BAWHOOOOMP!
ARRRRGH!
LATER...
--AND THE RECORDS RECOVERED BY THE STARSHIP CREW TELL THE WHOLE FOUL STORY! YOUR DISGRACE IS THE DISGRACE OF THIS COUNCIL, HAJARA! IT WILL TAKE MUCH TO REPAIR THE PUBLIC DISTRUST YOU HAVE SOWN!
A GREAT PIECE OF WORK, FRIENDS! I HOPE I NEVER HAVE TO -- BUT I AM READY TO DO THE SAME FOR YOU BOTH ONE DAY!
THOUGH NO LAB TEST WOULD SHOW IT, WE ARE BLOOD BROTHERS CAPTAIN!
I'M GOING TO GIVE YOU ALL DAY TO APOLOGISE FOR THAT STUNT YOU PULLED, CAPTAIN!
YEAH! SURE! BROTHERS IN BLOOD! CHUMS TO THE END!
WELL THEN, DOCTOR --I GUESS THERE ARE SOME THINGS EVEN BROTHERS DON'T SHARE!
THE END

ALIEN LEGION

ALIEN LEGION
FORCE NOMAD
ALIEN LEGION
PIECEMAKER
CHUCK DIXON
LARRY STROMAN
CARL POTTS
ALIEN LEGION
FOOTSLOGGERS

Alien Legion: Force Nomad
A premium collection of the first eleven issues of this critically acclaimed comic series about a fighting force a la the French Foreign Legion.

Alien Legion: Piecemaker
The follow-up to Force Nomad, the Alien Legion resumes duty in a series of far-flung combat zones.

Alien Legion: Footsloggers
Collects the first six comics from the original incarnation of the series in 1984.

Brought to you by

checker
BOOK PUBLISHING GROUP

Alien Legion: Force Nomad
ISBN: 0-9710249-0-1

Alien Legion: Piecemaker
ISBN: 0-9710249-4-4

Alien Legion: Footsloggers
ISBN: 0-9753808-7-7

Alex Raymond's
FLASH GORDON

Hardcover Collections

Alex Raymond's Flash Gordon: Volume 1
collects January 7, 1934 to April 14, 1935
100 full color pages
landscape hardcover format
ISBN: 0-9741664-3-X

Alex Raymond's Flash Gordon: Volume 2
collects April 21, 1935 to October 11, 1936
100 full color pages
landscape hardcover format
ISBN: 0-9741664-6-4

Alex Raymond's Flash Gordon: Volume 3
collects October 25, 1936 to August 1, 1937
100 full color pages
landscape hardcover format
ISBN: 1-933160-25-X

Brought to you by

checker
BOOK PUBLISHING GROUP

www.checkerbpg.com

Milton Caniff's STEVE CANYON

More action and adventure!
Starring Major Steve Canyon

Steve Canyon: 1947
features a 150 page story-
line from the inaugural year
of the strip.

Steve Canyon: 1948
features 182 action-packed
pages from year two of
the series.

Steve Canyon: 1949
150 action-packed pages,
circa 1949.

Brought to you by

checker
BOOK PUBLISHING GROUP

Milton Caniff's Steve Canyon: 1947
ISBN: 0-9710249-9-5

Milton Caniff's Steve Canyon: 1948
ISBN: 0-9741664-1-3

Milton Caniff's Steve Canyon: 1949
ISBN: 0-9710249-1-X